For my parents and for Maxine and Ken

Contents

Acknowledgements

I cannot thank Professor Geoffrey MacCormack enough. He inspired my PhD study in this area and has guided me through the whole research process ever since. I have benefited enormously from both his great library and his knowledge.

In the course of my research, I have sought and received help from many scholars: Professor Michael Palmer in London, Dr Heather Lardy, Dr Pak Chow in Aberdeen, and Professors Li Chuangan, Tian Tao, Tong Guangzheng, Yang Ruohe, and Zhang Yan in China. I owe special thanks to Professors Zheng Qin, Mao Haijian, and Zhang Jinfan. When I first introduced myself to Professor Zheng Qin in 1997, he helped me with accessing the First Historical Archive of China and took the trouble to invite me to attend the seminars he organized. On a couple of occasions I sought his help from Scotland, and he generously responded without delay. I felt extremely sad when he died in 2000. During almost a year of consulting original records I often met Professor Mao Haijian in the Archive in Beijing. His admirable study on the Opium War (1995) and his advice have greatly influenced me. Professor Zhang Jinfan played an important role in making it possible for me to study in Britain and I shall always be very grateful to him for this. He agreed to be my co-supervisor when I applied to enter the University of Aberdeen's split programme (which would save me a big proportion of the tuition fee). Later I received an Overseas Research Students Award and was able to register as a full-time PhD student in Aberdeen.

I should also like to thank the First Historical Archive of China and the Sichuan Provincial Archive. In particular, Tang Yinian, Ding Jianjun and Hu Zhongliang from the First Historical Archive of China helped me to recognize difficult characters and stamps in the records.

I am deeply indebted to the following scholarships for funding my research: the Overseas Research Students Awards Scheme; the Great Britain–China Educational Trust; the C. B. Davidson Bequest Scholarship; the Principal's Small Grant, University of Aberdeen; and the School of Law of the University of Aberdeen. I am extremely grateful to the British Academy (BA) for supporting my three-year research project and awarding me a publication contract for this monograph. Dr Ken Emond and Ms Janet English from the BA have helped me by smoothing things along.

Very special thanks go to my parents, and especially to my mother, who was my companion when things were most difficult. My husband, Professor Zhao Min, deserves my thanks for encouraging me to apply for the British Academy's publication award. But I shall always have a guilty conscience about my children Maxine and Ken, who suffered a lot as a result of my studies.

Finally, I thank the BA's reviewer of my early manuscript and my editor, Liz Paton, who put a lot of effort into making the book easier to read.

Chronology of the Qing Dynasty

Reign	**Years AD**
Shunzhi	1644–1661
Kangxi	1662–1722
Yongzheng	1723–1735
Qianlong	1736–1795
Jiaqing	1796–1820
Daoguang	1821–1850
Xianfeng	1851–1861
Tongzhi	1862–1874
Guangxu	1875–1908
Xuantong	1909–1911

Short Forms of Document Sources

Case Sources	
Baodi	Baodi county records, sections (*juan*) 95–195 of *Shuntianfu quanzong* [Imperial Shuntian Prefecture Archive]. Cited by *juan* number and document number — for example: Baodi, 95: 3–6.
Ba county records	*Baxian dangan* [Ba County Records]. Cited by *juan* number and document number if available.
Baxian	*Qingdai Baxian dangan huibian-qianlong juan* [Selected Ba County Archives of the Qing Dynasty — Qianlong Reign].
Baxian1	*Qingdai Qian-Jia-Dao Baxian dangan xuanbian* [A Collection from the Ba County Archives in the Qianlong, Jiaqing and Daoguang Eras], vol. 1.
Baxian2	*Qingdai Qian-Jia-Dao Baxian dangan xuanbian* [A Collection from the Ba County Archives in the Qianlong, Jiaqing and Daoguang Eras], vol. 2.
Shen Yanqing	*Huaiqing zhengji* [Administrative Achievement of *Huaiqing*]. In *Jindai Zhongguo shiliao congkan* [Serial Collection of Materials on Modern Ancient Chinese History], 1862.
Other Sources	
Bianlan	*Da Qing lüli huiji bianlan* [Qing Code with Sub-statutes and Commentaries], 15 vols.
Cunyi	*Duli cunyi* [Doubts Arising from the Sub-Statutes], by Xue Yunsheng.
Fujian shengli	[Regulations of Fujian Province]. In *Guanzhenshu jicheng* [Collections of Official Handbooks].
Hubu zeli	[Regulations of the Board of Revenue]. In *Zhonghua lüling jicheng* [Complete Book of Statutes and Regulations of China].
Huidian	*Da Qing huidian* [Collected Statutes of the Great Qing Administrative Law].
Huidian shili	*Da Qing huidian shili* (in the Guangxu reign) [Supplement to the Collected Statutes of the Great Qing Administrative Law].
Huilan	Xingan huilan [Conspectus of Cases from the Board of Punishments].

Huitong Xincuan	*Da Qing lüli huitong xincuan* [Comprehensive New Edition of the Qing Code]. 1873 [date of preface] Yao Run, Hu Zhang.
Jicheng	*Da Qing lüli zengxiu tongcuan jicheng* [Revised Comprehensive Compilation of the Great Qing].
Jizhu	*Da Qing lü jizhu* [Great Qing Code with Collected Commentaries], by Shen Zhiqi.
The Code	*Da Qing lüli* [The Great Qing code].
Tongkao	*Da Qing lüli tongkao jiaozhu* [Thorough Examination on the Qing *lü* and *li* with annotations], by Wu Tan.
Yuedong shengli	[Regulations of Guangdong Province]. In *Guanzhenshu jicheng* [Collections of Official Handbooks].
Zhizhe chenggui	[Regulations of Zhejiang Province]. In *Guanzhenshu jicheng* [Collections of Official Handbooks].

1

Introduction

Herbert Giles, a diplomat to China (1867–1892) in the late Qing, who became a professor of Chinese at Cambridge after studying at the University of Aberdeen, remarked in one of his books in a section entitled 'jurisprudence':

> A clever magistrate never hesitates to set aside law or custom, and deal out Solomonic justice with an unsparing hand, provided always he can show that his course is one which reason infallibly dictates.

He then told a story about one such official to demonstrate this:

> A poor man, passing through one of the back thoroughfares in Hankow, came upon a Tls. 50 note (= about 15 pounds at that time) lying in the road and payable to bearer. His first impulse was to cash it, but reflecting that the sum was large and that the loser might be driven in despair to commit suicide, the consequences of which might be that he himself would perhaps get into trouble, he determined to wait on the spot for the owner and rest content with the thanks money he was entitled by Chinese custom to claim as a right. Very shortly he saw a stranger approaching, with his eyes bent on the ground, whereupon he made up to him and asked at once if anything was the matter. Explanations followed, and the Tls. 50 note was restored to its lawful possessor, who, recovering himself instantaneously, asked where the other one was, and went on to say that he had lost two notes of the same value, and that on recovery of the other one he would reward the finder as he deserved. His benefactor was protesting strongly against this ungenerous behaviour when [this official] happened to come round the corner, who, seeing there was a row, stopped his chair, and inquired there and then into the merits of the case. The result was that he took the Tls. 50 note and presented it to the honest finder, telling him to go on his way rejoicing; while turning to the ungrateful loser, he sternly bade him wait till he met some one who had found two notes of that value, and from him endeavour to recover his lost property.[1]

Giles's comments, together with other similar remarks, once provided a heavily distorted version of Qing civil procedure. That view has not totally

[1] Giles 1876: 80, 81. According to Giles, the official was the 'Second Prefect' of Hanyang prefecture, Hubei Province.

disappeared. For instance, a popular textbook on comparative law, *An Introduction to Comparative Law* by Zweigert and Kötz, states in its chapter on Chinese law:

> Given that the great bulk of the legislation in ancient China appertained to criminal and administrative law and that the practice of law was mainly the practice of criminal law, how were conflicts of 'private law' decided?

The answer given is that 'there developed a wide variety of forms of conflict-resolution outside the courts'. Thus, '[o]nly a very small proportion of "private law" disputes ever came before the state courts in imperial China', for 'the procedures of the state courts were extremely prolonged and expensive, and the imperial magistrates had a reputation for being preoccupied, corrupt, and lazy'.[2]

If we turn to specific writings in English that have discussed the Qing legal system, we find, especially before 1970, similar distorted assumptions concerning the civil aspect of the Qing legal system. Three examples from the literature may be cited. In their celebrated book *Law in Imperial China*, Bodde and Morris clearly made the point that 'matters of a civil nature were either ignored by it [the Qing legal system] entirely (for example, contracts), or were given only limited treatment within its penal format (for example, property rights, inheritance, marriage)'.[3] In these circumstances, one Chinese maxim quoted by them — 'of ten reasons by which a magistrate may decide a case, nine are unknown to the public' — seems to represent the character of Qing litigation. In other words, a magistrate's decisions had little to do with the law.[4] Qu Tongzu wrote a monograph on the main aspects of the magistrate's administration. Although he discussed these aspects in great detail, he paid scarcely any attention to the magistrate's hearing of civil disputes. He devoted only three paragraphs (a total of 283 words) to 'civil cases' in the chapter on the 'administration of justice'. He did not come to any final conclusion about the role of the magistrate in the handling of civil disputes, but the brevity of his discussion suggests that he attributed little importance to it.[5] Sybille van der Sprenkel paid much more attention to informal and formal methods of mediation and arbitration, devoting a large number of pages in her book to discussing the mechanisms for dispute solution by the *tsu* (clan), guild tribunals, and village leaders.[6] If mediation or

[2] Zweigert and Kötz 1998: 290, 291.
[3] Bodde & Morris 1973: 4.
[4] Ibid.: 6.
[5] Qu Tongzu 1969: 118–19.
[6] Van der Sprenkel 1966: chs 7, 8, and 9.

arbitration failed to solve the dispute, the magistrate's court was the next resource. However, van der Sprenkel also pointed out that the official court was available only in theory — 'In practice, however, the inefficiency of the official courts left this need unmet'.[7] Despite the absence of a specific discussion of the handling of disputes by the magistrate, van der Sprenkel was still convinced that the magistrate would not welcome the dispute, his court was inefficient, and justice was not always achieved. On the basis of these presumptions, we must find it almost impossible to attribute to the magistrate a judicial role in the solving of civil disputes.

Thanks to 'the most significant material in existence relating to Ch'ing [Qing] law and administration',[8] Buxbaum was able to challenge the conventional view of the civil aspect of the Qing's legal system and the magistrate's duty in dealing with civil cases in his pioneering article of 1971. He argued that the Qing Code did recognize a difference between civil and criminal cases; that the courts very often handled civil cases; and that the cases we might designate as civil were not handled with penal punishment.[9] However, Buxbaum's study was too concise to be convincing.

In recent years, several studies drawing on the Taiwan archive and two similar archives in mainland China have enriched the subject from many aspects.[10] Philip Huang in particular wrote a book on Qing civil justice; drawing on 628 cases from Danshui Xinzhu in Taiwan and from Baodi and Ba counties in mainland China, he concluded that in practice the magistrate was a judge who made decisions on civil cases by following the 'principles' embedded in the law. However, because Huang makes only very brief references to the law in analysing the decisions, he fails to build up a strong connection between what he sees as the principles and the Code, and between the principles and the magistrate's decisions in the cases.[11]

My objective in this book is to conduct a constructive re-examination of past and current assumptions about the magistrate's role in the handling of land, debt, and marriage disputes. To carry out this task, it is necessary first to say something about the sources I have used and the approach that should be taken to them.

7 Ibid.: 120.

8 Buxbaum 1971: 255. Here he is referring to the Tanshui-Hsinchu Archives in Taiwan. These are original documents from the files of subprefectures and magistrates for the years 1789–1895. For more details about the archive, see Buxbaum 1971: 255–8.

9 Buxbaum 1971: 255–79.

10 Among them are Allee 1994a, 1994b; Zhou 1995; Huang 1996, 2001; Reed 2000; Liang 2005.

11 Huang 1996. Since his work is very relevant to my research, his arguments will be discussed in detail.

1.1 The sources

The sources fall into three groups: the Qing official law, the original case records (both those in the archives and those published), mainly from Baodi county, and other sources such as collections of judicial decisions, handbooks, and private commentaries on the Qing law.

The original case records from Taiwan and from Baodi and Ba counties comprise hundreds of cases. Although these show that land, debt, and marriage disputes were often dealt with by a magistrate, they cannot automatically provide answers about the performance of the magistrate's court in conceptual terms. Moreover, to understand these judicial decisions, we must find the root from which they sprang. Thus a more detailed examination of the Qing law for this purpose is of the utmost importance.

1.1.1 The official law

I take a broad view of the Qing official law.[12] It is official law first in the sense that it 'emanates from the emperor in whose person was concentrated all legislative executive, and judicial power'.[13] It is made up mainly of the *Da Qing lüli* (the 'Great Qing Code' — hereafter, the Code), the *Da Qing huidian shili* (Supplement to the Collected Statutes of the Great Qing Administrative Law — hereafter, *Huidian shili*), the regulations (*zeli*) of the Six Boards of central government (*liubu*), and the regulations of provincial governments (*shengli*).

It is well known that the arrangement of the Qing Code that contains both articles and sub-statutes was adopted from the Ming (1368–1644). Since the fourth Code of 1740, the articles (*lü*) underwent little change. So the phrase 'the Code' may refer to earlier versions but it usually refers to the one in 1740. In some places my discussion goes back to the original Great Qing Code with Collected Commentaries and Appended Sub-statutes. The situation with sub-statutes (*li*) was much more complicated. Because the sub-statutes were revised every five or ten years, the numbers and text changed from time to time.[14] The private commentaries on the Qing law are a good guide to the changes before and during the lifetime of their authors. I often consulted three such commentaries for this purpose: Shen Zhiqi's *Da Qing lü jizhu* (Great Qing Code with Collected Commentaries)

[12] Other sources such as customs and clan rules, although they have attracted the interest of some scholars, are not official. The scope of the Qing law is still a topic of debate.

[13] MacCormack 1996b: 19.

[14] For a general study on *li* see Su 1999.

of 1715, Wu Tan's *Da Qing lüli tongkao jiaozhu* (Thorough Examination on the Great Qing *lü* and *li*) of 1778,[15] and Xue Yunsheng's *Duli cunyi* (Doubts Arising from the Sub-statutes) of 1905. These commentaries covered important changes in the law over the whole period of the Qing dynasty.[16] I also refer occasionally to similar books, such as *Da Qing lüli huiji bianlan* (Qing Code with Sub-statutes and Commentaries).[17] These commentaries are regarded as the best of their kind and can supply us with reliable supplementary information on the Qing law.

Since the Code contained both *lü* and *li*, both terms will be used. When I use the term *lü*, it is usually clear that I am referring to the Code. The term *li*, in contrast, has several meanings and may refer to at least four different kinds of legislation: (1) the Code or, more exactly, the section on the general principles of the Code (*mingli*); (2) the sub-statutes of the Code (*fuli*); (3) regulations that came into force from time to time before they could be attached to the Code, being separately applied as settled rules (*li* or *dingli*); (4) the regulations of the Six Boards (*zeli*).[18] To avoid unnecessary confusion, I shall use specific terms such as sub-statute or regulation of the Board when mentioning *li*.

The last version of the *Huidian shili* was published in 1899 (Guangxu 25). This collection recorded the most important developments in and amendments to public policy and law during the Qing. In addition, it includes imperial decrees (*shangyu*[19] and *yuzhi*) and some precedents. Because it was

[15] The latest Qing law that Wu examined was 1778. His book was first published in 1780, but the recent book published by the China University of Political Science and Law Press, which is the one I have used, was based on the 1886 edition.

[16] For the influence of *Jizhu*, see Chen Fu-mei Chang 1980.

[17] For more on *Bianlan*, see MacCormack 1990: 52.

[18] The Qing legislation is much more complex at the highest level than is revealed here. There were also general circulars (*tongxing*) and rules promulgated by the various boards that did not require imperial endorsement (*bufu*). These legal rules are described with different terminology, although the exact meaning of the terms and the difference between them require more study.

[19] According to one study (see Wang and Lü 1998: 146–7), *shangyu* (imperial decrees) should not be regarded as *li*, because *shangyu* was an emperor's order to a particular official or board. It is true that some *li* were made in accordance with a *shangyu*, so such *li* would begin with 'in accordance with imperial order' (*feng shangyu*). Thus, the conclusion is right up to a point. However, a recently published book, *Qiangu zhinan* (Guidance on Tax Matters, 1999), which contains collections of regulations on tax matters, clearly marks many regulations with 'x year *shangyu*'. It is obvious to me that these are different from reports (*zou* or *ti*) submitted by an official or a board to which the emperor signified his approval (*zouzhun*). The *shangyu* reveals the emperor's active role in legislation. For example, a sub-statute of Article *Mousha zufumu fumu* (Plotting the killing of paternal grandparents and parents) was added directly by a *shangyu*

the final version, it allows us to see the whole pattern of important changes during the Qing dynasty.

Under official law, I also include the provincial regulations (*shengli*). They were promulgated by the provincial government in response to matters that were provincially significant. I refer to three of them: *Fujian shengli* (Regulations of Fujian Province), *Yuedong shengli* (Regulations of Guangdong Province), and *Zhizhe chenggui* (Regulations of Zhejiang Province).

1.1.2 Original records

Most of the data for this study derive from the case records for Baodi county. They constitute the main part of the Imperial Shuntian Prefecture Archives (*Shuntianfu quanzong*) stored in the First Historical Archive of China in Beijing. The Imperial Shuntian Prefecture Archive is divided into fourteen categories, of which law and lawsuits (*falü cisong*) is one (see Appendix 1). Baodi county was under the jurisdiction of the Imperial Shuntian Prefecture.[20] The city of Baodi was located 160 *li* (0.5 km) to the east of the capital city (Beijing). The Baodi magistracy was classed as an important post (*yaoque*) with three qualifiers: *chong* (frequent), *nan* (difficult), and *pi* (wearisome).[21] The 'difficult' qualifier implied that Baodi was a county with, at least, an ordinary rate of litigation.

The Baodi litigation cases are divided into eleven groups (see the bottom panel of Appendix table 2) and cover the years from Jiaqing 16 (1811) to Xuantong 3 (1911), the reigns of five emperors. In this sense, this study concentrates on the late Qing period. Disputes over land, houses, and debt comprise separate groups of cases. The land and house groups have a total of eighteen sections (*juan*), fourteen for land (*juan* 95–108) and four for

arising from a decision by the Board of Punishments. The decision said: 'The decision is quite right. I order that the Board of Punishments add it as a sub-statute in order to be applied' (*Tongkao*: 778). This *shangyu* was clearly direct legislation rather than an order to a particular official or board to make a *li*.

[20] The Qing divided local government into provincial and 'special' governments. The Imperial Shuntian Prefecture was a special government administering five departments and nineteen counties in which the city of Beijing stands.

[21] The Qing differentiated the importance of the post of the magistrate with four qualifiers: frequent (*chong*, meaning that the county was a centre of communications), troublesome (*fan*, meaning that the post involved a great deal of official business), wearisome (*pi*, meaning that the county had many overdue taxes), and difficult (*nan*, meaning that the county had a violent populace, prone to crime) (see Qu Tongzu 1969: 15). The most important post was designated with all four qualifiers; the least important (and easiest) post was, of course, that with only one or none of these qualifiers.

houses (*juan* 109–112). The debt group consists of eleven *juan* (185–195). The marriage group, categorized by the archivists as 'marriage and illegal sexual relations' (*hunyin jianqing*), has a total of twelve sections (*juan* 161–173).

Each *juan* contains varying numbers of documents of different kinds. *Juan* 97 contains the most documents (259 pieces). A simple calculation of the number of documents in the land, debt, and marriage cases, indicates a total of nearly 6,000 documents.[22] A document could be as short as a couple of sentences, or as long as ten pages. The following pieces, recording the progress of a case, may be found:

1. The cover, which recorded briefly the names of the parties, the cause, the date, the name of the office (*fang*) in charge, and the serial number (*bianhao*).
2. The original petition (*kongci*), with the magistrate's comments (*pi*). If the plaintiff had alleged a wound or fighting, a statement about the examination of the wound and a brief statement from the plaintiff would follow.
3. The rebuttal (*su*), together with the magistrate's comments.
4. The draft of particular orders (*piaogao*) — if the case was accepted — by the clerk of the office in charge, corrections or alterations, the magistrate's note of approval (*xing*) in his own writing, and the official stamp. The formal orders (*piao*) were rarely kept in the records because they would be cancelled as soon as they had been executed, or when an official holiday began.
5. The reports (*biing*) by the runners or the local headman (*xiangbao*) to the magistrate regarding fulfilment of the instructions contained in the *piao*, with the magistrate's comments.
6. The trial list (*shendan*). The decision (*pan*), if the magistrate wrote one, was usually placed at the end of the list. Few decisions were found in the court statements (see next).
7. The statements of the people questioned (*gong*), with personal signs of confirmation. These were summaries by the recorders rather than the original words of the people interrogated.
8. On most occasions the bond of confirmation (*ganjie* or *zunjie*) and the bond of guarantee (*baozhuang*) will be found.

[22] One should bear in mind that the categories are created by the archivists, and some cases are not quite correctly categorized.

9. The statement of money paid (*jiaozhuang*) and confirmation of receipt (*lingzhuang* or *shouzhuang*).
10. Evidence, such as contracts or maps, although many contracts were returned to the owner after a trial.
11. An application to close the case without a formal trial, with a note of the magistrate's agreement or refusal. This could be submitted at any stage.

I also draw on Ba county materials from both the published collection of the records and the Sichuan Provincial Archive. Ba county was the capital county of Chongqing Prefecture in the south-western province of Sichuan. The magistracy of Ba county was also classed as an important post with three qualifiers: *chong* (frequent), *fan* (troublesome), and *nan* (difficult). Ba records contain much more material than Baodi records — even the small collection of published records comprises about 1,754,000 words — covering the period from Qianlong 17 (1852) to the end of the Qing (1911). Unfortunately, the value of the Ba records is greatly limited for my purposes because only a few records have been microfilmed, and these are not very relevant to litigation, and because the published materials contain only selected parts of case records. Although a lot of contracts and petitions may be seen, they are in isolation. I could not find a complete package of records for one single case. It was therefore necessary for me to supplement these sources with other materials.

1.1.3 Qing officials' collections of decisions and comments, and handbooks

Collections of decisions and comments could be considered to be original official documents, whereas the handbooks contain magistrates' discussions and opinions on issues that arose during their administration.

Magistrate Shen Yanqing's collection of decisions is used as the main case supplement for this study. Shen Yanqing was the magistrate of the counties of Xingguo, Anyi and Taihe, which were all simple posts with one qualifier (*chong* or *nan*), and Poyang, which was an important post with three qualifiers (*chong*, *fan*, and *nan*), in Jiangxi province. He was a metropolitan graduate in the Daoguang era (1821–1850)[23] and was commended as being outstanding and distinctive during the Xianfeng period (1851–1861). He died in fighting during the Taiping rebellion. Magistrate Shen's book,

[23] There were three main degrees: licentiate or first degree (*shengyuan* or *xiucai*), provincial graduate or second degree (*juren*), and metropolitan graduate or third degree (*jinshi*); see Chapter 3.

entitled *Huaiqing zhengji*, was printed after his death. It brought together his official orders, trial decisions, and reports. Five of the chapters contain his trial decisions in 135 cases from 1839 (Daoguang 19) to 1852 (Xianfeng 2). His decisions have not often been used for studying the Qing, except by Shiga Shūzō.

I consulted several handbooks, such as *Fuhui quanshu* (A Complete Book Concerning Happiness and Benevolence), *Qinban zhouxian shiyi* (The Basics of the Magisterial Service Approved by the Throne), *Mulingshu* (Compendium on the Magisterial Service), and Wang Huizu's several handbooks.[24] Although these handbooks far from exhaust the magistrates' handbooks, they represent most, if not all, discussions, opinions, and suggestions relating to the duties of the magistrate. For example, *Mulingshu*, comprising twenty-four volumes, contains comments from about 150 officials on every aspect of the magistrate's duties. The most relevant part, called *xingming* (judicial tasks), consists of three volumes (*juan* 17 to 19).

The handbook *Qinban zhouxian shiyi* deserves a special mention. Emperor Yongzheng (1723–1735) commanded governors-general Tian Wenjing and Li Wei to draft a book for magistrates on the fundamentals of the magistrate's function in order to give them guidance, 'just as a south-pointing chariot is used for pointing in the right direction (*yiwei zhouxian zhi nanche*)'. The resulting publication consisted of twenty chapters, which were reviewed by the emperor. In this sense, it was not a normal handbook. To some extent it bore a much higher authority than any other handbook. Thus, the author of *Mulingshu* treated it as equivalent to law. Since it contained only the most important principles on a magistrate's duties, the text was rather brief and provided few details of the way in which the magistrate carried out his work. Perhaps because of this, the *Qinban zhouxian shiyi* has not received enough attention from scholars.

1.2 The approach of this study

This book examines the performance of the Qing magistrate's court in dealing with land, debt, and marriage disputes. Another important source of disputes — inheritance — is not dealt with here, mainly because I have not been able to obtain enough material for a satisfactory study. However, because matters concerning land, debt, and marriage cover a wide spectrum of Qing private life, the picture to be drawn can be taken as generally representative in terms of the magistrate's practice as a whole.

[24] Wang Huizu 1786a, 1786b, 1793, 1794, 1800.

My approach is to look at both procedural and substantive issues by commencing with an examination of the relevant Qing law. Without sufficient discussion on the law itself, the magistrate's performance in dealing with disputes would lack proper explanation. So, although my aim is to explore the magistrate's practice in solving land, debt, and marriage disputes, nearly half of this book is concerned with the relevant procedural and substantive law.

Chapters 2, 3, and 4 look at civil procedure in the magistrate's court, in order to provide a better understanding of the magistrate's performance in dealing with civil cases. The three chapters discuss the following issues: legislation on the competence of the courts to accept land, debt, and marriage disputes, and the bringing of such disputes by different groups of litigants; the routine procedure by which the magistrate accepted a petition and made comments; the steps and actions he would take in making a decision, as identified from various judicial documents. One noticeable phenomenon is that many cases were closed without a final hearing. This procedure is often regarded as the typical means by which civil disputes were solved in the Qing dynasty, and even in traditional China in general. Some scholars exclude such cases from the magistrate's formal system.[25] In the light of such accounts, I focus especially on these cases in one section and point out that the reason many cases were closed without a final hearing was not that the magistrate was reluctant to take action or that mediation played an extremely active role. The main reasons were that the dispute had been solved, that the magistrate was satisfied with the result, and that he felt no need to hold a further hearing. He could still deliver his order and control the outcome of such cases by making comments.

Chapter 5 considers the sources used for solving civil cases. It is in three sections, covering the laws governing land, debt, and marriage matters, respectively. I will pay special attention to the active role of legislation in meeting and shaping changing situations. The chapter argues that the relevant law was systematized under the Qing in its context and applicable to solve disputes.

If Chapter 5 answers the question of what were the relevant laws on land, debt, and marriage matters, Chapters 6, 7, and 8 answer the question of how the magistrate applied them. In another words, the magistrate's practice is explored by illuminating the main points of his performance in his decisions of cases. Each chapter discusses several typical types of case, one by one. The case types are chosen on the basis both of their frequency in terms of the Baodi records, and of concern that they should explore the main legal points in each area, that is, matters concerning land, debt, and marriage.

[25] Huang 1996.

Chapter 9 examines some other relevant matters concerning all three areas of cases. It first notes that the frequency of allegations of physical injury or false accusation rests upon the fact that the laws on injury (*shang*) were drafted too widely and that those on false accusation (*wugao*) were too complicated. As a result of such allegations, punishment was often meted out, whereas it was very rarely applied in land, debt, and marriage matters on their own. This chapter also contains a section on custom. Although custom played an important role in the process of solving disputes, it was not the fundamental principle applied by the magistrate in making decisions. However, Qing law played an active role in accepting, reforming, and making custom. Custom accepted by the law should therefore be considered as itself forming part of the law. Thus, Qing law actually covers a broader area of civil matters than had been thought. In the last section of the chapter, I argue that the magistrate enjoyed discretion in solving land, debt, and marriage cases when there was a gap between the law and the facts of the particular case, by taking into account the specific circumstances before applying a principle of law, that is, *zhunqing* (*qing* here refers to all the relevant facts) *zhuoli* (*li* refers to the principle and/or the reasoning of the law). *Zhunqing zhuoli* expresses a principle governing the application of the law in deciding hard cases, rather than a flexible tool allowing the magistrate to decide as he wished.

In the concluding chapter, I discuss how we can view the magistrate's performance in delivering justice in the Qing litigation culture. Given the specific background, the Confucian ideal world of an absence of litigation or 'no litigation' (*wusong*) and the recommendation of 'anti-litigation' (*yansong*) do not contradict the conclusion this study has reached, that is, that land, debt, and marriage disputes were solved fairly and efficiently by the Qing magistrate in accordance with the law. On the contrary, they show why the magistrate took so much trouble in trying to make the parties accept the decision willingly, and persuaded people through anti-litigation education. This perhaps can be seen through another often used phrase: 'ending litigation' (*xisong*). If the phrase 'no litigation' can be seen as representing an ideal and 'anti-litigation' as representing the educational approach of this ideal, then 'ending litigation' can be seen as having a more practical and realistic meaning, representing the judicial approach of this ideal.

In the remainder of this chapter and before the main chapters start, I introduce two fundamental issues. One is the Qing approach to matters concerning land, debt, and marriage, the other is the magistrate's multiple roles in terms of his responsibilities. The Qing approach to what we might call civil matters is based on the assumption that matters concerning land, debt, and marriage constitute the main area of private life. The second issue will draw attention to the magistrate's judicial role in the context of his inclusive responsibilities, which were many and varied.

1.3 The approach of the Qing Code to matters concerning land, debt, and marriage

When we look through the Code and the other elements of Qing law, it is clear that what might be called a system of civil law for the solution of land, debt, and marriage cases does not exist. Some scholars even deny the existence of fundamental principles guiding such matters, and argue further that, if there were any provisions on land, debt, and marriage, they took a criminal approach by imposing punishment on civil wrongdoers. On the surface, this view seems compatible with the Qing Code. A table of five punishments, among nine other tables, is incorporated at the beginning of the Code. The text opens with the five punishments (Art. 1).[26] The provisions of the Code were concerned with conduct that incurred various forms of punishment. How can such a Code be understood as providing the primary source for solving civil disputes? We must first provide an answer to this question before we probe into the Code to matters concerning land, debt, and marriage.

Those who see the Qing Code as solely a penal code seem to find support in the structure of the Code, but their perception is drawn from the distinction made in the West between criminal and civil matters. This approach has led to a severely distorted view of the Qing legal system.

We should bear in mind that 'criminal' and 'civil' are artificially devised categories. A criminal act is regarded as a serious violation of social order and public safety. The state prosecutes the offender on behalf of the victim. If the offender is found guilty, he has committed a particular crime. Generally, the definition of a crime reflects the attitudes prevalent in a society. By contrast, a civil matter is regarded as concerning only the relations between individuals over property and other personal relationships such as marriage. The state is involved only when the plaintiff brings a case to court. In any event, the distinction can be clearly identified from criminal and civil codes and acts, different trial systems, and the legal consequences.

The situation in the Qing is different. The Qing Code was an all-inclusive legal code that covered all areas of behaviour of concern to the

[26] Unless stated otherwise, I cite Articles and sub-statutes according to Xue Yunsheng's numbering in *Cunyi*.

government. The Qing also had no differentiated court system. Except for the Board of Punishments, many officials who were entrusted with executive functions also had judicial duties, as we will see clearly in the example of the magistrate in the following section. The structure of the Qing Code should first be understood in the context of the Qing government structure, which mainly consisted of a central government and provincial governments. The Qing assigned comprehensive responsibilities, both administrative and judicial, to most provincial officials. At the central government level, duties were divided and assigned to such main institutions as the Boards of Revenue, Rites, the Army, the Civil Service, Labour, and Punishments. Of course, the final authority in all matters was vested in the emperor.

Judicial duties were carried out by officials at each level, from the lowest, the magistrate, to the highest, the ministers. Officials at every level were either specifically responsible for judicial duties, such as those of the Board of Punishments and the provincial judge (*anchashi*), or responsible for a range of duties (including judicial), as in the case of the magistrate, the prefect, the governor, and the governor-general. Despite the mixture in its administration, the Qing judicial system was clearly identifiable within such a government system. When officials dealt with so-called judicial matters, they approached them in a judicial manner. They had to follow the procedures established by law or, more precisely, the procedures laid down in the Code and other authoritative sources.

1.3.1 Crime and non-crime

Buxbaum holds that Qing law distinguished between civil and criminal cases.[27] His argument has some basis. Although lacking the distinction between criminal and civil, the Qing Code did make a distinction between crime and non-crime. Given the fact that the theory of criminal and civil law is a product of modern Western thinking, the distinction between crime and non-crime is appropriate to the Qing context and obviously has a significance similar to the distinction between criminal and civil. The distinction between 'crime' (*zui*)[28] and 'non-crime' (*wu zuiming*) can be seen from the way in which several terms were used in the Code. Although *zui* refers either to wrongdoing in general or to named specific crimes, or both, when it is used solely to identify crimes it is combined with another term *ming* (meaning 'name'), forming the phrase 'named crime' (*zuiming*). This is evidence that the crime was a particular category of the law. Where *cisong*

[27] Buxbaum 1971.
[28] The term '*zui*' can be used in many senses, such as crime, wrongdoing, and to punish.

was used, provisions containing this phrase seem to refer to all law cases, including litigation over land, debt, and marriage matters. Apart from this term, several other more specific terms such as *huhun tiantu deng xishi* (minor matters concerning land, marriage, etc.) (Sub-statute 334-1), *huhun tiantu dengxiang* (matters concerning household, marriage, land, etc.) (Sub-statute 334-4), and *minjian cisong xishi* (minor matters such as lawsuits between local people) (Sub-statute 334-9) are used and they are clearly referring to litigation among individuals. The disputes concerning land, debt, and marriage matters also clearly constitute a separate category of cases in the Qing law. Thus, they reveal the nature of the distinction between 'crime' and 'non-crime'. For example, Sub-statute 336-17 regulated official adjudication in the capital. Its concern is to draw a distinction of jurisdiction between the Board of Punishments and the five city courts (*wucheng chayuan*).[29] It clearly states that cases concerning household, marriage, and land (*huhun tiantu*) and involving no named specific crime should go to the five city courts. Other cases should go to the Board of Punishments. The Supplement to Collected Statutes of the Great Qing Administrative Law (*Huidian shili*) also records a provision on appeals that discloses the same logic. It stipulated that, for serious cases involving 'named crimes' (*zuiming*), the provincial governor, after receiving an appeal, should take action. But, if the case involved only 'minor matters' (*xishi*) over land or marriage, it should be returned to the lower court (*Huidian shili*, vol. 9: 897–98). These provisions clearly suggest that matters identified as *huhun tiantu* that did not give rise to a named crime were not regarded as crimes. In this sense, they were non-crimes, or civil affairs.

A comment by a magistrate also shows the same approach. The magistrate defines *shuya quejiao* (literally, 'teeth of mouse and ears of birds', a phrase often used to refer to land and debt matters) as matters 'concerning no named crime (*wuguan zuiming*)' (*Mulingshu*, *juan* 18: *Bianshen* [Hearing pending cases]). When discussing false accusations, Shen Zhiqi also uses the concept of crime as the key criterion for deciding whether an untrue accusation should be treated as the offence of false accusation or not. He points out that the bringing of a petition 'in order to accuse somebody of a crime' (*Jizhu*: 810) was the key factor in forming the offence (see Chapter 9). The significance of this concept of crime is the existence of its opposite, that is, matters concerning land, debt, and marriage, which are not treated as named crimes.

[29] The capital city was divided into five parts: east, west, south, north and central city. The offices of the *yushi* (the chief official of each city) were called the five city courts (*wucheng chayuan*).

The recognition of matters concerning land, debt, and marriage as 'non-crimes' was the basis for their different treatment. The procedural rules for trials of both serious crimes and disputes concerning land, debt, and marriage matters were contained in the subsection of the Code entitled 'prosecution and litigation (*susong*)'. According to traditional interpretation, the term *su* means that the plaintiff petitioned for the prosecution of a crime, whereas the term *song* means the petition was to institute a (civil) action (*Jizhu*: 797).[30] Crimes were not allowed to be settled privately through compromise. They had to be brought to court for the official to decide, because crime was solely the responsibility of the state. Since a person could be convicted of a crime only by the state, amnesties could be applied only to crimes. One sub-statute makes this clear: an amnesty was to apply only to crimes committed prior to its grant. Offences involving land, debt, or marriage were excluded from its scope. However, disputes over these matters ought still to be clearly judged (Sub-statute 16-3).

Torture was allowed only, though notoriously,[30] in cases involving crimes, that is, when there was liability to the punishment of penal servitude, life exile, or death. In such cases, the magistrate might only recommend a decision, which then proceeded automatically through the review procedure to be confirmed or adjusted at a higher level. The emperor himself reserved the power to decide cases involving the death penalty.

For a crime, justice was achieved by the correct sentence on the basis of Qing law, here the correct punishment prescribed by the Code. As the *Huidian shili* put it, justice was achieved by imposing the right and proper punishment (*pingyun*) for the offence. The judge had to keep a balance between the offence and the law. In the case of civil disputes, the judge had to distinguish right and wrong between the two parties (*pouduan quzhi*). Justice was achieved by keeping the balance between the rights and obligations of the two parties (*Huidian shili*, vol. 9: 897, 915).

In these circumstances, the fact that civil matters were introduced in the Code with the phrase 'minor matters concerning family, marriage, land, and

[30] The word '*song*' consists of two parts, the radical 'speak' (*yan*) plus 'public' (*gong*). Since the element *gong* also means an official, *song* may be defined as 'speak in front of an official'. Commentaries of the Han dynasty (206 BC – AD 220) on the Zhouli (Rites of Zhou) distinguish accusations of crime (*yu*) from disputes over property (*song*). It seems to me that the term *song* implies a long history of officials handling arguments over property matters. Since the parties needed to argue with each other, the process for solving the disputes required the official first of all to listen to each party. Confucius uses the phrase *tingsong* (literally listen to *song*) to describe the formal process of deciding a case. So *tingsong* is also translated as 'try a lawsuit'.

[31] MacCormack points out 'a possible justification' for the use of torture (1996b: 147).

debt' (*huhun tiantu qianzhai xishi*) is just to follow the logic of the distinction between crime and non-crime. Matters designated as *huhun tiantu* that did not give rise to a named crime clearly bear a civil nature. Perhaps that was why the Code often qualified such matters with the term 'minor' (*xi*). This term should be understood as delimiting the scope of matters of a non-crime nature. It actually defined the jurisdiction of the magistrate's court for matters concerning *huhun tiantu* that did not give rise to named crimes. Any tendency to interpret the term *xi* as showing that the Qing legislator treated civil matters as insignificant, or as defining the nature of land, debt, and marriage matters as a whole, must be rejected. Matters such as marriage and land pertain to the most important values in traditional China. For example, Confucius' advocacy of family ethics or the complicated system of land administration give little support to the suggestion that matters concerning land or marriage were not important. The phrase *huhun tiantu qianzhai xishi* should be correctly interpreted as referring to the proportion of matters concerning land, debt, and marriage that were non-crimes, and thus civil matters. I shall show below that, in general, civil matters were treated carefully by the Qing legislators.

However, because, in the theory of modern criminal law, physical punishment is imposed only on a person who commits a crime, the feature of the Qing Code imposing physical punishment on offenders who committed a civil wrong is often criticized and used as grounds to argue that the Qing Code manifests little of a civil nature or treats civil matters from a criminal point of view. If we approach the Code solely from this aspect, this argument is valid. However, this far from exhausts the nuances of the distinction between criminal and civil. In a modern legal system, the same act may be both a crime and a civil wrong. For example, if a person entrusts his luggage to a staff member working in a left-luggage office in a train station, and then that staff member absconds with it, he has committed both the crime of theft and also two civil wrongs, namely, under English law, the tort of interference with goods and a breach of the contract with the person to keep the luggage safe. The point is that the true distinction resides not in the nature of the wrongful act but in the possible legal consequences. If the wrongful act is capable of generating conviction as a crime, that means it is regarded as a crime. If it is capable of generating a civil action, that means it is not regarded as a crime. If it involves both a crime and a civil action, it is both a crime and a civil wrong.[32]

[32] Williams 2002: 3–4.

The situation of a wrongful act under the Qing Code was exactly the same. Whether wrongdoers should be punished was a particular matter examined by the magistrate in the judicial process. The Qing legal system has often confused scholars because, apart from the fact that there is no separate court system or separate criminal and civil law for different classes of case, the fault of civil wrongdoers was not omitted in the Code. Mild punishments, for example blows with a light stick, were designed especially to shame wrongdoers, even though, in fact, the punishment was very rarely, if ever, imposed on civil wrongdoers by the magistrate (for more on punishment, see Chapter 9).

1.4 The magistrate's multiple roles

The magistrate's role in terms of conducting, hearing, and solving cases cannot be understood solely from the judicial point of view. His role was very different from that of the judge with which we are familiar today. The magistrate's judicial role was not confined to purely judicial work, nor was his power limited to conducting such work.

The Qing government, apart from the emperor, was typically constituted by the central government and local governments. The whole country was divided into, at its most, twenty-three provinces (*sheng*) as the biggest local administrative unit. The county (*xian*) and the department (*zhou*) were the basic administrative units in the province and the lowest level of government administrative structures. The magistrate (*zhixian* or *zhizhou*) presided over the county and the department, ranking lowest in the hierarchy of chief officials.[33] Superior to him were the prefect (*zhifu*), the intendant of the circuit (*daoyuan*), the provincial judge (*anchashi*), the provincial treasurer (*buzhengshi*), the governor (*xunfu*), and the governor-general (*zongdu*). The number of *zhou* and *xian* varied from time to time, the largest number reached being 1,523 (including the 11 counties of Taiwan province).[34] Although the magistrate was at the lowest level, he was supposed to take charge of all tasks such as the maintenance of order, the collection of taxes, the handling of cases, and the promotion of education. At the central level, these comprehensive duties were clearly divided between different administrative offices — the six Boards. Each Board had its own

[33] Since there is little difference between a department magistrate and a county magistrate, I use the term 'county magistrate' or 'magistrate' as referring to them both.

[34] See Qu Tongzu 1969: 2, 3.

responsibility, judicial matters, for example, falling within the remit of the Board of Punishments.

The magistrate was assigned numerous responsibilities by the law. One could even say that his duties knew no bounds. The following lists are summaries from different sources:[35]

> The magistrate's duty is 'superintending the government of a district, regulating its taxes and labour services, hearing and administering its legal suits, promoting education and culture, and controlling its customs. As to nourishing the people, sacrificing to spirits, providing for scholars, and explaining the law to the people, he is personally responsible and diligently manages.'[36]

> A magistrate takes charge of the government of a district. He settles legal cases, metes out punishment, encourages agriculture, extends charity to the poor, wipes out the wicked and the unlawful, promotes livelihood, and fosters education. All such matters as recommending scholars [to the public], reading and elucidating the law and imperial edicts [to the public], caring for the aged, and offering sacrifices to the gods, are his concern.[37]

In short, the magistrate was not only expected to take charge of everything within the territory under his jurisdiction and of all matters necessary to maintain public order, but also expected to improve the moral standard of the people and to nourish them. Among these duties, it was commonly believed that the management of judicial and fiscal affairs was the principal as well as a routine task.[38] The point is that his all-encompassing function assigned him multiple roles. He had to exercise different duties on different occasions. These different duties might occasionally be combined, and sometimes, if there was a conflict between them, one duty prevailed over another.

Different counties had different circumstances. In order to identify and classify these differences, and to designate the importance of the post of the magistrate, the Qing created four qualifiers: frequent (*chong*), troublesome (*fan*), wearisome (*pi*), and difficult (*nan*).[39] These factors vividly indicate the extent of the magistrate's task in correctly exercising his different functions. Furthermore, his various duties might be hard to compare with each other.

[35] Apart from the magistrate, the county government consisted of three groups of subordinate officials: assistant magistrate and registrar (*xiancheng* and *zhubo* in the county or *zhoutong* and *zhoupan* in the district); a chief officer; and miscellaneous officials (for more details about assistant officials and clerks, see Qu Tongzu 1969: 8–13; Antony 2002).

[36] *Qingchao tongdian*, cited in Watt 1972: 12.

[37] *Qingshi gao*, cited in Qu Tongzu 1969: 16.

[38] Qu Tongzu 1969; Watt 1972.

[39] See Qu Tongzu 1969: 15, and footnote 21 above.

For example, the duties of judicial and fiscal administration could be classified as specific or short-term duties that could be targeted in visible ways, as by the number of cases heard or the amount of taxes collected. In contrast, a duty such as 'promoting education and culture' or 'nourishing people' was a longer-term or overall duty that was not measurable in the same way. Not only might such duties be achieved in a relative way, but they also might be achieved only over a longer period of time. They could be accomplished in the sense that the people were better off than before, but a final achievement might never be reached. These duties rather constituted a future goal for the magistrate's administrative purpose, whose achievement was dependent upon the accomplishment of the judicial and fiscal duties. The various duties of the magistrate thus constituted a network in which the performance of each responsibility was more or less related to that of his other functions.

Bearing in mind the relationship between these duties is helpful in understanding the different aspects of the magistrate's administration, including his handling of land, debt, and marriage cases. For instance, Lan Dingyuan asked petitioners with degrees whether they had paid their land taxes when accepting their petitions on litigation open-days (*fanggaori*),[40] thus combining his judicial function with his tax-collecting function.

To take an example from Baodi county, a nephew falsely accused his uncle of taking his land, in order to obtain some financial support from his uncle. The magistrate, on learning the true circumstances, still ruled that the uncle should give financial help to the nephew and his mother (the uncle's sister-in-law) (Baodi 107: 114–120). The decision of this Baodi magistrate, if viewed solely from the judicial point of view, was obviously unjust. However, to explain the matter in this way does not take into account the whole spectrum of the magistracy, even in terms of the judicial role. The magistrate's action can be fully understood only through an understanding of his multiple roles. In another words, the Baodi magistrate's decision might be justifiable from a point of view other than the strictly judicial. The Code contains an Article (89) *Shouyang gulao* (Supporting Orphans and Old Persons). It states:

> As for widowers, widows, orphans, solitary persons, and persons who are critically or seriously disabled or poor, who have no relatives on whom they may rely, and cannot survive by themselves, if the official having jurisdiction who ought to support them does not support them, the punishment [for the official] will be 60 blows of the heavy stick.[41]

[40] Lan Dingyuan 1729/1989: 3.

[41] Jones 1994: 112–13. Unless noted otherwise, this is the translation I shall generally use.

It was also the magistrate's duty to ensure that the poor who had difficulty earning a living sought the necessary support from a close relative. How the magistrate helped the poor to obtain such support from a relative depended upon both how close their relationship was and how rich the relative was. The ruling could vary from ordering the relative to give ongoing regular support to ordering him to help just once. So some officials, for instance Bao Shichen, established rules in advance for fulfilling this function. He classified families under his jurisdiction as: extremely rich (*fuhu*, possessing 200,000 *liang* of gold); very rich (*raohu*, with over ten family members, each holding over 10 *mu* of land); rich (*shanghu*, each member holding over 6 *mu* of land); ordinary (*zhonghu*, each holding over 4 *mu* of land); poor (*xiahu*, each holding 2 *mu* of land); very poor (*pinhu*, each holding less than 1 *mu* of land); and extremely poor (*qionghu*, with no land or business, or with no son or grandson to give support, or with only one adult who had to feed four or five family members).[42] He picked out the extremely poor families, then traced their relatives in order to establish whether there were any extremely rich or very rich families among them. If there were, such families would be ordered to give support to their 'poor' relatives. If they complied, they would be rewarded with a board on their door bearing an inscription written in red, 'responsibly kind family' (*yihu*). Those who did not comply would also receive a board, bearing an inscription in white stating 'not kind' (*buyou*).[43] So when the magistrate ruled that a poor individual should be given some support by a rich relative, he was not acting on a whim, since supporting the poor was an integral part of his responsibility. 'Poor' was an administrative definition that carried a clear meaning. The Baodi Gazetteer, for example, identified 1,478 'poor adults' (*qiongding*) in Baodi county.[44] Thus, the magistrate was not solely a judge who could rule only on the particular claim of the parties, while ignoring or, to be more exact, being unable to take care of other problems involved.

In the light of a magistrate's multiple roles, it is not always easy to state whether he has carried out one particular duty correctly in some of the complicated situations. For example, in one case magistrate Lan Dingyuan arrested three litigation tricksters. But he did not report the case to his supervisors to have the case reviewed, as required by the law. Since the county had had a bad harvest for several years and many people were involved, if he sent the case to the higher officials too many people would have had to

[42] See Appendix table 3 for conversions of money and area.
[43] Bao Shichen 1872/1968: *juan* 28.
[44] *Baodi xianzhi* n.d.: *juan* 3.

give up their business. In these circumstances, Lan thought it better not to report the case in order to avoid troubling too many people.[45]

Although the magistrate's short-term and specific duties were his first concern in routine administration, his longer-term and overall duties gave him much more scope to play a benevolent role with respect to his subjects. The point is that the magistrate's multiple roles meant that he exercised different duties on different occasions. He had to exercise a duty in the correct way in terms of the particular role he was playing, while he might also combine different duties. It was the flexibility required by these duties that made the administration of different magistrates colourful and personal.

[45] Lan Dingyuan 1729/1989: 25.

2

Submitting and Receiving a Complaint in Minor Matters

Any procedural law on civil litigation will inevitably start by authorizing a certain state court to accept a complaint in order to take action on it. In the first article (Article 302) and its sub-statutes, the Qing procedural rules governing the litigation of such disputes logically regulated the order of jurisdiction of the courts at different levels on accepting petitions of all kinds. Procedural provisions were mainly grouped in the section entitled Litigation (*susong*), and classified as pertaining to the Board of Punishments of the Code. They amounted in total to forty-one statutes and nearly three hundred sub-statutes according to Xue Yunsheng's numbering.[1] Other regulations, such as *Liubu chufen zili* (the Disciplinary Regulations of the Six Boards), occasionally contained procedural rules on litigation. For example, these regulations stipulated that the time limit for the magistrate to close cases reserved for his own decision was twenty days.[2] The most relevant provisions in the Code were the following: which authority should hear a petition (Article 332), the responsibility of officials when accepting a petition (Articles 334, 335), petitions offending one's status and violating duties (Article 337), litigation involving military personnel and civilians, and litigation involving officials (Articles 341, 342), false accusation (Article 336), and encouraging litigation (Article 340). The first issue I will examine is the question of which authority is the proper one to hear a case.

1 For more details about the numbers of statutes and sub-statutes throughout the Qing, see Qu Tongzu 1980.

2 Disciplinary Regulations of the Six Boards: *juan* 47 (cited in Na Silu 1981: 265). For more details on regulations other than the Code, see Chapter 4.

2.1 Jurisdiction for accepting a complaint

The general principle of jurisdiction for all cases was that any case must first be heard by the court of the lowest level, the county magistrate's court. Petitioners who did not respect this principle were treated under the first statute in the litigation section (Article 332) as having committed the offence of '*yuesu*' (bypassing the immediate authority to submit a claim). This principle can be seen as the core principle of jurisdiction.

> Every complaint [lawsuit] brought by a military person or a civilian must be from the inferior to the superior [according to the proper order]. If someone brought a complaint to an authority other than his own superior authority (*benguan guansi*) he should be punished with 50 blows of the light stick. (*It is necessary that his own superior refuse to receive the action, or receives it and makes a mistake or irregularity. Only then is it permitted to go to the higher authority.*) (Article 332)[3]

The phrase 'his own superior authority' is the key to understanding the principle. Since most civilians were under the 'superior authority' of the county or district magistrate, in this sense we can say that the magistrate's court was the court of first instance for civil cases.[4] The principle was reconfirmed by a sub-statute added in 1800 (Sub-statute 332-17). The conditions under which the higher authority might accept petitions, stated in the official small commentary (the italicized commentary in the above quotation) on Article 332 in the above quotation, were rearticulated and put in the formal text of the Code as a sub-statute.

The phrase 'superior authority' should also be understood as referring to the magistrate himself rather than to his subordinate officials as well. Thus such officials as *xiancheng* (assistant magistrate), *zhubo* (registrar), *dianshi* (jail warden), and *xunjian* (subdistrict magistrate), who acted either as police commissioners and/or prison officers in terms of the judicial aspect of their duties, were not allowed to accept the complaint in minor cases. They were in charge of matters such as arresting thieves and absconding slaves.[5] They could neither investigate nor hear a civil case unless the magistrate entrusted

[3] Jones 1994: 314.

[4] Disputes among the military were dealt with in military tribunals, those among the *manzu* people by special officials. Disputes between the military or *manzu* people and ordinary people were dealt with in the magistrate's court.

[5] Should an assistant magistrate wrongfully receive a complaint, he was to be sent to another post with a rank lower by one degree. A magistrate who failed to examine his assistant's wrongful conduct and report it was to forfeit one year's salary (*Jicheng*, *juan* 30: 13; *Bianlan*, *juan* 30: 1b–3a).

them to do so. In such circumstances, their recommended decision was subject to verification by the magistrate. Occasionally some subordinate officials abused their power to receive petitions dealing with disputes between individuals. Qu Tongzu even noted that 'many magistrates allowed their assistant magistrates to accept complaints in order to give them some additional income'.[6] It is doubtful whether this is correct. The Baodi records provide a rather different picture, which does not support Qu's account.

As an integral part of this principle, the higher authorities — namely the prefect, the circuit or provincial judge, the governor and the governor-general — might accept petitions only once they had been before the magistrates. Both the higher authority and the magistrate were liable to discipline and punishment if they contravened the principle. For example, the magistrate who did not receive properly submitted petitions committed an offence punishable under the Code (Article 342). The superior official was to forfeit nine months' salary. The petitioner, as we have seen above, was to be punished with 50 blows with a light stick. In normal circumstances, higher officials became involved in the proceedings only after the magistrate's judgment had failed one or both parties in either procedural or substantive terms. In terms of procedure, a magistrate might fail to review the petition in the first place; in terms of substance, his decision in the dispute might be challengeable. Only in special circumstances, such as an official inspection (*xunli*), was the higher authority allowed to accept a petition directly from petitioners of the county being inspected. In other words, in this situation the petitioner was allowed to bypass his 'own superior' and to go directly to the higher authority (Article 334).

2.1.1 The jurisdiction of magistrates

Under the statute on the proper order of submitting a complaint, one of the attached sub-statutes further specified the jurisdiction of the county magistrates:

> In such minor matters as household and marriage, land, debts, fighting, gambling, and so on, the plaintiff should bring the dispute to the magistrate of the county where the defendant lives. No complaint is allowed to be brought to the magistrate of the county where the plaintiff lives. (Sub-statute 332-11)

This rule was also stipulated in Article 334 on the official's duty to receive the complaint. It made it the magistrate's duty to reject petitions wrongly

[6] Qu Tongzu 1969: 12.

submitted to the plaintiff's magistrate's court, but logically required at the same time that the defendant's magistrate should not 'make excuses and refuse to accept the complaint' (*tuigu bu shouli*). What was new about the added sub-statute was a clarification of the responsibility of the two magistrates. The sub-statute was first made a *dingli* in 1728 (Yongzheng 6),[7] and was later attached to Article 332 in 1740 (Qianlong 5) (*Tongkao*: 873). This development is evidence of the Qing's active efforts to provide a clear procedure for solving minor cases. The rule was reasonable in the sense of achieving a fair judgment in the case, as a commonly quoted commentary book on the Code made clear. The reason for preferring the defendant's magistrate to the plaintiff's was that the former was the nearest authority who could take action speedily to ascertain the essential facts on which a decision might then be fairly made (*Jicheng*, *juan* 30: 12).

The core principle of respecting the proper order and choosing the right magistrate was adjusted where the parties were merchants involved in actions over debt. The rule for this class of case was:

> If provincial business men who do business elsewhere have differences over matters of debt, they are only allowed to petition the superior officials of the district in which the business was conducted, who may interrogate and judge. Those who bring their complaints to the capital will be punished and sent back. The complaints will be rejected even though they are true. (Sub-statute 332-13)

The concern of the law here was, on the one hand, to prevent the merchant from submitting his complaint directly to the authority located in the capital, and, on the other hand, to recognize the difficulty for merchants in submitting a petition to the magistrate where the defendant lived. It might prove impracticable for a merchant plaintiff to follow this rule if he and the other party lived far away from each other or from the place where they had their business. So the parties' 'superior authority' was replaced with the authority of the place in which their business was conducted. The adjustment was fundamental in allowing a court other than the merchants' 'own superior authority' to accept the petition and make a judgment. The new rule provided merchant litigants with a procedure for solving their disputes that was relatively easy to follow.

We may take an example from Ba county. Liao, from Fujian province, had business in Chongqing (where the Ba county magistrate's court was located). When he had a dispute with Wang, who was not himself a resident

[7] See Chapter 1, section 1.1.1, for *dingli*.

of Ba county but had business there, Wang brought the complaint to the Ba county magistrate, who consequently tried the case. (Baxian1: 199–201)

The core principle might also need to be varied in other situations. When the dispute concerned the petitioner's 'own authority', it was not convenient for the plaintiff to submit the claim to the court so involved. In such circumstances, the petitioner was allowed to go direct to his higher authority to make his claim (Sub-statute 332-10).[8]

The above rules were generally followed in practice. The plaintiff would submit the complaint first to the county court where the defendant lived. If the plaintiff submitted the complaint to his own magistrate when the defendant was resident in another county, the records from both Baodi and Ba counties reveal that the magistrate made comments such as 'the defendant lives in *x* county, you should go to *x* county to submit your complaint' (*beigao xi* x *xian ren ziqu* x *xian konggao keye*). When the case was submitted and tried, the defendant's county magistrate would send a detailed report of the trial to the other party's magistrate (see Chapter 4).

However, the evidence also shows that the rules might be broken occasionally. A report from the magistrate of Qijiang county, where the defendant lived, to the Ba county magistrate clearly shows that the plaintiff went to Ba instead of Qijiang to complain and was accepted by Ba county.[9] Interestingly, when the Ba magistrate wished to bring the defendant from Qijiang for a hearing, the Qijiang magistrate did not act as requested by the Ba magistrate. Instead, he summoned the defendant and witnesses himself, then sent a report in which he stated that the defendant and the property in question were actually in Qijiang county. But he made this point through the defendant's statement, so adopting a polite way of refusing his colleague's request.

On other rare occasions the rule might also be deliberately broken for the purpose of delivering justice to an aggrieved victim by a competing magistrate. For example, magistrate Shao was one day stopped in his chair by a woman who poured out her story to him. Since Shao believed the woman had a great grievance and was determined to intervene in the case, he accepted the woman's complaint even though neither the woman nor the accused was a resident in his county. Also, interestingly, he reported his intention to get involved to his governor-general, who argued that Shao

[8] Furthermore, a small number of prefectures were allowed to accept the complaint in minor cases as the first level (*Huidian shili*, *juan* 816).

[9] It is difficult to ascertain why the Ba magistrate broke the law, because Baxian1 contains only an edited version of the report (Baxian1: 225).

might be regarded by other officials as exceeding his jurisdiction in taking action on a case that properly belonged to another county. Shao responded to the governor-general that, as long as the governor-general did not strongly disapprove, he had a way of making his interference legitimate. He made a thief in his custody confess that the person accused by the woman was his (the thief's) partner. Then Shao sent an official request to the magistrate of the woman's county to transfer the person accused by the woman to his court. He finally decided in favour of the woman.[10]

This story seems to show that the Qing judicial system lacked a strong procedural basis in terms of officials' attitude toward the procedures. To some extent the Qing judicial system placed its emphasis on the achievement of justice in a substantive sense. This emphasis might displace procedural justice. In other words, established procedural rules might be put aside if the officials believed that respecting them conflicted with the achievement of substantive justice in the case. The above story implies another interesting phenomenon: the avoidance of a particular procedure was achieved by bringing to the fore another procedure. Apart from this, the story certainly implies that breaking the law was by no means normal practice.

2.2 Requirement concerning time limits for submitting and receiving a petition

In theory, there was no particular provision in the statutes or sub-statutes of the Qing Code placing a time limit on particular claims in order to disbar them. In fact, the Code clearly stated in Sub-statute 93-6, added in 1767, that land disputes of 'many years ago' (*yuannian*) could still be brought to the court if there was strong evidence:

> In lawsuits disputing the status of burial land and hill land [the underlined text is missing in Jing's translation], if the matter is new, then the decisive evidence shall be the officially sealed contract or deed to the land. If the present proprietor has occupied the land for a long time, then it shall be necessary to obtain the number (*zihao*) and dimensions of the property in question, the fish-scale books (*yulin ce*),[11] and the sealed receipts for land tax payments and to investigate and compare them one by one; if they match one another and corroborate the argument of the party bringing suit, then he shall be

[10] Wang Shirong 1997b: 202.

[11] Fish-scale books recorded people's land-holdings, with entries being arranged in order of the size of the holding. See Zen 1961: 177.

> declared the true owner of the property. If investigation reveals that they do not match, or if the party bringing suit does not have sealed receipts for payment of taxes on the land in question, then whatever old contracts, steles, registers, or other items he cites shall not be admitted as evidence; whoever has brought false suit or has encroached upon the property of others shall be punished according to statute. (Sub-statute 93-6)[12]

If we compare this law with another provision inherited from the Ming Code, the difference can be clearly seen.

> In lawsuits relating to family property [the underlined text is missing in Jing's translation] and real estate (*jiacai tiantu*), if the matter is already five years old, or even if the matter is less than five years old, but investigation reveals that relatives have drawn up a document of division which takes account of the sale, and the sales contract is valid, then it shall be ordered that the present proprietor continue in his possession of the property, and redivision or subsequent redemption shall not be permitted, nor shall further lawsuits be accepted for adjudication. (Sub-statute 95-1)[13]

The Ming sub-statute created a general rule on time limits for certain cases in which petitions regarding family property (*jiacai*) and redemption of land (*tianchan*) were brought. Two circumstances were mentioned in each type of case. If the matter in dispute had arisen more than five years earlier, both kinds of case should be rejected, which meant that in no circumstances could the family property be re-divided or the land redeemed. If the matter arose within the previous five years, the magistrate should reject the petition and not let the petitioner redeem the land in question only if there had been a contract of sale; or should re-divide the family property only if there had been a contract of division as evidence.

Although the main concern of the new sub-statute of 1767 was disputes concerning land that had been occupied for a long time by a party, the Qing Code clearly established that whether an action was possible depended on the merit of the evidence of the case itself. It is clear that the phrase 'many years ago' (*yuannian*) in Sub-statute 93-6 refers to a period longer than the 'five years' of the earlier Sub-statute 95-1. In this sense, the change, or even the choice of language, is significant. This is especially the case if we read the practical requirements made later in the provision concerning evidence for a case like this. Such documents as the official register book, the fish-scale books, and the certificate of payment of taxes should be consulted in examining the land contract.[14] If necessary, the magistrate had to measure

[12] Jing 1994: 71.
[13] Ibid.
[14] See more on these documents in Chapters 5 and 6.

the land. Wu Tan once commented on the relation of the two different provisions by pointing out that the part of Sub-statute 95-1 on redemption of land that had been sold five or more years earlier should be abolished, since the new sub-statute had been substituted for it (*Tongkao*: 435).

The new stipulation added by the Qing clearly allowed more petitions concerning land to be made. As long as the evidence was strong enough, it seemed that it was always possible to go to court. In terms of time limits, the provision concerning the farming season (*nongmang*) is perhaps more interesting.

2.2.1 The farming season

Since 80 per cent of the Qing population were farmers and tenants, the country was heavily reliant on farmers to achieve successful harvests, for the sake of both supporting the government financially and providing for people's well-being. The government put great effort into securing and maintaining the basic conditions for farmers to sow seeds and harvest, including the offer of free loans and the lending of tools and other necessities. The issue of agriculture was taken seriously. In order not to interrupt cultivation, a sub-statute was enacted concerning the acceptance of complaints during the farming season:

> The farming season runs from the first day of the fourth month to the thirtieth day of the seventh month. Aside from rebellion, murder, robbery, corruption, bribery (*zang*) and other serious breaches of law, including the cheating by evil brokers or inn owners of their clients or customers when there is definite evidence, all of which should be handled as usual, the minor matters of household, marriage, and land, should not be received. They can be heard and decisions rendered from the first day of the eighth month. (Sub-statute 334-1)

This sub-statute was added in 1688 (Kangxi 27). It excluded one-fourth of a year from the period in which people could submit complaints about minor matters. To some scholars this might prove that private matters were truly minor in nature in the eyes of the government, since several months for hearing them were formally removed by the Code. However, if we track the development of this provision, the real concern — i.e. to safeguard the importance of farming — is not in doubt.

In 1761 (Qianlong 26), a new sub-statute (334-7) was introduced. The first part of this sub-statute allowed the magistrate to postpone the investigation of land cases arising during the farming season until the eighth month, should there be danger of harm to agriculture. Then the sub-statute continued:

> As to the investigation (*chakan*) of matters concerning water conservancy, land boundaries, etc. which are currently in dispute so that any delay in handling them will certainly harm the affairs of farmers, then the *zhou* or *xian* [magistrates] are ordered to go to the locality themselves and conduct a trial and render a decision and quickly conclude [the matter]. One should not issue a warrant for arrest and have them brought to the city or have them wait [and thus] harm the farmers. All the other complaints which will have no harm to farming should be dealt with as usual. [The magistrate] should not stop [hearing cases].[15]

The sub-statute ends with rules on punishment should the magistrate use the excuse of the farming season to stop hearing cases that he should hear (Sub-statute 334-7). It is very clear that the reason given for not hearing minor cases in such a way as to interfere with agriculture should be genuine. Whether the magistrate should conduct a hearing or not logically depended on whether such action would harm farming. This concern is even more obvious if we compare the procedure that was applied for the collection of taxes. During the farming season, or more exactly between the fifth and seventh months in this case, the collection of taxes was suspended as well.[16]

When we turn to the procedure in practice, a similar development can be seen. Huang Liuhong was a magistrate in the early period of the Kangxi reign. He followed the law on the farming season in his book *Fuhui quanshu*, and established the practice by hanging up a board on which was written 'stop litigation in the farming season' (*nongmang zhisong*) in front of his court without adding any explanation. The famous artist magistrate Zheng Banqiao, who held office from 1742 (Qianlong 7), that is before the revision of the sub-statute, also made such comments as 'This is a minor matter over land. It is the time litigation should stop. Petition rejected' (*tianchan xishi, tingsong, buzhun*).[17] It is worth noting that the reason for rejecting a petition was solely the timing of the petition. This early practice implied that stopping the receipt of petitions during the farming season had generally been followed.

The situation changed with the addition of the sub-statute in 1761. Yuan Mu, whose magistracy occurred after this date, clearly made the point that the magistrate should not reject all petitions concerning land, debt, and marriage matters during the farming season without considering whether the

[15] Buxbaum 1971: 262.
[16] Qu Tongzu 1969: 132.
[17] *Zheng Banqiao nianpu* 1991: 321.

case, if heard, would harm farming.[18] This is precisely what the new sub-statute intended. When the law was ambiguous and failed to make a particular point, the expected step was to revise it, as in the case we have just seen. The law was certainly revised after it failed to make clear that acceptance or rejection of a petition should be genuinely and solely for the purpose of protecting farmers' cultivation. In doing so, the law clearly changed its emphasis, from simply removing the authority of the court to receive petitions in minor disputes to establishing a reasonable condition for receipt. The decisive factor in the court's action was whether the petition would really influence the process of farming. This might also explain the Baodi practice. I have not seen a single case that was rejected for the sole reason that it was submitted during the farming season (see Chapter 3). This fact is also important evidence that the sub-statute of 1761 was subsequently applied.

2.2.2 The open day

It is common sense that the magistrate could not be available every day to accept petitions, and that it was necessary to set some limit on the days on which they might be submitted. When receiving petitions, the magistrate dressed in his official robes and sat in the main hall or the second hall of the court[19] to receive the complaints handed in by plaintiffs. The magistrate usually received petitions on fixed days called open days (*fanggaori*). In practice, magistrates tended to fix between six and nine days regularly in each month for people to submit complaints to the court.[20] Perhaps to give the magistrates greater discretion, this practice, often termed *fanggaori*, was not mentioned in the Code. Even so, the legitimacy of the practice of open days should not be challenged and the magistrate was bound to choose a certain days. The authoritative book *Qinban zhouxian shiyi* [The Basics of the Magisterial Service Approved by the Throne] advised that the magistrate did not have to stick too strictly to the commonly accepted open-day practice, which was to choose every third, sixth, and ninth day in every ten-day period of a month (i.e. the third, sixth, ninth, thirteenth, sixteenth, nineteenth, twenty-third, twenty-sixth, and twenty-ninth days).[21]

[18] *Mulingshu*, *juan* 18.
[19] See Appendix 4.
[20] The higher officials' courts also had 'open days' for accepting petitions on appeal. The responsible officials often set 'open days' to accept petitions as soon as they assumed office (Li Liwong 1663: *juan* 9, *Cisong* [Litigation]).
[21] *Qinban zhouxian shiyi* 1997: 666.

Different magistrates might have different practices in choosing open days. Magistrate Liu Heng designated the third and eighth days of every ten-day period. According to Zhou Guangyuan, Taiwan's practice was the same as that of Liu Heng.[22] The open days were decreased from nine days per month to six days. To some scholars, this practice revealed the magistrate's attitude towards civil disputes, i.e. they were only minor matters.[23] On the surface, if one adds up all the 'open days' of the year, excluding the farming season, 'only' sixty-three days are available to petitioners to submit their lawsuits. It is understandable that some scholars use the term 'only' in pointing out the small proportion of available days in a year. They clearly believe that civil matters were regarded as of little importance, and magistrates were discouraging people from bringing civil disputes to their courts.[24]

The practice of 'open days' has been considered to be a discouragement to litigation because it put an obstacle in the way of submitting petitions. Zhou Guangyuan quotes Liu Heng's comments regarding the open day as 'another way to reduce the number of weak cases, for the anger of the parties involved might have abated after a few days or few months of waiting'.[25] In fact, a similar comment can be found from Huang Liuhong, who deemed the open day to be a sort of screen for the filtering of minor cases. Interestingly, Lan Dingyuan had a different view of this practice. He said he fixed an 'open day' every three days as his bait to entice more people to come to his court.[26]

It is interesting that almost the same open-day practice was a sort of screen in the eyes of Liu Heng and Huang Liuhong, to stop some people from coming to court, but it was a bait for Lan Dingyuan, to increase the number of lawsuits. To understand why their views on the same practice differed so significantly, we need to examine the situations about which they were speaking. Liu and Huang were talking about disputes without any substantive conflict; in other words, the disputes were only quarrels arising from sudden anger. And Liu and Huang were comparing such fixed days with the absence of any fixed days at all. They were talking about people who could not come to the court immediately they had a quarrel because the day

[22] Zhou Guangyuan 1995: 20. I cannot find which days were open days in Baodi from the records, since the day shown on a complaint might have been added afterwards. This can be inferred from the different style of the handwriting.

[23] Huang 1996: 10.

[24] Allee 1994a: 149; Brockman 1980: 92.

[25] Zhou Guangyuan 1995: 85.

[26] Lan Dingyuan 1729: 5.

happened not to be the open day. For them, the rule about fixed days might lead to a change of mind. Lan, in contrast, focused on the regularity and commitment of such open days. Because they were fixed and highly predictable and would not be interrupted by the magistrate's other duties, more people would submit their petitions to the court. It was just these characteristics of regularity and certainty that made the open-day practice so important in terms of facilitating the procedure for hearing disputes.

First, the system of open days established a practical and convenient regular procedure for the discharge of the magistrate's duty to receive complaints. The magistrate's function was all inclusive — even a magistrate who supervised a district with a relatively small population and light tax quota still had to perform many other duties apart from his judicial ones. Should people want to go to the court, especially from far away, it was essential to know that the magistrate would be available. The practice of 'open days' was clearly an efficient and responsible method for both the magistrate and the litigants, by which the magistrate made a clear promise to be there to receive the complaint on open days, and the petitioner thus was able to make plans accordingly. Besides, receiving a complaint was only the start of the whole litigation procedure. Many other related matters such as making comments on the complaint, sending out summonses, preparing for trial, and sitting in the hall delivering decisions were to be undertaken by the magistrate outside the open days and within a limited time.

Moreover, if circumstances proved the open days were insufficient, the magistrate might post an official proclamation (*gaoshi*) to allow people to submit complaints on particular occasions. The Baodi records contain some documents about a case in which the defendant, Zhang, was considered to be an evil bully. Considering the possibility that many victims were too scared to bring a lawsuit, the magistrate posted a proclamation on the four gates of the city and Wangpu (or Wangbu) village where Zhang lived to give public permission for people to submit any complaint against him (Baodi, 97: 163). Moreover, the magistrate himself might take action in suspicious situations. The magistrate of Ba county one day saw a woman crying in the street as he was passing, so he questioned the woman on the spot and solved the case later when the woman submitted the petition (see debt case 1 in Chapter 7 and section 2.6 below).

2.3 Petitioners and their agents

2.3.1 Offending one's status and violating duty

In general, a person who brought a complaint against another was called the original complainant (*yuangao* or *yuanzao*), and the other was called the accused (*beigao* or *beizao*). The person who responded to a complaint already brought and made a separate counter-complaint was called the added complainant (*zaikong*). The law offered different treatment with respect to different groups of petitioners.[27] Before we discuss the different petitioners in detail, we need to look at a particular statute of primary importance, *Ganming fanyi* (Offending One's Status and Violating Duty) (Article 337).

The essence of this article was to encourage the family ethic, because the love between father and son and the relationship between husband and wife were in the eyes of Confucius inherent in human nature. This ethic was consequently interpreted and codified in the law as prohibiting sons, wives, concubines, younger brothers, and nephews from accusing a father, husband, elder brother, or uncle. Qu discussed this issue at length and concluded that 'the laws governing concealment and accusation could not be applied to cases of rebellion. Thus it is clear that when there was no conflict between sovereignty and family, between loyalty to the state and filial piety, both principles were recognized and encouraged. But when the two were in conflict, sovereignty took precedence, and loyalty to the state was the crucial issue.'[28]

Qu clearly points out that the exception in applying the principle of non-accusation was because the value of loyalty to the state prevailed over that of filial piety. This was certainly true. However, this theory does not cover situations that the law did not treat as offending one's status and violating duties. Here are the details of Article 337:

> If the accusation (*against the persons who are superior or elder*) is of plotting rebellion, high treason, hiding illegally obtained property, spying, or is against the official mother in the direct line, the stepmother, the caring mother or the natural mother for killing [the accuser's] father, or is against the adoptive parents for killing [the accuser's] natural parents, or if the accusations against the superior or elder relatives of the second degree and below are for wrongful

[27] The military and the Banner people had to take their cases to special tribunals rather than the magistrate's court. If a dispute over land, debt, or marriage occurred between a Banner or military person and a civilian, then the magistrate should hear the case (Article 341, Substatutes 341-1 and 341-4).

[28] Qu Tongzu 1965: 74.

> taking of [the accuser's] property, or for striking and injuring his person, (*then if the accusation is true*) he may of course make the accusation. This permission (*for the inferior or younger relatives*) to bring an accusation is not within the provisions of this law of violating status obligations and duties.[29]

Reading through the whole paragraph, we see that the provision not only excluded the application of the principle of non-accusation in such cases as rebellion, in view of the value of loyalty to the state, but also excluded its application in accusations against a senior relative for illegally taking away one's property. The significance of this exception was not only to allow the junior member to submit a complaint about matters concerning property against a senior relative, but also to show that such behaviour was not regarded as offending the senior relative's status. The reason given by Qu concerning loyalty to the state obviously did not apply. Nor is it likely that the matter concerning property contained a value of greater importance. The only reasonable explanation seems to be that litigation concerning property attributed nothing offensive to the senior relative. As I have discussed in Chapter 1, civil disputes did not involve crimes and thus could bring no shame on a senior relative so accused. Rather, this law decoded a secret of the Qing law on this important issue, i.e. disputes over property were neither crimes nor ethically wrong.

2.3.2 Male adults, the aged, women, and the disabled

There were several provisions concerning petitioners in terms of submitting an ordinary civil complaint. The different treatment accorded to different kinds of petitioner can be easily ascertained, although the situation was rather complex because such different criteria as artificial and natural identities were relevant. Examples of an artificial identity can be seen in the classes of the official and the degree holder, and of natural identities in the aged, women, and so on. The most differentiated treatment applied to certain petitioners, who were required to have an agent to submit the complaint to the court. Officials, the aged, physically handicapped people, and women all had to have agents, whereas male adults did not. In fact, male adults (*zhuangding*) — males over the age of 16[30] — were required to submit the complaint personally:

> If the male adult does not submit the complaint personally without a reason, and hides deliberately, or deliberately allows the aged, the young, the

[29] Jones 1994: 323.
[30] *Qingdai liubu chengyu cidian*: 154.

> disabled, a woman or servant of his family to do so, no action should be taken on the complaint. (Sub-statute 332-7)

The reason they had to submit the petition personally lay in the rules established to exempt the old, women, and the disabled from the punishment prescribed by the Code. That was also why the aged, the disabled, and women were required to employ an agent to submit the petition, since the agent could be punished in their place.

Article 22 (Redemption by Aged Persons, Youths, and Those Who Are Disabled) provided that redemption was to be allowed for anyone aged 70 or over or 15 or under, or who was seriously disabled, who committed a crime punishable with exile or a lesser punishment. The same possibility of redemption was also granted to women by a sub-statute (20-7). Because of these provisions, the people in question might take advantage of such exemption to avoid possible punishment if their accusations turned out to be false. This rule was emphasized by another Article:

> If a person is over 80, or under 10, or suffering from a critical disability, or is a married woman, that person may make an accusation in such matters as plotting rebellion, treason, or high treason, or a child or son's child being unfilial, or in the situation in which he himself, or those living with him, have had property taken by theft or fraud, or where property has been seized and taken away, or there has been killing and injuring. In other cases, he or she may not file a complaint. (*Since* [such persons] *can redeem offences, it is to be feared that they will accuse falsely in order to injure others*). (Article 339.02)[31]

We see this exemption often enough in the Baodi records. Decisions such as 'she is a woman and old' or 'he is blind so should not be punished according to law (*lide mianjiu*)' occur here and there. The small commentary on Article 339.02 (italicized above) makes it clear that the concern here was to prevent these persons from bringing false accusations and then escaping punishment under the provision on redemption (for more on false accusation, see Chapters 3 and 9). The problem was solved by introducing the intermediary of the agent. This meant that the people mentioned above could submit a complaint but they would exercise some care in so doing. The first sub-statute appended to this Article says:

> If a person is old, or suffering from a critical disability, that person may make an accusation in such matters as plotting rebellion, treason, or high treason, or a child or son's child being unfilial. In other matters, a relative who lives in the same family and knows the matter may make an accusation on behalf

[31] Jones 1994: 325.

> of the person. If it is a false accusation, the relative should be punished. (Sub-statute 339-1)[32]

The aged who had to have an agent to bring the petition were actually depicted differently in Articles 22 and 339, the former stipulating the age of 70 and the latter 80. In this case, Baodi practice supported the age of 70. All persons aged 70 or over either had an agent or else declared that they were bringing the case themselves because they did not have an agent for whatever reason. This might suggest that the general rule of Article 22 was respected in practice.

2.3.3 Degree holders and students of the Imperial Academy

Sheng or *shengyuan* are licentiates of the first degree, and *jian* are students of the Imperial Academy (Guozijian). From the Qianlong reign (1736–95), the lowest literary status (*jian*) was often obtained by purchase and *jian* holders did not actually attend the Imperial Academy, although they were on its roll. Three sub-statutes in the Code are relevant to the *shengjian* group. Although they speak of *sheng* and *jian*, higher degree holders such as *juren* (second degree holder) and *jinshi* (third degree holder) should also be included. It was one of the drafting skills of the Qing Code that a specific reference to the lowest category was deemed to include the higher categories. Here is one sub-statute:

> *Jiansheng* (students of the Imperial Academy) who lead a dissipated life devoted to wine and pleasure, neglect the warnings of their teachers, do not keep the

[32] If we read the Article carefully, we note that persons within the defined classes might bring a lawsuit to the magistrate's court in matters affecting property. However, according to the Qing Code, if a sub-statute has a particular provision that differs from a statute, it was the sub-statute that had priority (Article 43). Thus, these classes of person should use an agent to bring a petition in matters of property, as provided by the sub-statute. Allee noticed that the word '*furen*' (women) was omitted from the sub-statute, and concluded that 'the procedural regulation that women be represented by agents was not drawn from Qing legal statutes' (Allee 1994a: 168). Xue Yunsheng also raised the question with respect to the omission: 'will a woman be allowed to bring accusations herself or just be prohibited from bringing accusations in matters of marriage, land, and family property?' (*Cunyi*: 1019). The inconsistency is clear. Nevertheless, the law's intention was never unclear on this point, even though the word 'women' was omitted from the sub-statute. One of the attached instructions on the standard petition form, as will be seen in the next chapter from an example taken from the Baodi records, read: 'Petitions from the gentry, women, the aged, the physically disabled, or the mentally incompetent must be submitted by an agent.' 'Women' was simply added to the list of persons who should sue by agent. The real concern of the Code was to prevent these persons from bringing false accusations and then escaping punishment under the provision on redemption.

> rules of their university or school, visit prostitutes, give themselves up to gambling, frequent official tribunals and immerse themselves in litigation, make corrupt statements, and receive other people's taxes in order to pay them and other things of this kind will be reduced to the status of a commoner and receive the due punishment. (Sub-statute 374-1)

This sub-statute was originally enacted under the Ming and could be regarded as a general guideline applicable to *shengjian* (*Tongkao*: 961). It should be clear that degree holders were allowed to bring lawsuits, but the sub-statute was conceived to prevent degree holders submitting petitions not directly relevant to themselves. Although the principle was applied to all petitioners, degree holders were treated more severely when they violated it. The reason appears to be that they were sometimes involved in helping people with bringing a lawsuit either by drafting the petition or by being a witness. The concern of the law was clear — to impose a high standard of conduct on degree holders. In this sense, the Qing legislator was ready to invoke moral values in order to establish legal liability. Provisions about the degree holders added later made this concern more specific.

> Government students (*shengyuan*) who do not keep the rule of the school, being fond of lawsuits in many affairs, are all to be removed from school. In accordance with the code dispose of the case. Redemption is not permitted. (Sub-statute 1-16)

> Where a *shengyuan* on behalf of a person helps as a witness, but all the statements he makes belong to the class of false accusations, the appropriate territorial officials are to make an immediate report and request the removal of the button. In accordance with Article 340 on instigating lawsuits which defines the main offence, respectively increase the punishment by one degree and sentence the offence. If the amount of illicit goods when calculated would yield a heavier punishment than the original offence, sentence as subvert the law and follow the more serious offence. If inquiring into the affair clearly shows that there was a good reason and that the statements were not invented and there was no false witness, a stern warning is to be delivered to the said *shengyuan*. If the offender does not know how to reform and repent and again follows his previous practices, . . . the provincial educational commissioner will dismiss him. (Sub-statute 336-15)

As we can see, should a degree holder be involved in lawsuits not directly relevant to themselves, and they were proved to be false witnesses, not only were they punished, as required by the relevant law, but they were also stripped of their degree or dismissed from the school. Furthermore, if a *shengjian* was characterized as 'being litigious' (*haosong*), he was not allowed to redeem his punish-ment with money. The Code clearly showed its dislike of the dishonest involvement of *sheng* or *jian* in a lawsuit. What was not clearly stated was that *sheng* or *jian* should have an agent when submitting the complaint (although this was required by the instructions given at the end of the petition form — see Chapter 3). Degree holders, especially the *jinshi*, were often made officials and categorized together with official post holders. Because the law included a separate statute requiring officials to employ an agent to bring a lawsuit (Article 342), requiring an agent in the case of degree holders too would certainly fit with Qing logic.

Although officials, degree holders, the aged, and women were all required to have an agent, there was a difference between the agent of ordinary petitioners and that of petitioners with official rank, as revealed by Baodi records. The agent of an ordinary petitioner was usually a relative, and the petitioner still had to appear in court as well. If any punishment was to be imposed on the original petitioner, it was imposed on the agent in his/her stead. In contrast, the agent of a petitioner with official rank was usually a *jiaren* (hired servant)[33] instead of a relative, and the original petitioner did not have to appear in court. If the magistrate wished to communicate with an official petitioner, he addressed him through his agent, referring to him as 'your master' (*nijia zhuren*) so as to avoid a direct personal reference.

2.4 Scriveners and litigation masters

The position of scrivener (*daishu*) was established to assist illiterate people with the composition of a complaint. This was because the Qing was strongly against what were called 'litigation masters' (*songshi*), who previously supplied such help. The harsh treatment of litigation masters was in order to get rid of false accusations, because litigation masters were capable of making up a case entirely to meet the needs of their client. The scrivener was formally introduced by Sub-statute 340-10 in 1729 (Yongzheng 7). This provided that: (1) the magistrate should appoint scriveners by examination; (2) the scrivener should write the complaint according to the true facts; and (3) all complaints should be marked with the scrivener's stamp, and then could be received by the magistrate.

It is well known that the issue of assistance with the composition of a petition is inevitably connected with litigation masters. The social role of

[33] *Jiaren* here refers to people who lived in the same household. The official commentary on Article 287 states: 'one household (*means those who live together, including even slaves or hired servants*)' (Jones 1994: 273).

litigation masters has been well described by Macauley in *Social Power and Legal Culture*.[34] What I would like to make clear is that the law on litigation masters should be understood in connection with the provisions on scriveners, and vice versa. From the harsh provisions on litigation masters, it might appear that the Qing tightened attitudes to litigation. The original Article, inherited from the Ming, still allowed people to write petitions for others providing they stated the truth:

> If one is acquainted with another who is unlearned and cannot redress his wrongs and he gives him advice in accordance with the facts, or he writes the complaint for the other and the offence is not increased or decreased, there is no punishment. (Article 340)[35]

Such limited permission was discarded from later legislation. All the relevant sub-statutes added on litigation masters reveal a complete change. That is why Macauley opens her book with a story about a litigation master (Xu) who 'simply' wrote five legal documents and was sentenced to penal servitude. The position taken by the Qing toward litigation masters was so extreme that one cannot help sharing Macauley's belief that 'the issue no longer was simply litigation abuse, as it had been prior to the eighteenth century; it was facilitation of formal litigation'.[36]

However, that understanding, though correct as far as it goes, is only part of the picture. The Qing's attitude toward litigation masters was undoubtedly a very striking feature. But the issue in the story of Xu was not that 'he simply assisted another person in the composition of a legal document',[37] but that he should not have supplied any assistance at all, because the Qing at that time had formally established the facility of the scrivener, who was expected to compose legal documents. Xu not only composed a legal document, but did so five times. Thus he was punished one degree less than the punishment imposed on 'habitual litigation hooligans', that is, penal servitude for three years. We should not understand the provisions on litigation masters as targeting civil litigation as a whole.[38]

The change in the Qing law established the facility of the scrivener, on the one hand, and blocked the way for persons other than the scrivener to help with litigation, on the other. The law was concerned with two matters: first, illiterate people should have an easy way of finding a person to compose

[34] Macauley 1999.
[35] Jones 1994: 325–6.
[36] Macauley 1999: 19.
[37] Ibid.
[38] See also Bodde and Morris 1973: 415–16.

a petition for them; and, secondly, people should be prevented from getting help from litigation masters. One fact worth noting is that the practice of selecting scriveners through examination to draft complaints was adopted by Huang Liuhong before the law to this effect was finally put into the Code.[39] It is not clear whether Huang acted on his own or just adopted an already established practice. In either event, the legal position of the scrivener certainly does not support the view that the Qing adopted too strict an attitude towards litigation. Indeed, the employment of a scrivener was a very beneficial creation in terms of the help it brought to illiterate people, especially when we consider that most of the population of the Qing were illiterate.

Nevertheless, the problem of false accusation seems to have been a problem throughout the Qing dynasty. Although the law clearly provided that the scrivener should write exactly what the true facts were, otherwise he would be punished, in practice, exaggerated and false plaints did not stop. Scriveners were in fact rarely punished. Petitioners sometimes had their complaints drafted by somebody else, in which case the scrivener had only to rewrite them and then affix his sign. Sometimes, but not always, the original composer was traced by the magistrate. The reason there is no reported case of a scrivener being punished or dismissed perhaps lies in the fact that the scrivener was not in a position to judge the truth of what he wrote. It was the magistrate's obligation to make the facts clear in the performance of his judicial duty.

While the establishment of the scrivener did not succeed in stopping false accusations, the institution of scrivener brought a new problem. The law required that all complaints, at least those submitted by ordinary persons, should be signed by the scrivener. Actually, the Baodi records include many other submissions, apart from petitions, all stamped with the scrivener's sign. These documents include statements of confirmation (*ganjie*). Even the *xiangbao*'s report almost always contained one such stamp.[40] Only complaints from persons who had an official title needed no such stamp (Baodi, 107: 144, 145, 155). As a result, some scriveners took the opportunity to ask for an extra fee for the use of the stamp. And there were cases, for example the

[39] Huang Liuhong 1850/1972: 49.

[40] The *xiangbao*, as part of the *baojia* system, was appointed by the magistrate as 'head man' for a local community. There were 42 *bao* in Baodi. The people were organized into security units called *baojia*: 10 households comprised a *pai*; 100 households a *jia*; and 1,000 households a *bao* (Qu Tongzu 1969: 3). For more on the *baojia* system, see MacCormack 1996a: 121–33. Usually the *xiangbao* presided over a number of villages, ranging from just a few to over ten. The *xiangbao* was replaced by the *cunzheng* (the village head) and the *cunfu* (the vice village head) in the reign of Xuantong, as shown in Baodi (Baodi, 193–218).

case I quote later in this chapter from Lan Dingyuan, in which the scrivener refused to write a complaint.

The service supplied by scriveners, though still challengeable, shows that they were not as untruthful as litigation masters. At least they were registered and identifiable, whereas litigation masters often concealed their identity. Employment of scriveners was usually one of the most urgent tasks faced by a new magistrate. Once in post, the magistrate needed, as soon as possible, to appoint several qualified scriveners through examination. *Mulingshu* (*juan* 17) suggested that on the third day after taking up his office the magistrate should set an examination to choose scriveners and give them the wooden stamp. Some existing scriveners would keep their job by passing the test, but they still needed to change the style of their stamp, which would have the previous magistrate's surname carved on the top. During the interim, when a new magistrate was in the process of taking up his post and the new stamps were not ready, the scrivener would give his sign by handwriting. In the Baodi records we find such simple signs as 'the sign of scrivener so-and-so' (*guandaishu* x *chuoji*). Until the new scriveners came into operation, the original ones continued the task of maintaining the ordinary litigation process. Thus the civil litigation procedure experienced few interruptions even when the magistrate was changing. Smooth running during this time was especially significant because many counties were constantly changing their magistrates.

2.5 The form of the complaint

To bring a lawsuit, one needed to make a complaint openly (Sub-statute 333-1). Both the complaint and the counter-plaint had to be written on a standard form, called *zhuang*.[41] According to a decree of Jiaqing 10 (1805), the employment of standard forms would ensure that the composition of the complaint focused on the key point of the dispute and gave only the necessary relevant information (*Jicheng*, *juan* 30: 16). Although officials at different levels all employed a standard form for petitions, the available sources reveal that there was no uniform form used nationally.[42] The basic parts of all *zhuang* included the following four elements: (1) the petitioner's personal data, such as name, age, gender, status, address, and occupation; (2) relevant

[41] Gentry petitioners were excepted from the requirement of using the standard form. They used blank paper and wrote much lengthier plaints.

[42] I referred to Baodi county records, Ba county records, Huang Liuhong's *Fuhui quanshu*, and Dan-xin records from Allee 1994a.

information such as the name of the accused, the witnesses (in some places the identity of the *xiangbao* and the address of the inn[43] were also required), the evidence, and whether any comment had been made by the magistrate for the case (if it was a rebuttal or a follow-up petition,[44] or any other relevant submission, the magistrate would quite likely have made some sort of comment and this comment had to be copied for reference); (3) spaces left for the main accusation and the comment issued by the magistrate; (4) instructions to be followed in the petition.

The items included in each standard form varied from place to place and also from time to time. The Baodi forms had no entry for the *xiangbao* and the inn. This does not mean that the *xiangbao* was not important in Baodi county. On the contrary, in most, if not all, cases, the *xiangbao* assisted in the investigation of the facts or the execution of a summons or appeared in court when cases were heard. So the absence of an entry for the *xiangbao* implies that his role was too routine for specific mention.[45] In the Baodi records, I found a form that contained very detailed items at the beginning. These items included: whether the petition was brought for the first time (*xinan*) or not (*jiuan*), how much land (private or government) the petitioner farmed, how much tax he should pay and whether he had paid his tax, if not, how much was owed, whether he had borrowed any food or seed from the magistrate, and so on (Baodi, 102: 26; 167: 1). However, the more significant differences and changes concerned the space allowed for the main accusation and the magistrate's comment and the attached instructions. I shall consider the instructions in detail later. As for the space, there seem to be some changes. The space in Huang Liuhong's example contained only 144 squares, but all the records from Baodi county, Ba county, and Dan-xin had many more than that. The least number of squares in Baodi was 288 (some were 300) and the maximum in Ba county was 325.[46] We know that Huang Liuhong was a magistrate during the early years of Kangxi (1662–1722). If his information on this point was generally true at that time, then the Qing government may have been trying to adapt the form so as best to serve the purpose of litigation.

The form discussed above was the standard form (*zhengzhuang*) used by both plaintiff and defendant. The petitioner was asked to submit a copy plaint (*fuzhuang*) at the same time (see the instructions in Chapter 3). Since

[43] This was the small hotel where the petitioner lived temporarily during the litigation.

[44] For the follow-up petition, see later in this section.

[45] The reason for not needing information about where the petitioner was living, i.e. the name of the inn, is less clear.

[46] Dan-xin had 320 according to Allee 1994a.

the copy plaint was less formal, its usage by the magistrate varied, although usually they were used for the magistrate's review of the case in his inner court. Huang Liuhong used the copy form only for giving instructions to his office to draft the summons directive (*chuanpiao*).[47] The copy form he employed was very simple, including only information on the cause (the matter in dispute) and the names of the defendant, the witnesses, and the neighbours. Whatever the difference in the usage of copy plaints, they were usually kept by the magistrate and not placed in the court's files. They also showed some differences from the standard form. The cover page bears the handwritten words 'copy petition' (*fuzhuang*). The main space for the text was lines instead of squares. Except for these lines, there were neither printed items nor instructions. The scrivener's seal seems still to have been needed and the composition of the complaint was the same. The function of the copy form is perhaps the reason only a couple of copy complaints were found in the Baodi records (Baodi, 110: 121).

The characteristics of the complaint revealed by the forms are very interesting from both a technical and a non-technical perspective. The typical opening headlines the accusation in one sentence, and the closing formula expresses respectful submission to the magistrate. The petitioner employed a standard way of referring to him/herself. A person with any official rank referred to himself as *zhi* (official), one with a degree or the title of national student as *sheng* (degree holder), *jiansheng* (student), or *wusheng* (military student). A person of *manzu* nationality referred to himself as *qiren* (banner man), the ordinary people, usually of *han* nationality, referred to themselves as *minren* (male adult) and *shen* (body) or, in Ba county, *yi* (literally 'ant'). A woman referred to herself as *fu* (woman) or *shuangfu* (widow). In short, the personal data were recorded in an economical way.

Although the copy complaint took a form different from the formal complaint, it was also 'formal' in the sense that it was required at the submission of the petition. Apart from such formal complaints, another complaint called a 'supplementary complaint' (*touci*) also existed. *Touci* were used by petitioners to give more information, mainly to minimize the risk of a charge of false accusation, after the submission of the standard petition. They might first have submitted a petition using baseless language to fabricate charges to gain access to the court, then used a *touci* to change the original charge by way of further explanation.[48] Huang Liuhong strongly recommended his fellow magistrates to ignore the supplementary complaint, and

[47] See Chapter 4 for the *chuanpiao*.
[48] *Mulingshu*, *juan* 17, *Lun yiqie cisong* [Comments on litigation].

focus only on the original complaint in dealing with the case.[49] *Touci* were forbidden by a sub-statute introduced in the Kangxi reign (Sub-statute 336-4). Only a couple of supplementary complaints have been found in the Baodi records, called either 'details and reasons paper' (*qingyou dan*) or just 'attached paper' (*niandan*), which perhaps suggests that supplementary petitions were not often used (Baodi, 97: 40; 165:68), and this may be attributed to Sub-statute 336-4.

According to the Taiwan archive, it appears that a follow-up petition (*cuizhuang*) was more often submitted. As the name clearly implies, this petition was a submission in which a party asked the magistrate to take quick action after the original petition had been accepted. This was almost completely contrary to the practice that Baodi records revealed — there were no follow-up petitions. Although there might be other reasons for the popular usage of *cuizhuang*, one main reason could be that Taiwanese officials did not prohibit it; they might even have allowed it. This can partly be seen from the instructions attached to Taiwan forms revealed by Allee.[50] These instructions contained no relevant order comparable to that contained in Baodi forms: 'it is only permitted to have one accusation and one defence' (see instruction 6 in Chapter 3). By making such connections between the law, the magistrates' comments, and practice, we can deduce that the absence of follow-up petitions in Baodi county was certainly no mere accident, but was the result of a clear design.

2.5.1 An example form

For an example of the form of the complaint, I take a land case from the Baodi record[51] to demonstrate the details in its original order:

- the cover page;
- the two-page space in squares;
- the plaintiff (*yuangao*), defendant (*beigao*) and witnesses (*ganzheng*) with following margins;
- the surname and titles of the magistrate and the margin for his comments and the time (year/month/day);
- the statement of terms under which jurisdiction will be executed.

[49] Huang Liuhong 1850/1972: 121–2.
[50] Allee 1994a: 153–4.
[51] This example petition (Baodi, 99: 142) was actually the rebuttal in the case. The original petition was missing. However, either the plaintiff or the defendant used the same form of petition.

The cover page

This is the most common cover page for petitions in the Baodi records. The cover page included two items: one was the two-word printed phrase *chengzhuang* (plaint) placed vertically in the middle of the page; the other was the sign of the scrivener at the bottom to the left. The sign of the scrivener was composed of a rectangle with a small trapezoid on the top. The three words carved in the trapezoid were *zhengtang* (the chief official) and Dai (the surname of the magistrate at that time). There were three vertical lines in the rectangle: the right-side line contained the name of the scrivener Lu De — (one word was missing); the left side the *yue* (month) and the *ri* (day).[52] The most distinctive feature was the middle part, where a four-word phrase *yipian danxin* ('one piece of red heart') was carved in stylistic calligraphy.[53] Different scriveners chose different phrases with different cursive styles.

The two-page space in squares

> Complaint by degree holder Zhao Liankui, age 41, *minren* [male adult] Zhao Qitai, age 64, and Zhao Yongshun, age 52, all residents of Zhaojiapai village of Xingbaoli, 50 *li* south from the town.
>
> In the matter of obeying the endorsement to elaborate the following facts, we beg you kindly to condescend to take the responsibility to investigate the case and question the parties. On the complaint of Tian Youlai who accused Zhao Tongqing and *sheng* [a degree holder] (Zhao Liankui) and others of forcibly planting his land, an endorsement was written on the complaint: 'complaints concerning land should have the contract and certificate of tax submitted as evidence. There is no description of such documents or any statement of the reason to pay land tax, or the evidence held by the river runner Dong Zhongyuan, or the reason why Zhao Tongqing and others took the action of forcibly planting the land. There might be some other facts behind this. Wait, I will order the runner to investigate whether Dong Zhongyuan embezzled the land tax, and Zhao Tongqing and the others forcibly planted the land. After the runners have reported on the facts, I will verify them and take action.' From *sheng*'s ancestor there developed three branches of the family. *Sheng* Zhao Liankui is of the eldest branch, *shen* Zhao Qitai of the second branch, and Zhao Yongshun of the youngest. The three branches jointly possessed a piece of land of 4 *mu* left by the ancestor. The land is located on the western bank of Xiuzhen river without blocking the flow of the river.

[52] The left margin for putting in the time in the petition remained empty. The records show that sometimes this time was the same as the time at the end of the comments; sometimes it was different (Baodi, 104: 40).

[53] For details about the scrivener see section 2.4.

There is a record of tax collection in the name of Zhao Liangcai on the official registration book which may serve as evidence. The certificate of taxes is kept by Zhao Dachun, the head of *sheng*'s [Zhao Liankui's] clan. The land has been rented and planted by Tian Shengmei, who pays one third of the harvest to *sheng*'s clan, a payment used to defray the costs of sacrifice to our ancestors. Unexpectedly, Tian Shengmei occupied the river bank and blocked the river flow. Our clan was afraid that he would cause troubles for us (for the land was under the name of *sheng*'s clan), so tried to get back the land to plant it within the original bounds set in Daoguang's 16th year [1836]. Tian Shengmei asked his nephew-in-law Dong Zhongyuan, as well as his relatives Dong Yilong and Cao Shengzuo, to mediate as middle men, promised that he would plant the land as he did before, and wrote a contract of lease, which can be produced as evidence. Dong Zhongyuan, the middle man, also can be questioned. After Tian Shengmei died, it was his son, Tian Youlai, who paid our clan's grain tax. Now, because of the increasing numbers of *sheng*'s clan, we cannot pay the costs of the sacrifices and asked him for the land back. With his agreement in front of us, we three branches planted the land. Unexpectedly, he brought a false accusation and said that he had paid the land tax to Dong Zhongyuan. This land is the *sheng* clan's private property, which has nothing to do with Dong Zhongyuan. Furthermore, Dong has not any piece of land near this location and never received any tax payment from this land. He can be summoned and interrogated. How can Tian involve him as well as many members of the *sheng* clan in such trouble? Such behaviour amounts to promoting a false accusation. His occupation of the land does not accord with human obligation and moral principle. Now we have received your endorsement and have to state the truth. We implore that you, our kind and intelligent elder father, teacher, and great master, agree with benevolence to investigate and hear [the case]. This really is a favour to us. We will present our tax certificate and contract to the court when you hear the case.[54]

Names of plaintiff, defendant, witness

Yuangao (the accuser);

Beigao (the accused);

Ganzheng (witness).

Comment of the magistrate Dai and the date of the petition

Zhengtang [chief administrative officer] Dai's *pi* (endorsement)

[54] There are 144 squares on each page, which make a total of 288 squares. But the actual word count of this petition totalled 456, because the petition in fact ignored two instructions (instructions 13 and 16; see Chapter 3) and it contained more than one word in each square. Sometimes a petition could be much shorter. For example, the essential part of one petition (Baodi, 185: 50) contained only 60 words, which perhaps is the shortest petition in the Baodi records, but the magistrate's comment was 62 words.

The measurements of the land mentioned in the defence are not the same as those mentioned in the complaint. I suspect there may have been some deceit and false accusation. Wait until the runners have finished their investigation. Then I will check and make a decision.

The 10th of the second month of Daoguang 29th year (1849).[55]

2.5.2 Composition of the complaint

Shiga correctly observed the 'victim' feature of the complaint.[56] The main content was full of expressions stating how the other party had wrongfully and terribly done bad things to the petitioner, with a plea for the magistrate to take action at once to restore justice. The language was so emotional and metaphorical that even extreme literary allusions such as 'there is no trace of corpse and skeleton' (*shigu quanwu*) were employed in a complaint of a husband accusing another man of selling his wife. By creating such an atmosphere, the petitioner implied that the lawsuit was not intended to cause trouble without grounds. This feature was so strikingly pervasive in the composition of complaints that we would be justified in calling the phenomenon a culture of 'the plaintiff victim'.

Although the style in which complaints of the Qing period were composed and submitted was different from that of present-day petitions in civil disputes, the conclusion that such differences resulted from the fact that under the Qing 'the petition did not claim any right (*quanli*) in accordance with the law' was not true.[57] Very often, the emotional language depicted only one side or one layer of the incident, or managed to introduce exaggerations or even false accusations. In the original petition on which the above rebuttal was based, Tian obviously omitted to state the fact that the land belonged to the Zhao clan. He gave only part of the story, and made full use of the planting incident by the Zhao clan. He accused more than nine people and acted as though he was a powerless victim. In doing so, he was actually trying to keep his story in line with the law because, if the petition was true, he was obviously supported by the law. In the rebuttal by the Zhao family, a much more powerful party in terms of both the numbers of their family and their possessions, the victim strategy was not excluded. They claimed that they had experienced financial difficulty in order to justify their action in trying to take the land back, because the

[55] The next part was the magistrate's statement of the terms under which he would exercise jurisdiction, which will be listed and discussed in Chapter 3.
[56] Hiroaki Terada 1998.
[57] Ibid.: 214.

law forbids a landlord to evict a tenant without good reason. The most effective of the emotional appeals was the allegation of physical injury, since the person inflicting the wound was necessarily a wrongdoer. In the allegation of being the victim of great wrongdoing, the petitioner must drive the story in the direction of particular provisions of the law.

So far this chapter has shed light on some aspects of the state's attitude to civil litigation, or, more exactly here, of the law's attitude to civil litigation. The Qing Code laid down virtually no limits on a magistrate's power to accept civil complaints. The accessibility of the magistrate's court was as unrestricted as could reasonably be expected. As long as a petition had merit, it should be unnecessary to start the lawsuit by making false accusations or alleging physical injuries.

Philip Huang believed the reason was that 'the state took the posture that they [officials] did not . . . handle civil cases'. 'That posture was what led some litigants to represent civil disputes as criminal ones to gain the attention of the court'.[58] Macauley has a similar argument: 'Common people were easily convinced that a magistrate or higher official genuinely would not be interested in their "petty" complaints in both civil and criminal matters'. So, logically, people 'used the false accusation as a tool of judicial access'.[59]

It may be right to say that the use of false accusations as well as allegations of injury in the petition was a tool to obtain the magistrate's attention, although the reason was not because the state took an anti-litigation posture toward civil disputes or because civil matters were regarded as petty or were routinely sent back to the community to mediate. To understand this phenomenon, a much wider approach is needed.

The use of false accusation and allegation of injury as strategies to obtain speedy access to the magistrate's court actually resulted mainly from the provisions of the law itself. For example, the law required the magistrate to take action at once in injury cases, which did provide a shortcut for the plaintiff. The provision on false accusation also supplied an excuse, because those who brought untrue accusations left without being prosecuted. I shall discuses this issue in Chapters 3 and 9. In terms of the rejected petitions revealed in the Baodi cases, as we shall see in the next chapter, the magistrate made his decision on the merits of the case.

[58] Huang 1996: 194.
[59] Macauley 1999: 140, 141.

2.6 Submitting and receiving a complaint

To receive complaints, the magistrate had to sit in the hall, which was always a dignified performance. He followed a detailed set of steps in order to handle the flow of complaints in an efficient order and at the same time to create a solemn and respectful atmosphere. To a certain extent, magistrates followed a common procedure. They issued the notification of open days, usually received complaints in the early morning (*zaotang*, about 7 o'clock in the morning), and met every petitioner face to face. Nevertheless, some details in the procedure adopted by each magistrate could be very different. For example, both Huang Liuhong and Wang Fengsheng described their procedure in details that had very little in common. Wang had a record book sent in advance to the scrivener. The scrivener wrote down the names of the petitioners in the book and took this with him when he appeared in court where complaints were being accepted, in case the magistrate needed him. Wang interrogated every plaintiff himself about disputes brought to him for the first time (*xinan*) and always 'got to the bottom of the matter, and made a thorough inquiry into it (*qiongyuan jingwei*)'.[60] Liu Heng, too, emphasized the importance of questioning the plaintiff in order to obtain the true facts, so that petitions without merit might be rejected and the number of false accusations decreased. By questioning the plaintiff, Liu was able to reject petitions that lacked reasonable logic (*qingli*).[61] Huang Liuhong had a different practice. He allowed the plaintiffs themselves to hand in their complaints, and used a paperweight to hold them on his bench. After Huang had counted all the complaints, the clerk on duty called the names of the plaintiffs. The magistrate interrogated the plaintiff only when he thought there was something suspicious in response to the clerk's summons. At the end, he took the box in which all the complaints were put and returned to his inner court to decide on further action.[62] Many magistrates preferred to question petitioners on the spot when receiving the complaints, but the practice was not as uniform as Cohen suggested when he observed that all magistrates interrogated every plaintiff thoroughly.[63]

As we can see from the above, the big difference in magisterial practice lay in whether the questioning and the decision to accept or reject were made on the spot. Usually, if a magistrate such as Liu Heng or Wang Fengsheng interrogated the plaintiff for a specific purpose, he wished to

60 *Mulingshu, juan* 18: *Fanggao shencheng* [Reviewing complaint when submitted].
61 *Mulingshu, juan* 17: *Shuliao wenda* [Answers to some colleagues' questions].
62 Huang Liuhong 1850/1972: 120–1.
63 Cohen 1966: 1210–11.

decide on the spot whether to reject the case or agree to take further action. Huang Liuhong's practice, in contrast, was to make this decision later after careful consideration. Apart from Huang Liuhong, there were perhaps also newly appointed and inexperienced magistrates who wanted to avoid deciding on acceptance or rejection on the spot. In any case, as Wang Huizu pointed out, the magistrate should not force himself to make a decision on the spot if there were any points of obscurity and further information was needed. For such petitions, the magistrate should decide whether to accept or reject later, after further information had been obtained.[64] No matter how different the active steps followed by the magistrate, the aim was always the same, that is, to stop the bringing of false accusations.

The formal expressions for the magistrate sitting in a hall to receive complaints, whether on an 'open day' or not, were different. The receipt of complaints on an 'open day' was called 'receipt on open day' (*qigao shoucheng*); receipt on other days was called 'receipt while sitting on the hall' (*suitang shoucheng*). It was unusual, but not impossible, to receive petitions for civil cases on a closed day. Lan Dingyuan recited one of his own experiences:

> I had just begun my official business, then saw there was an old woman helped by a young woman kneeling outside the *yamen* [magistrate's office] with a piece of paper held over her head. So I asked the runner to let them in and said: if you want to bring a complaint, you should come closer to the hall, why kneel far away? I asked the runner to give the complaint to me, the runner said: it is a white paper. I said: it does not matter [whether it is in a standard form]. Women do not know the form of a complaint. The runner said: there are no words, the paper is empty. I said: even so, give it to me.[65]

Lan did not have to accept this petition, because the incident did not occur on an open day. Some magistrates, such as Liu Heng, strongly disagreed with the practice of acceptance on a day other than an 'open day'. But there was one kind of case that the magistrate had to accept on other days, that is, a petition brought by 'crying out' (*hanbing*). Once the petition had been 'cried out', the magistrate had to appear in the hall to make a response. Such cases had a degree of urgency that required the magistrate to take immediate action. An allegation of injury was the most common reason for 'crying out' a petition. Even where the plaintiff's injury was very minor, the magistrate was required by law (Article 303) to examine the injury at once.[66] Many

[64] *Mulingshu, juan* 18: *Shaozhun qinshen* [Avoiding easy acceptance through personal interrogation].
[65] Lan Dingyuan 1729: 62.
[66] For more on minor injury cases, see Chapter 9.

petitioners used the method of 'crying out' to gain access to the magistrate's court. Usually there was a drum (or gong, as Liu Heng had) in front of the court for this purpose. Baodi records contain many such petitions. On the cover page of several case files, the cause of the case was noted in only three words '*hanbingshi*' (crying out matter). Apart from this, the most unusual way to approach a magistrate, as I noted in the anecdote about magistrate Shao above, was to stop his chair to make a petition (*lanyu*).

Following receipt of the complaint, the next steps the magistrate had to take were making comments, investigating, summoning people to be questioned, and hearing and deciding. I shall turn in the next chapter to examine a magistrate's reasons for accepting or rejecting a complaint.

3

The Magistrate's Comments on Receiving the Complaint*

Theoretically, as I have pointed out, there was no limitation in the statutes or sub-statutes of the Qing Code on the persons who might bring petitions of minor disputes to the court. Nor was there any limitation on the period during which a dispute was allowed to come to the magistrate's court. As long as the petition was properly submitted, the magistrate had first to receive and then to review it. Magistrates who did not receive properly submitted petitions committed an offence punishable under the Code.[1] Obviously, the magistrate, as the only administrator in local government who was responsible for taking care of all tasks, could not, and was not expected to, act on all petitions brought before him. The magistrate had from the beginning to recognize cases with real merit and ignore those without. In other words, it was illegal for him to refuse to review complaints but, having reviewed them, he was entitled to decide to take no further action and to reject the petition. This possibility promoted a hostile atmosphere from the very beginning between the parties even in very minor disputes. Furthermore, the uncertainty encouraged the litigants to employ strategies to make the case 'strong' on the surface, including using exaggerated language or telling only part of the story in writing the complaint. All these circumstances made the magistrate's comments (*pi*) on the first petition of great importance.

Since the magistrate was required by law to close cases reserved for his own decision (*zili anjian*), which included generally what we term civil cases, within twenty days, a magistrate would be likely to make an immediate response to the petition by writing a comment (*pi*) at the end as to whether he would take further action or not. A magistrate who closed such a case

* A substantial portion of this chapter has appeared in the *Bulletin of SOAS*, 68(2), 2005, 276–94.

1 Art. 342. An exception was made for the time of the farmers' busy season (*nongmang*) (Substatute 334-1); see Chapter 2.

beyond the limit of twenty days would be liable to disciplinary action according to the regulation on exceeding the time limit.[2]

The quickest response the magistrate could make was on the spot during the process for accepting petitions on an open day. As the brief discussion in Chapter 2 has revealed, not every magistrate adopted this practice, like Liu Heng.[3] On the one hand, there was no strict legal requirement on this point, so that magistrates were not legally bound to decide the matter on the spot. On the other hand, it might not be convenient to make an immediate decision, especially for newly appointed magistrates, who still lacked court experience. No matter how soon this task was completed, the principle was the same, i.e. to make the comment without deliberate delay. For example, Huang Liuhong, though he did not make comments on the spot, read petitions on the day they were received.[4] Wang Huizu thought it better to interrogate the petitioner on receiving a complaint, and reject false accusations. Then he would take the remaining petitions and make his comments on the following day.[5]

These magistrates were certainly the best models the Qing had. However, the popular practice, though not as speedy as that followed by these model magistrates, seemed to be between three and five days.[6] In a book on the magistrate's court of the Qing by Tao Xisheng, son of a Qing magistrate, this point was made very clearly, i.e. comments within three to five days were routine in response to petitions. Tao's father was a magistrate of five counties of Shanxi province in the late Qing. The son had been with his father since the age of 11.[7] A diary from the early Qing (1699–1706) also described a similar routine. The author mentioned that he went to the court on 17 November of Kangxi 41 (1702) and received the comment 'investigate and report' on the 20th.[8]

The Baodi county records prove that the routine comment procedure could be very fast. The interval between the day of bringing the petition and the day of response revealed in the records was usually very short. Many responses were made on the same day or the following day, or at most on the third day after submission of the petition (Baodi, 96: 1, 5; 99: 6, etc.).

[2] *Jicheng*, *juan* 30, 14; also *Xingfazhi*: 109.
[3] *Mulingshu*, juan 17, *Lisong shitiao* [Ten suggestions on solving lawsuits].
[4] Huang Liuhong 1850/1972: 121.
[5] *Mulingshu*, *juan* 18, *Qindai zhifen* [The difference between energetic and lazy].
[6] *Qingbai leichao*, vol. 8: 2.
[7] Tao Xisheng 1972: 29.
[8] Zhan Yuanxiang 1983: 239–40.

Very few records show an interval of more than five days (Baodi, 98: 138).[9] Not only did the Baodi magistrates respond very quickly to petitions, but they would hear the case on the same day if the two parties brought their petitions together (Baodi, 188: 33–6; 188: 37–40).

Many magistrates and their secretaries expressed the importance of, and the principles for, magistrates' making good comments in the performance of their judicial duty. 'Magistrates who are good at trials can distinguish right and wrong only when the case reaches the stage of being heard; those who are good at making comments can solve the case and free the innocent at the beginning of the litigation.'[10] They 'should not reject all petitions, but neither should they accept all (*wu buzhun wu lanzhun*)'.[11] Good comments were 'to prevent false accusations at the beginning of a lawsuit' and 'to save trouble', so securing both efficiency and justice.[12] In other words, they accepted only complaints with merit and rejected those without. This could be done 'by taking into account both the *qing* of people and the *li* of things (*renqing wuli*), discerning false accusations, clarifying the fundamental principles, complying with the law, and using plain words'.[13] What the Qing officials tried to emphasize were two things. First, the decision about whether to accept or reject the petition had to be correct. Second, what was said in the comment about the decision should be convincing. To make a correct comment, the magistrate should consider things such as *qing*, *li*, and law. To make a convincing comment, the magistrate needed the ability to make his message clear to the parties. Miscarriages of justice might occur not just with wrongful rejection but also with wrongful acceptance. The magistrate should thus accept only legitimate cases rather than as many as he could.

[9] It should be kept in mind that many cases in Baodi involved minor injury claims, to which, according to the Code, the magistrate must make an immediate response. The opposite extreme I found in the records was ten days, almost the sole example.

[10] *Mulingshu*, *juan* 18: *Lunpi chengci* [Making comments on petitions].

[11] *Mulingshu*, *juan* 17: *Tingsong* [Hearing litigation].

[12] Wang Youhuai 1987: 69; Wang Huizu 1786b: 168.

[13] *Mulingshu*, *juan* 18: *Lunpi chengci* [Making comments on petitions]. *Qing* has several meanings — passion, feelings, affection, lust, circumstances, or facts. Scholars often accept *qing* as denoting human feelings (*renqing*), which was the source for solving disputes; see Shiga Shūzō, 1998a. *Li* means abstract right, the eternal fitness of things, principle, rationale, or to arrange or to manage. Scholars usually accept *li* as denoting heaven's principles (*tianli*). *Qingli* is commonly considered to be a key aspect of traditional Chinese legal culture. Some scholars have discussed the subject comprehensively (for example, Philip Huang 1996; Zhou Guangyuan 1995: Chapter 5; Yu Ronggen 1999; Shiga Shūzō 1998b; and Liang Zhiping 1996). For more, see the following discussion and Chapter 9.

3.1 Comments of rejection

Comments of rejection at the end of a petition indicated that the magistrate would take no further action in respect of the claim of the petition. How often did the magistrate reject a petition in minor cases? What were the reasons? Did magistrates reject a petition because they thought it was insignificant, as has usually been assumed in the past?

Table 3.1 offers an overall view of the rejection rate in the surviving Baodi land, debt, and marriage cases.

If we take a comment of rejection as a refusal by the court to take further action, the first group of reasons attracting our attention concerns the instructions attached to a petition form. These specified that petitions that did not comply with the conditions stated in the instructions should be rejected. The details of the instructions can be seen from the following example taken from a Baodi case.[14]

1. Petitions to reverse decisions on matters regulated by an amnesty will be refused.
2. Petitions with respect to cases decided by higher authorities will be refused.
3. Cases arising from fighting will be refused unless the weapon and the wound are described.
4. Cases arising from forcible theft will be refused unless the names of the neighbours, the month and day of the offence, and a list of the stolen property and goods are supplied (forcible theft includes secret theft).
5. The petition must be written on the basis of the facts without exaggerations and without bringing in irrelevancies or disclosing people's private affairs. Petitions contravening this will be refused.
6. When making a petition it is permitted to have only one accusation and one defence. If the accusation or defence is written on an unofficial form or mentions persons who have no connection with the case, it will be refused.
7. The number of persons accused is not allowed to exceed five and witnesses are not allowed to exceed three. Petitions contravening this will be refused.
8. Petitions from the gentry, women, the aged, the physically disabled, or the mentally incompetent must be submitted by an agent. Otherwise the case will be refused.

[14] In the original, every instruction begins with a '–'. Here I number them to facilitate discussion.

Table 3.1. The result of petitions in the Baodi county records.

Case type	Petition rejected[a]	Case resolved[b]	Per cent rejected
Land	9	127	7.0
Debt	12	126	9.6
Marriage	15	95	17.0

[a] 'Petition rejected' covers both petitions directly rejected and those in which a particular person was ordered to make a compromise without reporting back. It also includes petitions initially rejected but finally accepted for a reason other than the original one. My statistic is very different from that given by Huang, who counted only two rejected petitions (Philip Huang 1996: 241).

[b] I use 'Case resolved' rather than 'Petition accepted' because some cases lacked the original complaint but the continued court actions make clear that it was accepted. Another clarification is that 'Cases resolved' includes cases in which the dispute was resolved either with or without a formal hearing.

9. In cases concerning marriage, there must be a marriage contract or go-between. Otherwise the case will be refused.
10. For land or debt cases, there must be a middleman or a written contract or tax certificate. Otherwise the case will be refused.
11. For illicit sexual relations, there must be firm evidence. Otherwise the case will be refused.
12. Serious cases of illicit sexual relations, homicide, or theft that involve women will be refused.
13. Petitions should be about 250 words, and at the most 300. Otherwise they will be refused.
14. Petitions must have the seal of the scrivener and the city address of the petitioner or [his temporary residence].
15. Petitions must be filed with a duplicate.
16. Petitions must be properly spaced with only one word in each square, and there must not be extra attachments.[15]

Huang Liuhong gives a form of complaint in his handbook[16] which contains fifteen similar kinds of instruction. A comparison between his form and that of the Baodi petition showed that the instructions were not always the same. A Taiwan scholar, comparing Huang Liuhong's instructions with those contained in *Da Qing lüli huitong xincuan* (Comprehensive New Edition of the Qing Code — hereafter *Huitong xincuan*),[17] argued that there were no definitive rules determining whether a petition should be accepted

[15] Baodi, 99: 142.
[16] Huang Liuhong 1850/1972: ch. 11, 119–20.
[17] Hu Yangshan was the editor of this book according to Na Silu (1981); I have not seen this book myself.

or rejected since many of the instructions in the two examples were different — only three were the same and four were similar.[18] Although what he observed is true, the conclusion is not compelling.

The similarities between the instructions are more significant than the differences. Take instructions 13, 14, 15, and 16 of the Baodi petition as examples; they established the formal requirements of a petition. Instructions with a similar function were also included in Huang Liuhong's form and the *Huitong xincuan* form, although they were not exactly the same. For another example, the instructions of all three forms contained the rule that petitions concerning land, debt, and marriage disputes required the submission of appropriate evidence. Only the Baodi and *Huitong xincuan* forms required a contract, whereas Huang Liuhong's form required the insertion of the name of the agent or go-between as witness. All three forms required particular groups of litigants such as women, aged persons, and the disabled to have the petition brought by their agent.[19] It is clear that these instructions were established to secure efficiency in litigation for the sake of both litigants and the court. Although they mention the phrase 'will be refused' (*buzhun*), these instructions rarely constituted grounds for the rejection of petitions. They were not, as some scholars might think, in essence a way of blocking the litigants' access to the court.[20] Petitions complying with all the instructions did not automatically command acceptance by the magistrates, and on some occasions petitions that did not respect one or other of the instructions might not be rejected.

Many of the instructions certainly are based on the Qing law. In the Baodi example, instruction 8 can be traced to Sub-statute 339-1, instruction 14 to Sub-statute 240-10, instruction 9 to Article 101, and instruction 10 to Sub-statute 93-6. These instructions were also selected and attached to magistrate Huang Liuhong's form. However, instruction 6 in the Baodi example was not in Huang Liuhong's form. This one comes from Sub-statute 336–4:

> When submitting a petition it is only permitted to have one accusation and one defence. If the accusation or defence is written on an unofficial form or mentions persons who have no connection with the case, it will be refused (*buzhun*).

[18] Na Silu 1981: 80–1.

[19] Allee (1994a: 153–4) gives an example of instructions from the Dan-Xin archive. Since his example was the form used in the prefecture instead of the county, the difference was even greater.

[20] Zhou Guangyuan 1995: 85–7.

The reason Huang Liuhong did not include it in his form perhaps is because this sub-statute was enacted about the time that Huang Liuhong was living, so he probably did not have occasion to include it. The instructions of course varied from time to time.

Some provisions of the Code concerning litigation were not included in the above-mentioned three forms. Nonetheless, they were still equally respected. For example, Sub-statute 332-11 provided:

> In such matters as household and marriage, land, debts, fighting, gambling, and so on, the plaintiff should bring the dispute to the magistrate of the county where the defendant lives. No complaint is allowed (*bude*) to be brought to the magistrate of the county where the plaintiff lives.

This sub-statute established a very basic principle about which magistrate's court should have jurisdiction when the plaintiff and the defendant were resident in different counties (Chapter 2). Probably because this rule was so widely acknowledged, none of the available instructions included it. But clearly, if the plaintiff brought his petition before the wrong court, the magistrate would make a comment to the effect that he must go to the correct court.

It is hard to say when and how the instructions were first started and attached at the end of the petition form in terms of the whole country. Tian Tao observed that similar instructions, though much simpler, were found on the petition form used in the late Ming.[21] The instructions recommended by Huang Liuhong were developed since then. However, *Zhishang jinglun*, a book edited in the early years of the Kangxi reign (1662–1722), when magistrate Huang Liuhong lived, contained a public proclamation listing several similar instructions for bringing petitions to the court. This might imply that some of the instructions had not become attached to the form of the petition at that time, so a particular order was issued and posted publicly. It does not seem too wrong to say that the fully developed instructions discussed above were still not part of the form for all counties at the end of the Kangxi reign.[22]

Although these instructions might alone provide the reason for the magistrate to reject a petition, they were rarely discussed by magistrates who left handbooks for their successors, since they constituted only surface reasons for rejecting a petition. A more substantive reason for refusal was the nature of the case itself. *Mulingshu* clearly made this point: 'Cases which lacked *qingli*

[21] Tian Tao 2004: 17.
[22] *Zhishang jinglun*: 220.

or evidence, or which raised matters of no concern to the petitioner, or arose from temper and quarrelling' should be rejected.[23] According to this statement, the cases that should be rejected can be divided into four basic groups: (1) those that lacked *qing* and/or *li* (*wuqing wuli*), i.e. were unreasonable or not supported by the law, (2) those concerning another person's affairs (*shi bu ganji*), (3) those that lacked any evidence, and (4) those considered too trivial. Number (3) is easy to understand. Without evidence to support the facts, justice could hardly be achieved. It was necessary to exclude 'trivial' cases either because there might be no essential dispute for the magistrate to decide, or because the alleged claim was too insignificant to warrant a court process in terms of the benefit delivered to the petitioner after calculating the cost of the court session. Decisions were easy in these cases. The most difficult group was that in which the case lacked *qing* and/or *li*. *Qing* here refers to the story or the facts. The phrase 'lacking *qing*' means that the petition was fabricated and that the events as disclosed in the petition had not occurred. *Li* here has a double meaning. It could describe the eternal fitness of things, so lacking *li* also meant that the story in the petition was not true. *Li* could also mean what is legally right.[24] In this sense 'lacking *li*' refers to an absence of a right deserving legal protection.

The following examples illustrate each type of reason.

Case 1

A debtor accused his creditor of annoying him. The magistrate commented on the petition: 'You owe money to him and have not paid. Now you accuse him of being rough, which is hateful. Permission not granted.' (Baodi, 193: 45)

Case 2

Song accused Li of borrowing money from his father more than twenty years earlier and of refusing to pay him after his father died. The magistrate was not convinced by his story: 'If what you said was true, why have you not asked for the money back for over twenty years. Moreover, you have no witness and no debt contract. . . . It is obvious that you are making a false accusation after you failed to cheat him with an old, expired record book (*feiqi jiuzhang*). Permission not granted.' (Baodi, 190: 139)

[23] *Mulingshu, juan* 18, *Lunpi chengci* [Making comments on petitions]; also Wang Youhuai 1987: 70.

[24] Magistrate Liu Heng made clear the connection between *li* and the law when he discussed the matter of interrogating the plaintiff when receiving his petition. 'What if someone says that interrogating the plaintiff without summoning the defendant when receiving his petition does not comply with *li*?' Liu Heng argued that 'this is just following the statute and sub-statute. How should that be contrary to *li*?' (*Mulingshu, Juan* 17: 46).

Case 3
Li accused Zhang of owing him money for the purchase of a horse. He showed his tax invoice, which recorded the name of a different buyer. So the magistrate commented on the complaint: '[The accusation] is obviously untrue, permission not granted (*xianyou bushi, buzhun*).' (Baodi, 192: 188)[25]

Case 4
An uncle aged over eighty submitted a petition accusing somebody of occupying his nephew's land. Although the nephew's name was also on the plaintiff's list, the magistrate commented: 'If the situation is true, the nephew himself and his [the nephew's] son should submit a complaint themselves with the contracts and then I shall decide.' (Baodi, 97: 36)

Case 5
Zhang accused Qi of owing him money amounting to 4,310 *wen*. The magistrate commented: 'The money owed to you is only a small debt. You should go and ask him reasonably by yourself. Better not start litigation.' (Baodi, 187: 42)[26]

Case 6
Xiao's son was away from home for a relatively long time. The natal family of Xiao's daughter-in-law arranged for her to marry another man. Xiao, after being promised gift money (see Chapter 5), agreed with the plan. However, because he was not satisfied with what he obtained from his daughter-in-law's remarriage, he brought a lawsuit accusing her of remarrying another man by herself (which was forbidden by the law; see Chapter 5). The magistrate rejected Xiao's petition on the ground that he had approved his daughter-in-law's remarriage, thus it was wrong to accuse her now because of his dissatisfaction with the benefit. (Baodi, 170: 1)

In Case 5, the money in question was 4,310 *wen*. Baodi records of the Xuantong period (1909–11) reveal that the cost of litigation was 4.5 *liang* of silver, which was equivalent to about 5,400 *wen*. According to Huang, litigation in Ba county cost at least 4,000 *wen* for a case to go through a court session.[27] Although the cost might be shared by all parties involved, it seems certain that the plaintiff might recover only a small part of his little debt.

[25] In this case, the defendant submitted a follow-up petition, but the magistrate rejected it again on the ground that 'the decision of a case over buying and selling depends upon the account book. Now the account book does not show that Zhang San is the person who bought the horse, so how can the case be decided?' (Baodi, 192: 189).
[26] A similar comment can be found in Baodi, 172: 169.
[27] Huang 1996: 183.

Case 3 was rejected on the grounds that the evidence did not support the plaintiff's claim, in other words, there was not enough evidence. In a broad sense, lacking evidence can also be regarded as part of the reason for rejecting cases in group (1), i.e. *wuqing* (unreasonable or, here, untrue). But the emphasis here was rather on false accusations and those lacking a legal basis. Cases 1 and 2 illustrate these two aspects being decisive in terms of the essential cause of the dispute. Case 6 clearly shows that the main reason for rejection was that the father-in-law had no case, in other words, his claim lacked any legal ground. From this point of view, the magistrate's decision began with the initial handling of the submission of petitions. As for Case 4, although the magistrate believed there was a piece of land that had been illegally sold with a condition of redemption (*dian*), he did not make a comment of acceptance on the original petition brought by the aged uncle because he was not directly concerned. Later, the nephew brought a petition himself and the case was accepted.

Of course, the magistrate would not limit himself to one reason in rejecting a petition. He gave reasons based on the facts of the particular case. In a debt case after a debtor's death, the brother paid most of the debt to the creditor. But they quarrelled over the interest, and the creditor submitted an accusation in which he said he was hurt and 'several strands of hairs had been pulled out' (*luofa shujing*). The magistrate commented:

Case 7

'Meng Junyou owed you 10,000 *wen*. Since he died of illness, you almost had no chance to recover your debt. His younger brother Meng Junfu did not refuse to repay you on his behalf. You should let the matter drop. You were not content with the interest offered, quarrelled, and grabbed each other. How could you come to complain of such a minor matter? That your hair was pulled out in the fighting has been examined, and there is so little of it that there is an inconsistency with the description in your complaint. So I should not accept your complaint.' (Baodi, 193: 4)

The magistrate clearly showed his opinion of the case. He gave four reasons for rejecting the complaint: (1) the debtor was dead, (2) most of the debt was paid, (3) the unpaid amount of the debt was tiny and the quarrel was not serious, (4) examination showed that the injury was not as stated by the plaintiff in his petition. We can see that this comment was no different from a decision that the plaintiff would not be supported by the court. When a magistrate made such a comment, the effect of the comment was no less than an adjudication. Magistrate Gao of Baodi county clearly declared in one comment that his comment was indeed his final decision and that he

Table 3.2. Reasons for rejecting petitions in Baodi county.

Reason	Number of cases
Lacking *qing* and/or *li*	12
Lacking evidence or evidence not convincing	9
Trivial	3
Not relevant	1
Case has been closed	4
Should go to another court	2
Other reasons	2
Reason not clear	3
Total	36

would make it again if hearing the case (*cibi jishi benxian tangduan*) (Baodi, 172: 27). When a lawsuit was thought to be based on a false accusation, the magistrate especially needed to 'rule by comments' to prevent the innocent from being accused. When handbooks on good practice in relation to making comments specify that a comment is 'good', they are referring to properly motivated comments of rejection.

I found 36 rejected petitions in the Baodi county records. The reasons they were rejected by the magistrate can roughly be classified as shown in Table 3.2. As can be seen in this table, there were few rejected petitions compared with the hundreds of cases submitted to the Baodi magistrate. Although this may not represent the real ratio of rejection, the table can still give us a clue to the kinds of reason for rejection. We can see that the rejection of petitions was made on the basis of a particular reason or reasons, on the basis of the merit of the petition itself, not because these cases concerned disputes that were minor in comparison with criminal cases. Macauley's conclusion that 'lawsuits pressed at the county level were routinely bounced back to informal arenas for mediation' may not be true, at least in a county such as Baodi.[28] Huang's conclusion that 'rejecting a plaint was the magistrate's first line of defence against the problem of an excessive caseload'[29] is correct in so far as it relates to the result achieved by a 'good' comment of rejection. However, the magistrate should never make such a comment just to reduce his caseload. As many magistrates stressed, the best way to avoid an excessive case burden was to make the decision fairly and quickly. It was a decision made in the form of rejecting comments rather than the rejection itself that stopped some cases coming to the court. The following comment on a petition is a perfect example of this.

[28] Macauley 1994: 100.
[29] Huang 1996: 212.

Case 8

Jin Wende accused Yang Fugui of throwing him out after he had worked three years for his family, without paying him the wages due or giving him back the money he had deposited with Yang for safe keeping. He was beaten and kicked when he asked Yang why he was sacked the day before he submitted the petition. On the statement reporting the examination of his injuries, the magistrate made an order to a runner on duty to go to the Yang family with Jin. The magistrate commented: 'To drive away an impoverished man from afar who had lived a hard life working for three years does not seem a kindly thing to do. I order the runner on duty to accompany Jin to the Yang family to carry my order to Yang that if Jin Wende has not done anything inappropriate he should keep Jin and avoid the lawsuit.' The same day, the runner reported that the Yang family said Jin had done nothing wrong, and they would like to keep him, to which Jin also agreed. (Baodi, 188: 33–5)[30]

This comment was not a typical one of acceptance. However, it would be equally difficult to regard it as one of rejection, although the magistrate wrote nothing about further action. The magistrate clearly gave an order under a condition, i.e. the family should keep Jin if he had not done anything too wrong, which was most likely the case, for there were no follow-up petitions from either party. Although the petition was not accepted in terms of further involvement by the magistrate, the matter was settled. For this reason, the magistrate's initial comment could sometimes be regarded as resolving the case.

By rejecting a petition, what the magistrate intended to achieve was that the innocent were protected and unreasonable petitions were excluded from the court. The former depended on the latter, in the sense that the rejection of unreasonable petitions ensured the protection of the innocent. In contrast, if the accusation aroused the magistrate's suspicions and he believed that the innocent could be protected only by his taking further action, then he made a comment of acceptance.

Recall from section 2.5.2 on the composition of the petition that the plaintiff, in particular, often made an exaggerated claim or alleged physical injury. Some scholars believe that this occurred because the magistrate paid

[30] The relevant facts occurred on 8 July 1832 (Daoguang 12). Jin submitted the case to the magistrate on 9 July and the case was closed on the same day. This case is also mentioned in Huang 1996: 90, 91. He noted that, in making this decision, the magistrate appealed to the compassion of the employer. However, it was the condition ('if Jin Wende has not done anything inappropriate') attached to the magistrate's order that indicated the basis of his decision. No matter what the contract of employment, Yang, as the employer, should not unreasonably dismiss Jin.

little attention to minor cases — often either rejecting them or returning them to mediators. In fact, in very few cases (I found only two) were petitions sent for mediation (Baodi, 194: 2; 172: 79). Out of all the petitions rejected for any reason (only thirty-six), only three were rejected on the ground of being 'trivial'. Of course, acceptance by the magistrate in Baodi of most petitions might have something to do with the fact that many alleged an injury.

3.2 Comments of acceptance

Allee has observed that the most common reaction of the magistrate was acceptance and an order to investigate.[31] The previous section revealed that petitions over land, debt, and marriage matters might be rejected for various reasons, the most tricky being *wuqing* and *wuli*. Thus, it seems logical that, if the plaint showed the case to be the opposite of *wuqing* and *wuli*, it should be accepted. This point was made by magistrate Fan Zengxiang (1846–1931) in a collection of decisions and comments. He made a similar remark several times to the effect 'that where anything had really happened, anybody who is in the right (*youli youqing*) may feel free to come to court'.[32] The magistrate would accept a petition if he thought the plaintiff had a good reason and was owed an obligation. By *youqing*, Fan was clearly referring to the fact that the alleged complaints were true and had not been fabricated. By *youli*, he was referring to what was right in the eyes of the law. The question is, what are those reasons in the law in terms of land, debt, and marriage disputes?

There are more detailed discussions on the law governing land, debt, and marriage in Chapter 5. For the purpose of this section, I shall briefly summarize the main points. The section on land and houses in the Qing Code contained provisions for protecting rights regarding privately owned land. A statute usually consisted of three parts: it began by defining the particular offence, such as taking land or forcibly taking land (*qinzhan*, *qiangzhan*), then continued with a statement about the object in question, such as the type and amount of land, and finally specified the punishment to be imposed and the remedies available to the party suffering loss, such as return of the land to the owner or repayment of the price or the profits made from the land to the owner. The law also contained stipulations regarding the selling, conditional selling, or lending of land. For example, the parties

[31] Allee 1994a: 160.
[32] Fan Zengxiang 1912, vol. 1: 9, 15, 20.

had to make clear in their contract whether or not the land was sold conditionally by employing particular phrases (Sub-statute 95-7). Conditions were established for the redemption of land, and the consequences of non-redemption were regulated (Article 95, Sub-statute 95-3). In the case of tenancies, the law prohibited the landowner from reclaiming his land to cultivate himself without a legal reason.[33] The Baodi records show that the main types of land dispute were those over ownership, redemption of land, tenancies, and boundaries. They clearly reflected allegations based on the provisions in the Code and regulations.

In dealing with land-related petitions, the magistrate was very careful to determine such matters as whether the land in question was private land or government land, whether the contract was one of outright sale (*juemai*) or conditional sale (*dian*), whether the relationship between tenant and landlord had been broken, by either the landlord or the tenant, whether the land had been wrongly taken, and so on. The magistrate was concerned with these matters because the law prohibited people from selling or conditionally selling government land, prohibited the *dian* holder from not returning the land and the *dian* maker from not paying the money when redemption was due, prohibited a tenant from renting farm land to a third person, and prohibited people from the illegal occupation of land belonging to someone else (Articles 93, 95).[34] We find comments such as: 'arbitrarily to mortgage land owned by the Banner people (*qidi*) is contrary to the law (*yougan lijin*). Wait to be interrogated'; or 'How will the law allow rented land to be conditionally sold to a third person (*dianzhong tudi qirong si dian*)?' (Baodi, 96: 9), and so on.

Debt disputes could arise in a variety of circumstances, for the Code had a very broad definition of *sizhai* (private debt) and stipulated that all *sizhai* should be returned to the owner (Article 149; see Chapter 5). Thus, in handling debt disputes, the magistrate's focus was entirely on such matters as whether the debt was real or not, or whether there was evidence from witnesses or documents. He might suggest that the plaintiff consider his petition again if the debt was insignificant (Case 5) or reject the petition outright if the debtor wrongly complained (Case 1) or no evidence for the debt was provided. Otherwise, it would be unreasonable for him to reject petitions.

Marriage was regulated by detailed provisions in the Code, covering the conditions for a valid marriage, the requirement of an engagement contract

[33] The law on eviction was called *duodian li* in the Baodi county records. It is contained in the regulations of the Board of Revenue (see Chapter 6 for the details).

[34] For more discussion of the law concerning land in the Qing Code, see Chapter 5.

negotiated through a go-between, conditions for divorce, and a widow's remarriage (for a detailed discussion, see Chapter 5). Correspondingly, petitions were made on legal grounds such as breach of the contract of engagement, divorcing a wife without legal reasons, and so on.

These considerations explain the ratio of acceptance and rejection in Table 3.1 (although, as I have said, the table might not be an entirely accurate representation of the real percentages). Nevertheless, it is safe to say that the ratio of acceptance was larger than has usually been thought. This conclusion could be disputed, however, because of the striking occurrence of such matters as allegations of physical injury or exaggerated or false accusations. Referring to the frequency of false accusation, Wang Huizu (1731–1807) said: 'there is no petition called a petition if it does not tell a false story (*wuhuang bucheng zhuang*).'[35] As I have mentioned, according to some scholars the reason was 'that "trivial disputes" (over property, debts, marriage, and so on) were not enthusiastically accepted by officials. This was a realistic perception given the widespread government propaganda in *yamen* postings, circulars, and handbooks that such disputes were not worthy of constant and immediate magisterial attention. False accusations, or slight falsifications of accusations, were a perceived means of obtaining a formal hearing beyond the concatenations of clerks and village power holders.'[36] Although, as we shall see, it is true that some litigants did use the allegation of injury as a shortcut to access the court, the conclusion of these scholars seems too simple. As we have seen in the discussion of magistrates' rejection of petitions, the reason for rejection was not the fact that the complaint concerned land or debt. Petitions were rejected because they alleged what was self-evidently not true or because they clearly did not follow the rules for submission. Only one was rejected because the debt in question was small.

The explanation for the frequency of allegations of physical injury is rather complicated. According to the Code, petitions that involved physical fighting and injury were to be accepted and acted upon at once by the magistrate (Article 302). Should the petitioner claim to have been physically wounded, the magistrate had to examine the wound at once and deal with the matter. In Article 302, 'injury' (*shang*) was given the widest definition: '(*If the skin which is struck*) turns blue or red (*and*) there is a swelling, this is an "injury."'[37] Even for a very minor injury, the magistrate was required to

[35] Wang Huizu 1786b/1892, *Heci xuren benyi* [Reading the complaint to find out its core issue].
[36] Macauley 1999: 4.
[37] Jones 1994: 285.

act as soon as the matter was raised, because the evidence of injury might have disappeared if there was a delay. Not surprisingly, we often read statements of the following kind in the Baodi county records: 'The injuries were examined and Huang Lishi [née Li] had two scratches in the middle of her forehead and three scratches on the left side of her face. They all just broke the skin. No other wound was found' (Baodi, 96: 101); 'Shan and Chuan both had their braids untied. No other injury was found' (Baodi, 97: 136); 'Zhou Fulai had an injury of two scratches on the left of his forehead. No other injury was found' (Baodi, 99: 53). Obviously, it was rather easy to produce a '*shang*', as described above, no matter whether intended or not. The approach of the Code ensured that this was a shortcut means of access to the magistrate's court. In other words, the complaint was legally correct to allege an existing 'injury', even though the wound might have been caused with the purpose of securing a prompt hearing.

Some provisions of the Code on false accusation also encouraged petitioners to make an exaggerated or distorted allegation to obtain the immediate attention of the court. Although the Code imposed severe punishments for the offence of false accusation, at the same time it allowed the offender to escape liability under certain conditions, for example, the petition was made as a result of a misunderstanding or in a great hurry.[38] Such excuses gave the petitioners a chance to make serious allegations in a petition without being prosecuted for false accusation. Bearing in mind Wang Huizu's statement about the problem of false petition, I found only nine cases in the land section, twelve in the debt section, and seventeen in the marriage section in the Baodi county records, out of a total of over one hundred that were held by the magistrate to involve a false accusation. Although this number provides little indication of the real rate of false accusation cases, such a huge gap between Wang's statement and actual litigation practice rather supports the above observation. Many litigants escaped the punishment imposed by the Code for false accusation, not only because the law opened a window after shutting the door, but also because there was a distinction between an untrue statement in the initial petition and the offence of false accusation itself as finally decided by the magistrate.[39] Although some petitions showed

[38] 'Sometimes there may occur a case in which one has drawn a mistaken inference from hearing a person's words and hastily brings a wrongful accusation [of homicide]' (Sub-statute 336-9). Under this sub-statute, even a 'false accusation' of homicide was not punished.
[39] According to Shen Zhiqi, a private secretary in the reign of Kangxi, in the case of an offence of false accusation, the offender had to have had a motive for accusing the other party of a crime and for having him punished. For more on this, see Chapter 9.

that the parties were not telling the entire truth, the offence of false accusation was not always committed, especially in view of the escape clauses contained in the Code.

As we have seen, after receiving a petition the magistrate was entitled to reject it for certain reasons. This itself gave petitioners a strong reason for employing some strategy to secure access to the magistrate's court. These strategies included alleging injury and telling a false story. When the petition was not persuasive enough, or was not supported by the evidence, the only chance of securing its acceptance was to claim an injury or exaggerate the circumstances.

Case 9

Woman Wang complained that Wang Conggui did not allow her to redeem two *mu* of land belonging to her and her husband (who was away at the time), and that he had put a grave in the land. The magistrate summoned the witnesses and the parties. The truth was that woman Wang wanted to redeem the land without handing back the 130 *diao dian* price, and instead to make a debt contract with Wang Conggui. The latter, the *dian* holder, insisted on having the total price before giving her the land. The magistrate ruled in favour of the defendant by ordering woman Wang's husband to pay the money when he came back to redeem the land; the defendant should first move the grave to another place before returning the land. (Baodi, 97: 20–30)

Case 10

Liu employed Wang Han and Wang Chang to gather the wheat at harvest time. Liu offered them each 1 *diao* and 600 *wen* for the day they worked, but they wanted 2 *diao* each for the day. Since Liu did not give them this, they threw some of Liu's house goods to the ground and injured Liu's father. Wang Han and Wang Chang told the magistrate at the court that another man in their village paid 2 *diao* for the same work, and that Liu had agreed to this when he hired them. The magistrate made his decision on the trial list: 'Liu You employed Wang Han and Wang Chang to work. Because Liu paid less money [than the 2 *diao*] to both, the incident was created. However, Wang Han and Wang Chang should not throw his house goods about. I order that Liu You pay them the difference, which is 400 *wen* to each. Wang Han should be punished. All parties are to make a bond of confirmation and the case is to be closed.' (Baodi, 195: 41–2; 194: 213–14)

In Case 9, woman Wang used the strategy of claiming injury to have her case accepted. Otherwise, the possibility for her to involve the magistrate was small, because she really had no case. According to the law on conditional sale (*dian*), the landowner could redeem his land only when, on the due date, he paid the full amount of the price for which the land was conditionally sold. Although redemption of the land in question was sought, woman Wang intended to take the land back with a debt contract instead of the full price, which the *dian* holder refused. As for Case 10, it would have been almost impossible for the two plaintiffs to bring a petition accusing the defendant of not paying an agreed wage for labour without any convincing evidence, such as a contract. To them, fighting and claiming to have been injured was an easy way to compensate for their lack of evidence.

A comment of acceptance was only the start of a series of court actions, so many of these comments were intentionally shorter and simpler than comments of rejection. On a few occasions the magistrate accepted the case even after noting some reservation with regard to the cause of the petition, but generally his comments would be simple. Comments of acceptance can be roughly divided into two groups: one type was directed at an immediate hearing of the case without an investigation of the facts; the other consisted of an order to investigate the facts. The first type of comment could be as simple as 'wait for my hearing (*houxun*)', 'wait for my trial of you together (*hou jixun*)', or 'wait for me to hear you face to face (*hou zhixun*)'. Then the relevant office would prepare a formal document (*piao*) ordering the people involved to come to the court. The second type of comment ordered someone to investigate the facts or to submit particular evidence. The recipients of the order, if it was for investigation, were the runners, as well as the go-between, a witness, or a mediator, but most often the *xiangbao* or local head man (other than the runners). A typical order said: 'I order the *xiangbao* to investigate and report, then I shall check and decide' (Baodi, 97: 130). The recipient of the order was almost always required to report back to the magistrate. Until this was done no hearing would be heard.

Further explanation may be needed of this second type of comment. Baodi county records show that, in a small number of comments, the magistrate required the mediator, most likely the *xiangbao*, to effect a compromise and then report back the result. The key point here was the order to the *xiangbao* to report back, though the term 'compromise' (*tiaochu*) was used. When the *xiangbao* was involved in the litigation procedure, he was very often sent out by the magistrate to investigate the facts of the dispute. In such cases, the magistrate depended on the facts he reported back in order to hear the case. If the difference between the two sides was too great, the *xiangbao* would report back asking for an official hearing; otherwise, he would apply for the case to be closed without a hearing, no matter which term ('investigation' or 'compromising') was used. When the *xiangbao* applied for the case to be closed, a solution to the dispute was also reported to the magistrate. The magistrate might accept the application to close the case (Baodi, 187: 63–4) or reject it and order a summons issued (Baodi, 186: 112–15). He might not order the parties to be summoned at once but require them to clarify some confusion, and he would not close the case until he was satisfied with the result (Baodi, 100: 9–19). It was the involvement of the magistrate that played the greatest role in achieving a solution to a dispute. The *xiangbao*'s 'compromise' was no more than the result of his investigation and formed part of his report on the way the case had developed between the parties.[40]

Thus, most magistrates' comments can be regarded as ones either of rejection or of acceptance. On rare occasions the magistrate gave the petitioner the choice of whether the case would go further in the court (Baodi, 172: 27). On one petition the magistrate commented that, if the alleged wound was true, then the parties should come to court and a summons would be sent. If, on examination, it turned out that the alleged wound was false, the petitioner would be punished. It was up to the petitioner to decide whether he wanted to take the matter to court.

3.3 The magistrate's role in making comments

It is commonly thought that it was the magistrate's private secretary who actually read all the various petitions and commented on behalf of his master in the first instance. The magistrate needed only to confirm and sign.[41] This was deduced partly from the widespread use of the private secretary and some criticisms of their practices by officials, and partly from the fact that the magistrate lacked knowledge of the law. The phrase 'friend behind the curtain' (*muyou*, translated as private secretary) appeared formally at least in 1651, the eighth year of Shunzhi (1644–61) in an imperial edict (*shangyu*) to the Board of Officials (*Libu*).[42] One of the most influential commentaries on the Qing Code was *Jizhu*, whose author was a private secretary with over thirty years' experience. And there were many books of guidance for helping private secretaries make a success of their profession. Famous private secretaries, such as Wang Huizu, achieved a high reputation after being private secretary to many magistrates. In the Baodi magistrate's office, we know there was a room called *muting* (office of private secretary) specifically

[40] For the *xiangbao*'s role and closing cases without a hearing, see Chapter 4.
[41] Qu Tongzu 1969: 98.
[42] See Na Silu 1981: 23.

reserved for the use of a private secretary.[43] Fang Dashi, a nineteenth-century magistrate, described the 'typical practice' (*tongli*) of making comments in these words: 'a plaint would go first to the legal secretary, who would draft a preliminary comment on the duplicate copy and pass it on to the magistrate for approval; the comment would then be copied onto the original form by the "brush clerk" (*mobi*); he in turn passed that form on to be transcribed onto a "plaint placard" (*zhuangbang*) for public view.'[44]

This conception of the role of the private secretary has rarely been tested because scholars believe that the magistrates in the Qing lacked both administrative knowledge and experience and knew little about the law.[45] They were appointed to the post only because of their literary ability. So they were forced to let the secretary deal with all documents for them. The issue of the extent to which the magistrate actually depended on his secretary to make comments on the petitions and the extent to which the magistrate had to do so discloses two very different questions, and it is the latter that deserves most discussion. The relationship between the magistrate and his secretary as a whole involves complex factors and needs much more space. Here I offer only my initial findings in order to show not only that magistrates did have the capacity to make comments on the complaint, but also that they actually made many more comments on land, debt, and marriage petitions than has usually been thought.

Direct evidence of comments made by magistrates is still available today in examples left by some famous magistrates. The artist magistrate Zheng Banqiao's many comments on petitions are kept as art treasures by both private collectors and state museums.[46] Magistrate Fan Zengxiang also left many official documents, including hundreds of comments on petitions. His colourful style of composition and commenting on petitions, as well as on other documents, is so easily recognized that one would feel no difficulty in concluding that he was the author of these comments and compositions.

[43] *Baodi xianzhi*, *juan* 2.

[44] Fang Dashi 1878, 2: 31b, cited in Huang 1996: 213. Almost the same expression can also be found in He Shiqi's remarks on Litigation (*cisong*) in *Mulingshu*, *juan* 18.

[45] Recent researches on the secretaries are the exception. They include Gao Huanyue 2000.

[46] Zheng Banqiao took his third degree in 1736 (Qianlong 1) and was appointed as a magistrate of Fan county of Shantong province in 1742 (Qianlong 7). He is regarded as the best artist of bamboo paintings, and he is also famous for his outstanding calligraphy. Zheng left many comments when he was a magistrate. They are kept in the Museum of the Forbidden City and the Chinese History Museum and by private collectors in both China and Japan. The *Zheng Banqiao nianpu* (Records of Zheng Banqiao's Life) lists about 374 pieces of Zheng's comments on petitions. Most of them were on house, land, and debt matters (317–37).

There were also famous magistrates such as Liu Heng,[47] Huang Liuhong,[48] and Wang Huizu,[49] who either made comments on the spot on an open day (*fanggaori*) or on the same day on which the petitions were received, or made comments on some petitions immediately and on the rest as soon as possible afterwards. One might think that these magistrates were obviously the best the Qing had and should not be taken as demonstrating normal practice, although magistrate Zheng's achievement in art overshadows his performance as a magistrate. However, there is also evidence that ordinary magistrates might not differ too much from these exemplary magistrates. I have mentioned a Tao Xisheng, the son of a magistrate who administered five counties during his career, who stated in his book that his father had never consulted with his private secretary in deciding civil cases. He continued, 'for the magistrate's self-decided cases (*zili anjian*), the magistrate . . . closed the case after one session and hardly consulted with the secretary'.[50] It is very difficult to determine the exact role of the secretary in civil disputes, especially given the differences between each county, each magistrate, and each secretary. That is why the more important and fundamental issue is to make clear whether the average magistrate had the knowledge, experience, and ability to make comments himself, at least when he wanted and had to do so. Should he be capable of doing this in the first place, he would be able to control the decision in the sense that he understood and endorsed the decision, if made by the secretary. In other words, his overall capability meant that he was in control of the case. As long as the magistrate was the one to control the result of the case, even though he did not himself make the comments, the decisions were his rather than his secretary's. Of course, one possibility cannot be ruled out. Some lazy magistrates might rely much more on the private secretary than their colleagues did for routine tasks, including making comments on minor cases. This is, I believe, a different question that falls outside the scope of my discussion.

Qu Tongzu and Watt have made it clear that magistrates were people who had received a lengthy education.[51] There were three main degrees: licentiate (*shengyuan* or *xiucai*), provincial graduate (*juren*), and metropolitan graduate (*jinshi*). The provincial examinations were the crucial ones for those who aspired to public service, because this degree conferred the formal qualification for public office and the right to take the metropolitan

[47] *Mulingshu, juan* 17: *Lisong shitiao* [Ten suggestions on solving lawsuits].
[48] Huang Liuhong 1850/1972: 121.
[49] Wang Huizu (*Mulingshu, juan* 18: *Qindai zhifen* [The difference between energetic and lazy].
[50] Tao Xisheng 1972: 51.
[51] Qu Tongzu 1965; Watt 1972.

examinations for the third degree. In the eighteenth and early nineteenth centuries, there were a hundred or more competitors for each degree. There is no doubt that the successful candidates were people whose capability was, in theory, at least above average. Even the 'most of the rest' who 'had made their way into officialdom by purchasing examination statuses . . . had been educated for the examinations, but had failed because of the intense competition'.[52] On observing the qualifications of the magistrate, Watt summarized: 'First, they possessed a high degree of political consciousness. They knew the prevailing ideology and could express it unusually well. Second, they had proved an ability to analyse questions and form conclusions under intense pressure. These are not scholastic attributes, and this was a source of grievance to the many scholars who competed unsuccessfully for the only accredited tests of intellectual prowess. But the examination system was specifically designed to produce political administrators: it was perhaps more successful in doing so than is sometimes realised.'[53]

It is true that even successful candidates for the Qing's civil examination had not passed any examination in the law itself. And the law was well known for its complexity. On this question, some officials pointed out that, although the Code was very complex and comprehensive in terms of its content and structure, the parts relevant to matters concerning houses, marriage, land, debt, and fighting should be learnt first since they were easier to understand. Wang Huizu and Liu Heng had both discussed this easy way of starting to become familiar with the Code and pointed to the possibility of quickly mastering the parts the magistrate needed for routine trials.[54] Candidate magistrates usually had to wait for a long time, at least several years, before starting upon their career as a magistrate and they might, like Huang Liuhong, read the Code before taking up their post. They also sometimes had the opportunity to experience some administrative action.[55] When their waiting time was over, the actual post they took was usually classified as a 'simple' one.

I mentioned in Chapter 1 that the county magistrate's post was designated at a particular level according to the country's location, its size and population, its importance, and the difficulty in its administration. In Qing practice, magistrates were first appointed to a 'simple' or 'middle' post; and

[52] Watt 1972: 21.

[53] Ibid.: 32.

[54] *Mulingshu, juan* 17; Wang Huizu 1786a/1892: 144–5.

[55] Byron Brenan pointed out: 'These expectant officials, while awaiting a regular appointment, frequently get temporary employment, or *Chai shih* (*chai shi*). There are many duties to be performed in connection with provincial affairs for which provision has not been made in the regular administration, ... While residing at the provincial capital awaiting an appointment, the expectant . . . tries to get some knowledge of official work' (1897–8: 41).

there were many such posts. Even that most experienced secretary Wang Huizu when he finally became a magistrate was sent to Ningyuan county, classified as a 'simple' post. The difficult posts were often taken by those with experience in the same province. To take the example of a Baodi magistrate, Wu Lüfu had already had ten years' experience when he took up the post in Baodi county (an 'important' post qualified as 'troublesome', 'wearisome', and 'difficult') in Tongzhi 6 (1867). He had been either the acting or the substantive magistrate of Dacheng county (a 'middle' post qualified as 'troublesome' and 'difficult'), Pinggu county (a 'simple' post qualified with none of the four factors), and Yongqing county (a 'simple' post qualified with none of the four factors) before taking up the Baodi post. After Baodi, he became the magistrate of Changping county, which, like Baodi county, was an 'important' post (qualified as 'being frequently visited', 'troublesome', and 'difficult'). He served a total of twenty-two years as a magistrate (according to *Shuntian fuzhi*: 'Table 2 of the Qing magistrate'). This kind of progress meant that the magistrate could start with easily managed posts and had more time to learn administrative skills, even if they had not taken advantage of the waiting period. Wang Huizu said that, if a magistrate read a couple of statutes whenever he was free, he could understand the main points of the Code within a few months.[56]

A 'simple' post meant that the number of civil cases was perhaps very few, even only 50 per year according to Philip Huang.[57] Even in an important post such as Baodi, civil cases were those concerning people's everyday life. A magistrate who had succeeded in the competitive civil service examinations should not have experienced much difficulty in obtaining sufficient knowledge of the law and practical experience. He necessarily would have built up experience because the law required the magistrate to hear cases in person. As the relevant law on land, debt, and marriage matters was not difficult to master, after a reasonable period of practice a magistrate would be capable of resolving civil disputes, including making comments as his first response and final decisions as his final action. As Liu put it, 'after much practice, he [the magistrate] will be well versed in the Code'.[58]

The logical conclusion from the above reasoning has to be that the magistrate would have the capability to make the first comments on petitions himself. Whether a particular comment was actually made by him or not might not be significant, since he was the one who had the position of control and decided the case. Such active engagement becomes clear from the

[56] *Mulingshu, juan* 17; Wang Huizu 1800/1892.

[57] Huang 1996: 178.

[58] *Mulingshu, juan* 17: *Shuliao wenda* [Answers to some colleagues' questions].

comments of rejection on petitions. In fact, the magistrate had to maintain control of the case for it was the magistrate, rather than the secretary, who took responsibility should errors subsequently be disclosed. Thus the secretary's function was no more than to supply assistance to the magistrate, even though it might be very constructive assistance. Wang Huizu once made it very clear that if the matter 'does not concern hearing a case, it then may be trusted to the secretary. If it concerns such matters as land, marriage, debt, theft, homicide, and so on . . . [the magistrate] must know the law very well' in order to make a convincing judgment.[59] There is a clear difference between the active aspect of the magistrate's role and the passive aspect of the secretary's role. The power of a secretary could never compete with that of his master. Their relation was that of host and guest, in which the secretary as guest had the subordinate role; even a competent secretary such as Wang Huizu had to be ready to 'leave the magistrate when it was difficult to get along with him' (*buhe zequ*). The subordinate position of the secretary can also be vividly seen from the secretaries' own seals, such as 'always show respect' (*wu bujing*) or 'always cherish respect and fear' (*changcun jingwei*). The fact that a comment was made by the secretary, and the magistrate often agreed with whatever the comment was, cannot itself prove either that the magistrate lacked the capability to make comments or that the secretary in practice assumed more power in dealing with petitions.

It is clear that making proper and convincing comments was not a simple or easy task. The essence was to find a balance between too easy acceptance and too strict rejection. In other words, the magistrate should not accept too many petitions in order to acquire the reputation of loving his people, but nor should he reject too many just to decrease his caseload. Generally, a magistrate needed to achieve this balance by following certain rules on acceptance and rejection. As we have seen, the most important and most complex reason for rejection was that the claim was probably untrue and had no legal basis (*wuli*). Only the magistrate could make good comments, so that his judicial duty was properly conducted, the innocent were protected, people were educated, and, finally, disputes decreased.

[59] *Mulingshu, juan* 17. *Lüli buke budu* [The Code must be read].

4
The Magistrate's Actions in Approaching a Resolution

Following the magistrate's comment of acceptance on the petition, the case started the ordinary judicial journey. The case, as might be expected, would be resolved or decided through such court actions as the collection of facts and investigation of evidence, the hearing, and the judgment. In the magistrate's court, these actions probably can be seen more clearly through the formal documents used at each stage, namely, the directive (*piao*), the report (*bing*), the statement (*gong*), the decision (*panci*), and so on. In the following sections I provide illustrations of each type.

4.1 The directive

Piao (also *chaipiao* or *xinpiao*) were orders issued usually to the runners as an authority to carry out certain actions ordered by the magistrates. In short, the *piao* or *chaipiao* may be understood as evidence of permission, both for the particular order given by the magistrate and for the authority conferred on the bearer named in it. The orders could be infinitely varied, and the content of the *piao* could be of many different kinds. Shiga Shūzō has classified the *piao* of the Dan-xin records into investigating, submitting evidence, ordering, mediating, prohibiting, and summoning *piao*.[1] The Baodi county records could contribute a few more, such as *piao* ordering a person to follow the original decision. However, most *piao* can be divided into two kinds: the *chuanpiao* (summoning), which ordered somebody to come to court, and the *chipiao* (order), which ordered somebody to investigate, or submit certain information, or do other things. As the words 'order' and 'summon' clearly show, the difference between the two kinds was whether a person had to be brought before the court. The summons *piao* started with the words 'in the matter of summons' and the order *piao* with the words 'in the matter of investigation', 'in the matter of ordering', and so on.

1 Shiga Shūzō 1992b: 529–32.

Issuing a *piao* always involved sending one or more runners to find the persons involved for a particular purpose. These persons had to pay the runners a fee for the particular actions undertaken by the runners, which was called *lougui*. Many thoughtful magistrates were concerned to limit the issue of *piao*, to control both the number of *piao* issued and the number of either runners or parties involved in the *piao*. Some magistrates, for example Li Xuanfan from Baodi, issued a paper directly to the plaintiff, who then took the magistrate's order to the accused to come for the hearing if he lived in the town in which the court was situated (*Shuntian fuzhi*: 2717). Huang Liuhong even set up a sort of regular form for 'less important cases'. He called it 'the method of bringing in the defendant by the plaintiff himself'. In his book *Fuhui quanshu* [A Complete Book Concerning Happiness and Benevolence], he wrote: 'I had a piece of paper printed in the form of a *piao*, with the likeness of a runner holding a placard in his hand. The paper contained eight characters, *yuangao ziju kangwei najiu* (the plaintiff summons [the involved] himself, those who refused to come shall be arrested and punished). The following words were printed on the paper: "The Magistrate of X district, in the case of So-and-so, now orders plaintiff A with the assistance of the local elder and village headman (*yuedi*), to summon the following defendant and witnesses B and C to attend a hearing."'[2]

Perhaps influenced by this early practice, a magistrate's handbook approved by emperor Yongzheng (1723–35), 'The Basics of the Magisterial Service Approved by the Throne', advised this simple method of summoning the defendant by the plaintiff as a general rule for the magistrate to follow when a case was to be heard.[3] The practice adopted by magistrate Li Xuanfan of Baodi, mentioned above, might simply have been the result of following this rule. However, on most occasions, the parties lived not in the county town but in county villages, and the magistrate needed to make an investigation before hearing the case. That is why we can see from the Baodi records that the *piao* used most frequently were summons *piao* and investigation *piao*.

No matter what form a *piao* took, it was cancelled in the following situations: after the order in the *piao* had been completed; when the official holiday for the New Year began;[4] and when the current magistrate left and a new one came. In the first situation, the *piao* was cancelled for good; in

[2] Huang Liuhong 1850/1972: 123. See also Huang Liuhong 1984: 257. In fact, a Ming magistrate of Baodi, Yuan Huang, had already mentioned this method in his handbook, *Liaofan zazhu* of 1605 (stored in Beijing Library).

[3] *Qinban zhouxian shiyi*: 10.

[4] Qu Tongzu 1969: 17.

the latter two it was only temporarily stopped and would be continued when the holiday was over or the new magistrate ready for duty. Some civil cases were supposed to be suspended during the busy agricultural season, but since this regulation was flexible and not a strict rule, this is mentioned as the ground for cancellation for only a few *piao*.

Cancellation of *piao* was a routine and efficiently managed business in the magistrate's court. Every time a case was closed, the magistrate wrote the order 'the *piao* has been cancelled' on the reports submitted by runners or others in response to previous *piao*. The *piao* itself had the word 'cancelled' (*xiao*) written on it. Sometimes the parties submitted an application for closing the case without a hearing. Should the magistrate accept the application, he ordered the runner to cancel the *piao* on such petitions.

4.1.1 Drafting, correcting, and approving *piao*

Usually the magistrate set a deadline both for the preparation of draft *piao* and for completion of the order named in the *piao*. For example, Liu Heng set a deadline for the *piao* ready to be sent.[5] In one order given by the Baodi magistrate, the draft *piao* was required to be prepared within three days (Baodi, 190: 186). The number of days the *piao*, especially the summons *piao*, allowed the runners or relevant persons to report or to appear in person varied according to the distance of the destination from the court. Liu Heng allowed one, two, or three days if the distance was not very great, and one extra day might be added. If the place was a long way from the court, then a time of four to eight days was set, with two extra days allowed for completion.[6] However, some examples show that sometimes the runners took too long to summon the parties to the court and the magistrate had to punish them for this failure.[7]

After the magistrate had made his comments on the complaint, the clerk of the relevant office in charge of the case would draft the *piao* required by the comments. He identified himself at the end of the draft and impressed his personal sign. He might copy the magistrate's exact comments from the petition in drafting a particular part of a *piao*. On one Baodi complaint,

5 *Mulingshu*, *juan* 17: *Lisong shitiao* [Ten suggestions on solving lawsuits].

6 Liu set the deadline for issuing summonses in house, land, or marriage cases that had been accepted as before 9 o'clock the next day. He himself had a records book to check the issue (*Mulingshu*, *juan* 17).

7 In the Baodi records, comparison of the time when clerks finished the drafts with that of acceptance of the complaint shows that the gap could be as few as one or two days, or as many as five or ten days, or even more.

the magistrate wrote: 'an order to the village head in cooperation with the witness Ma to investigate whether what was said in the complaint is true and then to report and wait for my checking and interrogation' (Baodi, 95: 115). An almost exact copy of the comment can be found in the summons drafted by a clerk called Ling Zhenzong (Baodi, 95: 113).

The drafting of *piao* had its own regular and formal language. A *piao* usually consisted of four or five parts. It began with words indicating the nature of the *piao*, such as 'in the matter of ordering' or 'in the matter of summons'. Then followed a brief summary of the petition or petitions (if the defendant had made a counter-petition). The third part consisted of the magistrate's particular order, the time stipulated for carrying it out, and an order to the local headman (*xiangbao*) to assist the runner. The names of the runner or runners were given at the end of the *piao*. If it was a summons *piao*, then a list of names would be added. At the end of the draft, the writer always put the time of composition and his name, ending with such words as 'X office So-and-so drafts' (Baodi, 95: 125). In some draft *piao* from the Baodi records, we find a stamp containing times for the drafting, the correcting, the approving, and the issuing of the document (Baodi, 104: 19, 57; 103: 120).

After the clerk had finished the draft, it was sent to the secretary for scrutiny as to whether the summary of the case was accurate, or whether the list of names needed to be reduced (in order to keep the number of people involved as few as possible). Such corrections are very often found in the Baodi records. Sometimes the list of names is reduced to less than half the original. However, it is difficult to say that the clerk, by adding as many names as he could, wished to make an illicit gain by involving more people than necessary. It was not his responsibility to decide the final list of names to be summoned. On the contrary, he composed a long list to make the correcting easier, for it was always quicker to cross out names than to add some. After the content had been corrected, the name of the runner who was to execute the *piao* and the deadline for completing the order ('x day send x within x days') would be inserted. This is a crucial matter when examining the *piao* — an active magistrate such as Liu Heng always did this in person. Then the magistrate finally approved the *piao* with both a handwritten word 'all right' (*xing*) and the addition of the county's official stamp (*yin*). The following example is taken from the Tian Youlai case (see Chapter 2).

A draft *piao* of summoning from the Baodi records

A draft *piao* (*piaogao*)
In the matter of the summons. The matter was opened by a complaint filed by Zhaojiapai village in Shangjie *li*[8] alleging that Zhao Tongqing and others relied on their strength to bully the weak and forcibly plant the taxed land on the river bank without reasons, and so on. After a runner was ordered to go and carry out an investigation, a counter-plaint was filed by the licentiate Zhao Liankui and others to the effect that Tian Youlai occupied their land through trickery and so on. Also the local headman Liu Wanzeng made a report saying that the two parties both insisted on their own stories, [so it is] difficult to know the truth and settle the case. Now a summoning should be carried out. The runner is ordered with the help and cooperation of the *xiang-bao* speedily to summon those persons who should be interrogated as listed below to the court within —— days in order that they may give evidence at a hearing and judgment be given. The runner should not delay or cause any trouble. Otherwise, [the runner] will be brought up for prosecution with no mercy. Hurry! Hurry!
List (*jikai*)
Plaintiff: Tian Youlai
Defendants: Zhao Tongqing, Zhao Chunlin, Zhao Yongshun, Zhao Dacai, Zhao Qiheng, Zhao Qirui, Zhao Qihun, Zhao Wanqing, Zhao Qitai, Zhao Tingjun, Zhao Dachun, Zhao Liankui.
People mentioned (*cinei*): Dong Zhongyuan, Dong Yulong, Cao Shengzuo.
Xiangbao: Liu Wanzeng.
Daoguang 29th year (1849), third month, —— day drafted by Zhu Huiwu of Office of Work (*gongfang*).
The chief official (*zhengtang*) Dai. (Baodi, 99: 144)

The sentence underlined in the content was crossed out and replaced with two words: 'has come' (*zaian*). The blank space before the word 'days' was filled with 'four'. Eight names (underlined) in the list were crossed out and a mark (a tick) was added next to the last name (Liu Wanzeng). This made it impossible to add any new person to the list. The space for the day was filled with '17th'. The handwritten word '*xing*' (all right) appears just under the surname of the magistrate. An official sign, the 'seal of Baodi county', in both Chinese and *manzu* characters was affixed to the line giving year, month, and day. The handwritten *xing* had to be added by the magistrate himself, and the affixing of the seal had to be done at least in front of the magistrate. After the draft had been approved by the magistrate, it was ready for copying onto the official form.

[8] *Li* was a sub-county administrative division. There are twenty *li* in total in Baodi county.

4.1.2 The official form of the *piao*

I shall describe the formal *piao* using an example from the Baodi records, with a form from the Ba county records as a supplement. The formal *piao* was printed with enclosed double lines between which were burning flames, a vivid way of warning the carrier of the *piao* to carry out the order speedily. The lines in between were 32 cm in height and about 27 cm in width. The top trapezoid was about 6 cm high and contained two words *xinpiao* (in Ba county) (*Qingdai wenshu*: 229–30) or *huopiao* (Baodi, 193: 131).[9] The first vertical line from the right contained the magistrate's official title, rewards,[10] and surname. The text began with the word *wei* ('With regard to') much larger than the rest of the text. The contents were the same as in the draft. The *piao* of Baodi ended with the phrase 'return [the *piao* to be cancelled] within three days'. In specific places red ink marks (*biaozhu*) or words were added to highlight an important part of the *piao* or some key points such as a time limit, in order to stop the carrier from changing or adding anything. They were usually put at the beginning of the *piao* and the specific order to the runner and at the end of the text in the form of a tick or dot. The date of issuing the *piao* and the days for returning it were also added in red. Under the official sign, '*xing*' (all right) was handwritten in red, which meant that the *piao* had been approved by the magistrate. Apart from these typical places, the magistrate might add a red mark whenever he thought necessary.[11]

The *piao*, as authority for an action granted to its carriers, was directed at securing the performance of that action. Whatever the result, the *bing* (report), a counterpart of the *piao*, served the purpose of completing the process. The *bing* not only reveals the outcome of the order but also supplies the magistrate with the basis for any further order. It is for this reason that when, *piao* are examined, *bing* should also be examined.

9 *Xin* means reliable; *huo* means fire.

10 The Baodi example had: 'Zhang: Appointed (by the emperor) to hold normal rank as subprefect as the chief officer of Baodi county with a record of ten additional grades (*jia shiji*) and ten merits (*jilu shici*)' (Baodi, 193: 131).

11 In the Ba county example, the runner's name was in red ink and the surnames of the person to be summoned were dotted in red (*Qingdai wenshu*: 229).

4.2 The report

The people who implemented the *piao* or carried out the terms of the decision were required to report the result to the magistrate. A runner would have implemented a summons *piao*, with the help of the *xiangbao*, and reported the result. A particular order to investigate might have been implemented by a runner, the *xiangbao*, a witness, or the guarantor. The relevant person, usually the *xiangbao* rather than the runners, was required to report to the magistrate in such situations. Here are examples of reports (*bing*) taken from the Tian Youlai case.

Report 1

Report

Reporter Liu Wanzeng, *xiangbao* of Shangjie *li*

In the matter of reporting on obeying your order *piao*. In his complaint Tian Youlai said that his ancestors rented 7 *mu* of land on the bank of Xiuzhen river, for which a rent of 2 *diao* per year was paid to Dong Zhongyuan. The land was planted by Zhao Tongqing this first month, and so on. An order *piao* (*chipiao*) was issued which ordered me to investigate and report clearly, and so on. In accordance with the *piao*, with the assistance of the runner, I carried out the order. According to what Tian Youlai said, out of the 7 *mu* of land on Xiuzhen river bank planted by his ancestor, there are only 3 *mu* rented from the Zhao family. Now there are more than 4 *mu* of land which were forcibly planted by Zhao Tongqing. I questioned Zhao Tongqing about the matter. He is only 12 and knows nothing. I questioned Zhao Liankui about the matter. He said they had eleven strips (*long*) of land which consist of about 4 *mu*. They [the Zhao family] had planted the land [4 *mu*]. The other 3 *mu* of land were farmed by Tian Youlai and this land is not taxed. I questioned Dong Zhongyuan about the matter. He said he had never received the Tian family's rent, and so on. We went to the land. Zhao Liankui's family had planted 4 *mu* of land, but Tian Youlai had not planted the other 3 *mu*. Every side has his own story, and it is impossible to settle the differences. It is right for me to report to you, the magistrate, to check and take action. End the report.

[Comment by the magistrate]

Issue a summons *piao* to summon and question the parties. Order the original runner to return the *piao* and cancel it.

Daoguang 29th year (1849), 2nd month, 27th day. (Baodi, 99: 143)

Report 2

Report

Reporters: *kuaitou* (fast lictor) Zhang Xang, *zaotou* (lictor) Zhang Fu, *boyi* (runner) Zhang Xianting.

In the matter of reporting back. We were ordered to summon the parties in a complaint by Tian Youlai who accused Zhao Tongqing and others of forcibly planting his rented land on the river bank, and so on. In compliance with the order we summoned the persons at once. Now we have brought the plaintiff Tian Youlai; the defendants Zhao Yongshun, Zhao Qitai, and Zhao Liankui; the *cinei* (persons mentioned) Dong Zhongyuan and Dong Yulong; and the *xiangbao*, Liu Wanzeng. Zhao Dachun is too old and ill to come. Cao Shengzuo has died. His son has been brought to answer questions on his behalf. It is right for us to report to you, the magistrate, to check and take action. End the report.

[Comment of the magistrate]

In compliance with the court order, with the *xiangbao*'s assistance, you should lead the two parties to the land to survey its extent and the four boundaries. Then report back with a map for my checking and decision.

Daoguang 29th (1849) year, 4th month, 1st day. (Baodi, 99: 145)

Report 3

Report

Reporters: *kuaitou* Zhang Xang, *zaotou* Zhang Fu, *boyi* Zhang Xianting.

In the matter of reporting back. We were ordered to summon the parties for interrogation in the case in which Tian Youlai accused Zhao Tongqing and others of forcibly planting his rented land on the river bank, and Zhao Liankui made a counter-plaint. A hearing has been held and we runners have been ordered to measure the land in question. In accordance with the order, with the assistance of the *xiangbao* Liu Wanzeng, we have measured the land. . . . [explanations of the size and four boundaries of the land]. Now we have brought the plaintiff Tian Youlai; the defendants Zhao Yongshun, Zhao Qitai, and Zhao Liankui; the *cinei* (persons mentioned) Dong Zhongyuan, Dong Yulong; and the *xiangbao* Liu Wanzeng. Cao Shengzuo has died and his son is ill and cannot come. It is right for us to report with the attached map to you, the magistrate, to check and take action. End the report.

A map is attached for illustration.

[Comment of the magistrate]

The case has been tried and the *piao* is cancelled.

Daoguang 29th year (1849), 4th month, 14th day. (Baodi, 99: 154)

Report 2 was submitted in response to the summons *piao* quoted above and the other two reports responded to the order *piao*. Yet they all took the same form to explain the fulfilment of the directive. Their completion in each case was vital to the magistrate's next step. The smooth completion of the summons *piao* determined whether the magistrate could hear the case within the time he expected. On every report made in answer to the summons *piao*, the magistrate simply commented 'bring them for trial' (*daixun*). Sometimes people listed in the *piao* were not brought to him. The magistrate was required by law to hear the case if the missing person would not influence the investigation (Sub-statute 336-4). If the person the runner could not bring to the court was either the plaintiff or the defendant, or a key witness, the runners were not to bring any other person who might be available because 'it will be impossible to have them [the parties] confront each other' (*wuping zhixun*). Of course, the runners would have given reasons for their failure to bring somebody to court. The excuse most often used was that, owing to a bad harvest, the person had left his village to seek a living. The magistrate did not always believe the excuse, and sometimes accused the runners of making a false excuse or punished them with beating (Baodi, 152: 48, 49; 108: 38). In any event, such a report meant that the hearing would not happen as expected. In reporting back on the summons *piao*, no matter whether the parties summoned had been brought to the court or not, the runners usually did not explain the dispute itself. In contrast, this is the main focus in reports submitted in response to the order *piao* or, more exactly here, an investigation *piao*.

The order *piao* and its consequences, such as reports 1 and 3, were very important in the magistrate's plan for dealing with the case. In response to the magistrate's order *piao*, the *xiangbao* was often required to question the people involved in advance in order to investigate the facts of the case. His task was to clarify the issue, to ascertain the content of, and differences between, the stories of the parties, and, at the very least, to bring back everyone's story to the magistrate. This investigation was very helpful for the magistrate's preparation for his formal hearing in terms of obtaining more information to ascertain the truth. If the two parties stuck to their own stories, the reporter usually said 'the two parties stick to their own story and they both want to be summoned to court' (*gezhi yici junyuan chuanxun*). Then a summons *piao* would be issued.

To take report 1 as an example, when carrying out the investigation ordered by the magistrate the *xiangbao* questioned every person involved. Although each party questioned had their own story, two facts were revealing: Tian Youlai did rent a piece of land from the Zhao family, and the Zhao family did plant a piece of land that had previously been farmed by Tian Youlai. The *xiangbao* obviously had no authority himself to attempt to reconcile the stories and clarify the matter. So a summons *piao* was issued.

In the hearing, although Tian denied that the land, even the 3 *mu* that he seems to have admitted in the *xiangbao*'s report, belonged to the Zhao family, the Zhao family had evidence, i.e. tax certificates and witnesses, that Tian had paid the rent for a piece of land to the Zhao family. However, the exact size of the land in question still remained unclear, so the magistrate issued another order *piao* in which measurement of the land in question was ordered. Since measurement is the task of runners, the report (Report 3) was made by these special runners. The report with a map attached made clear the size of the land. So the magistrate heard the case again and delivered his decision.[12]

As we can see from the details of the procedure, the magistrate made every effort to determine the facts of the case, sending out two order *piao* to investigate. Even a formal hearing did not end the investigation process. In other words, before delivering his decision, the magistrate was prepared to repeat this procedure again and again, so that even his hearing could be regarded as one piece of the investigation, in the sense that the decision to close the case had not been made. It was through this (repeated) investigation that the truth was revealed; and from this emerged the magistrate's judgment and final decision.

4.3 Closing cases without further hearing

Should the two parties have resolved their differences and again become on good terms during the investigation, the report would ask the magistrate to close the case without taking further action (in the form of a formal hearing). Because the investigation *piao* was often carried out by the *xiangbao*, it was often the *xiangbao* who applied to the magistrate to close the case if the two parties were reconciled. On receiving the application by the party or

[12] Tian Youlai was ordered to continue to farm the land and pay the rent to the Zhao family without delay. In dealing with tenancy relations, the Qing law protected a tenant's rights by prohibiting the owner from taking back the land without legal reason. The Qing law expressed this rule abstractly as *duodian li* (the law on eviction). For a detailed discussion, see Chapter 6.

the report by the *xiangbao*, the magistrate, if he was satisfied with the result, would give his permission on the application or the report to announce that the case was closed and that no further action, mainly the hearing, would be taken by the court. In these cases, the magistrate made his decision by writing orders and comments on the relevant submission, which was called *piduan*. We will see that many cases were closed without a formal hearing or specific decision. These are often regarded by scholars as cases solved by mediation.

In the Baodi county records, 39 out of 126 resolved debt cases, 55 out of 127 resolved land cases, and 27 out of 95 resolved marriage cases were closed without a court decision being delivered by the magistrate. In other words, over 34 per cent of all civil disputes ended this way. Thus, Philip Huang excluded these cases from his discussion of the magistrate's formal adjudication in Qing civil justice and put them in a third realm 'in which lawsuits were resolved by informal mediation before they reached formal court adjudication, usually under the influence of some preliminary indications of the court's opinion'.[13]

Huang distinguished three stages of litigation: the initial stage, in which the plaintiff submitted the petition and the magistrate accepted this petition; the middle stage, which involved 'a considerable range of possible actions on the part of the magistrate, the runners and the *xiangbao*, and the litigants'[14] before the formal court adjudication conducted by the magistrate; and the final stage — the court session in which the magistrate usually made a decision on the spot. Huang's third realm was created during the middle stage, when the 'the informal justice of community and kin mediation and the formal justice of court adjudication . . . met and interacted'.[15] It constituted a 'realm of semiformal justice' because 'there was something of an institutionalized dialogue between the formal and informal systems'.[16]

The reason Huang arrived at this conclusion was the fact that the outcome of the case was not delivered by the magistrate on the spot. Although Huang believed that the court had a significant influence on these cases, in his view the magistrate 'simply' accepted the application submitted by the parties or other mediators. But this would undervalue the magistrate's power and overvalue the power of the informal mediator in these cases, if we confine the meaning of 'formal' in this limited way to 'the magistrate decided

[13] Philip Huang 1996: 9, 10.
[14] Ibid.: 116.
[15] Ibid.: 110.
[16] Ibid.

the case on the spot'. This is not consistent with the nature of the Qing's governing structure. Cases might end without a magistrate's hearing, but whether they did so was entirely dependent on the magistrate's agreement. This is evident in a sentence often employed by parties who applied for closure of a case without a hearing: 'although we have solved our problem, the unchallenged decision should come from you (*xiaqing suishun shengcai chuzi tianen*)'.

Furthermore, there were particular reasons for the magistrate to indicate his agreement. Theoretically, a case could be closed in this way because the dispute no longer existed, whatever the reason. The magistrate would therefore think there was no need to summon and question the parties and decide for them. This was the basic factor the magistrate had to take into account when he accepted an application to close a case. Although the parties could apply for closure for other reasons, such as exposure to some sort of pressure or a calculation of the financial costs, these were not common circumstances. Moreover, there is no example of closure on such grounds.

Case 1

Woman Yuan submitted a statement of receipt (*shouzhuang*) in which she said that Chen, whom she had accused of not paying her debt, had now paid, and that they neither had any difference any more. She was willing to end the litigation and asked the magistrate to be merciful and cancel the hearing. At the same time, Chen's statement of payment (*jiaozhuang*) was submitted and asked the same permission. The magistrate, of course, saw no need to hear the case and agreed to the application. (Baodi, 187: 63–4)

Woman Yuan submitted the statement of receipt directly to the court as the means of applying to the magistrate for cancellation of the formal hearing. Meanwhile, the accused submitted a corresponding application. The application for cancellation of the hearing in Case 3 in Chapter 7 took a similar approach. The debt had been paid and the creditor had received the money. It was clear that neither party would receive further benefit if the magistrate insisted on hearing the case. Nor was there any possibility that the magistrate could make a better decision than to close the case. That a debt had been settled was a typical reason and approach in debt cases.

More often, as I have pointed out, the application came from the *xiangbao* in his report to the magistrate asking for closure of the case on behalf of the parties (for example, Case 3 in Chapter 6). In playing the role of mediator, the *xiangbao*'s power was almost the same as that of other mediators in persuading the two parties to reconcile their differences. Indeed, the *xiangbao* might enjoy more power than ordinary people owing to his easier access to the magistrate and other government facilities. In the magistrate's eyes, however, he was just another runner or at best a clerk. This may be seen from the *xiangbaos*' reports, which always bear an official scrivener's stamp on them, as has already been shown in the Tian Youlai case (section 4.2).

Although the *xiangbao* played an important role in the process by which the magistrate handled civil cases, his function should not be overestimated. The *xiangbao* played two main roles: giving assistance to the runners by identifying people who were to be summoned, and investigating or helping to investigate facts and reporting his findings to the magistrate. The *xiangbao* was familiar with the situation in his community and had similar access to the magistrate as did the runners. Sometimes the summons *piao* had only the summoned person's surname. The magistrate relied entirely on the *xiangbao* to point out and hand in (*zhijiao*) the person summoned. When the petition was not clear or some suspicious matter needed to be clarified, the *xiangbao* was sent to investigate. He attended the court hearing to give evidence about what he knew or what he could prove to the court. For example, the *xiangbao* in the Tian Youlai case made a statement about the location of the land in dispute. Generally the *xiangbao* played a very important role in the whole process of solving minor disputes in terms of the help he supplied to the magistrate's court. However, it would be wrong to think that he necessarily played a particularly active part in helping people to compromise. The compromise was no more than the result of his investigation and formed part of his report on the way the case had developed between the parties. It was just the same as his other report in which he asked the magistrate to hear the case. In this sense, the function he played as a mediator was not, as Professor Huang observed, contrary to the Code. The relevant provision in the Code stated:

> Where people have lawsuits on trivial matters such as boundaries or irrigation and relatives are involved, the *xiangbao* may be allowed to investigate and report. The magistrate should personally review the case and decide. The magistrate must not assign the *xiangbao* to decide and close the case [on his own]. Should a case be closed [by the *xiangbao*] without the magistrate's personal hearing, the supervising officials are to report the magistrate at once and the magistrate will be reprimanded according to the regulations. (Sub-statute 334-8)

Careful reading of this sub-statute and comparison with the magistrate's practice regarding the *xiangbao*'s work in handling litigation make clear it is not right to say that 'the magistrate was in fact violating the Qing code'.[17] The concern of the Code was to make sure that the magistrate took active

[17] Ibid.: 113.

steps with respect to the case. He should not evade the responsibility of making a decision by relying on the *xiangbao* to close the case. If the case was closed by application of the parties made in the *xiangbao*'s report, it was not the *xiangbao* who closed the case. When the magistrate ordered the *xiangbao* to investigate and report back, he was not assigning to the *xiangbao* the task of solving the case and closing it. Thus, the way in which the *xiangbao* was involved in the magistrate's handling of the case was not contrary to the sub-statute. To report back to the magistrate was so well-established a procedure that, whether the magistrate ordered a 'report' or not, the *xiangbao* or person who was ordered to conduct a particular action would report back to the magistrate for his decision. On a few occasions the magistrate ordered the *xiangbao* to resolve the case (*lichu*). However, the *xiangbao* always still made a report regarding the result. He might report to the magistrate that the parties wanted a formal hearing or that the dispute had been solved, so that the case might be closed.

The relations between the magistrate and the *xiangbao*, and between each of them and the parties, can be clarified with an example from Baodi. The order given by the magistrate was partly used by Professor Huang, but for a different demonstration. 'The magistrate', he said, 'might express an opinion about how he wanted the matter settled, as for example: "Look into the complaint. If it is indeed the truth, then [do such and such]."'[18] The context is that the runner was ordered to cooperate with the *xiangbao* to investigate and clarify the matters raised in the petition. If the accusation was true, then the defendant was ordered to settle the debt and a report was to be submitted (Baodi, 190: 181–8). This comment was actually a very good example of the way the magistrate made a decision by writing on a document in the case. The *xiangbao*, in this case, reported after carrying out the order of the magistrate, and said that both parties insisted on their own story and wanted a formal hearing. The magistrate then ordered that a hearing be held later. One can see that the *xiangbao*'s power was indeed quite limited. He was just carrying out the magistrate's order. His power was not greatly different from that of any other person who simply carried out the magistrate's order in the case.

Of course, the *xiangbao* might abuse his power by not telling the truth in his report. Even one of the parties might tell a false story in order to get permission from the magistrate to close the case. This is even further evidence that the magistrate would not 'simply' agree with whatever was submitted to him. To get the magistrate's permission to close a case, the

[18] Ibid.

application or the report had to contain something that could satisfy the magistrate. It is thus not quite correct to say that the magistrate's agreement with the application for closure of a case was dictated only by his desire to encourage compromise. Here are some more examples.

Case 2
Rui brought the case against the defendant. He had tried to stop the defendant from stealing cotton from the cotton land he guarded and was hit. When the summons *piao* was sent, a group of mediators applied to the magistrate to close the case. They said the parties had only quarrelled, not fought. Because the defendant had walked through the land, Rui was afraid that he might steal something and so stopped him. Now they had come together, cleared up their misunderstanding, and apologized to each other. But the magistrate did not grant permission. He commented: 'Rui Cai took advantage of guarding the harvest to dare falsely to accuse somebody of theft and start the litigation. This is hatred. All are to be summoned until I inquire and punish.' The application for cancellation of the hearing was not granted. Several days later, the parties brought another similar application in which they emphasized that the litigation was really caused by a misunderstanding and that they were on good terms. The magistrate agreed this time: 'The two parties are now on good terms, how should I act too much.' He then ordered the parties to submit bonds that they would cause no further trouble. (Baodi, 97: 2–6)

Case 3
Woman Zhang accused Li, who had married her daughter-in-law after her son died and offered to feed her, of not keeping his promise. Moreover, he had sold her land and a donkey. The magistrate ordered the *xiangbao* and witnesses to investigate and report. The *xiangbao* reported that he could not settle the matter. Meanwhile, Li brought a counter-plaint in which he denied that he did not feed woman Zhang. As for the land in question, he said it had initially been given to him for farming. Woman Zhang later brought an application to close the case. She said this time that Li now knew he was wrong. She wanted to live by herself. Li had returned the land to her. She asked the magistrate to be merciful and cancel the hearing. The magistrate was not satisfied with the explanation. He asked: 'How much land was given to Li at the beginning, and now how has the land been divided between you and Li? Why do you want to live by yourself? I order you to answer these questions and submit statements concerning the delivery and return of the land for my decision. You should not make matters obscure any more (*wude hanhun*).' Later, woman Zhang and Li both submitted instruments of confirmation, as the magistrate asked. (Baodi, 100: 9–19)

Case 4

Zhang accused Li of encouraging his [Li's] brother to demand 10 *diao* which he had already paid back to Li. The brother had forcibly taken his door and some money from his home. The magistrate ordered the *xiangbao* to investigate the truth in an investigating *piao* dated 21st January. The *xiangbao* reported a similar story, and further explained that the brother did not know the money had been paid. Now both the door and the money had been returned to Zhang. However, the magistrate was not satisfied with the report. He commented on the report: 'The value of the cotton fabric Zhang owed to Li had been paid. How could the brother, who is neither the guarantor nor a creditor, demand the money from Zhang and even take off the door and steal some money? He must either have been put up to it by Li or have been very reckless. Both acts are hateful. This might also be the reason why there are many lawsuits from the locality. It is imperative to punish the parties seriously in order to prevent matters becoming worse. The parties should wait to be summoned for my hearing and punishment.' Five days later, a summons was sent out, but there was another report from the *xiangbao*, who came to the court instead of the parties and explained the reason for the brother's action. 'Li and his brother run a cotton business in partnership. The money Zhang owed should have been distributed between them. Now the summons has been sent, but we recently have had the spring rains which is good for seed sowing. So both parties wish to close the case without a trial, so as not to lose the chance to sow seed.' The magistrate was satisfied this time and agreed to close the case. (Baodi, 186: 112–15)

Case 5

One day, Wang cried out in the hall of the magistrate's court and submitted a petition. He owed Yue a debt of 2 *diao*. One day when they met, Yue asked that the debt be paid at once, and Wang promised to repay the debt after he returned from the market. Yue did not agree and seized his trousers, bag, sickle and 7 *diao* and 200 *wen*, and scratched Wang's neck. The magistrate heard the case at once and punished Wang for shouting in the court with 60 blows with the heavy stick. Then the magistrate had the summons for hearing the case drafted two days later. Another two days later, before the hearing conducted by the magistrate, Wang submitted an application asking the magistrate to close the case, since he already regretted his improper action (shouting in court) and the debt he owed had been paid. His goods and money that he left with Yue had been returned, and they were on good terms again. The magistrate commented: 'Since you cried out a petition to accuse Yue of seizing your property and money, whether your accusation is true or not should have been investigated and action taken. However, since this is the farmers' busy season and you have paid the debt, the court hearing is withdrawn and the case is closed.' (Baodi, 187: 160–4)

One can see that such cases were usually not very complicated, so that the magistrate could obtain the information he needed by communication with the *xiangbao* or the parties, rather than by interrogation of the parties personally. He showed no hesitation in disagreeing with the application at any point and asking the parties to do more, including appearing personally before him. He might comment that he cancelled the hearing because it was the farmers' busy season and so on, but that was a supplementary rather than the essential reason. For example, in Case 5 he had already dealt with the plaintiff's wrongdoing in court and finally granted permission to close the case because the debt had been repaid and the property seized by the defendant had been returned. Sometimes, even when the parties had come to an agreement and settled their difference, the magistrate insisted on hearing the case. However, he usually had nothing to do but to order submission of the bond of confirmation.

Case 6

Zhang accused Nan of buying flour on credit at the price of 8 *diao* and 400 *wen*. He wanted the debt to be paid but, when he asked for the money, he was hit. The mediators applied to the magistrate to close the case on the ground that the problem was solved, but the magistrate did not agree and insisted on hearing the case. The same day the magistrate heard the case and the parties confessed in court that the money owed had already been paid through mediation. Obviously the magistrate had no need to do anything except close the case. (Baodi, 190: 145–60)

I classify such cases in the group of 'hearing delivered' (see Tables 6.1 and 7.1).[19]

There were magistrates, such as Liu Heng, who disagreed with ending a case without a formal hearing, although most magistrates accepted this practice. The Code did not make any strict provision about whether or not the magistrate should close a case without a hearing. The law allowed the parties to apply to close the case (Sub-statute 336-9). However, whether the magistrate took this route to close the case without summoning the parties to court entirely depended on the magistrate from the very beginning. It is doubtful that the parties in the case could play an equivalent role. Thus the magistrate was not just 'simply' or 'routinely' accepting a compromise.

[19] In another example, one party stated when the magistrate heard the case that the debt had been paid. The other party said the money had been received. That was all the statements of the two parties stressed. The magistrate was left with no dispute to decide (Baodi, 99: 39).

This explains why all applications for closure were produced in a similar way, beginning with an explanation of the cause of the dispute, then describing developments since the submission of the petition, the result agreed by the parties and whether it had been fulfilled, and ending with a routine formula such as the parties 'had observed the appropriate ritual of apologizing to each other' (*bici jianmian fuli*)[20] and were on good terms again (*bicihehao*), so they both wished to end the case and asked the magistrate to be lenient and cancel the hearing (*mianxun*). Usually the magistrate asked the parties to submit bonds of confirmation for future reference. This suggests something different from Huang's third realm. Cases that were closed without a court decision were still part of the official process. The essential difference between these cases and those with a court decision was that the former finished without a hearing or a formal decision and the latter with a hearing and/or a decision. In the former the parties were willing to end the case and in the latter they might not be so willing. On an application for closure for which permission was granted by the magistrate, a statement was also made above the main text: 'Included [this case] in the entry of Cases Closed of April's Monthly Report' (Baodi, 168:126). There is no doubt that cases closed without a formal hearing were treated as closed by the court. To the magistrate, the fact that cases could be closed without a hearing was just a way of ending the case without the two parties confronting each other in court. Through ruling by comment, the magistrate could still control the case without a hearing.

4.4 The trial list

When the parties were summoned to court or when the magistrate ordered a hearing to be conducted at once, a trial list (*shendan*) was prepared by the clerks of the relevant office(s). The trial list was very simple. It started with the name of the office, followed by the names of the runners who were concerned with the case, then the list of the people who were to be questioned by the magistrate in court; it ended with the month and day of the case.

A trial list was a necessary preparation for a court hearing. The magistrate questioned people at least once during the trial according to the trial list and made notes on it. The notes were made against the names of particular people, such as 'who is also called x', or 'punish 20 blows with the light stick'. When we find a trial list in the case file, the implication is that a court hearing was held. The magistrate's final or semi-final decision might be found on the list. The people who had been questioned by the magistrate had their

[20] Huang 1996: 119.

surname marked with an ink dot, or two ink dots if they had been questioned twice. The examples I give are taken from the Tian Youlai case.

Trial list 1
Gongfang (Office of Work)
Yuanyi (the original runners): Chen Xiang, Zhang Fu. *Boyi* (added runner): Zhang Xianting.
Jikai (list):
Plaintiff: Tian Youlai.
Defendant: Zhao Yongshun, Zhao Qitai, Zhao Liankui.
Cinei (persons mentioned): Dong Zhongyuan, Dong Yulong, Cao Changling [Cao Shenzuo's son].
Xiangbao: Liu Wanzeng.
[Decision of this trial]
I order that the original runners with the help of the *xiangbao* bring the two parties together to survey the extent and four boundaries of the land in question. A map is to be made and a report returned, so I can check and decide.
4th month 1st day. (Baodi, 99: 146)

Trial list 2
Gongfang (Office of Work)
Yuanyi (the original runners): Chen Xiang, Zhang Fu. *Boyi* (added runner): Zhang Xianting.
Jikai (list):
Plaintiff: Tian Youlai.
Defendant: Zhao Yongshun, Zhao Qitai, Zhao Liankui.
Cinei (persons mentioned): Dong Zhongyuan, Dong Yulong,.
Xiangbao: Liu Wanzeng.
[Decision of the case]
I order that Tian Youlai continue to rent and plant the land belonging to Zhao Yongshun and the others as before. He (Tian) must not block the flow of the river and occupy the dam. Otherwise, he will be punished severely. Now all are to make a bond of confirmation (*jie*)[21] to close the case. The *piao* is to be cancelled.
4th month 15th day. (Baodi, 99: 152)

4.5 Statements and bonds of confirmation

Decisions might sometimes be written on the parties' statements (Baodi, 141: 142). For all the cases that progressed to a hearing the magistrate produced statements (*gong*) of what was said by the parties in court. However, it is not surprising to find that these statements were very brief. They were almost certainly summaries of what the parties said in response to questions by the

[21] The *jie* is also called *ganjie*; I shall say more about *ganjie* in the next section.

magistrate. They formed a clear logical basis for his decisions given at each stage. When magistrates discussed the matter of making good statements, they emphasized the skill in making statements simple, logical, and correct.

Dot marks were also made on the surnames, just as on the trial list. Every statement had the sign of the person who made it at the end. On most occasions this sign was in the form of a tick. The tick also marked the end of the statement, so that no more words could be added later. A very interesting feature is that the statement always ended with the same phrase '*shi shi*' (what I said is the truth). This looks as though the informant was making a pledge. Witnesses involved in petitions had to make a statement of confirmation or confirming bond (*ganjie*) together with the two parties. Should the witnesses supply false information, they were liable to punishment in accordance with the law (Sub-statute 408–5). What the witnesses and the two parties finally confirmed by their bond were just their statements. Here are two examples from the Tian Youlai case.

Statement 1

Dong Zhongyuan *gong* (states): I was a river runner. I have retired now. I kept two expired certificates. I did not receive 2 *diao* rent from Tian Youlai. [What I said] is true [tick].

Tian Youlai *gong* (states): I have 7 *mu* of river land and pay 2 *diao* rent to Dong Zhongyuan every year. The land does not belong to the Zhao Liankui family. [What I said] is true [tick].

Zhao Liankui *gong* (states): Tian Youlai farms about 4 *mu* of *mindi* (people's land) left by the ancestor of the *shengyuan* [here it is referring to the speaker Zhao Liankui]. The tax certificate can be evidence. We did not make a contract. [What I said] is true [tick].

Zhao Yongshun, Zhao Qitai *hegong* (state together): They say the same as Zhao Liankui. [One statement ends with a tick and the other with handwriting]

Dong Yulong, Cao Changling *hegong* (state together): Tian Youlai contributed the grain rent of six strips (*long*) to Zhao Liangkui's clan in the past. Later, Zhao Liankui complained that Tian Youlai was farming more land (than the six strips). So [Tian] increased the grain rent to cover eleven strips through our mediation. We know nothing about other things. [What we said] is true [tick].

Liu Wanzeng *gong* (states): The land disputed by Zhao Liankui and Tian Youlai is located on the river [bank]. [What I said] is true [tick].

4th month 15th day. (Baodi, 99: 147)

Statement 2

Tian Youlai *gong* (states): I planted eleven strips (*long*) of river land owned by Zhao Yongshun's clan and contributed half of the harvest to them for many years without any grain being unpaid. Zhao Yongshun's clan finally wants to take back the land (in disregard of my opinion). Today we attended your hearing and received your decision which orders me to continue cultivating the land and contributing the grain rent as before, and says that I must not owe grain rent and block the flow of the river, or occupy the dam. I willingly obey the decision, and will pledge a confirming bond (*ganjie*). What I said is true [tick].

Zhao Yongshun, Zhao Qitai, Zhao Liankui *hegong* (state together): Tian Youlai cultivated the *shengyuan* family's eleven strips of river land and contributed half of the harvest for many years without grain being unpaid. Because he occupied part of the dam and blocked the flow of the river, we want to take the land back. Today we attended your hearing and received your decision which orders that Tian Youlai continue to cultivate the eleven strips of land and contribute half of the grain harvest as before. He must pay the rent on time and not block the flow of the river and occupy the dam. We willingly obey the decision and pledge a confirming bond (*ganjie*). We have had our record book and tax certificate back. What we said is true [tick].

Dong Zhongyuan, Dong Yulong *hegong* (state together): If Tian Youlai cultivates the eleven strips of river land, the dam and flow of the river will not be affected. We willingly obey the decision and pledge a confirming bond (*ganjie*). What we said is true [tick].

Liu Wanzeng *gong* (states): If Tian Youlai does not plant the land within the eleven strips, and occupies the dam and blocks the river flow, I will report to the magistrate. What I said is true [tick].

4th month 15th day. (Baodi, 99: 156)

As one can see, the statements at each hearing were very brief. They focused on the essential questions of the dispute such as, in this case, what size the piece of land was, to whom it belonged, and what evidence the parties had. In Statement 1, Dong said that the land had nothing to do with him, which was consistent with what the defendant Zhao clan said in the rebuttal (see Chapter 2 on the petition form). However, Tian, the plaintiff, still affirmed what he had said in his original petition, namely, that he paid the rent to Dong, which implied that the land did not belong to the Zhao clan.[22] The

[22] Tian's original petition was not available in the archives. However, his statement on this part can be deduced from the magistrate's comment on it, which was given in the rebuttal (see Chapter 2).

statements of the Zhao clan members were similar to those they had given in their counter-plaint, i.e. they had 4 *mu* of land and they had proof. The later witnesses basically proved this point, that is, the land belonged to the Zhao clan. But they used the term strip (*long*) instead of *mu* to describe the size of the land in question. None of the above circumstances were known to the *xiangbao*, so the *xiangbao* simply made a statement about the location of the land, which was relevant to the Zhao clan's claim that Tian had blocked the river flow. We can see that the magistrate did not obtain a statement as to whether the Zhao clan had forcibly planted the land as the plaintiff accused, because this point actually depended on another more basic question, i.e. to whom the land belonged. The magistrate did not base his conclusion about such matters as the owner of the land and the size of the land solely on the statements. In other words, he did not achieve what was usually said: 'all statements can be matched to each other' (*gong yi shunhe*). Instead the magistrate ordered that the land be measured (see Trial list 1 for this decision) in order to clarify the facts.

Two weeks later, after the runners had carried out the measurement of the land, a re-hearing was held. The runners reported the details of their measurement: the land was '215 *gong* long from south to north, 5 *gong* and 5 *fen* wide throughout'. The land in question was actually a narrow rectangle, which was less than either party claimed. In the face of those facts, all the people involved this time made the same statement about eleven strips (*long*) when referring to the size of the land. Furthermore, Tian confessed this time that the land was the Zhao clan's property. However, he said that he paid the rent to the Zhao clan on time every year and never owed any unpaid rent, which implied that the Zhao clan should not take the land back and gave the real reason for bringing the case.[23] The Zhao clan agreed with what Tian said about the rent, but they pointed out that Tian had blocked the river flow, which also implied that they had a reason to take the land back. Since Tian had not actually failed in his obligations as a tenant, the magistrate ruled that Tian should continue to farm the land but must not block the river flow or occupy the river dam. This decision was noted on Trial list 2. However, relevant parts of the decision were also repeated by each informant in the confirming bond (*ganjie*). In this sense, the written decision made on the spot by the magistrate was not necessarily the whole decision for the case. For example, in this case, the order to the *xiangbao* that he should report to the magistrate if Tian blocked the river flow can be

[23] For the provisions on tenancy matters, see Chapter 5. For more tenant cases, see Chapter 6.

known only from the statements and *ganjie*. This also reveals that the magistrate's words in court when deciding the case could go further than the written decision on the trial list or the statements. From the statements, we can see that all words on the issues of the case were consistent with each other, and clearly formed the basis of the decision. But that is not the whole story.

The confirming bond that was made after the decision by each person involved was consistent with his statement and the decision as well. In other words, the decision can be traced not only from the magistrate's handwriting on the trial list or court statement, but also from the statement itself and from the confirming bond. The witnesses can also be traced from the confirming bond in this way. To see this feature clearly, the confirming bonds of the four persons involved, corresponding to their statements and the decision, are given below:

Ganjie 1
Ju ganjie (The person who makes the confirming bond is) Tian Youlai: In the matter of making the confirming bond. I agree to obey the decision in the case in which I accused Zhao Yongshun and others of forcibly planting [my] river land. You have kindly heard the case and made a decision that I shall continue to rent and plant the eleven strips of river land belonging to Zhao Yongshun, pay the rent on time, and not occupy the dam and block the flow of the river. I willingly obey the decision. The confirming bond I have given is true.

[The magistrate's comment]: *zhunjie* (the pledge approved)

Daoguang 29th year 4th month 15th day Tian Youlai [signed with cross]. (Baodi, 99: 157)

Ganjie 2
Ju ganjie (The persons who make the confirming bond are) Zhao Liankui, Zhao Qitai and Zhao Yongshun: In the matter of making the confirming bond. We agree to obey the decision in the case in which Tian Youlai accused the *sheng* of forcibly planting [his] river land. We have attended your kind hearing and received your decision that Tian Youlai shall continue to rent and plant our (*sheng*) eleven strips of river land which he rented and farmed, contribute half of the grain harvest to our (*sheng*) family, pay rent on time, and not occupy the dam and block the river flow. We willingly obey the decision and the agreement. The confirming bond we have given is true.

[The magistrate's comment]: *zhunjie* (the pledge approved)

Daoguang 29th year 4th month 15th day Zhao Liankui [signed with 'obey decision']

Zhao Qitai [signed],

Zhao Yongshun [signed with cross]. (Baodi, 99: 158)

Ganjie 3
Ju ganjie (The persons who are making the confirming bond are) Dong Zhongyuan, Dong Yulong: In the matter of making the confirming bond. We agree to obey the decision in the case in which such Tian Youlai accused Zhao Yongshun and others of forcibly planting [his] river land. We have attended your hearing and received your decision. Tian Youlai rented and planted Zhao Yongshun family's river land. We once mediated their dispute (about the amount of rent) and as a result Tian Youlai contributed grain from the harvest of eleven strips (*long*) of land, and did not damage the dam and block river flow. The confirming bond we have given is true.

[The magistrate's comment]: *zhunjie* (the pledge approved)

Daoguang 29th year 4th month 15th day Dong Zhongyuan [signed with cross]

Dong Yulong [signed with cross]. (Baodi, 99: 159)

Ganjie 4
Ju ganjie (The person who is making the confirming bond is) Liu Wanzeng: In the matter of making the confirming bond. I agree to obey the decision in the case in which Tian Youlai accused Zhao Yongshun and others of forcibly planting [his] river land. [They] have attended your kind hearing and received your decision that Tian Youlai shall plant the land within the eleven strips (*long*). I am ordered to report if Tian Youlai should occupy the dam and block the river flow. I dare not disobey your order. The confirming bond I have given is true.

[The magistrate's comment]: *zhunjie* (the pledge approved)

Daoguang 29th year 4th month 15th day Liu Wanzeng [signed with cross]. (Baodi, 99: 160)

If we compare these four confirming bonds with the corresponding statements by each person — i.e. the plaintiff's *ganjie* with his statement; the defendants' *ganjie* with their statements; the *cinei*'s (persons mentioned) with their statements; and the *xiangbao*'s *ganjie* with his statement — it is easy to see the remarkable consistency between them. The parties confirmed the decision made for them. If a punishment was imposed by the magistrate, the person who was so punished also stated that in his *ganjie*. The witnesses mainly confirmed what they had said in court, as in *ganjie* 3, which exactly repeated the court statement. The *xiangbao*'s *ganjie* was simply focused on the order given to him in the event that the plaintiff failed to carry out the decision. In short, the *ganjie* was a sort of written confirmation in which the *ganjie* maker stated that he agreed with what he had personally said in court and with what was decided by the magistrate in court or on the spot. The people involved were made to confirm both what they had said and the decision given by the magistrate. So I think a better translation of *ganjie* is 'confirming bond' rather than 'pledge of willingness to end the suit'.[24] It is clear that 'pledge of willingness to end the suit' does not exhaust all dimensions that the *ganjie* could cover.

4.6 The decision

We have seen the decision in the Tian case on Trial list 2 above, as well as the other non-final decision on Trial list 1. Decisions by the magistrate might be written on either the trial list or a statement of the parties. We may get the impression from the Tian case that the decision could be very brief. The magistrate seems afraid to waste ink by writing more sentences. And we find no reasoning or reference to any law on which the decision was based. This kind of decision, as we shall see later, was not uncommon in the Baodi records. This is very different from what we expect of a judicial decision. And it was also different from some model decisions in collections such as Magistrate Shen's decisions and Huang Liuhong's discussion of civil decisions and his examples. I shall examine a couple of Magistrate Shen's decisions in subsequent chapters. Here I quote one decision given by Huang Liuhong to indicate the difference from the decision in the Tian case given above.

> The following statement of decision is issued with respect to the case of infringement of property right and arrears in tax payments. The licentiate Zhang Xingji's father, Zhang Chengzu, bought a piece of land comprising forty-two *mou* [*mu*]. The claim of ownership of this piece of land has changed several times since; once it belonged to the Zhang family and at another time it belonged to a certain Hou family. The fact is that after the death of Zhang Chengzu, Hou Yang usurped the land while Zhang Xingji was still in his infancy. When Zhang Xingji returned to his old home at Wen-yang [modern Ningyang district in Shandong province], Hou Yang filed a petition with the governor's *yamen* to validate his claim to the property.
>
> During the hearing of the case, Hou Yang's son, Hou Jiazhen, presented as evidence a certificate of transfer dated in the fourth year of Shunzhi (1647).

[24] Huang 1996: 120.

> However, the subsequent decision in Zhang's favour was made by the governor in the twelfth year of Shunzhi (1655), and was validated by former magistrate Zhang who affixed the seal on the contract. Therefore the certificate of transfer of the fourth year of Shunzhi had long been invalidated.
>
> Hou Yang's second son, Hou Jiazhao, testified that his deceased father had filed a complaint with former magistrate Jin in the third year of Kangxi (1664) requesting the return of the land to the Hou family. But the documents of this case could not be found in the file. Hou Jiazhao produced a certificate of transfer signed by a certain person named Zhang Xiaoba. Upon inquiry Xiaoba turned out to be a pet name of Zhang Xingji when he was a child. But he swore that he had never signed that paper. Whereas Zhang Xingji passed his first degree examination in the fourteenth year of Shunzhi (1657), no paper signed by him could have used the pet name. Moreover, Zhang was already an educated man by then; why did he need a scribe to draw up a simple certificate of transfer? Would an old hand like Hou Yang have accepted such a document as a bonafide record? The piece of paper, therefore, cannot be accepted as valid evidence.
>
> In conclusion, there has been a great deal of controversy in this case. I, the magistrate, have decided that the decision of the governor made in the twelfth year of Shunzhi (1655) should be considered final. The land should be returned to the Zhang family. The accumulated cash tax in arrears should be paid by the Chang family after consultation with the heads of the local tax units, and the tax in kind shall be remitted.[25]

This decision is 281 Chinese letters in total, written in easily understandable language. It 'describes the proceedings, explains the reasons for his judgment', 'on the basis of the facts, and expresses the right and wrong of the two litigants (*xunqi liangzao zhi shifei*)'.[26] The emphasis of this decision is on the fact that both the contracts on which the Hou family relied were not valid evidence and thus established the fact that the land indeed belonged to the Zhang family. So the key point is the logical link between identification of the facts and the decision. As Hang Liuhong remarked, the difficulty of decisions lies 'in the magistrate's ability to detect the facts hidden by the litigants and by the duplicity of the witnesses for both sides, and in his adroitness at refuting them in a convincing way, so that both the litigants and witnesses will acknowledge the fairness of the judgment and this final settlement will not be challenged by either side'.[27]

[25] Huang Liuhong 1984: 299–300.
[26] Ibid.: 139, 292.
[27] Ibid.: 292.

The reason the decision in the Tian Youlai case was so brief was perhaps that the case was not complicated. Besides, we can clearly trace the magistrate's reasoning from the statements. And, as I have pointed out, the whole statement of decision might not be reflected just in the written decision. The written decision represented a summary of the hearing, but did not necessarily comprise the whole of the magistrate's reasoning. However, the immediate reason for its brevity was the fact that it was written on the spot, so contained only the most important points made by the magistrate.

Magistrate Yuan warned other magistrates to write their decision in the hall right after the case was closed, so there would be no opportunity for anyone to change it. We also find other advice such as suggesting that the decision should be made and communicated to the parties at the time of the hearing. Afterwards a more complete version of the decision could be written and posted on the front wall of the court the following day.[28] This might explain why Magistrate Shen's decisions are all in a more complete form.[29] The whole decision should have the confirming bond, the statement, and even the magistrate's earlier comments for reference.

As a matter of fact, Baodi records also contain decisions similar to the example given by Huang Liulong. In a case in which redemption of a piece of land was claimed, the magistrate ruled in favour of the defendant. He wrote a decision of about 250 words on the statement. It began with 'I have investigated and heard the case' (*chaxun*), and went on to summarize the cause of the case, the evidence (contract), and the facts, then mentioned the relevant law, and finally gave the decision in the case. It ended with the words 'the decision thus recorded' (*ciji*), one of the typical formulas used to end a decision.[30]

Whether expressed briefly or not, the decisions have two characteristics. One is that 'right and wrong' (*shifei* or *quzhi*) are always made clear. The other is that more weight is put on the facts than on the law.[31] Decisions were put in writing after the magistrate had actually given his verdict to the parties. Although the structure of the decision might not be regarded as exhibiting the best of reasoning, one thing is certain — it is not 'didactic conciliation',[32] but, rather, an adjudication.

[28] *Mulingshu, juan* 18: *Dangtang dingyan* [Making the decision right after the court session].
[29] There is another form of decision written in a special, literary style (*pianti*). This form of decision was rare in the Qing, so I shall not discuss it here.
[30] Baodi, 95: 105. The other typical ending is 'this is so decided' (*cipan*).
[31] For the reasons why the decision often did not quote the law, see Chapter 5.
[32] Shiga Shūzō 1992a: 419.

As we have seen, from the start of litigation to its close, both the magistrate and his assistants followed a highly systematic procedure. This procedure had a regular pattern, made use of regular forms and formulas in official documents, and had a regular practical style. Such a system could not have been achieved or changed without applicable provisions. I have cited a number of those regulations in this chapter. The civil trial procedure was followed in its general outline by all magistrates, although details might be varied by different magistrates in practice.

5
Law and Legislation on Land, Debt, and Marriage

Having discussed the framework of procedural rules concerning civil disputes and the magistrate's practice within these rules, we now need to look at the other main part of the picture of Qing civil justice. There is controversy about the sources on which magistrates relied to resolve disputes, with scholars suggesting custom, heaven's principle (*li*), human feelings (*qing*), and the law. This chapter, as the title suggests, will focus on the details of the relevant law. I shall demonstrate that the substantive provisions relating to land, debt, and marriage not only supplied applicable rules, but also were constantly and consistently revised to meet changing conditions. Other elements, such as custom, heaven's principle, and human feelings played different, though also important, roles in magistrates' decisions. These will be particularly discussed in Chapter 9.

5.1 Legislation concerning people's land

As an agrarian country, China depended for its prosperity to a great extent on the administration and usage of the land. Like preceding dynasties, the Qing took the matter of land very seriously. Consequently, the system of land administration was complex and burdensome. The extent of the system's complexity can perhaps be vividly demonstrated in the diversity of descriptions of land in the regulations of the Board of Household: government land (*guantian*), people's land (*mintian*), mature land, desert land, land of high quality, land of middle quality, land of lower quality, land burdened with two *dou* tax (*erdoutian*), etc. Out of over twenty names, the most important one in terms of our focus is *mintian or mindi*, land owned by the people.

Huang is right to argue that the principle of the protection of property rights was made clear in the Code.[1] Zelin also makes the point clearly that

[1] Huang 1996: 79–80.
2 *Qingdai liubu chengyu cidian*, 161–70.

property rights were well defined and enforced by the state.[3] Legal protection of private land was undoubtedly an effective final step in the administration and protection of private land. Before we turn to the law on land itself, it is crucial to know about the relevant measures and regulations concerning land.

5.1.1 People's land

Land (*tian* or *di*) was basically divided into people's land (*mintian*) and government land (*guantian*). Privately owned land was an essential part of the system and *mintian* was an official or legal phrase of the Qing governmental administration. Its scope was clearly defined as land owned by an individual, a private family, or a clan, and with the character of being freely tradable. The other main category was government land, which referred to land owned by the royal house, cultivated by troops, or distributed to a named official for a particular purpose, for example, *xuetian* (land given to schools at prefect and county level) and *jitian* (land under the control of the local government for religious worship). One may argue, as in the old proverb, that 'Everywhere under Heaven there is no land that is not the Emperor's' (*putian zhixia mofei wangtu*).[4] In theory, since the emperor had ultimate power, there would be no 'absolute freehold tenure exempt from taxes and services to the Crown'.[5] In practice, however, the emperors largely respected the established legal order. As MacCormack has noticed, emperors such as Kangxi (1662–1722) 'exercised a fine discrimination, acting in conjunction with his Grand Secretaries'.[6] In other words, the emperor had rules to follow. It was not easy for him to do whatever he wanted, especially if this conflicted with the established system.[7]

Land distributed by the government to *manzu* people — that is, *qi* people's land (*qidi*) — is difficult to fit into either of the main categories of land, because free trade in *qi* people's land was prohibited. For example, even the conditional sale of *qi* people's land to civilians was illegal, not to mention outright sale.[8] However, the point here is that there is a category of people's land. This not only indicates that the government admitted the existence of private land, but also implies that there were steps to follow for establishing, confirming, and protecting private land ownership.

[3] Zelin 2004: passim.
[4] Cited in Palmer 1987: 4.
[5] Jamieson 1921/1970: 90.
[6] MacCormack 1996b: 162.
[7] Zheng Qin noted that emperors of the Qing carefully followed the legal procedures in handling some of the most serious cases (*qinan*). See Zheng Qin 1988: 14.
[8] *Qi* people's land became freely tradable from the Xianfeng reign (1851–61).

Private land ownership in the Qing was established and supported through a variety of complex and detailed regulations. For instance, the registration book and the fish-scale books recorded both the owner's general and detailed economic status, including how much land was owned, and a full description of the land (its location, size, boundaries, and so on). The Qing Code clearly accepted these books as decisive evidence when there was difficulty in locating the owner of the land in question (Sub-statute 93-6). In the case of newly cultivated land, the magistrate was authorized to give the owner of the land an Owner's Certificate (*zhiye qingdan*). In the absence of this certificate, according to the regulations, the transfer of tax liability from the old owner to the new could not be accomplished.[9] When government land was changed to the status of private land, a certificate of land ownership was given to the owner as well. For example, with regard to the great quantity of land belonging to the Ming royal family and high officials, the Qing changed ownership by giving tenants the land they were actually cultivating as their private property forever. This land was known as *gengming tian* ('changing name' land). It formed a significant proportion of the land in China. Much military land of the Ming also had its ownership changed. Moreover, in the second year of Yongzheng (1724), the government gave an order to 'remove the name of *biandi* (military official land) from the book in which it was registered as government land and permit the individual tenant to sell and buy as he wished'.[10]

More private land was created by calling upon people to cultivate unoccupied land with no original owner and certifying the cultivator as the owner. Having encountered financial difficulties at first, the Qing instituted an important policy in Shunzhi 6 (1649). The government ordered that, 'for those lands without owners in the locality, the magistrates of the county and department shall issue official stamped certificates to people who then can farm and own them forever'.[11] These officials could be rewarded for having unoccupied land brought under cultivation. For such unoccupied land the government set up private ownership by issuing official certificates. Where an owner had abandoned his land, for example in the event of war or some natural catastrophe, the government set a time limit for his return. Should the owner not return within that time, other people were to be allowed to cultivate the land.[12]

[9] Yang Guozhen 1988: 80–1.

[10] Zhang Yan 1998: 53, 156.

[11] *Qingshizushilu*, *juan* 43, cited in Dai Yi 1991: 195.

[12] Zhang Yan 1998: 152. The Qing Code prohibition on the abandonment of land (Art. 97) could be seen as a restriction on the right of private ownership: where land had been abandoned for several years, the owner lost legal ownership. However, the reason for this rule was not to restrict the right of ownership but to make maximum use of a scarce resource in

As purchasing was the basic and the most common way to acquire ownership of a piece of land, perhaps the most important document recording the title of ownership of *mintian* (people's land) was the land contract or, more precisely, the land sale contract or hongqi. Although the land sale contract was not the only document that could demonstrate ownership of land, it was the first piece of evidence that had to be checked in resolving land disputes. This was because, at least partially, the land contract clearly revealed how the owner had obtained the land (by purchase) and indicated that the land had been obtained lawfully. The privately made contract was stamped by the magistrate's *yamen* (literally, official building) and had attached a 'tail' that officially endorsed the transaction. This official 'tail' was very important to the new owner, because it constituted an official record and official evidence in his favour as well as 'stopping the practice of making false contracts' (*yidu jianie zhibi*) (*Jizhu*: 237).

The purchase and sale of land are the hallmarks of land ownership. It is only if one admits that people's land was privately owned land, in other words, that private land ownership existed in the Qing, that events such as the change of name of Ming royal and official land and of military official land to private land make sense. In fact, about 70–80 per cent of land was people's land.[13] Once people's land is admitted to be privately owned land, the law is needed to protect the owners' rights. I shall discuss these legal provisions next.

5.1.2 The provisions concerning people's land

The people's land (*mintian*) is logically incorporated in the Qing Code. We shall see that the Code contains a substantial body of statutes and sub-statutes concerning private ownership of land (and houses). In the section on Land and Houses (*tianzhai*), which forms part of the Statutes regarding the Household (*Hulü*), eight statutes and twenty-five sub-statutes are directly relevant. Several provisions in other sections such as Articles 271 (Stealing Rice and Wheat from Fields), 276 (Uncovering Graves), 299 (Putting Pressure on Another so as to Cause Him to Die), and the sections on General

the context of an increasing population (on the tensions created by rising population density, see Buoye 2000). As a result of this policy, the amount of cultivated land increased very rapidly: from about 520 million *mu* in 1661, to 600 million *mu* by 1708, and 800 million *mu* by 1722 (although the figures given by the *Huidian*, *Hubu zeli* and other official sources vary, the general picture is the same – Dai Yi 1991: 195, 196, 325).

[13] Yang Guozhen 1988: 18. Also see Palmer's study (1987: 4) on Hong Kong, in which he observed that '[t]he dominant form of tenure in *Xin'an* (part of the New Territories of Hong Kong), as it had been in China since the southern Song Dynasty (A.D. 1127–1279), was private ownership in land'.

Public Disorder and Theft (*zeidao*) and Homicide (*renming*) are also directly relevant. Further relevant regulations can be found in other sources. For example, the Regulations of the Board of Revenue contained provisions on sharing public water and on tenants' rights, such as the right to remission of rent in years of bad harvests (see *Hubu zeli*: 161, 145, 667). The above provisions covered people of different nationalities (*han*, *man*, *miao*, etc.) as well as special groups such as civil officials and military officials. They also touched on different aspects of the ownership of land, such as using or drawing benefit from it, selling or conditionally selling it.

I shall first quote from Article 93 *Daomai tianzhai* (The Theft and Sale of Fields and Houses):

> Whoever illegally sells (*daomai*) fields or buildings belonging to another; or disposes (*huanyi*) of fields or buildings not belonging to him; or falsely claims (*maoren*) the real estate of another as his own; or makes out a contract of mortgage or sale with a false price (*xuqian shiqi*); or occupies (*qinzhan*) the fields or building of another — in each case, the offender shall receive 50 blows of the light bamboo if the amount of land in question does not exceed one *mu* [approx. 1/6 of an acre] and the house does not exceed one room. For each additional five *mu* or three rooms, the penalty shall be increased one degree, the maximum penalty not to exceed 80 blows of the heavy bamboo and two years of penal servitude. . . .
>
> The forcible seizure (*qiangzhan*) of government or privately owned mountainous wasteland, lakes, tea groves, reed marshes, or smelting works for gold, silver, copper, tin, or iron, shall be punished by 100 blows of the heavy bamboo and life exile at a distance of 3,000 *li* [900 miles], regardless of the amount of property involved.
>
> . . . .
>
> In each case of illegal sale or presentation, the property and the money paid for it, as well as all produce and profit derived from the land, shall be returned to the state or to its owner as appropriate.[14]

The test of ownership was whether the property was allowed to be sold by the owner and whether the law protected such a transaction. There is no doubt that the essential point in protecting the private ownership of land was to prohibit any violation of another's right to his land. The Code listed a variety of violations, including *daomai tianzhai* (illegally sell fields and houses), *huanyi* (dispose of fields), *maoren* (falsely claim fields), *xuqian shiqi* (make out a contract of sale with a false price), *qinzhan* (occupy the fields of

[14] Jing 1994: 43.

another), *qiangzhan* (forcible seizure of fields) (Article 93). The offences involved certain consequences depending on the type and amount of land in question and the seriousness of the offence itself. For a serious offence, punishment as severe as life exile at a distance of 3,000 *li* (900 miles) could be imposed.

Article 93 mainly concerned the aspect of the right to deal in land. Other aspects of property rights, such as the right to use and benefit, were stipulated in the following Articles:

> **Article 96**: *Dao gengzhong guanmintian* (Wrongfully Cultivating and Sowing Public or Private Land)
>
> Everyone who wrongfully cultivates and sows the fields (*orchards or other types of land*) of another (*not notifying the owner*), will, for 1 *mu* or below, be punished with 30 strokes of the light bamboo. For each [additional] 5 *mu*, add one degree. The punishment is limited to 80 strokes of the heavy bamboo. If the land was uncultivated, reduce the punishment by one degree. If there was force ([the act was] *against the will of the owner*), in each case (*whether the land is cultivated or uncultivated*), add one degree. . . . (*Moreover, levy on*) any profits that have been [received], (*and if it is government land*), they will be returned to the government, (*if it is private land*) they will be given to the owner.[15]
>
> **Article 98**: *Qihui qiwu jiaqiang deng* (Discarding and Destroying Tangible Personal Property, Growing Crops, Harvested Produce, etc.)
>
> Whoever purposefully discards or destroys another person's tools, or destroys or cuts down his trees or crops, shall be punished in proportion to the value of the property damaged, according to the scale of penalties in the statute on 'Theft' with the exception that he shall not be tattooed, and that the maximum penalty shall not exceed 100 blows of the heavy bamboo and life exile at a distance of 3,000 *li*. . . . If any private property is [accidentally] lost or destroyed by another, then the owner shall be compensated for its value, but no punishment inflicted.
>
> Whoever wilfully destroys the steles, monuments, or protective animal figures of graves not belonging to him shall receive 80 blows of the heavy bamboo. Whoever destroys the ancestral altar of another shall receive 90 blows of the heavy bamboo. Whoever destroys or damages walls, houses, or buildings of any kind belonging to others shall be punished in proportion to the cost of the materials and labour required for repair; if the damage is valued at one *liang* (tael) or less, the offender shall receive 20 blows of the light bamboo, and three years of penal servitude. In every case, the damaged property

[15] Jones 1994: 119.

shall be fully repaired at the expense of the offender. . . . If the damage is accidental, the party responsible shall make good its repair, but shall not be punished.[16]

Article 99: *Shanshi tianyuan guaguo* (Unauthorizedly Eating the Melons, Fruit, etc. of a Field or Garden)

Whoever, without permission, eats vegetables or fruits growing in the field or garden of another, shall be punished in proportion to the value of what has been consumed, according to the scale of penalties in the statutes on 'bribery' (as follows: if the value is one *liang* or greater, the offender shall receive 10 blows of the light bamboo; if two *liang*, 20 blows; and so on, the penalty increasing one degree for each *liang*, the maximum penalty not to exceed 60 blows of the heavy bamboo and one year of penal servitude). Whoever destroys such produce shall be punished in the same way.[17]

Violations of the right to use and benefit from the land were labelled *daogeng* (secretly cultivate another's land), *qianggeng* (forcibly cultivate another's land) (Article 96); *qihui* or *wuhui shumu jiaqiang* (discarding and destroying growing crops, harvested produce) (Article 98); *shanshi guaguo* (unauthorized eating of melons, fruit, from a field or garden) (Article 99). These Articles were designed to cover, in as much detail as possible, predicted violations of this aspect of the right of ownership by specifying both serious and minor offences. In Article 99, the punishment for an offender who ate fruit or vegetables started at ten blows with the light stick, if the value of the product so consumed was more than 1 *liang*. According to Shen Zhiqi, this punishment, even though physical, was rather light. This was because the starting penalty was the lowest in the Code and, further, it was almost impossible to reach the level of 1 *liang* worth of damage. For other minor wrongdoing (for instance, destroying grain unintentionally) no punishment at all might be imposed, only liability for compensation. However, most importantly, all these stipulations supplied civil remedies — the return of the land, the price, or the profits produced by land, if any, to the owner (*yezhu*).

Given that people were prohibited by law from stealing the harvest, from eating fruit, from cultivating or destroying the harvest, and from selling land to another, Huang is certainly not wrong to conclude that the Code has a 'principle: to sustain and protect the legitimate ownership of land or houses'.[18]

[16] Jing 1994: 46, 47 (1 *liang* = 1 oz of silver).
[17] Ibid.
[18] Huang 1996: 80.

The Articles cited above were not changed on being inherited from the Ming. To meet changing circumstances, sub-statutes were constantly added to the Code. The introduction of new sub-statutes and the emendation of existing sub-statutes enable us better to observe the attitude of the Qing in relevant legislation, by tracing the motives and purpose of changes. The biggest change or, rather, the biggest contribution of the Qing law was to distinguish between the sale (*mai*) and conditional sale (*dian*) of the land. To demonstrate this, we need first to quote from Article 95: Purchase of Fields and Houses by *Dian* (*Dianmai tianzhai*), which was originally copied from the Ming:

> Whoever conceals the fact that a piece of real estate has already been sold by mortgage, and sells it by mortgage to a second party (*chongfu dianmai*), shall be punished in proportion to the price of the second transaction according to the scale of penalties in the statute on 'Theft,' with the exception that he shall not be tattooed; the money from the second transaction shall be returned to its owner, and the real estate shall be returned to the first mortgagee-buyer. If the mortgagee-buyer, broker, or guarantor of the second transaction was cognizant of the situation, then he shall receive the same punishment as the offender himself, and the sum involved shall be confiscated; if they were not cognizant, then they shall not be punished.[19]

Article 95 established three rules: (1) tax should be paid on sales and conditional sales; (2) the owner who sold or conditionally sold the property to a second buyer, or the guarantor and buyer engaged in such a transaction who knew the circumstances, should receive punishment; (3) when the term of a *dian* contract expired, the owner might redeem the property with ready money and the *dian* holder should return the land — if the owner had no money to redeem the property, then the *dian* holder was allowed to redeem it. The three rules were all amended later. To facilitate comparison of the differences, here I summarize the final version of the sub-statutes (as presented by Xue Yunsheng in his commentary on the Code, *Cunyi*).

First, the tax applied only to the sale contract, not the conditional sale contract any more (Sub-statute 95-9). This sub-statute was added in Qianlong 24 (1759) and completely removed the possibility of confusing the sale and conditional sale contracts that arose from the ambiguous formulation of Article 95.[20] Second, Sub-statute 95-7 (which was added in 1753

[19] Jing 1994: 66.
[20] Philip Huang's study on '*dian*' misunderstands the Qing Code on one point: he says that the Qing taxed *dian* transactions (Huang 2001: 72) without commenting on the change in this policy.

according to Xue Yunsheng) required that, on the occasion of the sale of the land, the contract should specify 'redeem' or 'never redeem'. If the contract did not contain 'never redeem', and was less than thirty years old, redemption of the land was allowed. If it was thirty or more years old, and did not contain the phrase 'redeem', redemption was not allowed. Third, Sub-statute 95-3 dealt with the *dian* maker who asked for redemption before the term expired. He was to be liable to eighty blows with the heavy stick under Article 386 on 'Doing What Ought Not to Be Done'. Should the *dian* maker have no money to redeem his property, it was not just left to the *dian* holder as permitted by the Article. He could either ask the *dian* holder for extra money and then sell the land to him outright, or he could sell to a third person and return to the *dian* holder the price he had originally paid.

Clearly, the final provisions made a formal distinction between sale and conditional sale. The previous ambiguity had caused many disputes in practice.[21] This is perhaps why there was no change to the law on resale or conditional resale. These revisions would certainly have better equipped both officials and magistrates with clear and easy guidelines. However, this achievement was not just the result of a sudden whim on the part of the government. To achieve the changes, the Qing took a great deal of trouble adjusting the sub-statutes step by step. The following *li* reveal this feature.[22]

> **Qianlong 9th year (1744)**
> If a contract for the sale of land has been made many years ago and does not contain a clear phrase such as 'irrevocable sale' (*dujue*), the land is not subject to redemption. The children of the original owner must not request a further payment or seek redemption of the land. It is not necessary to mention persons other than the children or grandchildren. If a person sold the land many years ago and asks for a further payment or redemption, he commits the offence of 'deceit and cheating' (*ezha* defined in Article 274) and he should be sentenced according to the provisions of this Article. As for those contracts which permit a request for a further payment or redemption, should the later owner (the *dian* holder) require money for an emergency but the original owner (*dian* maker) is unable to redeem, then the former may transfer the property under a contract of *dian* to a third person. Should the original owner bypass the second owner and request from the third party a further payment or redemption after the second sale or conditional sale, he should also be

[21] According to two studies, such cases were common in the Ming (Tong Guangzheng 1998; Bian Li 2000).

[22] The quoted regulations are all from a book entitled *Qiangu zhinan*, a collection of sub-statutes on financial matters in the Qianlong reign (1736–95) from which I have extracted several provisions on *dian* (conditional sale).

> punished according to the provisions of Article 274. If the contract is one of *dian* (conditional sale) or even if it is one of *mai* (sale) but establishes a time for redemption using the term 'redeem', if many years have not passed and the 'purchaser' (second owner) has not already sold the land, the original owner should be allowed to redeem with ready money at the end of the period provided in the contract. The original owner should not forcibly redeem the land before the period covered by the contract, and the 'purchaser' (second owner) should not under any excuse refuse to surrender the land at the end of that period. Should either disobey, punishment is to be imposed in accordance with Article 274 on 'deceit and cheating'.[23]

This regulation marks an early stage in the attempt to distinguish between sale and conditional sale. It established the conditions under which the land could be redeemed or an extra price asked. It also established that the *dian* holder might become a *dian* maker himself.

> **Qianlong 18th year (1753)**
> When people sell land and houses (*chanye*), if they wish to redeem the property, they shall explicitly include the term 'will redeem' in the contract. This will be treated as a *dian* contract. If it is sold by a sale contract without such a term as 'will redeem', this will be treated as outright sale and the seller should not ask to redeem the land and houses. Anyone who stirs up confusion and asks for an extra price or redemption of the land under such a contract shall receive the punishment for 'deceit and cheating' (*ezha*) provided by Article 274.

This regulation clearly distinguishes between sale and conditional sale contracts according to whether the phrase 'will redeem' is included or not. However, if we compare it with the Code version of Sub-statute 95-7, which required the insertion of the words 'never redeem' in the contract, it is still not clearly required to do so. In the sub-statute, the punishment was eighty blows with the heavy stick under Article 386 on 'Doing What Ought Not to Be Done', which was different from the two regulations of 1744 and 1753.

> **Qianlong 18th year (1753)**
> If land has been bought within the last thirty years, the owner is allowed to redeem it. If thirty years have passed and the term 'outright' is not recorded in the contract, the original owner is not allowed to redeem the land.

[23] The text has '*ezha li*', where '*li*' is actually referring to Article 274: Obtaining Property from the Government or an Individual by Deceit and Cheating. Shen Zhiqi made the point that '*li*' could also refer to '*lü*' (see *Jizhu*: 18).

Qianlong 19th year (1754)
Even if land has been bought within the last thirty years, if the term 'to be redeemed' is not recorded in the contract, the original owner should not redeem the land. Punishment shall be imposed on people who violate this regulation.

We can see, especially from the two regulations of 1753 and 1754 dealing with the sale of land within thirty years or more than thirty years ago, that the Qing government was active in making new laws, including rules that guided civil matters.

The hallmark of private land ownership was the legal power on the part of the owner to sell his land. The action taken by the Qing government to regulate the details of sale and conditional sale reflected its wish to protect the individual's ownership of his land. For the better protection of land ownership, the Qing kept control of essential matters, including, as we have seen from Chapter 2, what should count as evidence of ownership and what should be taken into account by officials deciding land cases. The protection was thus consistent and wide.

5.2 The law concerning debt matters

The concept of debt (*zhai* or *sizhai*), as the Qing defined it in its early years, was 'the money that one person lends to another' (*Tongkao*: 522). Thus the core meaning of a debt resulted from the obligation of what one person owed to another because he had borrowed either money or goods. This definition still contained some of the original meaning of debt in Tang law, that is, the specific debt resulting from borrowing non-consumables without charging interest. *Zhai* as an abstract term for general debt can be traced back to the Song dynasty (960–1279).[24] The arrangement of the provisions on debt of the Qing Code also shows that the Qing later took *zhai* as an abstract term for general debt.

There were three Articles in the subdivision 'Money and Debt' (*Qianzhai*) under the head of Statutes Regarding the Household (*Hulü*): Taking Interest in Violation of the Prohibitions (Article 149); The Consumption of Property Received in Deposit (Article 150); and Finding Lost Objects (Article 151). Just from the titles of these provisions, one can see that the notion of debt covered more than just borrowing, for example, the debt resulting from a trust or from a benefit to which one was not

[24] Ye Xiaoxin 1993: 268, 355.

entitled. Another subdivision 'Markets' (*Shichan*), which is also included in the section on Statutes Regarding the Household (*Hulü*), has five statutes: License of Commercial Agents (Article 152); Valuation of Merchandise (Article 153); Monopolisers and Unfair Traders (Article 154); False Weights, Measures and Scales (Article 155); and Substandard Manufacture (Article 156). These Articles and their sub-statutes provided for commercial activities. Since the Qing organized its commercial transactions among business people through certificated agents called *yahang*, the laws governing business transactions were incorporated into those governing the *yahang*. If there was a debt among merchants, the principle of paying back the debt equally applied.[25] Although there were only a small number of Articles, they cannot be regarded as being too limited in scope in terms of Qing business affairs. More importantly, the basic rule for a debt was, as we shall see, to return the debt, which was not a criminal sanction from any point of view.[26]

Even though the concept of debt in Qing law encompassed more kinds of debt than just borrowing money or goods, the Articles on debt I am going to discuss focused mainly on the debt resulting from private loans. However, that does not limit the significance of the principle the law established. Here is the first section of this law:

> **Article 149**: *Weijin quli* (Taking Interest in Violation of the Prohibitions)
>
> Whoever privately lends money or accepts property in pawn shall receive no more than 3 per cent interest per month. No matter how much time passes, the total interest which accumulates shall not exceed the total amount of principal. Whoever violates this law shall receive 40 blows of the light bamboo. If the punishment calculated in proportion to the amount of excess interest, according to the scale of penalties in the statute on 'Bribery' (Article 345), is more severe than 40 blows then the offender shall receive the harsher punishment, the maximum penalty not to exceed 100 blows of the heavy bamboo.[27]

This section sets out the principles governing private loans. In the main, there were two kinds of private loan in the Qing, the ordinary loan (*fang*

[25] This general principle on debt is enshrined in the phrase 'law concerning being owed a private debt' (*fuqian sizhai lü*), which is employed in a sub-statute of Article 154. This sub-statute dealt with cases brought by businessmen who accused the certificated agent (*yahang*) of cheating and/or owing them money.

[26] In contrast, Brockman has stated, after giving a brief summary of the relevant statutes, that 'it is evident that the Code regulation of commercial activities was very limited in scope. Little of what is ordinarily considered commercial law today is mentioned at all. And what is mentioned is dealt with almost entirely in penal terms. There are no nonpenal remedies available. The only action that can be taken against a defaulting debtor is to apply a criminal punishment, flogging' (1980: 87).

[27] Jing 1994: 72.

qianzhai) and the loan secured through the deposit of certain goods with a pawnbroker (*diandang*). Goods were pledged with a pawnbroker in return for a sum of money as a loan at a certain rate of interest. The owner redeemed the pledged goods when he repaid the loan and the interest. The interest levied on these two kinds of loan might not exceed 3 per cent per month (36 per cent per year). No matter how many years had passed, the interest on the loan could not exceed the amount of the principal. Otherwise penalties up to a maximum of one hundred blows of the heavy stick were to be imposed. This principle was reconfirmed in the early years of the Qing by a special decree of emperor Shunzhi (1644–52). It emphasized that the total interest could not exceed the sum of the capital and no part of the interest could be added to the capital itself (*Huidian shili*, vol. 9: 419).

According to Jing's study, the monthly interest rate for private loans of money or goods was progressively reduced from the Tang dynasty's 5–6 per cent per month, to the Song's 4 per cent, then to the Yuan's 3 per cent.[28] Both the Ming and the Qing laws adopted the Yuan rule. As a matter of fact, we shall see later that some materials show that Qing officials reduced interest rates still further.

The Article continues:

> Any presiding official or clerk who lends money or accepts property in pawn within the area of his jurisdiction shall receive 80 blows of the heavy bamboo, even if he has not taken excess interest. If he has taken excess interest, then if the punishment calculated in proportion to that excess amount, according to the scale of penalties in the statute on 'Accepting a bribe for a purpose which is not itself illegal' (*buwangfa*) is more severe than 80 blows of the heavy bamboo, he shall receive the harsher punishment. In each case, the penalty shall be calculated based on one-half the total amount of excess interest; the offender shall receive 90 blows of the heavy bamboo if, in the case of a salaried official, the amount is 30 *liang* or more, or if he is an unsalaried subordinate, 40 *liang* or more; for each additional 10 *liang*, the penalty shall be increased one degree, the maximum not to exceed 100 blows of the heavy bamboo and life exile at a distance of 3,000 *li*. Moreover, the excess interest shall be recovered and restored to its proper owner, regardless of whether the offender is a commoner or an official.[29]

This section applied particularly to officials and clerks. They were prohibited from lending money within their jurisdiction, whether or not they charged illegal interest. The punishment for breach started at eighty blows with the heavy stick, with a maximum penalty of one hundred blows with

[28] Ibid.: 77.
[29] Ibid.: 72.

the heavy stick and life exile to a distance of 3,000 *li*. Here, the nature of the offence by officials and clerks lay in the abuse of power. The punishment was severe because the offence had crossed the boundary demarcating private and public matters. This section can be regarded as supplementing the general rules on private loans established in the previous section.

> Whoever owes a private debt and fails to fulfil his agreement with his creditor shall be liable for the following penalties, depending on how much he owes and how long the debt is overdue: Five or more *liang* three months overdue, 10 blows of the light bamboo; for each extra month, the penalty shall be increased one degree, the maximum not to exceed 40 blows of the light bamboo; fifty or more *liang* three months overdue, 20 blows of the light bamboo; for each extra month, the penalty shall be increased one degree, the maximum not to exceed 50 blows of the light bamboo. One hundred or more *liang* three months overdue, 30 blows of the light bamboo; for each additional month, the penalty shall be increased one degree, the maximum not to exceed 60 blows of the heavy bamboo. Moreover, both principal and interest shall be recovered and returned to their owner. (Jing 1994: 72–3)

This section was officially called in brief the 'law concerning being owed a private debt' (*fuqian sizhai lü*) and dealt with the matter of paying a debt. Should a debtor fail to repay on time, the penalty was ten blows of the light stick where the amount due to be returned was 5 *liang* or more and the delay was three months. The maximum penalty was not to exceed sixty blows of the heavy stick. Both principal and interest had to be returned to the owner. The loan usually was made by a contract (*yue*), the key evidence of a debt being such a contract. Scholars who have examined the format and the content of the loan contract point out that it usually contained the names of the two parties, with some other personal data, the sum of money loaned, the rate of interest, and the conditions for repayment. The debtor and the middleman usually gave their personal signs at the end of the contract.[30] The surviving examples of Baodi county records reveal several loan contracts entered into by store owners. They attract instant attention because of the following features: first, the document is endorsed with a large official logo of the store at the beginning of the contract; secondly, the content is short and simple. To give an example:

> [The store's official logo]
> Qingyun Tobacco Store to the South of Dongsi pailou (archway): The borrower Wei Jiuhao now has received from the Sun family 2,000 *liang* of

[30] See Tong Guangzheng 1998: 59.

> silver. We have agreed that the loan is to be repaid in ten annual instalments of 200 *liang* without interest.
> The premises of the shop are pledged as security for the loan.
> Borrower: Wei Jiuhao [sign]
> Middlemen: Wang Kui [sign]
> Lin Zifeng [sign]
> Liang Weiquan [sign]
> Guangxue 16th year (1890), 8th month, 15th day by Qingyun Tobacco Store to the South of Dongsi pailou. (Baodi, 193: 85)

Another contract is even simpler. Apart from taking the same format as the above, the content comprises only one sentence: 'x, through the contract, has received from y 50 *liang*, interest being agreed at 1.2 per cent per month'. (Baodi, 191: 185)

It was not only the original loan that was carried out through the contract. Usually both debtor and creditor would actively seek a way to confirm the debt by making another contract (for small loans or credit buying they might make only an oral agreement). Baodi also contains an example:

> Debt contract: Since —— [document not clear] owes Er Depeng capital of 1,400 *diao* exactly, we agree through the mediation of close friends and relatives that the debt will be repaid as following in —— [not clear] season 600 *diao*, in Daoguang 20th year [1840] 600 *diao*, and in the 21st year [1841] 200 *diao*. . . . This is agreed in front of each other. . . . Each is without regrets. . . . Now we wish there to be proof of our agreement, so we have created this written document.
> The witnesses: Cheng Xiaorui [sign]
> Kang Xurui [sign]
> Liu Xiangyuan [sign]
> [x year x month] the third day made by Li Hongsheng who takes the place of the debtor in repaying the debt [sign]. (Baodi, 186: 90)

If a new contract was drawn up, it seems logical to regard it as replacing the original one. Because the debtor and the creditor would usually take alternative measures such as the above contract or an oral agreement for the repayment of the debt, the debtor's fault in failing to pay the debt was mitigated. This perhaps largely explains why the application of punishment in debt cases was rare (see Chapter 7). Shen Zhiqi, in his commentary on Article 149, made clear that the level of fault of the debtor was the important factor to be considered when applying the law on punishment. He commented: where 'the offender had the intention of not returning the debt within the time limit of the contract to the creditor' and failed to repay for more than three months, the punishment should be imposed (*Jizhu*: 366). In other words, if the debtor had a good reason for failing to repay the debt, he should not suffer any punishment. For instance, if the reason for the delay was because of the debtor's insolvency or some other difficulty, it would be wrong to impose punishment in such circumstances. Many cases arising from delay in repayment resulted from such reasons (see Chapter 6).

Article 149 continues:

> If a powerful creditor whose loan is overdue does not report the default to the authorities, but instead takes matters into his own hands, seizing the debtor's crops, livestock, or other property, then he shall receive 80 blows of the heavy bamboo. If, however, the creditor has not seized property in excess of the amount he is owed, then the debtor is to be allowed to redeem the property taken, but the government will not force the creditor to return the items [this corrects an error in Jing's translation — see further below]. If he has seized an excess amount of property, and if the punishment calculated in proportion to the excess, according to the scale of penalties in the statute on 'Bribery,' is greater than 80 blows of the heavy bamboo, then he shall receive the harsher punishment, the maximum penalty not to exceed 100 blows of the heavy bamboo and three years of penal servitude. The excess property which he seized shall be returned to its owner.
>
> If a creditor accepts the wife, concubine, son, or daughter of a debtor in pledge for his debt, then he shall receive 100 blows of the heavy bamboo. If he uses that person sexually (*jianzhan*), then the penalty shall be increased one degree. If a creditor seizes such a person against the debtor's wishes, the penalty shall be increased two degrees to 70 blows of the heavy bamboo and one and a half years of penal servitude. If the creditor seizes such a person against the debtor's wishes and uses that person sexually, then he shall be strangled after the assizes. The person used in pledge for the debt or seized by force shall be returned to his or her family, and the debt shall be cancelled.[31]

The above paragraphs concern self-help by the creditor. Should the creditor take action on his own and seize the debtor's crops, livestock, and so on to satisfy the debt, without reporting to the authorities, he was to receive eighty blows of the heavy stick. But he might keep the property if the amount seized did not exceed the amount of his loan, unless the debtor was prepared to redeem it. If what the creditor had taken was the wife, concubine, son, or daughter of a debtor, he was to be punished with one hundred blows with the heavy bamboo. The wife, son, etc. should be returned to his/her family, and the debt should be cancelled. The Code imposed a severe

[31] Jing 1994: 72–3.

punishment upon a person who took a debtor's wife, concubine, or child to satisfy the debt.

Some aspects of the creditor's self-help need to be clarified. First, self-help was supported only to a limited extent by the law, for the property taken by the creditor was not to exceed the amount the debtor owed. Further, the creditor was liable to eighty blows with the heavy stick according to the Code. Then he might keep the property unless the debtor wanted to redeem it. The word 'redeem' here in the Code referred to the property the creditor had seized, rather than the punishment imposed on the creditor by the Code (Jing erred in this context). So, as MacCormack has observed, 'should the debtor refuse to repay, the creditor, if careful not to take too much, may resort to self-help'.[32]

The concern of Article 149 is clear. On the one hand, the creditor must not take advantage of the debtor by charging more interest than a certain rate, and he might be subjected to punishment by beating if he used self-help to recover the debt; on the other hand, the debtor must not break the agreement (*yue*) to repay the debt. The Code intended to balance the two sides, the creditor and the debtor. A comparison of the punishment of debtor and creditor shows that the Code in fact favoured the debtor because the maximum penalty for the debtor if he failed to repay the debt was sixty blows with the heavy stick, whereas the maximum penalty for illegally taking interest was one hundred blows with the heavy stick, and the starting penalty for a creditor who seized the debtor's property was eighty blows with the heavy stick. Nevertheless, the balance was still maintained in a broad way by the principle that the debt had to be returned to the creditor. It would not be cancelled unless the creditor took the extreme step, i.e. he took the debtor's wife, daughter, or son to satisfy what was owed.

In section 5.1 on the provisions relating to land ownership, I cited several regulations to demonstrate that Qing law was active both in amending itself to meet changing situations and in shaping the practice of people to bring about a more reasonable state of affairs. The provisions on debt may add further evidence on this point. Not only did amendment occur in the form of sub-statutes, it was also an important part of provincial regulations. Sometimes these changes may be uncovered from other sources. Here I first compare the Code of different periods as seen from three prestigious commentaries — namely, *Jizhu*, *Tongkao*, and *Cunyi* (see Chapter 1 for the three books) — then I look at other evidence of active adjustment as seen in the change in interest rates and provincial regulations on the pawnbroker.

[32] MacCormack 1990: 247.

In *Jizhu* (ca. 1715), the Code contained all six original Ming sub-statutes appended to Article 149. By the time of *Tongkao* (1778), three of the six original sub-statutes as well as a further sub-statute added in the Kangxi era (1662–1722) had been removed from Article 149 and five new sub-statutes had been added. *Tongkao* had a total of seven sub-statutes appended to Article 149 (*Tongkao*: 523–6). Although this number remained the same at the time of *Cunyi* (1905), the contents were not the same. The third, fourth, and fifth sub-statutes of Article 149 in *Tongkao* had been combined into one sub-statute (149-4) in *Cunyi*. Apart from this change, *Cunyi* added two sub-statutes. The essentials of the change may be summarized as follows:

1. The rule in the second section of Article 149 on officials and clerks was made more comprehensive by the provision (Sub-statute149-7 in *Tongkao* and 149-5 in *Cunyi*) added in 1736 (Qianlong 1). The new provision made officials accountable not only in terms of whether they took illegal interest or not, but also in terms of whether they had used force or not in lending money. According to Article 149, should the official make a loan, he was to receive a punishment of 80 blows with the heavy stick. According to the added sub-statute, the same punishment would be imposed on the official if he took a rate of interest between 30 and up to 40 *liang* (not including 40 *liang*), even if this was within the range of legally permitted interest. Even interest that was within the legal rate would be forfeit to the government. As for the situation in which the official took more interest than that permitted by law, the statute counted only the illegal proportion of the whole interest as *zang* (illegal interest) as the basis for the imposition of punishment, whereas the added sub-statute counted the total interest, including that which was within the range of 3 per cent per month, and that total was made the basis for punishment. The interest in excess of 3 per cent per month was to be returned to the borrower, and the interest up to and including 3 per cent per month was to be forfeit to the government.
2. The added provisions created new rules for military officials, for loans between ordinary people and Banner people, and for loans between ordinary people and minority people (Sub-statutes 149-3, 149-4, and 149-5 in *Tongkao*, which were later combined into one sub-statute (Sub-statute 149–4)).
3. Sub-statute 149-6 in *Tongkao* and 149-3 in *Cunyi* supplemented Article 149 by providing 'should any lender obtain illegal interest by means of some device such as *duanpiao*, he shall be punished severely.

The money will be forfeit to the government. The borrower who confessed to be exempt from punishment and payment of interest.' According to Jing, *duanpiao* was a device for extorting an illegally high rate of interest while disguising the arrangement in a legally enforceable contract. The contract would state an amount of principal far in excess of the amount actually lent; the borrower would be required to 'repay' the higher amount given in the contract at the stipulated interest rate.[33] Xue pointed out that this provision was specially made for officials (*Cunyi*: 399). But the earlier book by Wu Tan (*Tongkao*: 525) did not mention this and the sub-statute does not use any specific word to limit its scope to 'officials'. The Ba county records supply a case that falls under this provision, suggesting that it was not limited to officials (see Debt Case 1 in Chapter 7). There was no change made to the matters concerning repayment of the debt and creditors' self-help.

This list of laws is no more than a very brief summary. Some provisions once enforced in the Qing might not be attached to the Code. Changes in both the legislation on debt matters and the practice of enforcing the relevant law were much more complicated than was expressed in the text of the Code. The following evidence on loan interest with regard to pawnbrokers may give us a better view of this feature.

I mentioned above that some materials show that the Qing officials reduced interest rates below 3 per cent per month. There is an example in a book by Bao Shichen.

> Private loans should bear no more than 2 per cent per month as interest. Overcharged interest which is higher than 2 per cent but less than 3 per cent per month should be forfeit to the government. If the interest taken is higher than 3 per cent per month, the principal should be forfeit as well.[34]

The rule given by Bao Shichen implied that people had generally been able to respect the legal rate of interest of 3 per cent per month in making ordinary loans. Otherwise, there would be no sense in officials reducing the interest further.

However, Brockman noticed that in Taiwan small pawn shops took too high a rate of interest. So he concluded that the provision on the limitation

[33] See Jing 1994: 295, n3.

[34] Bao Shichen 1872/1968, *juan* 28: 13b.

of interest was 'not uniformly applied' in Taiwan.[35] Although this might be true, the limitation of interest for pawnbrokers seems to have been a more complicated issue. On this matter, the Regulations of Fujian Province (*Fujian shengli*) provide us with a good opportunity to explore some features of both the position of pawnbroker and the process of provincial legislation. Since Taiwan was once part of Fujian province, it might also help us to understand the situation of the Taiwan pawnbroker.

These regulations are rules given to the whole province in the name of the provincial treasurer on receiving approval from the governor-general of a report from a magistrate or prefect, often on the basis of a particular case. They did not have a standard formula, and appeared with no unified names. And the style of the text is often informal from the legal document's point of view, more concrete than abstract. The regulations contained six items relevant to our discussion.

In a regulation of 1764 (Qianlong 29), a distinction was made between large and small pawn shops. A large pawn shop was to charge interest at no more than 2 per cent per month, with a maximum of thirty-six months for maturity of the loan. A small pawn shop was to charge no more than 2.4 per cent per month, with a maximum period of twenty-four months (*Fujian shengli*: 457–8). The concern was twofold. On the one hand, the regulation aimed to improve the business of vulnerable enterprises in order to give them more security. Thus they were allowed to charge a higher rate of interest and stipulate a shorter period in their loan contracts. On the other hand, the intention was to maintain a certain number of small pawn shops in order to provide a source of loans for the poor in difficult times.

A regulation of 1774 (Qianlong 39) clarified the nature of the distinction between large and small pawn shops, the criterion being 500 *liang* of silver. Shops that registered their capital as 500 *liang* of silver or over were categorized as large, and those with less were classed as small (*Fujian shengli*: 459–60).

However, the regulation remained problematic. First, it said nothing about whether a small pawn shop was allowed to increase its capital, and if so by how much. When people experienced a poor harvest and needed loans from a small pawn shop, quite often the store needed to add more capital to keep the business running, since many people were unable to redeem their goods. Since the regulations provided no ruling on this issue, should a small pawn shop increase its capital, debtors might demand that their loan

[35] Brockman 1980: 88.

be charged at the lower interest rate, just as for a large pawn shop. Secondly, some pawn shops with a lot of capital might take advantage of this principle to register as small ones in order to gain more benefit. In either event, the law needed to be revised in order to balance the different aspects.

That brought about the regulation of 1873 (Qianlong 48), which was clearly fairer and more practicable, in that it thoroughly considered the interests of both sides, the pawnbroker and his customers. Interest, whether at the higher or lower rate, was to be charged according to the amount of the loan. Pawnbrokers who made a loan of 3 *liang* of silver or more might charge interest at 2 per cent per month, with a redemption period of thirty months, and those who made loans of less than 3 *liang* might charge interest at 2.4 per cent per month, with the same redemption period (*Fujian shengli*: 462–9). This principle appears to have been in force thereafter, for no further regulations were made on this issue.

It is also worth mentioning the light this regulation sheds on the provincial legislative process. The regulation started by recalling the regulation of Qianlong 29, then the revision of Qianlong 39, and finished by noting the change to be made. It provided many details of the procedure for the consideration of proposals by the governor-general.

I use a couple of examples to elaborate the process of reporting, rejecting, and accepting between the provincial treasurer and the governor-general. The provincial treasurer proposed to allow both small and large pawn shops to increase their capital. Small pawn shops were to be allowed to increase their capital to 5,000 *liang* of silver. The governor-general rejected the proposal on the grounds of impracticality, because it would be impossible to ascertain the particular situation of every pawn shop. The revised proposal suggested that capital should be allowed to increase to match increasing business from the time of initial registration. The governor-general rejected it again, because no distinctions were drawn between different situations. A later proposal was made with reference to the practice of other provinces, making a distinction not between large and small pawn shops but between specific loans: for those of 3 *liang* or 3,000 *wen* or more, the interest rate should be 2 per cent per month with a redemption period of thirty months; for loans of less than this, the interest should be 2.4 per cent per month, with a redemption period of twenty-four months. This proposal obviously gave a more balanced consideration to different businesses. The governor-general also agreed that it removed the problem of large pawn shops registering as small ones. But he was still not satisfied that the interests of the poor had been fully considered. Obviously those who could afford only a loan less than 3 *liang* or 3,000 *wen* were the poor, who would find it difficult to redeem the pledged property in a short period. After further consideration, the provincial treasurer proposed that the redemption period for goods pledged for a loan of less than 3 *liang* should not be made too short, in order to benefit the poor. This time the governor-general approved the proposal, and finally the official pronouncement was posted and kept on file from then on (*Fujian shengli*: 462–9).

Taiwan was mentioned in this regulation on account of its remoteness and the difficulty of communicating the new rule. The Taiwan government was therefore given more time before the rule came into force (*Fujian shengli*: 466). However, Taiwan seems to have been troubled by some problems relating to the pawn shop loans, such as charging too high interest. Another regulation was specifically made to deal with this problem: 'Should anyone in Taiwan who opens a small pawn shop lend money at interest higher [than 3 per cent per month], taking clothes and other items as pledges from the poor people, the local official who has ignored the matter will be moved to another post one degree lower' (*Bianlan*: 2198).

The rate of interest that pawn shops might levy seems to have been a matter for provincial decision. An official proclamation (*gaoshi*) by the provincial judge of Jiangxi province provides another example of how provincial legislation was maintained and respected. Since the pronouncement is a perfect example of the form of local legislation, I cite the main part of it below:

> An order to all people of the province: in the matter of returning some interest to borrowers by the pawnshop owners. The matter has been jointly reviewed by officials of the province. Pawn brokers should keep to loans at the interest of 2 per cent per month as usual. Moreover, if the pledged goods are kept more than a whole year before redemption, one month of interest should be cut from the whole interest charged. If the goods are kept more than two years before redemption, then two months of interest should be cut. This has applied with no exception for a long time, and official proclamations have been posted and kept on file. It is nearly the end of the year, the time at which both the pledging and redemption of goods take place very frequently. I am afraid that the law has been in place too long to be respected. It is necessary to order again that owners of pawn shops adhere to the provisions that have been made in detail.[36]

Official proclamations might also be made at lower levels, such as the prefecture and the county. We may take an example from the Ba county

[36] *Qingshi ziliao*, vol. 3: 213. The judicial commissioner was in post from 1733 (Yongzheng 11) to 1743 (Qianlong 8).

records, although it is not clear that the proclamation emanated from Ba county itself since the records also contain documents from Chongqing prefecture and other counties. The proclamation states:

> Businessmen gathered in inns are required to pay attention to theft. It is ordered that businessmen should record the money they have brought with them and hand it to the inn for safe keeping. The inn should record the money and keep it safe. Should anybody ignore the order and not hand their money to the inn, any loss would not be considered the responsibility of the inn. If they respect the rule, then the inn should compensate them for any loss. [In its conclusion, the proclamation took an example of a real case in which a businessman named Li lost his money. Since he had not handed it to the inn for safe keeping, the inn had no responsibility for the loss. What he had lost could be returned only once the thieves were caught.][37]

The nature of the rules established by the lower level of officials such as the county magistrates may deserve more study. But one point is clear from the regulations of Fujian province: most of the proposals originated in reports submitted by a magistrate. It is certain that county magistrates often reported their proposals to obtain approval from provincial officials. The rules contained in the approved proposal supplied guidelines for the magistrate in resolving relevant disputes. The magistrate obviously had been authorized to make such rules, subject to their being consistent with the principles of the law. In this sense, the authority of these rules, just like that of the provincial regulations, was mainly derived from their being consistent with the law. But, unlike the rules of the Code and other promulgations of the central government, they might readily be changed by other officials of the same or higher rank and position if their application caused any problem.

5.3 The law on marriage

The family was highly respected in traditional Chinese society and played a key role in the Qing. It was believed that when people are happily married, there is always harmony in society. In the administration, the relationship of members of a family, especially that of father and son, was the model for the emperor in ruling the state like a father leading his family. The state and family were even combined into a single term *guojia* (state-family) as an abstraction for the country. In economic and general administration, the family was the basic unit for managing many things such as tax, labour, and

[37] Ba county records, *juan* 203.

registration. In the judicial system, family values were also the most important consideration for the law on many matters. 'The Chinese family life compared favourably with the somewhat too loose bonds of the Occidental, — in fact, in family life China is presented at her best'.[38] One may not agree with this positive estimation, but it is true that family was never a 'loose bond' in China.

'Marriage' (*hunyin*) was a subdivision under the division of Law concerning the Board of Household. At the beginning, it consisted of seventeen statutes and eight sub-statutes, according to *Jizhu*, increased to nineteen sub-statutes in *Tongkao*, and had reached twenty-three by the time of *Cunyi*. The Qing marriage law originated in the Tang Code of 653,[39] about one thousand years prior to the Qing. However, the principles of marriage law remained the same and even the exact text of the Tang Code can be found in the Qing.[40]

Some provisions from other divisions of the Code also concern marriage. For example, 'buying and selling a divorce' (*maixiu maixiu*) was in 'Toleration by a Spouse of a Wife's or Concubine's Infidelity' (Article 367); 'abducting and selling a woman as a wife' was in 'Abducting Persons and Selling Abducted Persons' (Article 275). Generally speaking, marriage law can be summarized in four parts: three forms of lawful betrothal and marriage; prohibited marriage; situations in which the betrothal/marriage could or should be withdrawn or dissolved; and the punishments when the relevant laws were not observed. My discussion on marriage law will focus on the marriage agreement, divorce, and a widow's remarriage. These were the issues that most concerned people and were the most popular reasons for litigation.

5.3.1 The marriage agreement

According to the first statute of the law on Marriage — The Marriage of Men and Women (Article 101) — legal marriage should be established through two steps, the marriage agreement and the marriage ceremony. The marriage ceremony could not be undertaken without having first made the marriage agreement. Thus, the marriage agreement was clearly the prerequisite for a legal marriage. Generally speaking, the conditions that had to be fulfilled for the marriage agreement were the same for the marriage itself.

[38] Jamieson 1921/1970: 13.
[39] For the history of the Tang Code, see Johnson 1979: 39–40.
[40] For the changes to the law of marriage from the Tang (618–907), to the Ming (1368–1644), and to the Qing, see MacCormack 1990: 268–82.

Because of the significance of the marriage agreement, I examine in detail the conditions required by the law for the marriage agreement.

The first section of Article 101 dealt mainly with matters concerning the marriage agreement. Because of this, this statute was regarded as establishing the basic principle for marriage matters, and was to be generally consulted when dealing with cases of marriage.

> When a marriage is being arranged for a man and a woman, if (*it should be the case that*) there is a defect (*a disability or an*) infirmity (*sickness*), or if there is [great] age or [great] youth, or if one is the offspring of a concubine, or an adopted son (*of the same clan*), or an adopted son (*of a different surname*), it is the responsibility of each family to inform the other clearly of the matter, so that each may do as it wishes. (*If one party does not wish to proceed, it may withdraw* [from the negotiations]. *If both wish* [to proceed], *then, in agreement with the marriage broker*) they will write out the marriage contract. [The young people] will be engaged and married according to the rites. If [the head of the bride's family] who has agreed to the marriage of the daughter has already signed the marriage contract, or if there is a private agreement (*this means he already knew of such matters as the man's defect, infirmity, age, or his status as the son of a concubine or as an adopted son*), and he changes his mind, (*the member of the woman's family who is in change of the marriage decision*) will receive 50 strokes of the light bamboo. (*The woman will return to the husband.*) Even though there is no marriage contract, when engagement presents have already been received, this is also the case. (Jones 1994: 123)

The first part thus expressed the principles for entering and finishing the process of marriage. The heads of the two families (*liangjia*) had to honestly inform each other of the real status of the boy/girl when entering the marriage agreement (*dinghun*). For example, it had to be acknowledged whether he/she has a disability. Whether the families continued with the agreement was completely dependent on their own willingness to proceed. 'If one party does not wish to proceed, it may do so' (*buyuan jizhi*). If they were both in agreement, they were to write a contract of marriage (*hunshu*) through an employed go-between (*tong meishuo*). Then in due course the couple could marry each other.

The second part focused on the girl's family. What were the consequences if, having made the marriage agreement by a written contract (*yibao hunshu*) and/or having agreed with each other privately (*jiyou siyue*), for example, having accepted the boy's disability,[41] the girl's family withdrew from the agreement (*hui*). This situation was not the one covered by the

[41] For more on the private agreement (*siyue*), see below.

clause stating 'If one party does not wish to proceed, it may do so'. Once the contract had been made, it was too late for the girl's family (and the boy's family too, as we shall see later) to change their mind. Thus, the head of the family was liable to punishment, and the girl had to return to the first engaged boy. The last sentence of this section stated the other possibility for a marriage agreement: 'Even though there is no marriage contract, when engagement presents have already been received this is also the case.' So, the engagement to marry could be made and substantiated by written contract, with or without the negotiation of a go-between, or by the acceptance of engagement presents.

Despite its brevity, this section contained every essential element for a legal marriage and expressed the principle that the marriage agreement should not be broken. These elements were: (1) bona fides, (2) mutual assent, (3) the principals' decision, (4) employment of a go-between, (5) the written contract, (6) a private agreement, and (7) engagement gifts.[42]

(1) Bona fides

To be honest was not just a requirement for entering into a marriage agreement. It was also the universal principle for entering into other civil contracts. What was emphasized here was that the parents should in particular disclose any personal disadvantages of the boy or girl, such as that he/she might be older than the average age of marriage, or had serious physical problems, or the boy was an adopted son or a son of a concubine. In cases where one party actively cheated, for example by letting a sister of the girl with a defect be seen, or a brother of the boy with a defect be seen, and afterwards used the girl or the boy with a defect to complete the marriage, the head of the family was to receive punishment — eighty blows with the heavy stick for the girl's family head, ninety for the boy's. The person without a defect who had actually been seen had to complete the marriage unless he/she had already been engaged to another (Article 101), or he/she was not from the same family.[43] Should the boy or the girl with a defect have completed the marriage, because it had been achieved by cheating, the couple had to divorce. When one party cheated by ways other than the use of a substitute, and had completed the marriage, the other party might bring an action to the court for divorce.[44]

[42] I use 'marriage agreement' to refer to the agreement of the two parties to the marriage and 'written contract' to refer to the particular document that concluded the agreement.

[43] Hoang 1898: 27.

[44] Ibid.: 28.

(2) Mutual assent

Mutual assent (*yuan*) refers not to the agreement of the boy or girl themselves but to that of the head of their respective families. So, only the family head could withdraw, if at all, from the marriage agreement. He might ask for the opinions of the boy or girl before entering into an engagement, but whether the latter agreed or not was not even a matter for concern. Consistent with this principle, the liability, if any, for breach of the law on marriage agreements fell on parents (or other relatives) as responsible persons. Should the marriage have been contracted by force, the responsible person was subject to more severe punishment (Article 112).

(3) The principals' (zhuhunren) decision

The position of the heads of the two families was the key factor for a marriage, as shown above. The term 'two families' (*liangjia*) and the reference to the head of the girl's family (*nüjia zhuhunren*) in the opening section of the Article (101) indicated that the family principal was empowered to arrange and decide the marriage agreement. Later, the first attached substatute (Sub-statute 101-1) made this emphasis crystal clear by further dividing the principal into two levels: the closest relatives, such as grandparents and parents of the boy/girl, and the 'remaining principals' (*yuqin*). The 'remaining principals' are listed in the last two statutes (Articles 116 and 117) of the Marriage Law. An often-used phrase, 'the go-between's suggestion does not constitute an agreement [by the principal]' (*meishuo weiyun*), expressed a situation where the principal did not approve a marriage agreement negotiated by a go-between, whether or not the couple had consented. If a widowed mother remarried another man, she was the principal for her daughter if she took her into her second husband's home (Sub-statute 101-1).[45] She would lose her power to arrange a marriage if she separated from her daughter.

The only exception to this rule was the absence of the male on government service or business. He was then allowed to make the marriage agreement by himself (Article 101.5). It is obvious that there might have been a conflict between an engagement contracted by the parents and one contracted by the absent son. The principle in such a situation was simple and clear. Should the marriage not have been completed by the son, the marriage agreement made by his parents took priority, and the girl engaged

[45] Since the son usually remained with his deceased father's relatives, the Code mentioned only the daughter.

by the son might marry another. Should the son have completed the marriage himself, then the one agreed by his parents or grandparents could be cancelled.[46]

Whether the marriage was legitimate or not depended first on whether the heads of the families had agreed or not. If two people lived together on their own as a couple without the agreement of the principals, they were treated as having illegal sexual relations rather than as husband and wife (*sizi gouhe*) (Sub-statute 117-4). Because the principals were the people responsible for the agreement and were de facto the decisive factor for consent, punishment when the law was breached was logically inflicted on the heads of the families first rather than on the couple (Article 117). So, as MacCormack emphasizes, 'Generally to be borne in mind is the fact that the persons incurring the punishments were those responsible for the marriage, that is, the elders in the two families who had arranged it, not the boy and girl themselves.'[47]

(4) Employment of a go-between

The go-between (*mei*) was introduced in the commentary in smaller letters on the Article in the context of the written contract. The importance of the go-between was unquestioned. However, it is doubtful that the employment of a go-between was a prerequisite for a legal marriage. On the one hand, from the point of view of the Code, negotiation conducted by a go-between was a normal presumption for a legal marriage. As an old Chinese saying expressed it, 'the marriage is willed by the order of the parents and negotiated and witnessed by the go-between (*fumu zhiming, meishuo zhiyan*)'. Thus, the go-between was recognized in a general provision (Article 117) as a responsible person whose importance was second only to that of the principal. Go-betweens would be liable to punishment for any breach of the law committed with their knowledge. On the other hand, the recognition of an agreement made privately without the negotiation of a go-between was also clear. And we shall see from the next two sections that a marriage contract could be made by the two families without the intervention of a go-between. Nevertheless, the employment of a go-between could indicate without any doubt the seriousness and willingness of the two parties in making the marriage agreement. So, in marriage disputes, the go-between was the key witness and was interrogated in the court. It was quite normal for a

[46] The same principle applied in a conflict between marriage agreements made by both the parents and the grandparents. The one made by the grandparents had priority.
[47] MacCormack 1990: 270.

magistrate to reject a go-between's request not to be involved in the hearing (*zhaishi*) (Baodi, 168: 182–205).[48]

(5) The written contract

A written contract (*hunshu*) was clearly required by the Code: '(*If both wish* [to proceed], *then, in agreement with the marriage broker*) they will write out the marriage contract. [The young people] will be engaged and married according to the rites.' What can be understood generally from this provision are two things: first, the marriage contract was a written one and was to be the conclusion of the marriage agreement; secondly, the contract was made through the go-between. So, the written contract was the most important step, the concluding step, of the marriage agreement after serious negotiations. The agreement could not be regarded as finalized until the written contract had been completed. In this sense, the written contract can be seen as a symbolic mark of the achievement of a marriage agreement.

However, despite being given a unique status, the form and the content of the contract were not mentioned. The Code seemed deliberately to leave room for people to develop their own details. If we read the provision on marriage where the boy is called in to the girl's household (Sub-statute 101-3), the law clearly required that some basic statement should be made, such as whether the son-in-law who lived with his wife's parents would stay with the girl's family for the parents' whole life (*yanglao*), or, if not, how long he was expected to stay for (*chushe nianxian*). So the written contract that marked the conclusion of the marriage agreement might vary from place to place and from time to time.[49] What we must understand is that this contract was essential for proving the marriage agreement. We shall see in the

[48] However, since the private agreement could be understood as an agreement without a go-between (see below on private agreements), if the go-between was omitted, the legal status of the marriage might not be influenced.

[49] The situation was the same in terms of the various customary practices in making the written contract. People might make the contract in a more formal way, which included several documents. For example, the boy's family might make a formal proposal of marriage with a less formal letter regarding the boy's status or physical condition, and, if any, a list of the betrothal presents. The girl's family would also reply with a formal acceptance of the marriage proposal with a similarly less formal letter regarding the girl's personal information (Chen Peng 1990: 330–40). In some places, people might regard exchanging and accepting the boy's and the girl's name card as creating the contract. Even sending the girl's name card to the boy's family might have alone been sufficient to conclude the marriage engagement (*Minshi xiguan diaocha baogao lu* 2000: 859). The content of the contract also varied. In some places it contained a lot of details, in others it was very simple. The key point here is that the document that served as the contract had to be commonly accepted in the local community as the contract.

discussion of cases that the written contract played an unchallenged role as evidence of the legal status of the marriage agreement.

Although the marriage agreement was best made with a written contract, achieved through the negotiation of a go-between, a go-between might not have been present when the contract was made.

(6) A private agreement

The commentary in smaller letters on the term 'private agreement' in the Code explained what it meant. It referred to personal exchanges and confirmed, orally rather than in writing, the condition of the boy or girl, for example, whether the boy was an adopted son, or other situations that particularly required the two parties to be honest (see the bona fides subsection above). It was concluded by the two families without the negotiation of a go-between. Thus, 'private agreement' referred to a particular part rather than to the marriage agreement as a whole. If the contract was written, this part was an exception; in other words, the particular situation of the boy or the girl was not necessarily part of the content of the written contract. This commentary can actually be traced back to the Tang Code, according to which the 'private agreement' was clearly a supplementary part of the marriage agreement.[50] Although both the Ming and Qing Codes almost copy the Tang's explanation of 'private agreement', from the language of the Qing Code we can deduce that the understanding of the Ming and Qing officials and scholars seemed to have changed. In this sense, there was another understanding of 'private agreement'.

For example, the Ming collected commentary clearly stated that a 'private agreement is the marriage agreement made privately without employing the go-between'.[51] This explanation differed significantly from the meaning given by the Tang, Ming and Qing Codes. It implied that the 'private agreement' was made without the negotiation of a go-between and was itself the final marriage agreement. As to whether it also referred to an oral agreement remains unclear. The Qing seems to have accepted this understanding and expanded the dimension of the 'private agreement' to cover the marriage agreement (*Jizhu*: 252). Because of this explanation, many scholars, Shiga for example,[52] regard a private agreement as one of the three alternative prerequisites of a legal marriage (the others being the written contract and the engagement gift).

[50] Ye Xiaoxin 1993: 291.
[51] Chen Peng 1990: 323.
[52] Shiga Shūzō 2003: 379.

(7) *The engagement gift*

The engagement gift (*pincai*) was introduced at the end of the first section of Article 101 as another possibility for a marriage agreement: 'Even though there is no marriage contract, when engagement presents have already been received this is also the case.' Thus, the engagement gift was also the mark of the marriage agreement (Article 101). Since the engagement gift was introduced in the context of withdrawal from the marriage agreement by the head of the girl's family, the recipient of the gift was clearly the girl's family. Although the gift was introduced as a replacement for a written contract for the conclusion of the marriage agreement, it bore the same significance as the written contract.

A further important question concerned the nature of the engagement gift. What we can deduce from the name given by the Code is that the engagement gift had a specific meaning, that is, the gift was delivered by the boy's family and accepted by the girl's as a commitment to the marriage agreement. Shen Zhiqi pointed out that there were no strict rules about the value and the form of the gift; anything that passed through the go-between and was given as a symbol of agreement could be the gift. Objects that were exchanged just to affirm good relations between the families were not the engagement gift (*Jizhu*: 252). The underlying principle was that the gift was accepted with a clear understanding that it was the engagement gift. The sender expected that the particular marriage agreement would be concluded when he sent the gift, and the accepter received the gift knowing the meaning behind it. The difference between the engagement gift and an ordinary present was that there might be a Gift List (*Lidan*), which would list every single aspect of the gift, including the colour, the nature, and the fabric (*Jizhu*: 252). In the Baodi records we can see examples of Gift Lists that were submitted to the magistrate as evidence.

Breaking the marriage agreement

Once the marriage agreement was made, it was protected by the law. Either party had the right to have the marriage ceremony completed in due time. The fifth section of Article 101 concerned completion of the marriage ceremony according to the time scale agreed by the two families. The responsible person on each side would have received fifty blows with the light stick for breaching the rule. Examples of breach were if the boy's family used force to complete the ceremony before the due date, or if the girl's family refused to have the ceremony on the due date. If the agreement was broken, the principals were to be punished and the marriage reinstated (Article 101). If one girl was engaged to two boys or one boy was engaged to two girls, more severe punishment would be inflicted on the responsible persons. The punishment for the principals was seventy blows with the heavy stick if the second marriage had not yet been completed, and eighty blows if the marriage had been completed. The first engagement was upheld. However, if the first intended husband did not intend to keep the girl any more, then double the amount of the marriage gift had to be returned to his family and the girl was allowed to enter the other marriage. As for the family that agreed to the second engagement, if they were aware of the real situation, the principal received the same punishment as was imposed on the principal of the party making the engagement. If they did not know the real situation, they were free from prosecution. In the former case, the gift would have been forfeited to the government; in the latter, it would have been returned to the boy's family.

The protection of the marriage agreement had some exceptions. The third section of Article 101 stated: if 'there is the commission of a sexual offence or theft (if the man has committed an offence, the woman may marry someone else, or if the woman has committed the offence, the man may marry someone else), this law is not used.' In other words, if the boy or girl committed theft or had illegal sex with someone else, this constituted grounds for the other side to withdraw from the agreement.[53] There were three other exceptions: (1) if either of the parties died after the betrothal although 'the marriage presents shall not be returned' (Sub-statute 101-1); (2) 'if the boy's family fails to complete the marriage ceremony for five years after the period fixed, or if the boy leaves his home and has not been heard of for three years, the woman, on application to the magistrate, shall be issued a certificate allowing her to marry another person, and she shall not be obliged to return the first engagement gift' (Sub-statute 116-2); (3) if the son had entered into a marriage contract by himself while his parents had made another one for him, either his own contract (should he not have married the girl) or the one made by his parents (should he have married the girl) could be cancelled (Article 101).

The concern of the law was to achieve a twofold outcome. On the one hand, it set out clear principles for the agreement of the marriage conducted by the heads of the families of the boy and girl. There were two kinds of evidence for the marriage agreement: a contract and/or a gift. The law upheld the first properly made marriage agreement. Except for reasons given

[53] Hoang (1898: 37) noted that such an offence by the boy referred only to theft, and did not include illegal sexual relations, although there is no such implication in the text of the Code.

by the law itself, the marriage agreement had to be followed in due time by the wedding ceremony. On the other hand, the advantage of establishing the clear principle was a great saving in government resources. In other words, a legal marriage could be achieved without too much governmental participation. As Jamieson commented, the marriage 'requires no registration or celebration by any public authority, civil or religious'.[54]

5.3.2 Ending or annulling a marriage

Some marriages were made illegal from the beginning by the law, and others needed or might need to be ended for various reasons. Although I shall mention the legal prohibitions on marriage in this section, I pay more attention to the conditions under which a legal marriage had to be, or might be, ended. The law either retained the power to compel the dissolution of a marriage or conferred that power on the husband. On most occasions the law had the power to decide whether the marriage was legal or could be ended. It also conferred significant power on the husband to divorce his wife.

Marriage should not be established

The major prohibitions on marriage derived from kinship and social status. Three statutes (Articles 107, 108, and 109)[55] and their four attached substatutes placed wide-ranging restrictions on marriage between people standing in a kin relation. In general, marriage was prohibited between people with the same surname or between individuals related to each other within the five degrees of mourning. Should any marriage be considered to be in breach of these prohibitions, not only was the marriage void but the persons involved were punished. In some situations, punishments were extremely severe. For example, if a man married a concubine of his father or grandfather or the wife of his father's elder or younger brother, he was liable to be beheaded. If the wife he had taken was his deceased brother's wife, the penalty was hanging (Article 109). Restrictions on marriage also derived from social status. Marriage was prohibited between an official and a woman under his jurisdiction (Article 110); if a Buddhist or Taoist monk was one of the parties (Article 114); and between an honourable and a mean person (Article 105).

[54] Jamieson 1921/1970: 44.
[55] Marrying Someone with the Same Surname (107), Marriage between Superior and Inferior Relatives (108), and Taking in Marriage a Relative's Wife or Concubine (109).

The object of marriage in China had long been regarded as being to combine two different surnames and to build a lifetime relationship between the couple. A marriage should be entered into in good faith with mutual assent, and so on. Such beliefs and principles logically resulted in certain provisions. The law prohibited the hiring out of a woman as a wife to a man for a certain time (Article 102), and prohibited a husband from having a second principal wife.[56] Marriages that involved dishonesty, such as the use of a substitute (*wangmao*, Article 101), or forcibly taking a woman as a wife (*qiangzhan*, Article 112)[57] were also prohibited. Marriages were prohibited to be completed at certain times : (1) during a period of mourning for the parents, grandparents, or other senior agnates (Article 105); and (2) during the time when parents were imprisoned (Article 106).

Although the law required that all the marriages mentioned above be annulled, some, for example marriage completed during a time of mourning or while a parent was in prison, were not per se illegal marriages. Thus marriages such as those completed during a time of mourning might not be annulled. An edict issued by emperor Yongzheng in 1735 stated:

> There are people of low status who do not know the rites. Fearing not to be able to make a marriage in times of mourning, they complete the marriage when the father or the mother is still very sick, or even has already died, but not yet been buried. This practice is followed by numerous merchants, as well as by scholars and magistrates, and even, now, by men of the eight Banners (*baqi*). We see this with great sorrow. From henceforth, we forbid all families whose members hold the office of magistrate or whose members have the degree of simple graduate or graduate of the Imperial College to celebrate marriages during the period of three years' mourning. Whoever infringes this prohibition will be deprived of his dignity or rank. But there are poor people, who, when their father or their mother, tortured by illness, groans on a bed of pain, lack the help of a daughter-in-law in the household. We allow them to be brought home as daughter-in-law (*yingqu*), so that she may be of real service, but the boy and the girl can not live as husband and wife (*chenghun*) before the parent has recovered or, in the event of death, before the end of the period of mourning.[58]

[56] In 1779 (Qianlong 44) there was a change, because emperor Qianlong promulgated a decree that allowed a single son to succeed to two family lines, and to marry one woman for each family he represented. However, the girl who entered the second marriage was never given the status of wife by the authorities.

[57] Many provisions dealt with the different situations in which force or cheating was used to seduce or abduct women by people of varying relationships to the woman involved.

[58] Hoang 1898: 86–7; Chen Peng 1990: 517.

By this decree, an engaged girl of ordinary family was allowed to enter her would-be husband's household at a time when her help was very much needed by the husband's family. In such circumstances, certain rites might be dispensed with, such as the bride being brought in with a red chair and music being played. This decree opened a window for such marriages among people of lower status to be exempt from the strict prohibition. The magistrate when dealing with such a case had the discretion to annul or not annul a marriage.

Established marriage should be ended

The Code recognized certain actions committed by either husband or wife or certain members of their families as 'breaking the bond' (*yijue*), as a consequence of which the marriage should, on most occasions, be ended. The provision of *yijue* was attached to Article 116 (Repudiate a Wife), and the explanation was given in the commentary in small letters on Article 337 (*Ganming fanyi*). This commentary listed nine examples, including the wife's parents marrying her to another man or repudiating the son-in-law who lived with them, or a husband marrying another woman, forcing his wife to commit adultery, or hiring her out to be another man's wife. The conditions set out in the commentary were not exhaustive. Other actions more serious than those listed in the commentary all constituted 'breaking the bond', such as the killing by the husband of the wife's parents or other close relatives of her natal family, or the beating or killing by the wife of her husband's parents, grandparents, or brothers and sisters.[59]

An exception to ending a marriage when the bond was broken occurred in the circumstance of a wife's parents repudiating their son-in-law who lived with them. Here, the law especially protected the marriage and required the wife to return to the son-in-law. However, since the bond had been broken, the couple had to live separately from the wife's parents, even though the original contract required the husband to live with his wife's parents for the duration of their lives.[60]

Ending marriage by the husband

There were seven grounds on which the husband might lawfully repudiate his wife (Article 116). Some of these appear to be very trivial, such as talking too much or jealousy. The other five grounds were: bearing no son, shameless behaviour, disregard by the wife of her parents-in-law, theft, and

[59] See also MacCormack 1990: 280–2, and Qu Tongzu 1965: 122–3.
[60] Hoang 1898: ch. 22.

incurable illness. In theory, the wife's position was extremely vulnerable. Her husband might repudiate her upon any of the above grounds subject to three excuses or exceptions: she had mourned three years for her parents-in-law, her husband's family was richer than at the time of the marriage, and she had no home to which she might return.[61]

This provision obviously favoured the husband. Not only were some reasons really insignificant, but also he did not need to go to the court to divorce his wife. However, the power of the husband to repudiate his wife had some limits. The marriage bound not only the couple but also the two families. The wife's family often played an important role in matters concerning their daughter. This was especially true in a situation in which their daughter's future was at risk. Their life too would certainly have been affected should their daughter be repudiated and return to stay with them. Thus the support of her family should not be ignored in observing the disparity in status between man and woman. The law was concerned to prohibit the husband from repudiating his wife if she had no family to which she could return. When the wife had her family to back her, the strength of the family played an important, if not a decisive, role. The husband perhaps was forced to consider the effect of the repudiation in ending the relationship between the two families. If the husband failed to justify his intention to repudiate, the wife's family often challenged the repudiation. As a last resort, the wife's family or the wife herself could bring the case to the court, on the basis that the repudiation was groundless (*wugu*). Then it would be the court, instead of the husband, who decided.

In this sense, the balance drawn by the law might not incline to the husband as much as had been thought. To support this point, we can compare the stipulations on punishments imposed on the parents of the husband and of the wife. If the husband was 'repudiated' by his wife's family, the wife's parents received one hundred blows with the heavy stick for throwing away (*zhu*) the son-in-law who lived with them without a reason (Article 104). The punishment for the husband who repudiated his wife without a reason was eighty blows with the heavy stick. The point is that, given that the husband had a more privileged position than the wife, the slight difference in punishment shows that the gap might not have been as wide as has usually been thought.

[61] Adultery would make the three excuses inoperative.

Divorce by mutual consent (heli)

It might not be right to analyse 'mutual consent' as a separate ground for divorce, because it 'is not presented in the Codes as a distinct ground of separation'.[62] 'Mutual consent' appeared in the Article on Repudiation at the end of the section on 'the breaking of the bond' (*yijue*): 'If the two spouses do not get along together, but wish to divorce, there is no punishment. (*If in spirit they are already separated, how can they be united by force?*)'.[63] These words explain why a separation was to be allowed when the husband and wife disliked each other. Thus, there was no follow-up provision on ending a marriage in this way. Indeed, marriage was expected to be one of the roots of moral ethics. Once it had been established with the proper rites (*hezhi yili*), its maintenance relied on mutual responsibility and virtue (*chizhi yien, weizhi yiyi*). Although the term '*he*' meant that both the husband and the wife agreed to separate, divorce without any substantial ground conflicted with the theory and morality of the purpose of marriage. As many scholars have pointed out, if feelings never played an important part in building up a marriage, how could they formally be made a legal reason for divorce? It was beyond the Qing's thinking to set up both a rule and a procedure for a divorce lacking any substantial grounds.

5.3.3 A widow's remarriage

Although the classic Confucian literature regarded the chastity of a wife so highly that she was expected to be faithful to one man for the whole of her life until she was buried in the same grave with him,[64] the Code did not prohibit a widow from remarrying. However, she should conduct the second marriage only after she had completed the period of mourning for her husband (Article 105). The person in charge of such a marriage was usually the deceased husband's parent or other close relative. The widow's family could arrange a marriage for her by giving back the formal marriage presents to the deceased husband's family (*Huidian shili*, vol. 9: 336). Some historians have rightly observed that the person who would have been in charge of the widow's remarriage was actually the one who would receive the remarriage gift.[65] But in any event, the widow should not be forced to marry against her will, otherwise the person in charge of such a marriage should

[62] MacCormack 1990: 280.
[63] Article 116, Jones 1994: 134.
[64] MacCormack 1990: 269.
[65] Chen Peng 1990: 311.

be punished by eighty blows with the heavy stick. If an element of force was involved, the woman was to return to the home of her former husband and the betrothal property was to be returned to the giver. If the forced marriage had been completed, the marriage could stand if the widow wished it, but the betrothal present had to be forfeited to the government. The punishment was or was not imposed on the second husband depending on whether he knew the circumstances (Sub-statute 105-1).

Generally speaking, it is true that the marriage law remained relatively unchanged during the Qing. However, this was not the case with the law governing a widow's remarriage. The most significant change in the marriage law thus concerned the widow's remarriage.

Issues concerning a widow's remarriage were regulated mainly in five provisions: Article 105 (Marriage during Mourning) and its attached sub-statute; Article 109 (Marriage with Widows of Relations) and its two attached sub-statutes. The original statute (Article 105), inherited from the Ming (1368–1644), was changed significantly in 1725 (Yongzheng 3). In the original Article, the widow's natal parents and grandparents and the deceased husband's parents were not to be prosecuted should they force the widow to remarry. The reason, according to Shen Zhiqi, was that the widow's parents should not be punished for arranging another marriage for the widow for her own sake. As for the parents-in-law, there was no prescription in the rites stating that parents-in-law might arrange their daughter-in-law's remarriage (*Jizhu*: 262). A widow's other relatives who forced her to enter into another marriage were liable to a punishment of eighty blows with the heavy stick if they were related within the third degree of mourning and sixty if they were within the second degree. The punishment of sixty blows with the heavy stick was also imposed on the deceased husband's grandparents and his relatives within the second degree of mourning should they force the widow to remarry (*Huidian shili*, vol. 9: 335–6).[66]

These provisions were changed significantly in the revised Article. According to the revised Article 105, the widow's parents and grandparents, as well as the deceased husband's parents and grandparents, all were to receive the same punishment of eighty blows with the heavy stick should they use force to arrange another marriage for the widow. The punishment for these principals was rather severe, especially since originally there had been no punishment at all (except for the husband's grandparents). The

[66] See also MacCormack 1996b: 96. Shiga mistakenly states that only the widow's grandparents and parents were free from punishment. Actually, the widow's parents-in-law were treated in the same way (Shiga Shūzō 2003: 351, n.18).

punishment imposed on other relatives was also increased. For example, the punishment imposed on the widow's relatives within the third degree of mourning was increased to one hundred blows with the heavy stick, and on those within the second degree of mourning it was increased to ninety blows (*Jizhu*: 262; Article 105, *Huidian shili*, vol. 9: 335–6). The original Article 105 also provided that, where the marriage had been completed, the woman (despite the use of force) was to remain with her second husband.

In 1740 (Qianlong 5), another two significant revisions were made. One was with respect to the rules on who was in charge of the widow's remarriage: 'If a widow is willing to enter into a second marriage the parents of her late husband shall have the right of negotiating the marriage, and shall be entitled to receive the marriage presents' (Sub-statute 105-1).[67] This provision was actually a development of a decree of 1673 (Kangxi 12), which recognized the position of the widow's in-laws but still preferred the widow's parents to arrange the marriage for her. The condition was established that the parents should return the marriage gift to the deceased husband's family (*Huidian shili*, vol. 9: 336). If we recall here Shen Zhiqi's comment that 'there was no prescription in the rites permitting parents-in-law to arrange their daughter-in-law's remarriage', the changing of the law was significant. The other revision was that the widow was given the right to choose whether or not to remain with the second husband if the remarriage had been forcibly completed (Sub-statute 105-1). As Xue Yunsheng observed, 'violating one's duty to exercise compulsion to remarry the widow was revised and attracted more and more severe punishment' (*Cunyi*: 296). This seems to support the conclusion by Kathryn Bernhardt that the bond between a woman and her husband or his family was made closer in the Qing,[68] and by MacCormack that 'to some extent in the thinking of the Ch'ing legislators the value of chastity outweighed that of filial obedience'.[69]

Although a widow was allowed to remarry, she could not marry any person of her deceased husband's clan. The lightest punishment (one hundred blows with the heavy stick) for a marriage between agnates outside the degrees of mourning was imposed by a specific Article entitled 'Marriage with Widows of Relations' (Article 109). But if a man took the widow of his elder or younger brother, whether divorced, remarried, or not, the punishment for the couple was hanging.

[67] Jamieson 1921/1970: 36.
[68] Bernhardt 1996: 42–58.
[69] MacCormack 1996b: 96.

5.4 Summary

The Qing provisions on land, debt, and marriage have been briefly discussed. The Qing Code contained both the key principles and specific rules, as well as, in some cases, detailed provisions relating to land, debt, or marriage. Philip Huang is quite right to hold that principles for protecting people's rights in civil matters were contained in the Code.[70] What I need to add is that these principles were not mainly implied or stated in only a few Articles. They were consistently and explicitly established throughout the Code and systematically incorporated in other regulations.

Regulations such as *dingli* (settled rules), *tongxing* (general circulars), and *zeli* (the Regulations of the Six Boards) were constantly being made, applied, and added to the Code if necessary. The Regulations of the Six Boards also contained many useful rules and they were amended at regular intervals. For example, the Regulations of the Board of Revenue were revised fourteen times from 1776.[71] Many specific rules were established by the local government, including the county magistrates. The authority of these rules came mainly from their consistency with the law. The local officials had to honour the principles laid down in the Code.

The concern of the Code is clear — the achievement of consistency and certainty in the law through the upholding of certain important values[72] and the employment of two basic principles in drafting provisions. One principle considered the offender's motive, whether he behaved with or without intention (*youxin* or *wuxin*); the other looked at the nature of the offence and the actual level of damage.

To give an example of the first principle, the offence of unintentionally destroying grain was not subject to punishment. This was clearly stated in the Code (Article 98). In other cases, no clear distinction was made between offences with and without intention. This was because some offences already implied intention — for example, illegally selling or forcibly seizing another's land or unauthorized cultivation of another's land. On the other hand, if someone planted a couple of rows of his neighbour's land just next to his own land, whether by mistake or confusion, he had not committed the offence of taking another's land, and thus should not be punished.

[70] Huang 1996.

[71] Ye Xiaoxin 1993: 521.

[72] See MacCormack 1996b for a discussion of some of the most important values in traditional China.

An example of the other principle — that is, dealing with offences in accordance with the nature of the offence and the actual level of damage caused by offender — is that the highest punishment for *chongfu dianmai* (selling fields to a second party) was one hundred blows with the heavy stick and three years' penal servitude, two degrees higher than that for *daomai* (illegally selling another's land), which was eighty blows with the heavy stick and two years' penal servitude. The reason for this difference was that the offender in the former case not only received the price from his first sale but also caused the first buyer to lose his property. 'His heart is more evil' (*Jizhu*: 237). Another example is that *qiangzhan* (forcibly seizing another's land) was more serious in nature than just *qinzhan* (occupying the fields of another). In the former case the punishment was one hundred blows with the heavy stick and exile to 3,000 *li*, whereas for the latter case it was one hundred blows with the heavy stick and three years' penal servitude. Not only was the sentence imposed for the former offence (*qiangzhan*) higher, but there was no need to calculate the amount of the property that had been seized. The reason was, according to Shen Zhiqi, that the land was taken by 'force', so the degree of fault was higher. A further example is that a severe punishment was imposed on sons or grandsons who made a gift to another of the collective burial grounds of their ancestors or made a fraudulent contract of sale or mortgage. They (as well as the recipients of the property) were to be sentenced to military exile at a distant frontier (Sub-statutes 93-1 and 93-4). This was because the offences involved two factors: on the one hand, the recipients of the property often abused their position when they accepted the property; on the other hand, filial duties had been breached on the part of the son and grandson. Where the fault was less, so was the punishment less.

I have demonstrated that the Code did not treat matters concerning land, debt, and marriage mainly as crimes. However, the level of fault did often involve a minor punishment. In other words, civil matters were not isolated from the issue of motive, and thus were not automatically exempt from punishment (see Chapter 9).

Although the Code covered matters that generally, in the sense of their individual nature, corresponded to the concept of civil, some details were missing in the Code. We have seen that the details of land transactions, the particular obligations of debtors and guarantors, the content of the marriage agreement, and so on, were subject to local variations. As some scholars have compellingly pointed out, the contract played a key role in people's social and economic life.[73] In practice, people's contractual activity can be seen in almost all aspects of everyday life. Apart from the part played by local legislation in filling gaps in the Code, custom also had an important role, as will be discussed in Chapter 9.

[73] Zelin 2004.

6

Cases and Judicial Decisions Concerning Land

The Qing dynasty strongly encouraged the development of agriculture and an increase in the population. As a result, both the amount of cultivable land and the population increased dramatically. The population was around 300 million by the end of the Qianlong era (1736–95) and had reached 400 million in 1834 (Daoguang 14). The quantity of cultivable land was 5.4 million *qing*[1] in 1673 (Kangxi 12), and the amount of taxable land reached over 7.91 million *qing* in 1812 (Jiaqing 17).[2] Although some new techniques were introduced and high-productivity plants such as sweet potato and corn were promoted and spread in Qing agriculture, the increased population placed pressure on the limited sources of utilizable land. In general, peasants' individual landholdings became smaller, and disputes concerning land made up a large part of civil cases.

This chapter discusses the magistrate's performance in resolving disputes over land matters. Through detailed reference to several typical kinds of land case, I reveal some important aspects of the magistrate's judgment regarding land disputes. Other matters that are generally significant, such as petitions of false accusation, claims of minor physical injury, and the question of whether the magistrate imposed any punishment during the trial process will be left to Chapter 9. The material covered by the land cases is one of the best illustrations of the interrelation of individuals in their daily life. Such cases provide us with an excellent platform for understanding the Qing magistrates' practice in the solution of so-called civil disputes.

6.1 Sources for this chapter

The main cases, those from the Baodi and Ba county records and magistrate Shen's case book, were introduced in Chapter 1, and Table 3.1 showed the

1 1 *qing* = 100 *mu*
2 See Du Jiaji 1997.

Table 6.1. The result of land cases in the Baodi records

Result	No. of cases	Form of resolution		
		Court decision	Hearing delivered	Closed by application
Petition rejected	9			
Result unknown	37			
Resolved	127	45	10	55
Total	173			

pattern of solution in Baodi cases. For the purpose of the discussion of this chapter, I provide further details, including the number of Baodi cases whose result is unknown (see Table 6.1).

Table 6.1 provides some very rough statistics in terms of the end result, but it allows me to indicate the groups of cases upon which this chapter draws. By 'result unknown', I refer to those cases that did not have a known solution, for whatever reason. According to Philip Huang, the main reason, apart from such obvious circumstances as the loss of documents or mistakes by the archivist, was that 'few plaintiffs, once satisfied, in fact took the trouble to advise the court and get the case closed'.[3] However, this is very unlikely to be true. Sub-statute 336-5 in the Code specifically deals with situations in which one or both parties were absent from the investigation and hearing. According to this sub-statute, the case had then to be cancelled if it had been pending for two months. The application of this law can be seen in the Baodi records. Shiga Shūzō noted that there were cases finally cancelled after being pending for two months, although he failed to find the relevant rule in the Code.[4] Furthermore, the magistrate often blamed the plaintiff for 'bringing a lawsuit and then withdrawing it very quickly' (*qimie ziyou*). Finally, if the case was not closed properly, there was always the possibility of a formal hearing. This might cause much more trouble to the petitioners than the submission of an application to close the case in advance. Because there was no clear outcome, cases with 'result unknown' will generally not be used in the following analysis.

When the magistrate made a decision in court, I classify the result as a 'court decision'. This group will be the main source of cases in this chapter. If a resolution was achieved by the parties outside the court and the case was closed because they had applied for a cancellation of the hearing and

[3] Huang 1996: 119.
[4] Shiga Shūzō 1992b: 522.

this was permitted by the magistrate, it is classified as 'closed by application'. Where the dispute was solved through a formal hearing, the result had the same status as that of cases closed by application. Some cases received one or more hearings from the magistrate, but ended with cancellation of a further hearing after the conclusion of some sort of agreement satisfactory to the magistrate. I therefore also consider these cases, because they were an integral part of the magistrate's jurisdiction. Some cases were ended at the court hearing but the magistrate did not make a particular decision, because the dispute had already been resolved by the parties. I classify these results as 'hearing delivered'.

The real purpose of a dispute was often obscured by the emotional and exaggerated style of the plaint. The category to which a case belonged is not always clear until one has gone through the whole record. Even then one might not find it easy to classify the case because it involved a variety of issues, on all of which the magistrate made a decision. Consequently, the statistics used in this study should be understood as giving a general picture, not as providing answers to particular questions, since that might distort the truth from the very beginning.[5] The discussion in the rest of the book will try to follow as exactly as possible the way in which the magistrate dealt with land, debt, and marriage cases. Once his method has been identified and analysed, we may hope to decode the nature of the magistrate's role in terms of the performance of his judicial tasks.

Magistrate Shen's cases were generally more complicated than those in the Baodi records, especially the land cases. The reason is that the counties he governed were in the southern area, where the power of the clans was much stronger and their property more extensive than in the north. Disputes over land matters made up the majority of his collection — 75 cases out of a total of 135.

In chapter 5, I discussed the ownership of land by individuals in the Qing. The factors indicating ownership included the right of use, the right to collect fruits, and the right of sale. Although cases concerning land broadly speaking were connected more or less with ownership of land, the records show that several further distinctions among different types can be made,

[5] According to Baodi records, cases involving physical injury were usually in the charge of the Office of Punishment (*xingfang*), whether or not land or debt was the essential issue. Land cases were in the charge of the Office of Revenue (*hufang*), and debt cases were in the charge of the Salt Office (*yanfang*). Marriage cases were in the charge of the Office of Rites. If the case involved the measurement of land, as in the Tian Youlai case, it was the Office of Work (*gongfang*) that took charge.

namely cases concerning ownership, conditional sale (*dian*) and redemption, tenancy, and boundaries. These types are based mainly on the Baodi records. Because economic and social conditions varied in the different parts of China, some margin should be allowed for the typicality of the cases in terms of the whole country. Even so, the causes of the disputes and the judicial decisions delivered by the magistrate are representative of the general pattern of land disputes and the performance of the magistrate court as a whole.

6.2 Cases concerning ownership

I mentioned in Chapter 5 that, according to some studies on Ming civil cases, it was not uncommon in the Ming (1368–1644) for an owner of land fraudulently both to sell his land and to sell it conditionally to different people.[6] The right to the land in such cases was abused by the owner owing to an ambiguity in the law. Although the Ming law strictly forbade this activity, at that time sale and conditional sale were not clearly distinguished, so it was easier for the owner to abuse his right. The Qing kept the same provision as the Ming on the prohibition of the dual sale and conditional sale of land. It further developed a number of its own provisions both in the Code and in the Regulations of the Boards. I noted this aspect in Chapter 5 and pointed out that it was the Qing legislation that effectively intervened and shaped customs in this area. This would be a major reason for the available case records from Baodi, Ba, and Dan-xin providing little evidence of such cases.

Another significant feature in the Qing concerns land transactions. The procedures for a particular transaction — such as the amount and quality of the land, the time and place for exchanging payment and the land contract, guarantees and witnesses, and other factors — were well developed, so disputes over such transactions were also very rare.[7] Understandably, disputes over land ownership were caused more often by other reasons. We shall see that the magistrate handled such trials in a consistent and regular way.

Case 1

The plaintiff's father sold the land to Xiao A and Xiao B. After his father died, the plaintiff brought a petition accusing A and B of illegally occupying his land with a faked land contract. Having ascertained the truth, the magistrate

[6] Tong Guangzheng 1998; Bian Li 2000.

[7] See also Huang 1996: 39–40.

punished the plaintiff for false accusation. The plaintiff made a bond guaranteeing obedience in which he said that he would never cause trouble again. (Baodi, 100: 191–3)

Case 2

When a land transaction was blocked, the intending buyer brought the case to the magistrate, citing the owner, née Gu, as the defendant. The magistrate made the following decision: 'The witnesses Wang and Zhang have been summoned to the bench and have stated that the land in question had been allocated under the name of Gu Zhangshi [née Gu] when the family property was divided. Hence, the land belongs to née Gu[8] and the sale of the land is allowed (*zhunqi chumai*). The selling price was presented to the court before I heard the case. Née Gu should have the money and the buyer should now pay the sale tax. All should make a bond of confirmation. The case will then be closed.' [A tick marked the end of the decision] (Baodi, 106: 136–49)

The key issue in the above two cases was to make clear who was the owner (*zhu*) of the land in order to follow the principles in the Code of 'return the land to the owner (*huanzhu*)'(Article 93) and 'rule and order the owner to take care of his land (*duanling guanye*)' (Sub-statutes 95-1 and 93-6). Obviously, questioning the parties and witnesses and examining the written evidence such as the stamped land contract (*hongqi*),[9] the family division contract (*fendan*), and the land tax payment certificate (*chuanpiao*) were fundamental procedures required by the Code (Sub-statutes 93-6 and 95-1).

In Case 2, the procedure for resolving the case was especially significant. To make sure of the facts, every point arising from the interrogation was considered and resolved with careful rationalization and consistent hearings. Within nine days, the magistrate had heard the case three times. Each subsequent hearing was for the questioning of new witnesses. Since the uncle stated that the land belonged to him and that the land contract (*qizhi*)[10]

[8] When a father died, the Qing law basically gave the son(s) the right to inherit the family property rather than the wife (see Articles 78 and 88 and the sub-statutes). However, the division would not be arranged until the son(s) were living separately (Article 87). Usually the widowed mother could administer the family property as she wished. Here the magistrate named only the woman Gu as the owner of the land, because her son was still living with her.

[9] If it is clear that the tax had been paid and the contract stamped by the local government, which the phrase '*hongqi*' reveals, the translation for such a contract is 'stamped land contract'. Sometimes the parties used '*qi*' (contract) or '*qizhi*' (contract paper). In these cases, whether it was stamped or not remains unclear. I shall translate these phrases as 'land contract'. However, 'land contract' could also actually refer to the stamped contract.

[10] I have translated the term as closely to the original text as possible.

submitted by née Gu to the court had been stolen by his own son, the magistrate summoned the key witnesses, i.e. the middlemen who witnessed the family division. Two middlemen gave positive evidence that the land had been allocated to née Gu and her son. In these circumstances, the uncle changed his statement concerning possession of the land in the final hearing by saying that the land belonged to the clan rather than to him, but he still insisted that the contract was stolen by his son. In this case, the written evidence née Gu submitted not only included the documentary evidence consisting of two stamped land contracts (*hongqi*) for the proof of the land ownership, but also the 'family division contract (*fendan*)', to prove the source of her ownership. One point worthy of clarification is that the family division agreement was defined here as evidence. The family division contract was not usually necessary in cases concerning ownership. The reason for its appearance in this case was only because it was alleged that the land contract had been obtained illegally. That was why the magistrate summoned more witnesses. The fact that a family division agreement was enforced like other contracts was because the agreement (or the contract) was valid in terms of the law. It was not the case that the magistrate based his decision on custom instead of law, as Allee has argued.[11] The magistrate's intention of securing consistency between every aspect of the case, including the written evidence, the parties' statements, and the statements of the witnesses, is very clear. All those efforts were to decide whether or not née Gu was the owner (*yezhu*). If she was, then she was entitled to manage her land, including selling it. The important parts of this decision, such as the return of the sale price to née Gu and the order to the buyer to pay the sale tax, were all logical consequences of the decision. It is clear that the magistrate's ruling in favour of née Gu in Case 2, and of the defendant in Case 1, was the result of applying the law according to the evidence. As for the allegation of theft, the magistrate orally ordered the uncle to find and send his son to the court for further consideration (this was not stated in the written decision), but before the question of theft was investigated the case was closed.

Case 3

An uncle brought a complaint in which he said that he had been bitten by his nephew when he went to his nephew's home to ask for the return of the sickle that he had lent to his nephew. The magistrate commented on the uncle's complaint: '[I] order the *xiangbao* [local headman] to investigate the truth then submit a report and I will take action (*chaming queshi bingjiu*).'

[11] Allee 1994b: 134–8.

More than twenty days later a report came, in which the *xiangbao* said: 'The two parties were members of the same clan. There was only a quarrel but not fighting between them. The dispute actually resulted from the sale of a piece of land. Since the land was originally registered under their (the uncle and the nephew) common ancestor's name, they did not formally change the registered owner's name to the new buyer's and transferred the land tax to the new owner (*gengming guoge*). We have gathered the parties together to have the registered name changed. The new owner paid the sale tax and received a tax paid certificate. The nephew did *koutou* to his uncle; they are on good terms again.' The magistrate was satisfied with the result and felt no need to take action himself and so commented on the report: 'The result is known. The closure of the case is permitted.' (Baodi, 1842/DG22, 97: 130–2)

Although the case was not brought to claim ownership of the land, it illustrates a key aspect of ownership, that is, the requirement for a legal transaction when ownership of land changed. I discussed the change in the registered name in Chapter 5. This case demonstrates its significance. The two parties finally amicably changed the name in which the land was registered to that of the new buyer. The issue of the 'name' of the land was an especially decisive matter for owners who belonged to the same clan. The serious way in which the common people treated the 'name' of ownership of the land is apparent. The Qing actively established and kept records that could identify the owner of the land. The name in which the land was registered recorded the ownership of private land. In some cases, such as the next one, the records provided the key evidence for deciding who was the owner of particular land.

Case 4

The Huang clan and the Xiong clan were historically involved in a suit regarding the Huang clan's two hills (A and B). With the supporting evidence of the fish-scale book, a decision was made in favour of the Huang clan, that is, the hills belonged to them. The Huang clan was even supplied with an officially stamped record of the decision (*yinyan*) as approved. The Xiong clan accused the Huang clan of illegally occupying their hills (C and D) on which they intended to put graves. Magistrate Shen investigated the facts and heard the case. He ascertained that hill C according to the Xiong clan was actually the Huang clan's hill A, and hill D was actually the Huang clan's hill B. The Xiong clan had put graves, some with and some without tombstones, on both hill C and hill D (or A and B). To support their claim to ownership, the Huang clan had the fish-scale books, in which the hills were separately numbered 8767 and 8768. The Xiong clan, as *junji* (registered as a military family), provided the military registration book, which recorded only half a *mu* of land, without marking the four boundaries. The military registration book was made after their first lawsuit. Apart from the military registration book, the Xiong clan had no further evidence such as a land contract (*qi*) or tax certificate (*chuanpiao*). Hence, the two hills were undoubtedly the Huang clan's property that had been handed down by their ancestors. Other persons should, of course, not interfere with this. But how was the fact to be explained that the Xiong clan's graves were in the hills if they belonged to the Huang clan? 'According to my investigation,' magistrate Shen said, 'the two clans had good relations by marriage for generations. That is why the Huang clan allowed those graves to be put in their land. The permission was given purely out of friendship. Thus it is wrong for the Huang clan to deny that those graves belonged to the Xiong clan. Their statement about these graves is obviously wrong, since two tombstones with the surname Xiong are still there. As to the Xiong clan, they should not take Huang's two hills as their property simply because they had graves established on the hills.' Finally the magistrate ended with the words: 'In consideration of the circumstances of the case I decide (*zhuoqing dingduan*) to whom the two hills belong. Since the graves were indeed the Xiong clan's, I order the clan to heap up the graves and enclose them with a wall and worship forever, no further graves being allowed. The Xiong clan must not take advantage of the graves to plot the occupation of the hills. The Huang clan may administer the land outside the grave walls as they wish and should not damage the graves.' (Shen Yanqing: 450–4)

Cases 1–4 paint a clear picture of the performance of the magistrate's court in dealing with disputes concerning ownership of the right to land. The essence of the judicial process was to locate the owner of the land (*zhu* or *yezhu*) in question. For any situation the magistrate would first establish that the land was not government land.[12] To decide the owner of land, the magistrate's goal was to follow the law to give legal protection to the ownership of private land and enable the owner to administer or sell his land if he wished. With respect to the key issue in the cases, that of deciding which party was the owner, the magistrate did not follow his personal preference, but, on the contrary, established the facts based on the evidence required by the law, namely the land contract, the family division contract, the registration book, the fish-scale book, and so on. If all these proofs were still not sufficient to clarify the facts, the magistrate was authorized to examine the land on the spot and act on what he found out. In the sense that the magistrate was fundamentally following the law in making decisions, the litigation took a logical and predictable direction. That is, the decisions would

[12] In one case, the land in question was government land. The magistrate simply cancelled the land contract, commenting: 'it is government land. It is illegal [to make a contract for it]. The contract is to be cancelled' (Baodi, 101: 15).

be that the owner (*zhu*) had the right either to administer (*guanye*) or to sell (*mai*) the land.

One could say that Case 4 is a different example. The magistrate did not completely support the Huang clan in their claim to the two hills, even though the evidence revealed their unchallengeable ownership of the hills. To rule in favour of the Xiong clan on the existing graves, the magistrate particularly invoked the phrase '*zhunqing dingduan*' (to decide in the light of the *qing*) to justify his ruling. To supplement the discussion of *qing* in Chapter 3, I now analyse *qing* in the context of Case 4 (see more in Chapter 9). In this case, the term *qing* clearly referred to two overlapping meanings. It pointed to both the fact of the existence of the graves and the 'human feeling' explaining their presence. The friendship of the two clans was the reason for the establishment of the graves and, thus, a part of the facts of the case. In this sense, *qing* here referred to the particular facts of the case, that is, the situation of the Xiong clan's graves. The reason that there was a difficulty in deciding their fate was precisely because the magistrate clearly intended to protect the Huang clan's ownership as required by the Code. The graves of the Xiong clan had been lying in Huang's hills for many years, but the two clans were no longer on good terms. The reasoning of the magistrate is clear: although there was no question as to the ownership of the hills, it was not only wrong but also highly impractical to ignore the existence of the graves and to order the Xiong clan to remove them to another place. On this point the magistrate explained the friendly relationship between the parties established by marriage and pointed out that the Huang clan had actually allowed the graves as a symbol of their friendship. This implied that the owner would allow the graves to stay because, once a grave was dug, it was likely to remain there permanently. In these particular circumstances, the magistrate ruled that the graves should stay. If we understand *qing* here as referring to the particular facts, the magistrate's ruling, being based on these particular facts, was a supplementary part of the decision and posed little challenge to the Huang clan's ownership.

Case 5

In 1845 (Daoguang 25), members of the Wu and Li families decided to build a dyke against flooding. To the east of the proposed dyke was a parcel of land for the worship of ancestors belonging to Chunluan, which was needed as part of the wider base of the dyke, so that the dyke might have its full effect. However, Chunluan did not agree to sell his land. Out of disappointment, two persons from the Wu and Li families built a wall across a pool to block the flow of water to Chunluan's land, preventing its cultivation. The dispute was brought to Magistrate Shen. He ruled: 'For Chunluan, he is following *li*

> but ignoring *qing* if he considers only his land but not the public dyke; for the other people, they are following *qing* but ignoring *li* if they consider only the public dyke at the expense of Chunluan's land.[13] I order that Chunluan give the land to the public at a reasonable price for the building of the dyke. As for the pump point [the place where the pump was situated], the previously established practice should be respected by all when they cultivate and water the land. The two [defendants] who had built the wall to block Chunluan's water flow should be punished for causing trouble. Thus both *qing* and *li* are followed.' (Shen Yanqing, 656–9)

This case seems to have been brought to magistrate Shen by Chunluan when he was unable to use the pool to water his land. Shen employed a comparative analysis of *qing* and *li* in explaining and giving his decision. Shiga has pointed out that Shen was using *qing* to mitigate the strictness of *li*.[14] Although this is correct, more still needs to be said on this.

In this case Chunluan refused to sell his land. Shen commented that this was in accordance with *li*. I have pointed out (see Chapter 3, and more in Chapter 9) that the term *li* and law are sometimes interchangeable. This was the case here, because Qing law gives the owner the right to sell or not sell his land. In magistrate Shen's usage, *li* indicated Chunluan's legal position, that is, he had the legal right to keep his property.

What did the magistrate mean by '*qing*'? The people planning to buy Chunluan's land were a small community who wanted to build a dyke against flooding.[15] Chunluan's land was right where the base of the proposed dyke needed to be built. The plan could not be implemented without this piece of land. The magistrate commented that the small community had *qing* in respect of the purchase of Chunluan's land, so Chunluan did not have *qing* for refusing to sell it. Obviously, *qing* here did not refer exactly to a common meaning of *qing*, namely 'human feelings'. It had a wider implication, encompassing both the public benefit and the individual's obligation to his community. In essence, this case does not show that the individual's right to his land might be in danger. Rather, it reveals the conflict between the individual's right and the claim of public benefit. In this situation, the magistrate did not rule in favour of Chunluan because Chunluan's land would also have been in danger if the building of the dyke turned out to be a failure.

[13] I explore Shen's use of *li* and *qing* below.

[14] Shiga Shūzō 1998a: 38.

[15] Throughout the history of traditional China, effective measures against flooding were one of the major challenges for the government. There was a special institution, the River Circuit (*hedao*), for this purpose in the Qing.

The facts of this case may be said to illustrate a gap in the Code. Nevertheless, the magistrate's decision should not be regarded as contrary to the law. Rather it was a special decision for a 'hard case'. If the strict application of a particular principle might result in injustice, the magistrate was able to exercise 'discretion'. This very significant feature will be discussed in Chapter 9.

6.3 Cases concerning the *dian* contract

Dian is usually translated as 'conditional sale'. I made clear in Chapter 5 that this was a unique land-use practice among individuals in traditional China. Under the *dian* contract, the *dian* holder had the right to use someone else's land and to harvest fruits there after paying a price and taking possession of the land. The *dian* maker gave his land to 'another, taking a proportionate sum of money, fixing a period of years, and redeeming'.[16] Another similar practice in traditional China was *dang*. It had the same characteristics as *dian* but, in addition, the *dang* holder had to pay rent for the land to the *dang* maker. Thus, *dian* and *dang* were not just different terms for the same practice, as Philip Huang believed.[17] Under the terms of a *dian* or a *dang* contract, the *dian* or *dang* holder had the right to cultivate the land himself, to rent it out (including to the original owner), or to become a *dian* maker himself by conditionally selling the land to a third person.[18] As I have pointed out, this last practice resulted in very frequent lawsuits by the owner of the land, according to some studies of civil cases in the Ming.[19] This was not the case in the Qing, at least in Baodi county. The main reason was the introduction of several new regulations during the Qianlong period, especially a sub-statute of 1753 (Qianlong 18), which required people to write 'redeem' or 'never redeem' on the contract (see Chapter 5). Before that time, there was no clear difference in form between the sale and the *conditional sale* of land in terms of the content of the contract and paying taxes (see Chapter 5). In cases from Baodi county, the relevant contracts could often tell the magistrate whether the land was redeemable or not. I found both a *dian* contract (Baodi, 95: 107) and a sale contract (Baodi, 95: 98) in the Baodi records. The *dian* contract clearly provided that the land had to

[16] McAleavy 1958: 404.
[17] Huang 1996: 82.
[18] Yang Guozhen 1988: 41–2.
[19] Tong Guangzheng 1998; Bian Li 2000.

be redeemed after five years. This contract was left in the records because the case was not resolved. If it had been resolved, the contract would have been returned to the relevant party. That was why so few contracts of any kind remained in the records. The sale contract was left in the records because it was an illegal contract — the land in question was government land and so should not have been an object of sale or conditional sale. The content and form of the contract demonstrate its difference from the *dian* contract. The term 'never redeem' (*yongbu huishu*) was clearly put in.

Case 6

Wu accused Wang of redeeming his land without paying the amount of money necessary for redemption, and that, furthermore, he had taken away his chairs and a door. In his counter-plaint, Wang said Wu actually owed him a couple of years' land rent (it seems that this case was actually one of *dang* in which the *dang* holder paid rent to the *dang* maker). The magistrate heard the case. Witnesses gave evidence about the *dian* relation between the two parties. Wang had made a *dian* (*dang*) of his 20 *mu* land to Wu at the price of 76 *diao* plus 3 *diao* as rent every year of the term covered by the contract. The magistrate cross-examined them and found out that they actually owed money to each other. Wang owed Wu some wine costs and Wu owed Wang some land rent. After setting off their debts, Wu still owed Wang 8 *diao*. The magistrate ordered Wang to give Wu 60 *diao* to redeem his land. This price was 16 *diao* less than the original *dian* price of 76 *diao*. The debt of 8 *diao* owed by Wu to Wang was deducted from the redemption price. As for the remaining 8 *diao*, Wu kindly gave up (*yirang*) his right, so Wang actually was able to reclaim his land at the price of 68 *diao*. Meanwhile, Wang was ordered to return all the chairs and the door to Wu. To secure the execution of the decision, the magistrate ordered both sides to present a guarantor who separately guaranteed that Wu would return the land to Wang on receiving the money, and that Wang would have the 60 *diao* paid to Wu. One month after the trial, 60 *diao*, which was actually borrowed, was submitted to the magistrate by Wang's son. The magistrate at once informed Wu to come to the court and receive the money. Then, on the following day, a written statement confirming the receipt of 60 *diao* was made by Wu. The case was thus finally resolved. (Baodi, 97: 60–76)

This case, and Case 9 in Chapter 3, reveal two key principles of the law concerning the *dian* contract. First, when the term of the *dian* was over, the money had to be paid in full by the *dian* maker and, on receipt of the money, the *dian* holder had to return the *dian* contract and the land to the *dian* maker (the landowner). Second, redemption was allowed only when the term of the contract had expired (this is why Case 9 in Chapter 3 was simply decided in favour of the defendant). Since Case 6 above involved a matter of debt, before applying the rule permitting redemption the magistrate cleared the debts of both parties and ruled that Wang should redeem his land at the price of 60 *diao*. In both cases, the magistrates used language exactly echoing that of the Code — for example, '*beijia qushu*' (to redeem land with ready money).

I shall discuss the part of the decision in Case 6 involving '*yirang*' (to give up part of a debt to do the right thing) further in Chapter 7. The two parties had actually made a *dang* contract in which the *dang* holder had to pay the landowner rent every year of 3 *diao*. He did not pay the money for a period of time, thus breaking the contract in terms of the *dian* (*dang*) relationship. But he justified his action on the ground that the landowner owed him money and had failed to pay it back. From the landowner's statement of payment (*jiaozhuang*), it is clear that the 60 *diao* that he was later made to pay by the magistrate was actually borrowed for the purpose of the decision. So the landowner's difficulty in paying back the whole amount of the money, 68 *diao*, was obvious and it would have been impossible for the magistrate not to notice this. That was probably the reason for introducing *yirang* to exempt a relatively small proportion of the whole price from repayment. As part of his decision the magistrate asked both parties to find a guarantor to ensure that the landowner paid the money and the *dian* holder returned the land within one month. Exactly one month later, the landowner submitted the money to the magistrate and asked the magistrate to summon the *dian* holder to return his land deed and receive the money. The next day the *dian* holder was summoned and submitted a statement of receipt (*shouzhuang*) saying that he had received the money and had returned the land deed.

The magistrate's performance in handling this case was actually very impressive. He gave comprehensive consideration to all the issues involved, for example, the debt, the financial difficulty of one party, and, of course, the core issue of the redemption of the land and, most importantly, the law and its practicality. He exempted the landlord from some repayment owing to his financial difficulty, and he asked him to have a guarantor to ensure that the required payment would be successfully made. The concern of the magistrate was that the conflict between the two parties should be fully resolved, while keeping them possibly still in a working relationship.

When a case was decided in accordance with the law to allow the *dian* maker to reclaim the land, the exact timing of the redemption would take into consideration the farming situation of the land in question, as the next case reveals.

Case 7

Ma accused Qu of preventing him from cultivating his own land. But Qu said the land in question had already been made a *dian* to him by Ma's son. Ma could redeem it only one year later after the harvest. The magistrate interrogated both parties and their sons, the go-betweens of the *dian* contract, and ruled: 'According to the statements, Qu has sown the land on 12 March. No redemption is to be allowed now. The money for redemption should be paid after the autumn harvest when the land is empty, in accordance with the contract.' (Baodi, 103: 117–27)

This case allows us to see a problem concerning the time of redemption of the land. It is understandable that the time for redeeming the land in question should first have been decided on the basis of the term inserted in the contract. However, once the land had been cultivated, the practical time for returning the land, if there was a dispute, ought to be decided by taking the actual situation of the land into account. In this case, the magistrate ruled that the land would be better returned when it was empty.[20]

The redemption of land could sometimes be difficult because the *dian* holder — who had the right to use the land as he wished — had planted trees or built a house. The next case reveals such situation.

Case 8

Yang had received under *dian* a parcel of land from Zhang, on which Yang built a one-room house and planted some trees. When the land was due to be redeemed by Zhang, Yang cut down the trees he had planted and intended to pull down the house. Zhang stopped him pulling down the house by offering to buy it. The two parties disagreed over the price and began to fight. An examination of the wounds was made at the court, and the magistrate issued a summons for a trial. Twenty days later, before a formal trial had been heard, an application to close the case without trial came to the magistrate. The parties had resolved the problem themselves: Zhang finally reclaimed his land without buying the house, and the house was pulled down by Yang. The magistrate considered there was no need to take any action. (Baodi, 109: 22–8)

Although the *dian* holder had the right to use the land as he wished, when the time came to redeem the land it had to be returned as it was prior to the contract. So the trees and the house all needed to be removed from the land before its return (as was the grave in Case 9 in Chapter 3). On the other

[20] This case seems to have implied that, despite the father's unchallengeable status in trading the family property, the son also shared limited responsibility. Otherwise, there would have been a risk for the other party that the magistrate would cancel the *dian* contract.

hand, anything produced by the *dian* holder belonged to him and the landowner had no right to share it. However, sometimes difficulties arose, as, for example, in the following case:

> **Case 9**
> A nephew once accused his aunt (née Li) of forcibly seizing his land and a house. The magistrate ruled that the house in question should still be shared, that the land still be planted by the nephew, and that the harvest be shared. Only 200 *diao* was to be paid to the nephew, then the house and land might be redeemed by the aunt. Both parties confirmed the decision by bonds. The two parties petitioned the magistrate again only two months after their first lawsuit, because they had a dispute over sharing the coming year's harvest. The magistrate had an investigating summons sent to the *xiangbao* to order him to find out the truth and report back. The two parties were ordered to wait to be summoned for further interrogation. The report by the *xiangbao* stated: 'I obeyed the magistrate's order to help the runner to gather together the two parties and witnesses. They both regretted bringing the case. Now the house the nephew built on his aunt's land would still be shared as before, and the land would stay with the nephew to farm. The aunt was to share the harvest, and that year's share had been fairly divided between them. I thus report this agreement of both parties according to the facts.' The magistrate commented on the report: 'The report was read, the case can be closed.' (Baodi, 96: 100–6)

This case discloses a *dang* relation as well, for the landowner (the aunt) shared the harvest of the land with the cultivator (the nephew). But the relationship between aunt and nephew was more complicated. The *dian/dang* holder (the nephew) had built a house on the land and he shared it with the landowner (aunt). Since the owner herself lived in the house, in redeeming the land she would have had to pay money for both the land and the house. The house builder would then have had to move out when he received the money for the house built on the landowner's land. For some reason he did not move, as the decision indicated. They must have experienced a difficulty in carrying out the decision, so their relationship remained unchanged.

Case 9 highlights the complicated interrelations of the parties to lawsuits in the Qing. Cases such as this often involved multiple duties and rights, representing the complex network of relations between individuals in traditional China. It is not possible completely to understand magistrates' practice in resolving cases without taking account of these subtleties in relationships.

Sometimes a dispute was complicated in the sense that it involved more than one issue of legal significance.

Case 10

Jia Xungong wanted to redeem a piece of homestead from Jia Xunchen and injured Jia Liushi [née Liu] when redemption was refused by Jia Xunchen. But the case turned out to be much more complex than the primary quarrel suggested. This can be seen from the summary of the decision of the magistrate noted on the trial list: 'I interrogated the parties and witnesses and found out Li Fu's land,[21] left by his ancestors, should have been confiscated. Since too many years have passed and there are over thirty graves buried there, I will be lenient and no further prosecution will be made. Jia Xungong should continue to rent and farm. The sale contract of the house land was examined. It discloses an outright sale (*juemai*). Jia Xunchen is not allowed to redeem. Jia Xungong (the buyer) should pay the sale tax which should have been paid when the contract was made. Jia Liushi [née Liu] has recovered from her injury. Jia Xunchen is old and blind. The law allows no punishment to be imposed on him (*lide mianjiu*). Now all the people involved are to write a bond of confirmation and the case is closed.' [End marked with a tick] (Baodi, 96: 95–8)

This case is another good example of the magistrate's active role in dealing with disputes. He handled five legal issues: (1) the liability to confiscation of Li Fu's land — Li Fu was involved only because the parties mentioned him in their petition; (2) confirmation of the tenancy relationship between Li Fu and Jia Xungong; (3) determination of the sale of Jia Xunchen's house land as an outright sale — he had to pay the sale tax that he did not pay when the contract was made; (4) Jia Liushi's recovery from injury; (5) Jia Xunchen being old and blind and therefore exempt from punishment by law.

The above cases have revealed the most common type of issue dealt with by the magistrate in relation to the *dian* contract. The issues were simple, and to some extent the disputes may not appear to be very significant from our point of view. The decisions in Cases 6 and 9 in Chapter 3 were to permit redemption of the land subject to the payment of money; the decision in Case 7 above was for the land to be redeemed after the harvest according to the terms of the contract. Other decisions also demonstrate that what the magistrate had tried to establish through his investigation of the facts and interrogation of parties and witnesses was whether the *dian* contract was

[21] This case arose because Jia Xunchen wanted to redeem a piece of land that had been sold outright by Jia Xungong. Both parties had something to do with Li Fu's land: first Jia Xunchen farmed the land, then Jia Xungong farmed it, and Li Fu was involved as *cinei* ('person mentioned'; see Chapter 3). The magistrate noted in his decision that 'Li Fu's land, left by his ancestors, should have been confiscated'. This was because Li Fu's family had not registered the land for the assessment of land taxes. According to Article 90 (Fraudulently Concealing Fields and Their Produce from the Tax), the fields that were concealed should be forfeit to the government.

legal, and when and how the *dian* maker should redeem the land. The magistrate would quote phrases from the Code, such as 'prepare the money to redeem the land', in his decisions; and he would make specific decisions about how and when to permit redemption in accordance with the *dian* contracts. We turn now to a case of a different kind.

Case 11

During the time of the Jiaqing reign (1796–1820), the Chuan family sold the vacant land to the front and back of their memorial temple to the Zhang family. Thirty or forty years later (the case occurred about 1843 or Daoguang 23), Chuan Tinglan, a member of the Chuan family, suddenly came back from elsewhere asking for redemption of the land sold to Zhang on the grounds that he was planning to extend the memorial temple. So Zhang brought the case to the magistrate. The magistrate expressed doubt about Chuan's real reason for wanting to redeem the land. Nevertheless, since 'everyone may want to worship his ancestors', he allowed Chuan to redeem the parcel of the land in front of the temple for 7,200 *wen*, double the original sale price. Zhang was ordered to enter into a contract for this matter on the spot in the trial hall. The land to the rear of the temple was to remain the property of the Zhang family, since trees planted there by that family had given good protection to the temple and should not be cut. The two parties were ordered to make a joint contract for that matter on the spot as well. As for the Zhang family's other land to the left of the temple, it was bought by Zhang (from other people), was far from the temple, and should be under the Zhang family's full control with no disturbance by Chuan. Only one person among those who had sold the land to Zhang was still alive. Although it was wrong privately to sell clan-owned property, the survivor was old and lived alone. Thus, on the ground of mercy, the magistrate imposed on him only a light punishment. (Shen Yanqing: 525–7)

Although the land had been sold outright (*mai*), and not conditionally (*dian*), many years earlier, the magistrate still allowed redemption of part of the land to a member of the seller's family. From the magistrate's analysis, we may deduce the following reasons: (1) the land that had been sold was the clan's collective land, which meant that the plaintiff shared in the right of ownership, but did not know this when it was sold — this implied that he was entitled to assert a claim of ownership; (2) the land the plaintiff wanted to redeem was designated for the purpose of ancestral worship — compared with normal use of land by a new owner, this seems have had privileged status, as the Code conferred a more important status on land destined for sacrifice to the ancestors;[22] (3) the new landowner was still allowed to keep the

[22] The Code provided for more severe punishment for action that contravened the protection accorded to land reserved for the worship of ancestors (Sub-statute 93-1).

other land. On these grounds, the magistrate did not follow the provision of the Code that 'outright sold land should not be redeemed' (Article 95, Sub-statutes 95-3 and 95-7). He decided that the parcel of land was to be redeemed, but at twice the original sale price. This allowed some compensation to the other party.

The magistrate selected this case for his case book because he thought it was a good model for the handling of difficult cases. Indeed, it seems at first glance that the law was not applied, if 'law' is interpreted only in relation to specific sub-statutes (Sub-statutes 95-3 and 95-7) that provide that land sold outright should not be redeemed. However, the relevant circumstances of this case certainly involved more than that the land in question was sold outright. The point is that, since the land belonged to the whole family, the original sale, which was made without agreement by all members of the family, was legally null. If these circumstances are considered, it is not right to conclude that the magistrate did not apply the law. As the other 'hard case' showed, the magistrate enjoyed significant discretion in terms of deciding how a specific provision should be handled in the light of complicated circumstances (for the limitations on his discretionary power, see Chapter 9).

6.4 Cases concerning tenancies

A tenant was generally someone who rented and farmed land and paid rent to the landlord.[23] Tenants can be generally categorized according to whether or not the tenancy was granted with a time limit — unlimited tenants and ordinary tenants.[24] The most striking feature of an unlimited tenancy was that the tenant and his children had the right to farm the land with no time limit. As for other tenants, the characteristics varied.[25]

About 30 per cent of the population in the Qing period were self-employed farmers. Even though it is believed that this is the highest proportion ever reached in traditional China, most of the population were farming land owned by other people. Issues relating to the relationship between tenant and landlord have attracted much scholarly debate. Their changing contractual relations, the development of fixed rents and permanent tenancies, and the custom of land having two landlords, and so on, are

[23] Zelin divided landlords into six categories (1986: 508).
[24] Yang Guozhen 1988: 43.
[25] For the details, see Yang Guozhen 1988: 43–73.

very complicated issues.[26] There seems some evidence that the Qing legislators were reluctant to legislate formally for the practice of land having two landlords. Although some provincial regulations repeatedly prohibited the practice (see below), Baodi cases reveal no such case. This section will therefore focus on the key points as seen in the available cases and regulations. For example, what was the cause of a dispute between landlord and tenant and was the point of view of the law recognized in the disputes and the decisions? Although many studies show that the relationship between tenants and landlords became more tense owing to the large increase in the population, tenant cases of all kinds in Baodi records are rather rare. A noticeable feature in the Baodi magistrate's handling of tenancy cases was his reliance on what he called 'the law on eviction' (*duodian li*).

I pointed out in Chapter 1 that the term '*li*' referred usually to either the general principles of the Code (*mingli*), or the sub-statutes of the Code (*fuli*), or specific stipulations (*dingli*). They were all, of course, part of the law (see *Jizhu*: 18). What is not clear is which law the phrase 'law on eviction' was referring to. The only sub-statute in the Code that mentioned tenants was 312-3. This dealt with the punishments for gentry-landlords who bullied their tenants, and the punishments for tenants who failed to pay their rent. To find the 'law on eviction', we have to turn to regulations other than the Code, such as the Regulations of the Board of Revenue and the provincial regulations. The following quotations are from the Regulations of the Board of Revenue:

> When [*han* nationality] people rent land from *manzu* people, though the land may be transferred to another landlord, the original tenant should stay. The new landlord should not take back the land without a reason and should not increase the rent. But if the tenant owed rent to the landlord, the landlord is allowed to take back his land. (*Hubu zeli, juan* 10)

> In the tenancy relationship, if the landlord intends to use part of the land for graves, he is allowed to take it back. The rest of the land should remain with the original tenant to farm. If the landlord takes back his land for the above reason, but in the event he rents it to a new tenant instead of using it for graves, the matter should be solved according to *duodian li*. (Ibid.)

Although it is not clear which provision exactly created *duodian li*, the particular law seems to have been established by then and widely known. Its content may be roughly outlined as: (1) the tenant could stay unless he owed

[26] For the details of the various relationships between tenant and landlord, see Buoye 2000 and Zelin 1986.

rent to the landlord, and the tenant should not rent the land to any other person; (2) if the tenant owed no rent to him, the landlord should not take back the land and he should not increase the rent; (3) the landlord had very limited grounds on which to take the land back for his own purposes.[27]

Provincial regulations, for example the Regulations of Fujian Province, also contained rules on tenancy. The Fujian regulation on tenancy was made in 1764 (Qianlong 29). It required the officials of the province to communicate the principles governing tenancy by inscribing them on stone tablets (*leshi*) and posting proclamations. It did not accept the custom of land having two landlords, and ordered that disputes over such a practice should not be heard. As for tenancies, the essential rules were the same as those established by the Board of Revenue, that is, the landlord should not increase the rent or evict the tenant if he paid the rent without delay (*Fujian shengli*: 445–7). That these basic principles were followed by the magistrate can be seen from the following cases:

Case 12

Zhang Rong accused Jia of refusing to accept his rent and wanting to revoke the tenancy. The magistrate commented on his complaint: 'According to law, the tenant should not be changed if he owed no rent to the landlord (*rubu qianzu, li buzhun chedi*). According to your complaint, you not only did not owe any rent but also paid the deposit for holding a long-term tenancy. Why does the landlord still want to revoke your tenancy? It is not understandable. I will order the runner to investigate the truth, and decide after his report.' Then an investigating order (*piao*) was sent to the *xiangbao*, ordering him to investigate why the landlord had acted against the regulations of the tenancy by refusing to accept the rent. The defendant told a different story in his rebuttal. He accused Zhang of illegally making a *dian* (*sidian*) of part of the rented land to a third party. On this point, the two *xiangbao* reported differently. One report was in favour of the tenant, the other in favour of the landlord. But they both admitted that they could not arrange a compromise between the parties and that a formal trial by the magistrate was necessary. The magistrate had a summons sent to the two parties and the witnesses. During the hearing, Zhang did not admit that he had illegally made *dian* of part of the land to a third party. He had let this person pay the rent on his behalf and farm the land only during the time he was away. Two people confirmed his statement. Jia, the landlord, said: 'since Zhang did not sub-let the land to another person, I am willing to accept the rent on the 15th of the ninth month as before.' The case was closed with bonds of confirmation and a statement by the landlord acknowledging that he had received the rent. (Baodi, 100: 146–60)

[27] See also Buoye 2000: 121.

Case 13

A tenant, Bo, could not pay his rent to the Ding family. The magistrate ordered that Bo return the land to Ding. A new dispute arose when the Ding family sent a new tenant to cultivate the land. Bo's mother wounded herself in order to ensure acceptance of the case. The magistrate interrogated the Ding family's agent and Bo, then wrote on the trial list: 'Bo is given five days to move from Ding's house. The original runner will escort Bo after five days to the village to hand back the land. Bo's mother's wound was self-inflicted. Bo should submit a bond of agreement and obedience.' But the process of handing over the land was not fulfilled until two months later owing to Bo's mother's continuing interference. (Baodi, 102: 152–76)

Cases 12 and 13 clearly indicate the legal points and the reasons for the magistrate's decisions: the tenant should not sub-let the land to a third party (Case 12);[28] the landlord should not evict a tenant without a good reason (Case 12); and the tenancy relation was ended if the rent was not paid (Case 13). The legal reason for the landlord to take his land back was default on rent payments. In certain circumstances, for example where the tenant was the original cultivator of the rented land, the Regulations of the Board of Revenue provided that the landlord might evict the tenant only if the rent had not been paid for three years. If the tenant failed occasionally to pay the rent, the landlord had to bring a petition accusing him only of default on payment (*Hubu zeli, juan* 10).[29]

Case 14

In December 1850 (Daoguang 30), Liu accused Xu of intending to increase the rent. He was hit when he went to Xu to ask why. The two parties and a witness were summoned to the court, where the magistrate heard the case. Xu denied that he had intended to increase the rent and the magistrate agreed that there was no substance to the complaint. The case was closed after the two submitted bonds of confirmation. (Baodi, 100: 178–87)

Case 15

Zhu complained in his accusation that he had rented (*yindian*) two parcels of land originally planted by Duan for a deposit of 215 *diao*, Li and Wu being

[28] Some studies show that sub-letting often happened (Zelin 1986; Buoye 2000).

[29] It seems reasonable to suggest that it was difficult for a landlord to evict a tenant who had paid a rent deposit. Buoye 2000 provides us with some cases in which tenants resisted an attempted eviction. If we consider the rule about non-payment of rent for three years, the cases discussed by Buoye seem not to have infringed the rule allowing eviction on default on rent payments. So the tenant does not seem to have been 'without legal recourse' (2000: 115). This is especially interesting when Buoye points out that the rent deposit might be as much as three years' rent (2000: 108).

> the go-betweens. Now Duan, in concert with Sun and Tian (the owners of one parcel of land), first took back one parcel and then refused to accept the rent for the other parcel. The magistrate sent three runners to order the *xiangbao* to deal with the dispute impartially, and then to report back. In the report, the *xiangbao* said: 'Now Duan has returned his own parcel of land and the other parcel was also returned to Zhu Kun. The result is fair to both and they all agreed.' The magistrate commented: 'Since the dispute was settled, the case is closed. I still order the two parties to submit their bonds of confirmation for later checking.' (Baodi, 104: 1–5)[30]

The magistrate thus demonstrated the key points of the law relating to tenancy: the landlord should not increase the rent (Case 14), and the landlord should let the tenant stay if he had no reason to evict him (Case 15 and the Tian Youlai case in Chapters 2 and 3). However, the law did allow the landlord to take back his land for a good reason. Given how difficult it was for a landlord to evict a tenant, landlords might use this particular situation or even invent one, saying that they had experienced a financial difficulty, in order to renegotiate an increase in the rent with the tenant. Zelin has cited several cases in which widows took advantage of their husband's death to claim that they were suffering financial difficulties.[31] This is evidence that the law governing the tenancy of land was generally respected.

The four cases examined here, as well the Tian Youlai case, though not complex, reveal different aspects of the law of tenancy. In each, the magistrate's decision clearly followed the law (*duodian li*), either by way of a sentence such as 'according to the law, the land should not be taken back if the tenant owed no rent to the landlord' (*rubu qianzu, li buzhun chedi*) (Case 12), which is only slightly different from the text of the law ('*rubu qianzu, li buzhun duodian*'), or by way of the simple phrase '*duodian li*', or even just by the term '*li*'. The fact that the law was intended to protect the right of tenants can also be seen from the claims of petitioners. For example, in Case 15, the petitioner claimed that his rent was refused by the landlord; in Case 14, the petitioner accused the landlord of wanting more rent. These causes of conflict are clearly recognized by the law.

Both the law and the case files shed light on some common features of tenancy. The tenant had the right to farm the land for the time determined by the contract, subject to the payment of the rent; the landlord had the

[30] The magistrate did not hear the case and make the decision in the court, contrary to Professor Huang's interpretation (1996: 83). According to Zelin, 'suits in Baxian filed by tenants invariably focused on one feature, rent deposits' (1986: 522).

[31] Zelin 1986: 514.

right to collect the rent and take back the land if the rent was overdue. The three key points governing a tenancy were, first, the rent must be paid, second, the tenant should not sub-let the land, and, third, the landlord should not either increase the rent or take the land back without a good reason. It is not surprising that all tenancy disputes arose from a failure by either the landlord or the tenant in carrying out one of these obligations.

6.5 Cases over boundary disputes

It is not difficult to understand that disputes over boundaries of land occur very easily. Not only did the long cultivation of land often cause confusion over boundaries, but two parcels of land might be so close that their owners might easily cross the boundary when carrying on their work. In consequence, damage might be done; furthermore, people might take advantage of geographical confusion over some piece of land to challenge or claim the ownership of the land.[32] For most of such cases, examination of the land was often the most important step to be taken. Once measurements had been taken, the parties would readily reach agreement.

Case 16
One day, Shan and Chuan came to the court, each accusing the other of taking two ridges from his land. They quarrelled and fought, and both were injured. The magistrate ordered a runner to measure their lands. In his report the runner said: 'Shan should have 3 *mu* of land and now only has 2.7 *mu* according to my measuring. Chuan has now given Shan 0.3 *mu* of land back to make his land 3 *mu* again. However, Chuan's land, which is next to the river, is also less than he should have according to my measuring. That was why he destroyed Shan's grain. Now Shan has accepted compensation from Chuan for the damage.' Although the boundaries of their land were ascertained, the two parties were still brought to the court to be interrogated by the magistrate. They both wrote bonds of confirmation, and the case was then closed. (Baodi, 97: 133–43)

Case 17
Zhou accused Du of planting one strip (*long*) of his land and of wounding him with a pick when he asked him to explain. The magistrate had Zhou's wound examined, 'bestowing on him the medicine' (*ciyao*) for his recovery, then heard

[32] Buoye discusses boundary conflicts in some detail, drawing on the evidence from homicide cases (2000: 72–82).

> the case after Zhou had recovered from the injury. The magistrate first punished Du for injuring Zhou. Zhou stated in the court that he farmed 10 *mu* of land, but that now one strip (*long*) of his land was occupied by Du. Du said that he farmed 7 *mu* of land himself. Then, a runner was ordered by the magistrate to measure the land and report back. He reported back on the following day, stating that he had measured the lands, in the company of the two parties, according to their land documents, which clearly recorded the four boundaries. 'Zhou possessed 10 *mu,* as he said, but actually occupied 9.6 *mu*, that is, 0.4 *mu* less than he should have according to my measuring. Du possessed 7 *mu* as he said, but actually occupied 6.96 *mu*, that is, 0.04 *mu* less than he should have. Through the mediation of their relatives, Du has given 0.4 *mu* land to Zhou to make his land up to 10 *mu* again. As for the shortfall of Du's land, Du would claim it back from his other neighbour, Li, before the land was sown next year.' The magistrate gave his order to the runner on the report: 'To bring the two parties to the court for my interrogation, then write the bonds of confirmation to close the case.' (Baodi, 103: 152–66)

Whether the parties were brought to the court in Case 17 remains unknown. However, the caution shown by the magistrate in these two cases is much more significant. This was perhaps because the decision or the solution would depend almost entirely on the runner's personally conducted examination, and this examination might favour one party or the other. This especially reminds us of the bad reputation of runners. The magistrate clearly wanted to take the matter into his own hands for the final hearing. His attention and desire to control the result of the case are very obvious, even though cases like this did not give him much scope. Neither the parties nor the magistrate could do much when confronted with the result of the examination of the land. In this sense, the result of the measurement had determined the solution of the case. From the process of such cases, we know that, since established practice had so much to do with the legal protection of the land, the magistrate no doubt often ruled that the parties stick to their established practice in cultivating their land. This can clearly be seen from the next case:

> **Case 18**
>
> One day in 1869 (Tongzhi 8), Wang and Li made simultaneous mutual accusations. Each complained that the other had planted one strip of his land and hurt him. Eighteen days later the magistrate heard the case. The truth was that Li's seedlings could not grow because they had been covered with soil by Wang. Their lands were extremely close to each other. That was why they scratched each other with nails. The magistrate punished Wang with slapping of the face since he should not have brought the accusation after he had damaged Li's land. (Baodi, 103: 87–96)

A similar case was caused by Zhu's damaging his neighbour's cotton plants. The magistrate simply ordered that the offender should never cross his neighbour's land and cause damage. But punishment was not imposed, since the parties were relatives of the same clan (Baodi, 104: 101).

6.6 Cases over water rights

Shared rights to water or passage through the fields also caused lawsuits, especially in the south where small ponds and springs frequently appeared.

Case 19

Jiang had a pond for watering his surrounding land. Above Jiang's pond there was 0.7 *mu* of land belonging to Liu on which was a spring to water this land. Below Jiang's land next to the pond Liu also had several *mu* of land rented by Menzu, watered from a pond called Chenjia. Since the Chenjia pond was lower than Menzu's land, to water with a bailing bucket was hard work. In June 1847 (Daoguang 27), Menzu dug a channel on Jiang's land next to Jiang's pond so he could bring water from the pond to his land through Jiang's land. After Menzu had been stopped by Jiang, Liu, the landlord, brought a case to the magistrate stating that the water Menzu brought to his land through Jiang's land was actually his spring water from his 0.7 *mu* of land. The magistrate analysed the facts: not only was the spring too small to water any more than his own land, but also the two parcels of land owned by Liu were a long distance from each other. 'How could such a meagre spring water land one hundred paces away? Who will believe that this spring has unlimited water? As Menzu can water his land from the Chenjia pond, all should water their land according to established practice.' The person who was too lazy to water his land should have been punished. But since they had revealed the whole truth, and assured him that they would not again offend, the punishment was not imposed. (Shen Yanqing: 612–13)

There was a regulation concerning the offence of watering one's land from another's pond. A person who used water from someone else's pond was to be punished according to the principle of Article 93 (The Theft and Sale of Fields and Houses), in which the severity of the punishment depended upon the amount of land watered.[33] Clearly, Menzu should not have used someone else's pond to water the land he farmed. But he was not punished because he had confessed his offence and showed real regret for what he had done, matters that were to be considered when making a decision.

[33] *Zhonghua lüling jicheng*: 161.

Case 20

Two villages, Sun and Cheng, were located on the same river. They both watered their lands from the river. Sun village was in the upper reaches of the river. It had a Bridge X and three earth weirs A, B, C across the river to collect water from the streams. Next to weir C were five stone weirs that belonged to Cheng village. The stone weirs collected water from the streams once Sun village's weirs A, B, and C had become full of water. In 1820 (Jiaqing 25), Sun village made the walls of their weirs higher and thus stopped the flow of the stream. Cheng village fought with Sun village and brought the case to the magistrate. The magistrate ruled in favour of Cheng village by ordering that Sun village rebuild the weirs with the insertion of stones so that each contained a gap to allow a flow of water. The height of the gap was to be the same as the depth of the river under Bridge X. Sun village obeyed the decision to rebuild weirs A and C with stones and put in the gaps in accordance with the decision. In 1845, Sun village plugged the gap of weir A with earth, thus they faced a lawsuit again. Magistrate Peng decided the case by ordering them to obey the previous decision. Then Sun village tried again to block the water in weir A, so Cheng village removed stones from weir C and accused Sun village of evilly blocking the gap and violating the previous decision of the magistrate. Then the magistrate wrote: 'I checked the two decisions by the former magistrates and conducted the interrogation, the whole truth being revealed as I showed above. I believe agriculture and irrigation are most important for government. To make use of something equally and take advantage of it can benefit all. If someone wants to monopolize the benefit, the advantage the thing can give to us cannot be achieved. . . . The most important rule is the right of all to equal use of water. Now Sun village was in a higher area than Cheng village, so Sun village had already benefited a lot from the river. They have now repeatedly disobeyed the judgments and even wanted to dam the river. The lower reaches contain almost no water. It was wrong for Sun village to look after themselves alone. However, that Cheng Jinyun removed the gap stone in retaliation for what Sun had done to weir A was what I call one wrong in reply to the other wrong. Both parties are wrong for losing the sense of equality. I should have punished them both, but since they are neighbouring villages I leniently do not punish them. Instead, I decide that both parties should pay 500 *wen* to the witness to remove the stone in weir A and restore the stone in weir C. Then report to me after this has been done.' (Shen Yanqing: 588–91)

This case was brought to court three times, and the final decision was no different from the previous two, which had applied the rule that public water resources should be shared. This rule can be seen from the regulation mentioned above. The magistrate emphasized this rule. To implement the decision, he ordered both parties to pay a sum of money and required them to report back when the work he had ordered had been done.

6.7 Summary

The types of land case presented in this chapter represent some typical patterns in the Qing in terms of the legal points they dealt with. Land disputes mainly concerned claims to the ownership of a plot of land, graves, or hills, or the right to water. They might also concern claims to redeem a *dian* contract or arise from a tenancy. As the decisions collected by magistrate Shen revealed, the details of the case could vary significantly between areas. Many of the cases from Baodi county were rather trivial and uncomplicated. The land in question was usually not large, and this was especially true in the cases concerning boundaries.

The law in terms of both the principle and the letter was applied clearly by the magistrate in his rulings. In some, though not all, decisions, particular phrases — such as '*beijia qushu*' (to redeem the land with ready money) — or legal principles — such as '*duodian li*' (law on eviction) — were quoted, showing the strong connection between the law and the magistrate's decision. As a result, as far as the translated cases reveal, land ownership was upheld, land boundaries were maintained, the *dian* and tenant contracts were supported, and so on. Cases that took specific circumstances into account were very rare; they usually involved complex relationships and obligations of the two parties.

Investigations were usually conducted thoroughly by the runners and the *xiangbao*. Evidence such as the contract, records of land registration, witness statements, and the runners' examination played an important role in ascertaining the facts. As the result of the application of the law, the legal contracts were often either enforced or else cancelled by the magistrate. The hearing was usually arranged within a reasonable time, the parties and witnesses were carefully interrogated, and the decision, unless challenged, was executed. In general, disputes were solved efficiently within an established judicial procedure. These cases show that the magistrate was responsible and capable enough in terms of carrying out his judicial duty. Because land was the most important form of property in the Qing, one might think that the magistrate's performance in handling disputes other than those concerning land might be less satisfactory. To find out the answer, I shall now turn to debt disputes.

7
Cases and Judicial Decisions Concerning Debt

This chapter focuses on the magistrate's performance in solving debt cases. Like the land cases, the material covered by debt disputes provides another good illustration of the way in which the lives of individuals are interrelated, especially with respect to commercial activities. The concept of debt in the Qing law was enlarged to denote any kind of just demand for money. Apart from private loans — small or large, with or without a written contract — the most typical actions that might result in debt were buying and selling in the market, especially on credit, employing a person, etc.[1] Some cases of debt might be typical only in a society like the Qing — for example, debt disputes arising from attempts to recover from the guards employed by one or more landlords to keep an eye on the harvest the value of what was lost while they were on duty.

This chapter cites cases from Baodi and Ba counties almost exclusively. Magistrate Shen's case collection is generally not relevant, because it contains few debt cases. Table 7.1 gives a general idea of the pattern of debt cases in Baodi.

7.1 Loan cases

We have seen that the Code took a strict approach to private loans. The loan maker could charge no more than 3 per cent per month and, no matter how many years passed, the interest was not to exceed the amount of the principal. This maximum rate of interest for loans was generally respected in loan contracts. A diary dating from an earlier time (1699–1706), whose author was a first degree holder, recorded many private loans in his community, most of them to his clan. The 3 per cent interest per month was the highest rate charged in these loans.

[1] A debt produced by gambling was not recoverable because gambling was illegal in the Qing. A debt from gambling would be forfeit to the government according to law (Article 378).

Table 7.1. The result of debt cases in the Baodi records

Result	No. of cases	Form of resolution		
		Court decision	Hearing delivered	Closed by application
Petition rejected	12			
Result unknown	34			
Resolved	126	73	14	39
Total	172			

There is some evidence that the interest rate was even further reduced in some places (see Chapter 5). The Ba county materials actually show that Sichuan might also have applied a similar rule. There are 127 loan contracts in a published Ba county archive. In most of these, interest was charged at 2 per cent per month or less. In a few, interest was charged at 3 per cent per month (Baxian2: 105–39). The Baodi records, though they contain few loan contracts, seem quite strongly to support this suggestion. I quoted two such contracts in Chapter 5, one loan charging interest at two per cent per month, the other charging no interest.

Theoretically, cases over loans arose because either the loan was overdue or the loan interest exceeded the legal rate. In practice, cases over illegal interest arose very rarely. The Baodi records do not supply a single case on this point. The only one I have discovered comes from the Ba county materials.

Case 1

One day, the magistrate of Ba county saw a woman crying in the street. He questioned her in the street, and she told her story. She had borrowed 12.6 *liang* of silver and some pork and tobacco from Qu, and had made a loan contract for a total of 30 *liang* in which the interest was calculated as part of the principal and the pork and tobacco were accounted for in money. Later she made another loan contract for 20 *liang* in the same way, since she borrowed more pork and tobacco from Qu. Thus, she had a total of 50 *liang* due under the loan contract. She agreed that the interest would be 6 per cent per month, but wrote 3 per cent in the contract. She had already paid him 28 *liang* of silver, but Qu had asked her to pay more that day and she had no money to pay. So she had tried to commit suicide but was rescued by Li. She could not help crying in the street. The magistrate summoned Qu and the woman the following day. What the woman had told the magistrate was true, and Qu was found to 'have overcharged the interest and to have treated the interest as capital' (*dali duisuan*). The magistrate decided that Qu's 50 *liang* of silver

[2] *Qingshi ziliao*, vol. 4: 184–274.

was to be forfeited within three days. The woman was exempt from any prosecution. Since the contracts between Qu and the woman were illegal, the magistrate also invalidated them. (Baxian2: 163)

The above facts are based on the statements by the woman and Qu in the court hearing. As I have said, the publication of Ba county records was too selective. In this case, the magistrate's decision was not contained in the published Ba county records and the magistrate's exact words are hard to deduce. Nevertheless, it is clear that the magistrate was enforcing Article 149 and the third sub-statute of the article (see Chapter 5). The word '*li*' of '*dali*' (higher interest) refers clearly to the legal loan interest (3 per cent per month), so *dali* meant charging interest higher than the legal limit, and '*duisuan*' (literally, to accumulate and calculate) meant to treat the interest as capital. Since Qu had made a contract that was legal on the surface, this was certainly a sort of '*qiaoqu*' (cunning way) under Sub-statute 149-3. Accordingly, the magistrate ordered forfeiture of the capital of the loan and dismissed any charge against the woman. This is exactly in line with the sub-statute.

One could say that this case shed light on the reason why illegal interest cases were rare. As this case shows, illegal loans could take a legal form in the contract, and a creditor who entered into an illegal loan would make every effort not to bring the case to the magistrate. Although this is true, it does not answer the question of why the debtor too was so reluctant to bring the case to the court. As I have said, the law exempted debtors from punishment for an illegal loan if they voluntarily came to court. More research is needed before any solid answer can be provided. One possible factor might be that illegal loans among ordinary people did not occur very often. What then were the most common cases in a county such as Baodi? Here are some examples:

Case 2

Zhang Fa and Zhang Furui quarrelled and fought with each other when Zhang Fa asked Zhang Furui to pay him the debt the latter owed. The magistrate punished both for the fighting and ruled that Zhang Furui must pay the debt (12,700 *wen*) within three days. (Baodi, 186: 72)

Case 3

Woman Ma accused Yu of refusing to pay a debt of 10 *diao* and the interest at 2 per cent per month. She alleged she had been kicked by Yu's son when she asked them to repay the debt. She had an account book (*zhangben*) as evidence. Three days later, a summons *piao* was drafted in which Yu, his son, his son's wife, woman Ma and her agent (her son) were summoned for interrogation by the magistrate. Woman Ma was also ordered to bring the evidence [her account book] to the court. More than twenty days later, Yu's son submitted a statement of payment (*jiaozhuang*) in which he said that he had sold some grain and repaid his father's debt to woman Ma, and she had accepted the money. Now they were on good terms again. The magistrate was satisfied with the solution. So he closed the case. (Baodi, 190: 140–4)

The magistrate's decision in Case 2 is not available and Case 3 was closed without a hearing. However, the two cases were simple and the magistrate's performance is clear. The debts were proved, so they had to be repaid, as required by law. That was exactly what the magistrate ruled in Case 2 and no doubt would have in Case 3, had he held a hearing. Not only would the magistrate order the debtor to pay back the debt, but he would set a time within which the payment must be made, as in Case 2. Phrases such as 'to return the capital and interest' or 'to return the confirmed sum' to the creditor 'within so many days' or 'in so many instalments' appear very frequently. Understandably, the time limit was set on the basis of the debtor's ability to repay the debt. In some cases, it could be very long (see later). The magistrate clearly applied the law concerning being owed a private debt (*'fuqian sizhai lü'*) in the above solutions, that is a legal debt must be repaid (Article 149). For his decision, the most important matter was proof of whether the debt existed, which was sometimes a more difficult matter for him than the application of the formal law.

Case 4

Meng accused Du of wounding him with a farming fork (*cha*) when he went to claim repayment of a debt. But Meng had no evidence to support the debt. The debt claim was rejected and Du was punished with ten days in the cangue [a wooden board affixed around the offender's neck] for the injury he had inflicted. (Baodi, 188: 187–208)

Case 5

A accused B of repudiating a debt. The parties told their own stories when the runner went to investigate, so the magistrate heard the case. Not convinced by A's petition, he ruled: 'Han Yanshou (A) submitted several account books called *wanjinzhang* [what kind of account book this was remains unclear]. Except for that, he has not any strong evidence (*shiju*) for the existence of the debt. He should be punished for this. Since they [the two parties] were members of the same clan, I leniently exempt him from punishment. His [Han Yanshou's] brother Han Fushou confessed that there was no such thing as a debt. The conflict arose because Han Yanshou wanted to borrow some money from (B) and was rejected. All the facts have been established (*anwu xunqing*). All should submit the bond of confirmation and the case is closed.' (Baodi, 193: 151–8)

Article 149 stressed that the debt should be returned in accordance with the contract (*yue*). The instructions at the end of the standard petition form also made it very clear that for debt cases the contract should be submitted when the case was brought (Chapter 3). It is not difficult to understand that the contract was the key evidence for the existence of a debt. People made a contract and left it with the lender when they borrowed money and asked for the contract back when the debt had been paid. The practice of asking for the return of the contract left with the creditor was called *jieyue* (getting back the loan contract) in Ba county. The Ba county records contain public pronouncements issued by the magistrate reminding people not to forget to take the loan contract back when repaying the debt (Baxian2: 285). However, the contract was not the only evidence for the debt. Other written evidence, such as the account book in Case 3, might also prove the debt. In this case, it was important that the account books were in valid form and did not have any alterations, as in Case 4 and some other debt cases in Baodi (187: 135).[3] If none of the above evidence was submitted, or the evidence submitted was found to be invalid, as in Case 2 in Chapter 3, the magistrate would probably take no action.

However, sometimes he made a great effort to prove a debt, even though there was no written evidence, as shown in the next case.

Case 6

Chen accused Ren and Li of owing him money amounting to 2 *diao*. He asked them to pay the debt and was injured. But both Ren and Li denied the claim at the court. Ren stated that the fighting was because Chen went to him to borrow some food and he did not agree. Li, who happened to be there, separated Chen and Ren and did not fight. It was not until the third hearing that Ren confessed that he did owe Chen 2 *diao* and paid it back. He was punished. (Baodi, 188: 163–86)

It might have been because Chen was injured that the magistrate thought it was necessary to prove the debt. What is surprising was the length to which the magistrate went. He had no difficulty in ruling on the fight and punishing Ren for the trouble he had caused. Nevertheless, he heard the case three times until the statements given by both sides matched. He did so just to prove a small debt of 2 *diao*. Evidently, debt cases, even as small as this, were regarded as worthy of receiving justice in the eyes of such an ordinary magistrate.

[3] The account book in this case (187: 131–7) was not clear owing to some correction marks.

In discussing debt cases, some scholars have noted that punishment was rarely imposed, as required by the Article on debt.[4] The above exploration of the magistrate's rulings shows this to be correct. The punishments that were imposed in Cases 2, 4, and 6 were for the offences of fighting or making a false accusation, rather than for the fact of owing a debt.

Two factors will help to explain this. As a contract I quoted in Chapter 5 shows (Baodi, 186: 90), the parties to a debt sometimes made a follow-up contract for the debt or part of it. In this contract, it was agreed that 600 *diao* should be paid in 1839, another 600 *diao* in 1840, and 200 *diao* in 1841. When that case was brought to the Baodi magistrate in 1839 (Daoguang 19), the decision on the repayment of the debt was that 856 *diao* of the debt should be returned in 1839 and 544 *diao* interest in 1840 (Baodi, 187: 122–9). When the case was brought to the court, the periods for repaying the debt given in the follow-up contract had not even passed. Therefore imposing no punishment on the debtor was not really contrary to the provision on punishing the debtor. In cases of small debts when both parties lived in the same neighbourhood, they would naturally seek a way of securing the recovery of the debt by either making another oral agreement or postponing the repayment. This might make the Article imposing punishments according to overdue time inapplicable. Another relevant factor is the debtor's financial difficulty. This perhaps was seen as making the debtor's fault in his delay to pay the debt only a minor one.

7.2 Debt for other reasons

It goes without saying that when one buys something one has to pay for it. The Code stressed the principle that both buyer and seller should be equal and deal with each other honestly in the market or in business (Article 154).

Case 7

Zhou complained in his petition that he sent some stalks to Wang's home. Wang did not pay the price of the stalks worth 1.8 *liang* of silver. When later he asked for the money, Wang offered only 0.18 *liang*, which he refused to accept. Wang was angry at this and hit Zhou with his fist, hurting his left eye. The incident was witnessed by Li. Wang did not admit the story told by Zhou. He told the court that it was 1.8 *liang* he wished to pay, also witnessed by the same Li. Only after Li gave his testimony did Wang confess that what Zhao had said was true. The magistrate punished him by slapping on the face

[4] MacCormack 1996b: 48.

and ordered him to pay. He paid the debt to the court the same day as the decision was given and Zhou confirmed that he received the money. On the statement of receipt, the magistrate wrote: 'It has been established that Wang Er hit you because you demanded what was owed. He has been punished with slapping of the face. The debt has now been paid and he owes you nothing more. The case can be closed. The confirmation of receipt of the money is kept on file for record.' (Baodi, 187: 37–41; case closed in one day)

Philip Huang has pointed to a clear difference between the case patterns of Baodi and Ba counties.[5] In Baodi county, as seen from the records, the cases show that commercial activities usually involved small sums of money and that the two parties were often members of either the same clan or the same small community. In contrast, Ba county in Sichuan was a commercial city (*wufang zaju*) and debt cases were more complicated than those of Baodi, as seen in the following case:

Case 8

Deng rented Jiang's ship through Xiao to transport coal from Ba county to Shehong [Shehong is a county in Tong Chuan prefecture, Sichuan province]. He paid for both renting the ship and the transport work at 37,000 *wen*. Since he did not receive the coal, he went to check and found out that Jiang had sold the coal on the way to Shehong without telling him. Thus he brought the case to the magistrate of Ba county. Jiang confessed and said he had acted thus because he was poor and heavily in debt. The magistrate ordered that Jiang be taken into custody until he had sold his boat to repay Deng the money he had paid for renting the boat and for buying the coal. (Baxian1: 421)

The most significant feature of this case is perhaps the measure the magistrate took for recovery of the debt. He kept the debtor in custody and ordered him to sell something first to satisfy the debt. This seems dramatically to disprove Brockman's observation that the magistrate was not capable of forcing a debt to be paid.[6] Similar measures can also be seen in other Ba records. For example, the magistrate ordered that an employer who owed his employee his salary be kept in custody until he had sold his ship to pay the debt (Baxian1: 421).

Understandably, a debt often resulted from the buying and selling of goods between people who had little relationship with each other. The magistrate would clarify the rights and wrongs to the parties and decide which side should pay, if any, the debt to the creditor. However, family

[5] Huang 1996: ch. 6.

[6] Brockman 1980: 87.

members or close relatives were sometimes also trapped in a debt situation with which they themselves could not deal. The next case clearly demonstrates that, in handling debt disputes among family members, the magistrate resolved the case in the same way as he did in other debt cases.

Case 9

Three families of the Liu clan, family A, family B and family C, wanted to sell the roller they shared. The two go-betweens valued the roller at the price of 65 *diao* and B offered to buy it. After deducting the money that family B should be paid for their share, 21.66 *diao*, and the money B already paid, i.e. 7 *diao* 200 *wen*, B owed family A and family C 36 *diao* and 100 *wen*.[7] Thus family A brought the case to the magistrate. The magistrate heard the case and made a long decision of about two hundred and seventy words on the trial list: 'to order B [family B are the two brothers] to pay 43 *diao* and 320 *wen* to A and C after a deduction of 21 *diao* and 66 *wen*. After further deducting 7 *diao* and 220 *wen* that B had already given, B should pay 36 *diao* and 100 *wen* to family A. Then family A should give family C the money representing their share. (Baodi, 192: 132–42)

When cases were brought to the court in which there was no problem as to the existence of a debt, the most important matter for the magistrate to decide was the amount of the money in question and how it was to be paid. In some cases, it is quite possible that there was only an oral contract (Case 7), or at best a go-between (Case 9). He very often needed to question the parties and witnesses until their statements matched each other, and the two parties agreed with the exact debt.

One may also note that the decisions in the above cases were made quite efficiently. If the case was not a hard one, the magistrate could close it with astonishing speed. For example, Case 7 was closed the same day the petition was made, and Case 9 was closed within nine days.

Employment matters were another source of debt cases. Again, the magistrate had to clarify the reward the employer had offered to pay. The decision by a Ba county magistrate mentioned above about payment of a salary has shown the strict application of the law on repaying a debt.

In Case 8 in Chapter 3, Jin Wende accused his employer of throwing him out without paying him the wages due. The magistrate sent a runner with a conditional order: 'if Jin Wende has not done anything inappropriate',

[7] Family A, family B and family C each should roughly have had 21 *diao* and 66 *wen* from the selling of the roller. Family B offered to buy it and therefore owed 21 *diao* and 66 *wen* each to family A and family C, a total of about 43 *diao* and 320 *wen*. They had paid 7 *diao* 220 *wen*, so they still owed 36 *diao* 100 *wen*.

Yang 'should keep Jin and avoid the lawsuit'. In practice, the contract of employment was made according to a person's needs in either the short or long term. Usually, if the term was more than one year, this counted as long-term employment. The legal status of a long-term employee was that of '*gugongren*',[8] a status roughly equal to that of a servant. The Code distinguished between short-term and long-term employment (Sub-statute 314-5). It is not clear exactly which kind of employee Jin was in the family, although he was quite likely one of *gugongren*. But, whatever the type of employment, the two parties had to follow the contract they had agreed (according to Yang, many long-term employees made only an oral contract instead of a written contract[9]). Neither party could breach the contract. An employer was not allowed to dismiss an employee without recognized reasons. That was why the magistrate ordered the family to let Jin stay, subject to the condition that he had not done anything improper in the family. This condition implied the basis for the magistrate's decision.

The magistrate sometimes clearly intended to support the side of the employee. As in Case 10 in Chapter 3, where there were contradictory statements as to the salary agreed between the two parties, the employees cited another employer in the same village who paid 2 *diao* to his employees for similar work. The magistrate admitted this evidence, ruling that the employer should pay them 2 *diao* each. When there was no clear evidence (such as a contract) of the agreed price, commonly accepted practice was considered. One party in another case in Baodi (189: 68) also said that he was doing the work at 'the price generally accepted in his village' (*zhao benzhuang guchejia gulan*). It might look as though the magistrate was calling upon local custom to decide the case. However, he did this only in terms of establishing the truth. When the facts were not clear, he needed something other than his feelings to rely on to decide the facts. Custom had little to do with his ruling on the payment of the debt itself.

7.3 Debt cases involving self-help, the pledging of property, and guarantors

It is understandable that, if someone was in debt, they or their creditor would be forced to seek some way to resolve the matter. When the creditor could no longer endure the overdue debt, he might take matters into his own

[8] Yang Guozhen 1988: 57.
[9] Ibid.

hands by seizing the debtor's livestock or other property either to satisfy the debt or to put some pressure on the debtor to pay. This kind of self-help was defined as *zhunzhe* in the Code. Although the Code did not invalidate this means of satisfaction of a debt, it clearly discouraged it by imposing a punishment.[10] This was perhaps because self-help was often connected with force. The recommended form of petition against self-help in Fujian province suggested the following: 'form for complaining against a local tyrant (*tuhao*) *zhunzhe*' (*Fujian shengli*: 967).

Case 10

Jin accused Gao of seizing his donkey in satisfaction of his debt, and injuring him. The magistrate heard the case and ruled: 'According to the statements, Jin Yongzeng borrowed from and owed to Gao Qi 82 *diao*. This is proved to be true. Jin should by law return both the principal and interest (*lidang zhao benli changhuan*). Now, I noticed that Jin Yongzeng is poor and lives a hard life. Gao Qi should keep in mind that they are neighbours. Apart from the 12 *diao* that Jin has returned and the donkey that is equivalent to 34 *diao*, making a total of 50 *diao* paid,[11] the remaining 32 *diao* should be paid within two years in succession until the end of 1877 (Guangxu 3). As a favour, the interest is cancelled (*qingrang*) and will not be demanded. This will do. All should submit the bond of confirmation for keeping the record.' (Baodi, 193: 7–17)

If the debtor did not have enough money to pay, then the property or livestock seized was to be priced in money to satisfy all or part of the debt, as Case 7 shows. However, the magistrate would usually rule that the debtor pay the debt and the creditor return the seized property or livestock, as the Code provided. In another Baodi case, after the magistrate believed there was a debt, he simply ordered the debtor to pay the debt and return the leather jacket and other things he had taken within three days (Baodi, 191: 1–11). But in Case 10 the interest was cancelled as a favour, the remaining debt to be returned within two years. The magistrate's decision reveals his flexibility and determination.

[10] Jing (1994: 72–3) has misunderstood the relevant provision (Art. 149): 'If, however, the creditor has not seized property in excess of the amount he is owed, then he may redeem his punishment by paying the allotted fine, and he may keep the property he has seized.' It was not the punishment that was to be redeemed, but the property seized. Jones (1994: 162) gives the correct translation. See Chapter 5.2.

[11] I am aware that 12 plus 34 does not total 50. I may have introduced this error, since most of the materials I collected were hand-copied.

Case 11

The plaintiff, a woman, lent money to a Mr. Lin, who gave her a deed to guarantee the debt, thereby creating a mortgage over his land. The debtor was now dead and the plaintiff went to his tenant to obtain rent, as interest on her loan. The tenant and a relative of the debtor refused to pay the rent. The magistrate in his comments on the complaint, noted that, despite the fact that this land was inundated by water, nonetheless, the money and interest on the debt should be repaid. The magistrate sent a runner to check the facts and asked that the original mortgage contract be brought to court. The runner attempted to conciliate the dispute but was unable to do so, thus the parties were brought to court for trial. In his decision the magistrate noted that despite the fact that this land was inundated by water for a period of time, the water had receded and the land had been reclaimed by the tenant, although it was still not yet cultivatable as rice land. He noticed that custom (*suli*) holds that three years after reclamation of the land, rent is once again due and payable. He, therefore, ordered the debtor's heir to give all rentals to the plaintiff three years after reclamation of the land. He also held that the mortgage may be redeemed upon payment of this outstanding balance in a lump sum. The magistrate requested and received bonds from all parties manifesting their willingness to abide by his decision. (Dan-xin case, No. 23306; quoted from Buxbaum 1971: 277, 278)

Although the decision took into account the custom (*suli*) that, three years after reclamation of the land, rent was once again due and payable and ruled that 'the debtor's heir is to give all rentals to the plaintiff three years after reclamation of the land', the fundamental decision to return the debt and redeem the land upon payment was the result of application of the law. In other words, the decision that 'money and interest on the debt should be repaid' had little to do with this custom. In this sense, to regard the case as illustrating the importance of local custom for the decision when the relevant contract was obscure in its language missed the essential point of the decision.[12] When the magistrate resolved debt cases, he had to think about the practicability of a decision on repayment of the debt. A decision would be ineffective unless it could be enforced. In this case, in order to establish when the debt should be repaid, the magistrate first had to establish when the land would become cultivable in terms of paying the rent. An order like that in Case 11 was no more than a particular means for making repayment possible. Even the custom itself might have had its root in official stipulations. For example, a regulation stipulated that, should land be uncultivated on account of water or sand, the rent should cease to be payable at the time

[12] Allee 1994b: 137.

and payment should resume only after it was possible again to cultivate the land (*Jicheng*: 667).

If a property was pledged to secure a debt (*diya*) and the debt failed to be recovered, the creditor was entitled to keep the pledged property, but, understandably, at a similar price (see Chapter 9). Sometimes the debt was guaranteed by a person, and it was the guarantor (*danbao*) who was required to make the repayment if necessary, as the next case shows:

Case 12

Wei was the guarantor of Feng for a loan from Zhou of 200 *diao* at interest of 2 per cent per month, counting ten months as one loan year. Zhou had already received 131 *diao* back. Owing to bad harvests, Feng could not pay the rest and neither could Wei, the guarantor. Wei submitted a petition accusing Zhou of coming to his house twice to ask for payment of the debt, and of damaging his family belongings and throwing a one-year-old baby to the ground. When Wei offered to pay the debt by selling a parcel of his land on behalf of Feng, Zhou sometimes demanded 600 *diao*, and sometimes 700 *diao*; although Zhou failed to tell Wei the exact sum of the debt, he continued to harass him. Thus Wei asked the magistrate to make clear the amount of the debt and allow him more time to pay. Not convinced by Wei's story, the magistrate made a long comment on Wei's complaint: 'You were Feng's guarantor for a loan of 200 *diao* from Zhou Yifu in June 1838 (Daoguang 18) at interest of 2 per cent, which was many years ago. Between 1837 and 1845 (Daoguang 17–25) 131 *diao* was paid to [Zhou] Yifu. This sum does not even cover the interest. I am not surprised if Yifu desperately wanted his money back. Now instead of criticizing yourself, you bring a complaint, which is very unreasonable. You admitted in your petition that you agreed to pay the money when Yifu went to your home, and you seemed to intend to sell your land in satisfaction of the debt. Why now ask for more time until after the autumn? This is contradictory. The complaint is not accepted.' But, one month later, Wei submitted another complaint stating that he had made a *dian* (conditional sale) of a parcel of land that had allowed him to pay in total 214 *diao*. For the rest of the debt, Zhou wanted a parcel of 12 *mu* of land from him, and Wei had agreed at a price of 186 *diao*. However, Zhou's younger brother, wanting only money, came to his home and seriously harassed him again. Still not convinced, the magistrate wrote: 'What has the matter to do with the younger brother. He even harassed you. It is obviously an exaggeration. The complaint is, again, not accepted.' It was not until Wei's third petition that the magistrate finally ordered the *xiangbao* to investigate the truth. The reason he agreed to take action this time was because the younger brother's behaviour was very unreasonable. 'In private loans, no matter how many years have passed, the money returned should not exceed *yiben yili* (the capital amount and an equal amount of interest). You acted as guarantor for Feng when he borrowed 200 *diao* from Zhao. The

> amount repaid has reached 214 *diao*. If you pay the rest with the land valued at 186 *diao*, that is enough for the capital and an equal amount of interest. Zhou Yifu has already agreed. Why was Zhou Yide [the younger brother] not satisfied with that and made trouble more than once?' The village head brought the magistrate two different stories. Zhou said that the money Wei was lent was 22 *liang* of silver, so he wanted 44 *liang*, and did not want any land. Wei said he would pay the rest of the debt after the harvest in *diao*, since the loan was 200 *diao*. They both wanted a formal trial by the magistrate. The magistrate agreed to hear the case after the farmers' busy season. In early July, just after the farmers' busy season, Wei submitted another complaint accusing Zhou of forcibly taking his horses in satisfaction of the debt. The magistrate conducted the case at once and ruled that Zhou should return the horses to Wei and that Wei should pay Zhou 220 *diao* within ten days. Then they submitted a joint statement of confirmation in which they said that they had already returned the money/horses to each other. The case was finally closed. (Baodi, 187: 149–57)

This case is interesting, first of all, for the role played by the guarantor. Throughout the whole process, four petitions were made to the magistrate before he heard the case. But the real debtor was not even a party. He was mentioned as a *cinei* (see Chapter 3), someone who was not involved in the litigation. The guarantor was completely responsible for repaying the debt, even to the extent that he had to sell his land. The magistrate made this clear in his comment by rejecting the guarantor's petition at the beginning and treating him in the same way as a debtor. Once the guarantor had paid the debt on behalf of the debtor, he would himself become a creditor to the debtor. The Code implied the guarantor's position in Sub-statute 149-2 on loans by official candidates. When recovery of a debt from a debtor was impossible, the creditor was entitled to turn to the guarantor and the guarantor could not refuse to pay. Otherwise, he risked being accused (see also Cases 13 and 14 below).[13] The initial response of the magistrate indicated that there was no need to question anyone, since the debt was clear and it should be paid. The case is also interesting for other factors. The comment of rejection made by the magistrate on the initial petition exactly followed the Code, and so did the result of the case.

[13] In one case, a 'guarantor' was accused on the ground that he had refused to pay the debt he guaranteed (Baodi, 137–41). Although the case turned out to be unfounded, the position of the guarantor is clear.

7.4 Decisions involving cancellation

In the Baodi records, in five out of the total number of debt cases, *yirang* or *qingrang* was applied in waiving part of the debtor's debt. *Yirang* most often meant to give up or waive part of the interest of a debt in order to do what was right. In one of these cases a compromise was reached before the formal hearing by the debtor's returning the principal without the interest, which was waived by the creditor. The magistrate confirmed this solution in the trial of this case (Baodi, 189: 78–9). Although this did not often happen in Baodi county, the role of *yirang* is very interesting. It suggested that the magistrate might sometimes apply human feelings (*qing*) instead of the law on debt, especially if the decision employed the equivalent term *qingrang* ('kindly give up'). Before I analyse Baodi cases that applied *yirang*, some background on the term '*yi*' needs to be considered.

Yi was one of the five basic concepts of Confucian ethics, which were *zhong* (conscientiousness), *yi* (righteousness), *li* (rite), *zhi* (wisdom), and *xin* (faithfulness). *Yi* was usually explained as *shan* (virtue) or as *yi* (proper), as being what the *tianli* (heaven's principles) required. In other words, it involved doing what was right regardless of material benefit. In Confucius' eyes, *yi* was an obligation to society; to others it meant what a person should have. 'It is not right to refuse to enter the public service. For if it is wrong to ignore the duties arising out of the relations between the members of a family, how is it right to ignore the duties a man owes to his sovereign and country' (*Analects*, 18). The great thinkers differed on the question of the source of the obligation to behave with *yi*, Confucius pointing to social relationships, Mencius to human nature, Zhuxi to heaven's principles (*tianli*), and so on. The theories nonetheless had one thing in common, in that *yi* was always discussed in connection with *li* (material benefit). And, although the relationship between *yi* and *li* varied, the meaning of *yi* was always the same, implying the surrender of, or the refusal to take, a material benefit. Several terms contain the word '*yi*' — for example, *yi* land (*yitian*), *yi* school (*yixue*), or *yi* action (*yijue*) — in which it has such a meaning. If we recall from Chapter 1 that magistrate Bao Shichen rewarded those families who supported their poor relatives with a board bearing the inscription *yihu* ('responsibly kind family'), it is clear that resorting to *yi* means either making no profit from others or contributing material benefit to others.

Yi appears in the Code as *buyi* (failure to fulfil one's duty), the ninth of the ten great wrongs (Article 2), and *yijue* (breaking the bond between a husband and a wife) (Article 116). The commentary by Shen Zhiqi on '*buyi*' states: 'the crimes in this provision involve the relations of senior and junior, teacher and student, husband and wife, where the relationship is not based on the blood tie (*tianhe*) but rather on the bond of righteousness (*yi*)' (*Jizhu*: 10). So *yi* in a legal context expressed the duty arising from particular relationships. However, in the context of debt cases, as shown by the following cases, the meaning of *yi* seems extremely broad.

Case 13

Zhang stood as guarantor for Zou when he borrowed 910 *diao* from Bai. Since Zou could not pay back the debt, Zhang made a *dian* contract of his land and handed the contract to Bai as a deposit while at the same time Zou promised to sell his house to pay the debt. Zhang brought the case to the magistrate because, according to Zhang, Bai had forcibly taken this pledged land, destroyed his wine vat, and hit him. Bai stated at the hearing that he wanted to share Zhang's harvest because Zou, the debtor who was supposed to have sold his house, intended to repudiate the debt. They both said at the hearing that before the court session Bai had agreed through the mediators to give up (*yirang*) 150 *diao*, the debt remaining to be repaid by Zou who had sold his house. The magistrate approved the solution, and ordered Bai to hand back the land contract Zhang had pledged to him at the court and pay compensation for the wine vat he destroyed after the hearing. (Baodi, 194: 61–79)

Case 14

Zhang Suyu stood as guarantor for Zhang Yiqiu when he borrowed 200 *diao* from Zhang Yuwen. Zhang Suyu had once paid 8 *diao* as the cost of a meal for Zhang Yuwen. When Zhang Suyu asked Zhang Yuwen to pay back the 8 *diao*, Zhang Yuwen bit his finger, so Zhang Suyu brought the case to the court. The magistrate ordered Zhang Yuwen to pay the 8 *diao* and Zhang Suyu to urge the [debtor] to pay the debt of 200 *diao*. When he failed to do so, the case was brought to court again. This time the magistrate ruled: 'Since Zhang Yiqiu has died and his post as land manager [*zhuangtou*, a person who looked after royal family land] was given to his young brother Zhang Muhong, I order him [the younger brother] to pay 150 *diao* of the total debt over three seasons. Since Zhang Suyu failed to make the debtor repay in due time (as he was so ordered in the previous decision), he should contribute 50 *diao*. However, since he is poor, I order him only not to claim the 8 *diao* meal cost which Zhang Yuwen owed him, and order Zhang Yuwen to waive the remaining [42 *diao*] with *yirang*.' (Baodi, 188: 136–45, 189: 94–5)

Despite the fact that the concept of *yi* was strongly advocated by Confucians, and that *buyi* (failure to fulfil one's duty) was one of the ten great wrongs (*shie*), *yi* did not have a clear place in the provisions on debt in the Code. Cancellation of a debt was allowed in only one specific circumstance: when a creditor, by using force, took the debtor's wife or children as an alternative method to satisfy his debt (Article 149). Although the official explanation of the law on the interest rate on private loans often clearly stated that the reason for making this law was to help people with difficulties, the principle that the debt had to be repaid was crystal clear (see Chapter 5). In this sense, the decisions giving effect to *yirang* indeed appear to be a form of abuse of the law on debt. Alternatively, when the term *qingrang* ('kindly give up') appears in the decision, we may understand it as an appeal to human feelings.

However, careful examination of these cases and decisions provides us with more interesting information on *yirang*. The above two cases, as well as Case 10, were simple rather than complicated. One person had to return to another a sum of money that was proved by evidence. Decisions invoking *yirang* could be applied only to a proven debt, and when the magistrate applied *yirang* he also first emphasized that the debt was legitimate.

As we can see from the *yirang* cases, the part of the debt that was waived by the creditor was small. It might be coincidence that the most that was waived in the above two cases was 21 per cent of the whole debt. And it always happened when the debtor was in a very difficult situation and if the debtor and the creditor were relatives, neighbours, or in a close relationship. In other words, if these two conditions were missing, the magistrate could not just order the creditor to cancel part of his debt in order to do what was right.

'Poverty' in itself could not be regarded as an excuse by the magistrate to waive part of the debt in favour of the debtor. Rather it was the debtor's economic status that was relevant, which was confirmed by the Code as a factor that had to be considered when making policy (see Chapter 1).[14] The Code distinguished between people who were 'economically capable' (*youli*), 'possibly economically capable' (*shao youli*), or 'economically incapable' (*wuli*).[15] Although the standard for these distinctions was not given precisely, they clearly referred to people in different economic circumstances. When employing *yirang*, the magistrate did not deny the creditor's right to recover his debt; on the contrary, he always confirmed it. However, economic circumstances might be taken into account as an element of the facts if the relationship of two parties is more than just a debtor and a creditor.

[14] This feature in debt dispute was reflected in the fact that a debtor sometimes brought a case accusing the creditor of being over-zealous in forcing him to repay the debt (Baodi, 189: 44).
[15] See the table on exemption from punishment in *Jizhu*: 44.

Although decisions invoking *yirang* took the two parties' relations and the debtor's repayment ability into account, it is notable that they did not introduce the principle of 'taking specific circumstances into account to apply the law' (*zhunqing zhuoli*). That seemed to have caused confusion because, where the two parties were involved in debt decisions invoking *yirang*, human feelings appear to have been taken into consideration and to have played a limited role. We see from the cases above that sometimes the magistrate ordered the debtor to sell his property to satisfy a debt. A debtor experiencing difficulty who was a complete stranger to the creditor still had to pay his debt. In contrast, in decisions in which the phrase *zhunqing zhuoli* was employed, *qing* usually meant 'the facts' or, more precisely, the particular facts. The difference between decisions invoking *zhunqing zhuoli* and those invoking *yirang* or *qingrang* was that the former aimed to avoid an unjust decision, whereas the latter aimed to avoid an inhumane decision.

When a magistrate waived part of the debt in favour of the debtor because of his difficulty, he was to some extent forced to do this by having no other, or no better, choice. If the magistrate's decision could not be carried out, justice remained an empty word. Obviously, in a debt case, the key factor was the actual repayment of the debt to the creditor. Thus, how much exactly the debtor could pay had a limited role to play in the final decision. The following examples might give us some clue as to this difficulty.

Case 15

Liu submitted a petition to the court asking for the magistrate's help to recover a debt confirmed by a previous court decision. In the earlier case, because the debtors, the Li brothers, could not pay, they asked the magistrate to allow them more time. The magistrate agreed and ruled that they need pay only part of the debt immediately, leaving the rest to be paid one year later. But, one year later, the debtors again failed to pay and the case was brought to the court for the magistrate to take stronger action in forcing the debtors to pay. The order *piao* was drafted at great speed (in two days) and issued to the runner, who carried the magistrate's order to the debtors to pay the debt at once. Three days later the runner reported back stating that he could not carry out the order because the elder brother was away. So he brought the younger brother to the court. The magistrate ordered the younger brother to pay his part of the debt within three days in court and the rest was to be paid by the elder brother when he returned and was summoned to the court. The younger brother was released under a guarantor's agreement. Even then, he paid his part of the debt eight, rather than two, days later to the court. (Baodi, 187: 66–83, 187: 99)

This case involved the magistrate's court in much effort to deliver the decision and make sure that the creditor received the money. With great difficulty, the debtor was pressed in every possible way to pay the debt he owed. In cases where the two parties were in different locations, such difficulties could make recovery almost impossible.

A decision in the Ba county records demonstrates how recovery of a debt could bring disaster to the people involved. In this case, the accused (the debtor's employer) died in custody while the magistrate tried for three years to recover the debt. The magistrate then had to decide to release the other people involved and suspend the case until the actual debtor, who had been absent, could be summoned to the court to pay the debt (Baxian, 268–9).[16]

Because decisions that invoked *yirang* meant that the law on debt was not strictly applied and that the parties' relationship was taken into consideration, we may regard them to a limited extent as appealing to human feelings. If the creditor and the court both had difficulty in obtaining repayment of a debt, the magistrate could not do better than to decide with *yirang*. Nevertheless, observations by some scholars to the effect that the magistrate in many cases disregarded the debt and imposed an unreasonable compromise on the parties,[17] are not supported by the evidence from the Baodi county, and possibly also the Ba county, records.

[16] Since only selected documents are published, the exact circumstances of the death of the accused (Yao) were not clear. Yao was accused because his employee used his business stamp to do business with the plaintiff. Yao appeared not to have agreed to the employee's act.

[17] Shiga Shūzō 1998a: 34.

8

Cases and Judicial Decisions Concerning Marriage

Discussion of the marriage law of the Qing has revealed some aspects of the codified rules governing marriage. Turning to the decisions of the magistrate's court, we will see how these rules were applied. An apparent question that arises is this: whereas the resolution by the magistrate of land and debt disputes seems unlikely often to have been influenced by elements other than the law, did the magistrate insist more strongly on a compromise when resolving marriage cases, or did he often invoke moral values?

Because disputes over marriage were frequent, both Wang Huizu and Liu Heng strongly recommended that, after his appointment, the magistrate should first become familiar with the law on marriage, together with some other important rules (see Chapter 3). We should note also some specific discussions by magistrates on marriage disputes. Under the subheading 'Marriage' (*hunyin*) in the chapter 'Judicial Duty', Huang Liuhong particularly discussed the principles that should govern disputes over the marriage agreement.[1] He made the following two points:

1. Although the existence of the marriage agreement could be decided by checking such factors as the contract and the betrothal gift and interrogating the go-between, there were engagements that 'are agreed through people who are not really matchmakers' or lack 'proper betrothal ceremonies'. They might be made at a party when two people just make up their mind to engage their daughter and son by appointing another guest as their go-between, with the exchange of a cup of wine as the gift on the spot. When a case like this was brought to the court, the magistrate should question the boy and the girl personally to decide whether they were willing. If they themselves agreed to marry each other, the marriage agreement should then be upheld.

[1] Huang Liuhong 1850/1972, *juan* 20.

2. In cases where the agreement was properly made with clear evidence, the magistrate had to uphold the agreement in order to 'preserve social relations in the community (*yizheng renlun*)'. A properly established marriage itself was the foundation of morality. Once the status of the husband and wife to be had been properly defined, the rites required that they stayed together and should never separate, even if the marriage was unhappy. This principle, which was established by the ancient sages (*shengren*), ought not to be challenged.[2]

Huang Liuhong's point is clear. When the merit of the marriage agreement itself was challengeable because either the go-between or the gift had a flaw, the magistrate should take the extra step of asking the opinion of the boy and girl. To Huang Liuhong, enforcing a properly made marriage contract was not a problem at all. Since the process designed for making such a contract would enhance moral standards, to enforce such a contract was to respect the foundations of morality. Huang Liuhong emphasized the moral element embedded in the legal procedure for making the contract.

Huang's point was later repeated by another magistrate, Xu Wenbi.[3] Many of his comments were just copied from Huang Liuhong. He, too, clearly pointed out that the magistrate should enforce a properly made contract in order to preserve the foundations of social relations. The difference was that Xu Wenbi did not appeal too much to the moral values embedded in proper procedure in making the marriage agreement a justification of the magistrate's judicial duty to enforce the agreement. On the contrary, he simply emphasized that the magistrate should 'abide by the statutes and sub-statutes', and so ultimately appealed to the law (*Mulingshu*, *juan* 19: *Pan hunyin* [Making decision over dispute concerning marriage]).

Although Huang and Xu made the point that, in disputes over the marriage agreement, the law should be followed, their opinions can still be understood as being generally applicable to marriage cases as a whole. As we shall see, the magistrate's decisions in general followed the law clearly, whether the principle or the text, the old or the new.

In discussing the magistrate's performance in dealing with marriage disputes, I bring in cases and decisions from sources other than the Baodi or Ba archives and Shen's collection, since these sources provide good illustrations of important aspects of the issues. However, the main types of dispute

2 See also Huang Liuhong 1984: 448–50.

3 Xu Wenbi was recognized in *Mulingshu* as a magistrate of good reputation.

Table 8.1. The result of marriage cases in the Baodi records

Result	No. of cases	Form of resolution: Court decision	Hearing delivered	Closed by application
Petition rejected	15			
Result unknown	8			
Resolved	72	45	not clear	27
Total	95			

are still based mainly on Baodi case records.[4] Three types of case — breaking the marriage contract, divorce, and a widow's remarriage — will be discussed separately at length. Table 8.1 provides an overall view of the pattern of resolution of the cases contained in the Baodi records. Cases concerning illegal sexual relations, which were not directly relevant to marriage, are not included.

8.1 Breaking the marriage agreement

Cases of breaking the marriage agreement did not constitute a large proportion of marriage cases as a whole in Baodi county. With the help of other supplementary case decisions, including those from higher courts, we can draw a relatively full picture of court performance in solving marriage agreement disputes. First, I consider two Baodi cases.

Case 1

Two boys were engaged to the same girl by her father. Both the boys' families employed go-betweens and gave marriage presents to the girl's father. Though the father denied that he had made a promise to Huang, one of the two family heads, the magistrate found out that Huang's family in fact made the engagement with the girl earlier than the other family. Thus the magistrate ruled in favour of the Huang family, deciding that Huang's son should have the girl. (Baodi, 168: 183–205)

Case 2

A father broke his marriage engagement with Zhang by accepting marriage presents from another. Having discovered this, Zhang took back by force the

[4] Baodi, *juan* 161–73 (see Appendix 2). They are categorized by the archivists as 'marriage and illegal sexual relations' (*hunyin jianqing*) — see Chapter 1.

girl engaged to him. The magistrate punished Zhang with slapping of the face for taking the matter into his own hands without reporting to the court, but ruled that he should have the girl back and upheld the engagement. (Baodi, 170: 44)

These two cases were simple and the decisions are clear. Both girls' families broke the law on marriage agreement because they broke the legal marriage agreement, which was protected by law. According to the law, the girl had to marry the first engaged boy and the responsible principal should be punished. The magistrate ruled that the girl should return to the first intended husband in both cases. The punishment imposed on the intended husband in Case 2 for his action in taking back the girl was set in accordance with Sub-statute 101-4, which stipulated that the intended husband should actually be punished with thirty blows with the light stick. Why the magistrate punished him more lightly, that is, slapping his face, is not clear.[5] The crucial evidence to prove the legal status of the first marriage agreement in the above cases was the gift accepted by the girls' fathers.

The gift alone could serve as decisive evidence to prove the existence of a marriage agreement, as the Baodi cases show when no written contract had been made. If the contract was made and available, it alone might be sufficient to prove whether the marriage agreement existed, as shown in the next case.

Case 3

Yang's second daughter died young after being engaged to Xong and entering Xong's family as a *tongyangxi*.[6] Yang orally agreed to marry another daughter to Xong but a go-between was not employed nor was a formal contract made. Because Xong's family became very poor, Yang refused to complete the marriage. Xong brought a case accusing Yang of breaking the engagement (*kenhun*). Perhaps realizing his weak position in terms of the evidence required by the law, he forged a marriage contract as evidence to support his complaint. Yang counter-claimed by accusing Xong of fabricating the contract. On finding out the truth, Magistrate Shen ruled in favour of Yang by giving his daughter permission to marry another man and cancelled the forged contract by Xong. He also ruled that Yang should give a parcel of land to Xong. (Shen Yanqing: 471)

[5] The girl's father in the first case was not punished. It is not clear whether the girl's father in the second case was punished for engaging his daughter to two boys. More explanation on punishment will be given in Chapter 9.

[6] A *tongyangxi* was a girl who was engaged to a boy at a tender age and was brought up in the boy's family. The wedding ceremony was completed when the girl reached maturity.

In this case, the contract was the decisive factor proving the existence or non-existence of the marriage agreement. The plaintiff certainly knew that he was not in a good position in the absence of this evidence, so he forged a contract, which seemed easily detectable. Without a contract or any other evidence, the boy's father failed to prove that the girl's father had accepted his alternative arrangement for the marriage. Even though the magistrate seemed to believe that the oral agreement had been made, the reason for his decision is clear, that is, the defendant obviously had the law on his side.

If the parties claimed that they had not only made the contract but also exchanged the gift, the magistrate would check both the contract and the gift.

Case 4

A boy engaged to a girl died after the girl of tender years entered his family. The boy's family wanted the boy's adopted brother to marry the girl instead, but the girl's father refused. And he took back his daughter. 'According to law,' Magistrate Shen wrote, 'whether the boy is a formally adopted child (*guofang*) or an informally adopted child (*qiyang*) must be fully communicated to the other side and their consent obtained. Should both parties still be agreeable, then a formal contract is to be drawn up through the go-between and the marriage completed with the procedure required by the rites.' Now the boy's family had a contract of marriage but it did not name the adopted boy. The go-between gave evidence that he once sent some rice and pork to the girl's family on behalf of the boy's side, which should not be deemed to be the betrothal presents, but were a friendly gift. Finally, Magistrate Shen ruled that the girl's family should give 20 *diao* to the boy's family for both the cost of the rice and pork and the expense of the girl's living in the boy's family. The contract was dismissed and the girl allowed to marry someone else. (Shen Yanqing: 462–3)

In this case, the contract turned out to be insufficient to support the plaintiff's allegation, for it failed to show the correct name of the boy as he claimed. Shen quoted Article 101 to make clear that the girl's father was entitled to refuse the substituted boy. Since the contract was not sufficient to prove the marriage agreement, Shen then turned to the goods sent to the girl's family, because the plaintiff alleged they were the marriage gift. The goods were found to be not convincing enough to be the betrothal gift, but rather were a friendly gesture. The magistrate thus refused to uphold the plaintiff's claim and cancelled the invalid marriage contract.

As this case shows, the go-between, the contract, and the gift, which were all relevant for the establishment of a valid marriage agreement, revealed the nature and importance of the marriage agreement. Huang Liuhong and Xu Wenbi had made it clear that, as long as the marriage agreement was properly made, the marriage must be upheld. Of course, if breaking of a marriage agreement was mutually agreed, it should not be considered to be against the law, and so the court would not intervene. The message from the court, as from the law, was rather simple: the legal marriage agreement was protected and would be restored if necessary.

Case 5

Hao engaged his daughter to Zhou Jingzhi's son. Zhou later withdrew from the engagement owing to the death of his son. Hao then engaged his daughter to Zhou Qingyun. After Qingyun's fortunes declined, the marriage contract was lost. When the family wanted to complete the wedding ceremony, Hao refused, but asked Zhou Jingzhi to accept his daughter as a daughter-in-law despite the death of Zhou's son. Hao brought a petition accusing Jingzhi of making up the story of his son's death, alleging that the son had actually been abducted and had not died. The magistrate ruled: 'Jingzhi withdrew from the marriage agreement due to his son's death, so the bond between the girl and Zhou's family has been cut off. Now although Qingyun lost his contract, he has the go-between as witness to prove the marriage agreement. And Hao should not break the contract because Qingyun's family became poor. I order the wedding ceremony to be arranged by Qingyun for his son and Hao's daughter within a limited time. Hao and his son are both degree holders. However, if they are deprived of their degrees, the girl will very likely be upset, thus the two families will not be on good terms. So I lightly punish them with a warning (without reporting them to the higher authority for cancellation of their degrees).'[7]

Two key points were involved in this case. First, according to law, the death of one party was a legal reason for the other party to end the marriage agreement and enter into another one. Thus, and secondly, the engagement made by the girl's father after the death had to be upheld, subject of course to compliance with the proper procedure. We can see in this case that, although the guilty father strongly objected, the magistrate had no hesitation in upholding the second agreement. However, he did take the matrimonial relationship into account when making the decision about whether to remove the titles of Hao and his son.[8] Obviously the girl, and her

[7] *Qingshi liezhuan* [Biographies from Qing History], cited in *Qingdai mingan*: 454.

[8] Three provisions (Sub-statutes 1-16, 335-15, and 374-1) from the Code are relevant to degree holders. Sub-statute 374-1 required the removal of a *shengjian*'s degree if he started a petition without grounds (see Chapter 2).

family as well, would have found it difficult to get along with her future husband and his family if both her father's and her elder brother's titles had been removed as the result of the case.

A marriage agreement, irrespective of whether it was made through a written contract or acceptance of the gift, once it was properly finalized, would be enforced by the magistrate. This is certainly the conclusion from reading the above cases. Since in practice a written contract was often made, enforcement of the law to support the marriage agreement sometimes was the same thing as enforcing the written contract. The lengths to which people might go in trying to possess such key evidence as a written contract were sometimes excessive, as we can see in Case 3. On very rare occasions, the contract even caused loss of life. The records of the Board of Punishments contain a case in which a father wished to withdraw from a marriage agreement, but was unable to do so because the written contract would prove that he was wrong and the contract would be enforced by the court, should the other party bring the case to the court. He employed and plotted with Zhang to obtain the contract for him by deception. Subsequently things went wrong. Although Zhang finally obtained the contract, this was by getting the other party drunk and killed.[9]

Although the contract played the key role in proving the marriage agreement, when the magistrate upheld the marriage he was applying the law. To believe otherwise, that is, that by enforcing the contract the court was calling upon people's commonly accepted practice, would be to overestimate the judicial importance of the contract. As we have seen, and will continue to see, the magistrate, and his higher authorities, enforced the contracts only when they had legal merit. Otherwise, the magistrate would cancel them, as in Cases 3 and 4 above. The court was of course applying the law by enforcing the contract. As long as the evidence had real merit, the decision was not hard to made. However, that was not always the case.

Case 6

After Wang Duer became engaged to Qu's daughter, he went to Xinjiang province and, according to the news he sent back, worked with his uncle. Since Wang Duer had been away and not come back for ten years, Qu applied for permission from the magistrate to allow his daughter to marry again under substatute 116-2. He was granted permission, and married his daughter to Wang Wanchun. Wang Duer's father appealed and won. Wang Duer was ordered to complete the marriage without delay. Refusing to let go of the girl, who was also his wife, Wang Wanchun falsely claimed that the girl was

[9] *Xingke tiben*, 1785/ [Qianlong 50], cited in Wang Yuesheng 2003: 19.

> pregnant. Later the girl really became pregnant and gave birth to a son. When the case went to the provincial level, he argued that the bond between a mother and a son could not be broken. The case was reported to the Board of Punishments for decision. The Board analysed: substatute 116-2 is only applicable while there is no information about the boy's absence. If the intended husband is away for business or for visiting relatives, and the place of his stay is clearly located, though the wedding ceremony is postponed, the bond between a husband and a wife to be cannot easily be cut off.' The Board ruled in favour of Wang Duer, and was even prepared for the worst happening, that is, the girl might commit suicide.[10]

This case went right up to the Board of Punishments. Although there might be some confusion about the details of the case owing to the concise style of summarizing the facts, the most striking feature was the strictness of the court in enforcing the original marriage agreement. Shiga commented on the decision of the Board in this case: 'we can see clearly how the marriage contract was strictly enforced by the court'.[11]

In this case, strict enforcement of the contract precisely meant applying the law, that is, the first marriage agreement was upheld. This practice is a perfect example of the point on resolving disputes concerning marriage agreements made by Huang Liuhong and Xu Wenbi. Except that, in this case, the marriage supported by the Board would have been doomed to failure. Perhaps fearful of this result, soon Wang Duer himself said that he did not want the girl any more. According to the law, if the first would-be husband refused to accept the girl back, he could recover double his marriage gift. In this case, since the girl had already been married to Wang, Wang was ordered to pay this amount.

This case vividly exposes the intention of the officials in carrying out their judicial duty to apply the law. Human feelings, the bond between a mother and a son, although it seemed reasonable to appeal to them, were almost not considered at all in the support given by the Board to the first engagement. We may even regard the application of the law as mechanical. One factor we should bear in mind is that this rigid decision was made by the Board of Punishments. Because it was responsible for the judicial unity of the whole country, it tended to apply the law very strictly. Even so, given the strong connection between human feelings and a family, the disregard of a mother's feelings for her son in order to apply the law was very significant.

[10] *Xingan huilan* [Conspectus of Cases from the Board of Punishments], cited in Shiga Shūzō 2003: 396.

[11] Shiga Shūzō 2003: 397.

However, upholding the first marriage agreement in such circumstances carried problems. In a case such as this, when the boy was away for an unreasonably long time without coming back to complete the wedding ceremony, even though the marriage agreement had been properly made, it was certainly not easy for the girl to wait, especially after she had reached the age of maturity.

I found two cases of the late Qing in which the decisions revealed a change.

Case 7

Chen and Shi had a marriage agreement. The Chen family was away for seven years without any news. Shi married his daughter to Ge when she was mature and she gave birth to a son. When Chen came back, he submitted a petition to his magistrate who ruled in his favour, ordering Shi's daughter to be restored to him. The decision was overruled by the independent district and reported to Fan, the provincial judge of Shanxi province. Fan commented: '. . . According to law, when there are disputes between two suitors, then the one first engaged should marry the girl. However, if the intended husband is away for three years without any communication, and the girl is mature, it is permissible for her father and elder brother to engage her to another man. This is also *dingli* (a settled regulation). There was no news of the Chens for seven years. Thus, the girl married another man, which is, of course, consistent with heaven's principles (*tianli*) and human feelings (*renqing*). . . . So the decision can only be made to order the return of the marriage presents to the Chen family, not dissolve the marriage.'[12]

The next case was almost the same:

Case 8

Luo and Rong had a marriage agreement. Accompanied by his family, Luo went to Taiyuan for business. After nine years had elapsed without any communication with Rong, the girl was married to another man by her father at her age of maturity, and gave birth to a son. When Luo came back, he submitted a petition accusing Rong of breaking the engagement. The magistrate reported the case to the provincial judge of the province, Zhu. Zhu analysed: '. . . . According to law, when there are disputes between two suitors, then the one first engaged should marry her. However, if the intended husband is away for three years without any communication, and the girl is mature, it is permissible for her father and elder brother to engage her to another man. This is also *dingli*. There has been no news of the Luos for nine years. Thus, the girl married another man, which is, of course, consistent with heaven's principles

[12] *Qingdai mingchen pandu*, vol. 4: 6–7.

> (*tianli*) and human feelings (*renqing*), not to mention the fact that a son was born to Rong. So the decision can only be made to order the return of the marriage presents to the Luo family, not dissolve the marriage.'[13]

The noticeable change is the reference to *dingli* (settled regulation)[14] in both decisions, which permitted the girl's father and elder brother to engage her to another man without reporting to the magistrate when she reached the age of maturity, whereas originally the girl's family needed to obtain a certificate from the magistrate to do so (Sub-statute 116-2; see Chapter 5). Nor did this *dingli* emphasize that the absence of the boy must be due to his absconding (Sub-statute 116-2). The new regulation seemed designed in particular to give the girl's family more freedom to enter into another marriage and the officials a legal basis for ruling that the later marriage was valid. However, it is not clear when exactly this 'law' was made. It is noticeable that such cases were still treated as difficult at the lower level. So the magistrate might report to the higher authority for his decision, as in the two cases above.

8.2 Ending the marriage

Going through the divorce cases in the surviving records, especially in Baodi, I immediately noted that divorce cases constituted the largest group of marriage disputes, numbering about twenty out of a total of eighty cases in Baodi. To illustrate these cases better, we may divide them roughly into four types: applying for a divorce because the husband was absent; mutual agreement; repudiation; and selling a wife. The following grounds for dissolution of a legal marriage were given by law (see Chapter 5): the husband had fled from home for three years; the wife's conduct provided one of seven reasons for repudiation; breaking of the bond (*yijue*); mutual consent. The first three types of divorce roughly reflected the legal grounds for divorce. Disputes concerning selling a wife had no legal basis, but they actually accounted for over ten divorce cases in the Baodi records.

8.2.1 Application for divorce

Case 9

Woman Ma married Zhang Lao. She later returned to her natal family after her husband went away. The husband had been absent without news for six

[13] Ibid., vol. 3: 26.

[14] See Chapter 1.

years and woman Ma's parents found it difficult to support her. Woman Ma's mother asked the magistrate for permission to remarry her daughter. The magistrate wrote a relatively long comment on her petition: 'According to the law, if the husband has fled (*taowang*) elsewhere for six years already, his wife should be allowed to marry another man. The term "flee" means to hide in some place in order to avoid prosecution for a crime. If the husband is away on business, or visiting relatives and friends, or touring, although the location is unknown, and even if there is no message from him, he should not be treated as "fleeing". Now your son-in-law left for business. He should, of course, have a permanent address. It would be wrong if I allow your daughter to marry another man just on the ground that you have not received news from him. If indeed you live a very hard life, I order you, with the help of the Zhang clan, to ask Zhang Lao's brother to take your daughter back now and find out Zhang Lao's whereabouts.' (Baodi, 162: 142)

This case reveals that the magistrate was ready to support an existing legal marriage according to law. The ground that the husband had fled for three years was not applicable to this case. The magistrate analysed the facts and did not grant the divorce by applying Sub-statute 116-2, but at the same time he ordered the husband's relatives to support the wife and to find out the location of her husband.

Case 10

In an application to the magistrate, a father requested that his daughter-in-law be allowed to return to her natal family, since his stepson, the woman's husband, had gone away to work for thirteen years and no news at all had been received. The magistrate required the woman's brother to report back on whether the woman herself wanted to stay. Several days later the brother submitted a report in which he said that his sister did wish to remarry and did not want to stay in her husband's home any longer. The magistrate gave his permission and issued the certificate. (Baodi, 162: 91–2)

Although the husband in this case was also away for work, permission was granted to the woman to marry another man. Perhaps the reason was that the father could not afford to keep the woman and the husband's absence had been rather long. The magistrate carefully checked the woman's willingness before he permitted the application.

It is worth mentioning that the cause of the petition brought by the father was very simple: 'In the matter of reporting the reason for ending the marriage and to place this in the records of the court (*wei chengming fuqi liyi qingyou enzhun cunan shi*)'. He even applied only to put the matter in the file rather than to ask the magistrate to decide. Sometimes the application was even shorter: 'in the matter of reporting to place in the records (*wei cheng-ming cunan shi*)' (Baodi, 170: 232). This style of petition was seen only in petitions brought by the husband's family. This might suggest that divorce was easier when requested by the husband's side.

8.2.2 Mutual consent

Mutual consent was defined in the Code as a situation in which the couple disliked each other and both wished to end the marriage. I found not a single case of mutual consent owing to dislike. As I have pointed out, marriage in traditional China was sustained by responsibility rather than personal feelings (see Chapter 5). So we have to understand 'mutual consent' very loosely as indicating that the couple jointly wished the dissolution of their marriage, as in the following application.

Case 11
The person who has drawn up the divorce contract is Li Guozhen. His house is in bad repair and he does not have enough food and clothing to feed and dress a family, owing to the flood and a bad harvest. 'I have to beg food in the street and still sometimes fail to take food home. My wife has to go back to her parents to enable her to live but her parents are in the same difficulty. Then she has to come back. I have a father of over 70 years old whom it is difficult for me to support. So my wife and I have decided to separate, with the agreement of my father, in order to avoid starving to death. I will be solely responsible if any member of either family has regrets. Should I repent of the divorce myself, the separation agreement on which I have placed my palm and foot prints may be the evidence to prove that I had agreed to the separation.

May you, magistrate, please conduct an investigation. The divorce money is 400 *diao*.'

Person drawing up the contract: Li Gouzhen

[signed with whole foot print and whole palm print] (Baodi, 176: 157)

In this case, the wife returned to her parents and later they arranged another marriage for her. Although, in theory, this divorce was agreed mutually, the application was still brought by the husband. As I have pointed out in Chapter 5, the law did not stipulate any procedure for divorce by mutual consent. And I have reason to suspect that all applications for divorce by mutual consent, even though very rare, were made by the husband.

Case 12
Xia Shigeng submitted an application to divorce his wife: 'In the matter of having a record of ending my marriage owing to poverty. I married Ke

> Zhanzhou's daughter née Ke several years ago. I was born in a poor family, which can only be supported by hard labour. Now the rice price is very high. Although I am willing to work harder, I have nowhere to work. Thus I cannot afford every day's meals . . . . it is better for us to be free of the marriage and seek to survive separately. I discussed the divorce with née Ke who has agreed with me. Her father, Ke Zhanzhou, witnessing my poverty, also has not interfered.' He then briefly spoke about the arrangement for née Ke to marry Li by following the proper procedures. He finally made an allegation that he was forced by poverty to let née Ke marry another man, that neither she nor her father agreed because they despised his poverty, and that Li did not plot to take and marry her. Thus he would like to report to the magistrate to keep the facts on record. The magistrate agreed but warned the husband to let the woman return to her family and remarry from there. (Ba county records, 1801/Jiaqing 6, *juan* 200)

The reason for divorce was almost the same as in Case 11. Consent was given not only by the wife, but by her father as well. After all, the burden of a divorced wife fell on the father if he did not remarry her. Interestingly, consent by the wife's father was also often seen in contracts of repudiation. As we shall see, this feature made the issue of repudiating a wife more balanced towards the wife's side than it might appear at first sight.

8.2.3 Repudiating a wife

To illustrate the issues regarding the husband's power to repudiate his wife, I first translate a contract of repudiation from Baodi, which bears a similarity to the above cases.

> **Divorce contract**
>
> I, Chen Mengling, aged 37, married née Liu, Liu Shiling's daughter, and am the person who has drawn up the contract of repudiation. First, she cannot keep a wife's good behaviour, . . . , always blaming and hitting. So I called my father-in-law who agreed to take her back . . . to marry to another man. . . . There is to be nothing to do with Chen Mengling after the divorce. The divorce is witnessed by three sides and agreed by both families. . . . Anyone who repents will be sent to the magistrate's court for punishment. . . . The contract is drawn as evidence.
>
> Jiaqing 21st year month date 21 The contract maker:
>
> Chen Mengling [sign] (Baodi, 161: 116)

According to the text of the Code, a woman was clearly subject to her husband in a marriage. As we saw in Chapter 5, any one of the seven wrongs (*qichu*) by the wife constituted a legal ground for the husband to repudiate her, subject to the three exceptions (*san buqu*). Although this was true, the importance of the wife's own family should not be underestimated, for marriage unites two families rather than just two individuals. Cases concerning repudiation reveal the practical consequences of this view.

As the above contract of repudiation and Cases 11 and 12 reveal, the difference between repudiation by the husband and divorce by mutual consent might be very little in terms of the procedure and the form of the divorce contract, except that the term 'repudiate' (*xiu*) was employed in the contract of repudiation. However, although this term was not used in the divorce contract of Case 11, because it was a divorce by mutual consent, the documents of the case clearly show that the husband used the term 'repudiated' to express his divorce from his wife. So, the term was also quite likely to be used to refer to a divorce not owing to any improper behaviour on the part of the wife. In this sense, *xiu* might bear both a strict sense, implying the wife's wrong, and a less strict sense. If the wife had not done something wrong, and the term *xiu* was still applied, then inevitably the term lost something of its strict meaning. The significance of this is that the theoretically favourable position of the husband was declining.

This had a lot to do with the effort of the wife's family in protecting their daughter's marriage. In the Baodi records, petitions brought by a wife's family accounted for the second-largest group of marriage cases, totalling eight. Their legal ground for bringing the petition was that the husband was exercising repudiation without a good reason. This action itself might save the marriage without the necessity of a hearing by the magistrate.

Case 13

A petition brought by the wife's family accusing the husband of repudiating their daughter without a proper reason (*wugu xiuqi*). Even though the magistrate believed that the repudiation was backed with a reason, he accepted the petition and ordered the parties to wait until he heard the case personally. Later the plaintiff brought an application for closing the case without a formal hearing because the husband had withdrawn the repudiation. The magistrate permitted this. (Baodi, 164: 52)

The outcome of the case might have been due to the influence of the magistrate's comment, as Philip Huang has commented.[15] What is more

[15] Huang 1996: 125–7.

interesting is how easy it appears to have been for the wife's side to accuse the husband of intending to repudiate her without a legal reason. The wife's family certainly appealed to the provision that prohibited the husband from repudiating his wife without a good reason. Even a wife might herself submit a petition to the magistrate to seek his help in saving her marriage.[16] However, in doing so, the wife's family sometimes abused their right.

Case 14

A father accused his son-in-law of intending to divorce his daughter, since the son-in-law did not let her into their home. The truth was actually that the daughter had a physical problem and the couple could not lead a normal life. Later, the father submitted his explanation for withdrawing the petition and expressed his agreement to allow the husband to return the marriage contract to him, so he could marry another girl. (Baodi, 1907/Guangxu 33, 170–227)

It is very likely that the wife's family sometimes served significantly to restrict the husband's power over his wife, and their support should not be underestimated. Thus, although to insert the agreement of the wife's family in a repudiation contract seems unnecessary in terms of the law on repudiation, in fact it was logical if we consider the provision that barred repudiation when the wife had no natal family to which to return. Thus we can assume that the wife's family was able to serve as a check on the husband's abuse of his power. Reliance upon support from her natal family might also be one of the reasons a woman was reluctant to marry someone far away from her family and relatives. In one case from Ba county, a woman was married by her deceased husband's parents to another man who lived in a county situated in the lower reaches of Yangzi River, whereas her relatives lived on the upper side of the river. The magistrate ruled in favour of the woman by prohibiting her deceased husband's parents from marrying her to someone in the area of the lower reaches of the Yangzi River (Baxian2: 487).

It might, therefore, not have been as easy as has been thought for the husband to repudiate his wife. Indeed, the fact that the wife had to return to her parents if she was repudiated by her husband added further pressure, at least financially, on the woman's family. So it is very understandable that in practice the husband did not often exercise his power of repudiation. Wang Yuesheng has observed that, even if the wife had committed one of the seven wrongs (*qichu*), she was very often not repudiated. He looked at

[16] Wang Yuesheng mentions a case in which a wife submitted a petition to the magistrate and the magistrate decided in her favour by ruling that the husband should take her back (2003: 120).

562 cases where wives had committed adultery. Surprisingly, in only nine cases was the wife repudiated. According to law, adultery was an absolute ground for repudiating a wife, even nullifying the three exceptions that protected the wife from repudiation.[17] Thus, although there might have been several reasons for husbands deciding not to repudiate their wives, the unpopularity of repudiating a wife is clear, even when the husband had a good reason for divorce.

In terms of court performances, the magistrate gave constant and resolute support to the original marriage rather than just to the husband. Sometimes, the husband failed to repudiate his wife even though he had a good reason. In one case, a husband applied to the magistrate for permission to repudiate his wife. Although the wife had behaved badly, the magistrate did not grant the divorce. It was only when the husband appealed that the divorce was finally permitted. The appeal judge criticized the magistrate for sticking too strictly to the principle that the original marriage should be protected.[18] On the other hand, whereas repudiation of a wife was not easy, selling a wife seemed very popular, and I shall discuss this next.

8.2.4 Selling a wife

In Case 11, the couple was divorced, the wife returned to her parents, and, from there, she was married by her natal family. In Case 12, it appeared that the divorced wife might be married to another man by her first husband, despite the magistrate's warning that she should be married by her natal family, otherwise he could be treated as selling his wife. Sometimes the difference was hard to detect between properly remarrying a divorced woman and the selling of a (divorced) 'wife' by the husband.

In cases of 'selling a wife', the 'wife' was, in legal terms, a divorced woman. The essence of selling a wife can be roughly understood as the transfer of a wife from one marriage to another, at a price. The second marriage might have been arranged by her first husband, or a by person other than her first husband without reference to him. On most occasions, it was the first husband who organized the second marriage, because understandably other people would find it difficult to do this while the marriage lasted. When selling his wife, for whatever reason, the first husband needed first to divorce her by making a contract of repudiation, then to give her to the second husband in exchange for the gift money from him.

[17] Wang Yuesheng 2003: 97.
[18] *Qingdai mingchen pandu*, vol. 3: 14–15.

Scholars usually connect the case of selling a wife with Article 367: 'Toleration by a Spouse of a Wife's or Concubine's Infidelity'. As the title reveals, this statute provided rules on illicit sexual relations. It started with a stipulation relating to a husband who facilitated and tolerated his wife or concubine engaging in fornication with someone else. The husband, the adulterous lover, and the adulterous wife were each to receive ninety blows with the heavy stick, and the wife was to return to her family. The Article went on:

> If consideration is used to buy a divorce or to sell a divorce [i.e. someone gives the husband money to cause him to get rid of his wife] (*in order*) that [the one giving it] may marry another man's wife (*by agreement*), the husband and the wife and the one who is buying the divorce, will each be punished with 100 blows with the heavy stick. The wife will be divorced and returned to her own clan, and the wedding gifts will be forfeit to the government. If the one buying the divorce and the wife use tricks to put pressure on the husband to divorce her, and if otherwise the husband would not have sold the divorce, he is not punished.[19]

The Baodi records contain a case that clearly applied this law:

> **Case 15**
> Wei, a resident of Baodi, accused Zheng of a neighbouring county, Sanhe, of privately selling his wife and daughter. The case was heard and decided by the Sanhe magistrate. Then he sent Wei and the others involved to Baodi with a detailed report (*yiwen*). According to the report, the facts were that Wei had fled with his wife and daughter to Sanhe because of the flood. When they one day rested in a temple, Wei approached Zheng asking him to act as a go-between to marry his wife. It was arranged that Li would marry the woman for a gift of 70 *diao*. Later, because of a problem with the money, Wei submitted a petition to the Sanhe magistrate's court. In his reasoning, the magistrate said: 'According to my investigation, Wei, owing to his poverty, employed Zheng as a go-between to marry his wife Liu to Li as his wife. Then he brought a false accusation since he was not satisfied with the marriage presents he had obtained from marrying his wife, and he thought Zheng had more than he should. Li and his brother dared to buy a divorce of a wife clearly knowing her real status. Zheng was also wrong to serve as the go-between for he too knew the woman's real status (*zhiqing shuomei*), and took some money, which was not right. Thus Wei, Li and his brother, Zheng, are all to be punished under the law of buying and selling a divorce (*maixiu maixiu*). Liu unwillingly married another, which is forgivable, and punishment will not be imposed on her. She should divorce Wei and return to her natal family.' (Baodi, 1823/Daoguang 3, 163–70)

[19] Jones 1994: 348–9.

The transferring report (*yiwen*) sent to the Baodi magistrate by the Sanhe magistrate gave a clear statement of the law. In this case, the husband was driven by poverty as a result of the natural disaster of flood to divorce his wife and marry her to another man in order to secure survival for them both. This was not a case that Article 367 envisaged. However, the Article was still applied and the magistrate did not exercise mercy for any of the parties and based his decision strictly on the letter of the law on buying and selling a divorce (*maixiu maixiu*).

Some officials also noted the gap between Article 367 and wife-selling cases such as this. Shen Zhiqi's commentary on Article 116 (Repudiation) contained an explanation. He commented: 'if the husband was too poor to afford his wife and had no means of repaying debt, as a result of which he sold his wife, he should be judged under Article 386: "Doing That Which Ought Not to Be Done (*buyingwei*)".[20] However, the wife should be returned to the first husband' (*Jizhu*: 287). Bao Shichen, who became a magistrate after 1808 (Jiaqing 13) when he obtained his degree in the capital, also discussed the law applicable to such cases in his book. He specially pointed out that wife-selling cases should not be judged under the law on *maixiu maixiu* (Article 367): 'the ordinary cases relating to selling and buying a wife on the ground of poverty should certainly not be judged under buying and selling a divorce (*maixiu maixiu*),[21] because that is not the right law for such a situation. The law of *maixiu maixiu* is for the situation in which the wife commits adultery, the husband then deliberately divorces her in order to make her the adulterer's wife, and accepts money for this marriage.'[22] Bao suggested applying the principle of Article 117, 'Making Marriage against the Law'. His suggestion is particularly significant in understanding the practice of the court in dealing with such cases, because he considered this point when the Board of Punishments sought his advice on several legal difficulties, including the law governing buying and selling a

[20] Article 386 imposed punishments on wrongdoers of forty blows of the light stick, if the matter was adjudged to be less serious, and eighty blows of the heavy stick, if the matter was more serious.

[21] Bao Shichen 1872/1968: *juan* 31.

[22] Summer (2000: 61–4) discusses the phenomenon in detail. He points out that the wife-selling cases highlight the gap between official priorities and the needs of normal people. He is quite right to point out that a case such as this did not fit under Article 367 concerning illegally marrying an adulterous wife to the adulterer. However, he is wrong to conclude that this gap resulted from the legislator's incorrect treatment of such wife-selling cases as illegal sexual relations. The confused position of the law arose from the fact that it did not cover such situations in the first place.

wife. Since there was no commonly accepted belief about which law should be applied to such cases, we might expect court practice to vary, as the following cases show.

Case 16

A husband married his wife to Meng, and brought a complaint later accusing Meng of forcing him to sell his wife. Meng said he was not particularly happy about marrying the plaintiff's previous wife, but his grandmother said she needed somebody to take care of her. That was why he agreed to the marriage. The magistrate first punished Meng for marrying another's wife and ordered him to take the woman home until the husband was summoned to the court for a further decision on the marriage. The husband, before he could come, committed suicide. (Baodi, 1814–1816/Jiaqing 19–21, 161–9)

Case 17

A husband prompted by poverty married his wife to Zhao at a price of 110 *diao* marriage gift through her father, Wang. The husband drew up the repudiation contract, which was kept by his wife's family, who received 50 of the 110 *diao*. The husband now brought the case by accusing the father of privately selling his wife to another man. The magistrate's decision can be seen on the second husband's counter-plaint. 'The parties and the witnesses have been clearly interrogated. You [Zhao] married Wang's daughter through a go-between and did not know that woman Wang was a married woman. You were deceived by the go-between Bai. I decide to fine Bai 40 *diao*, and you should give 20 *diao* to the former husband Li. Woman Wang should be taken home by you. All should signify their willingness to accept the decision and close the case.' (Baodi, 171: 82–3)

Case 18

The uncle of née Zhang accused her first and second husbands and her younger brother of conspiracy to sell her. But the truth seemed to be that née Zhang herself was not happy to stay with her former husband, and frequently left him. Her younger brother, having failed to persuade the former husband to have her back, arranged for her to marry another man at the price of 50 *diao*, of which he kept 10 *diao* and the former husband had the rest. Although the uncle's allegation was unfounded, since née Zhang's former husband had agreed to repudiate her, the magistrate stated that both the younger brother and the second husband 'were not good citizens' (*fei anfen liangmin*). For example, 'the fifteen year old brother dared to require a repudiation contract from his brother-in law', and the second husband offered the marriage gift too late, the woman having already lived with him for one year. They should be punished 'in order to deter someone else from committing the same wrong' (*yijing xiaoyou*). (Baodi, 172: 80–5)

These cases were all brought on the ground of selling a wife. Although many such cases resulted from the husband's poverty, they could be very different. For example, the second husband in Case 16 married the divorced wife because his grandmother needed somebody to serve her, in other words, the factor of the filial duty owed by a grandson to his grandmother was involved; the second husband in Case 17 did not know the woman he had married was another man's wife; and the woman herself in Case 18 was the one who resolved to end the first marriage. As these cases have explored, the situations in which a woman ended the first marriage and entered another varied dramatically.

Encountering cases such as these, the law on buying and selling a divorce (*maixiu maixiu*) was even less applicable. This contributed to the difficulty facing the court in resolving such cases. The magistrate might have been able to apply a particular principle by following the main accepted practice in dealing with similar cases. For example, Hoang noted that, if the first husband was forced to divorce his wife on the ground of poverty, the commonly accepted practice in the courts of Zhejiang province was to rule under the law of 'Doing That Which Ought Not to Be Done' (*buyingwei*) (Article 386), and that the marriage gift might be kept and the wife remain with the second husband.[23] Nevertheless, the problem of which law should be applied to such cases remained.

This problem is indicated by the six such cases that appeared in *Xingan huilan* (Conspectus of Cases from the Board of Punishments), under the application of Article 367 (Toleration by a Spouse of a Wife's or Concubine's Infidelity). It seems that the common practice in judging such cases was to apply Article 367. I quote from two of the cases.

Case 19

Quan, with the help of his brother-in-law, sold his wife to Yuan because of poverty. Both Quan, his brother-in-law, and the second husband were punished with one hundred blows of the heavy stick according to the law of *maixiu maixiu*. The woman should have returned to her natal family according to the law. But, since her brother was involved, she should not be sent back until it was ascertained whether her parents were still alive or not. (*Huilan*: 3286, 1795/Qianlong 60)

Case 20

Chuan sold his wife on the ground of poverty to Zhang through a go-between. Since sale for this reason was different from the situation given in the law of *maixiu maixiu*, Chuan, Zhang, the wife and the go-between should

[23] Hoang 1898: 132.

> be punished with eighty blows of the heavy stick according to the law of 'doing what ought not to be done' (Article 386).[24] The wife was to remain with the second husband since her former husband was too poor to feed her and she had no family to which to return. (*Huilan*: 3289, 1827/Daoguang 7)

Most husbands in these six cases claimed to be forced by poverty (and/or illness) to sell their wives. Cases 19 and 20 represent more or less the two ways of dealing with such cases given in the *Huilan*. Case 19 was the earlier (1795/Qianlong 60), and Case 20 the later (1827/Daoguang 7). The key issues in these cases were whether the woman could stay with her second husband and whether the marriage gift was to be forfeited. Out of the six cases, four were decided according to the law of *maixiu maixiu* (Article 367). In two of the cases, however, 'specific circumstances were taken into account to apply the law' (*zhunqing zhuoli*), and the point was clearly made that Article 367 was not completely applicable to the facts of the case — for example, the husband was poor and ill, or the second husband did not know the truth. In Case 20, the woman, instead of being returned to her natal family as stipulated by the Article, was rather to remain with the second husband and the money kept by the first husband.[25] Finally, Case 20 reveals that the gap between the facts of the case and the law of *maixiu* was clearly recognized, and another law (the law of *buying* — Article 386) was applied instead. This decision suggested a general trend, as in the commonly accepted practice in Zhejiang province (see above).

Interestingly, if we go back to Yuan and Ming legal history, it is surprising to find that a similar problem was experienced by Yuan and Ming courts, and that both the Yuan and Ming actually had clearer, and maybe better, rules on dealing with cases of wife-selling. In general, in dealing with such cases, if the husband had divorced his wife in order for her to marry the adulterer, the law of *maixiu maixiu* should be applied; if the husband had married his wife to another man for money, the law of *buyingwei* should be applied; if the husband had acted under the pressure of poverty and illness, then no punishment was to be imposed.[26]

History may sometimes repeat itself. In the so-called wife-selling cases, what the three dynasties had in common was a firm intention to apply the law. When a particular law was not completely applicable, the court might

[24] See footnote 22 above.
[25] See also Bodde and Morris 1973: 428.
[26] Xue Yunsheng, *Comparative Edition of the Tang and Ming Codes*, quoted in Chen Peng 1990: 586.

exercise discretion. It is quite clear that *zhunqing zhuoli* was introduced to help resolve the difficulties of applying a particular statute. Compared with the two previous dynasties, law makers in the Qing were more conservative in this matter than their earlier counterparts.

Although we do not have clear evidence of the Qing's failure to provide a revised regulation, development was very slow, at least at the level of central government. The evidence from the Baodi court shows no sign that the Qing had made any widely applicable law on the difficult issue raised by the selling of a wife. However, by exercising their discretion, magistrates still achieved reasonable decisions, even though no statute or regulation appeared to be applicable.

8.3 Cases concerning a widow's remarriage

A widow was allowed to remarry, subject to completing the mourning period for her deceased husband. I have pointed out in Chapter 5 that the law on a widow's remarriage was the most revised part of the Qing marriage law. The privilege of arranging for remarriage was transferred from the widow's natal parents to her in-laws. Should she be forced to remarry, she was the one to decide whether to stay or divorce. Most importantly, she had the right either to remain faithful to her dead husband or to remarry. In dealing with cases concerning a widow's remarrying, the magistrate clearly applied the relevant law, as, for example, in the following comment by a magistrate of Baodi county: 'If the husband is dead, the widow is allowed to remarry by law. Your cousin is dead and your cousin's wife has no parents-in-law. She can decide herself whether to remarry or not' (Baodi, 173: 6).

Case 21

A widow's father-in-law accused her brother of breaking a promise to give him [the father-in-law] the 165 *diao* marriage gift after having engaged the widow to a man. Before a formal trial was conducted, the father-in-law submitted an application to close the case without the formal hearing. He explained that the widow's family had returned the marriage presents to him. 'Since we live a hard life, if my daughter-in-law wishes to remarry I cannot stop her. But all the wedding presents she received [from her deceased husband] should be returned to me. Now through the mediation of relatives they have been returned.' The magistrate gave permission and closed the case. (Baodi, 161: 112–15)

Case 22

The widow's father-in-law accused the widow's father of privately arranging for her to marry another man. The widow's father, in his counter-plaint, rejected the allegation and said that he had told the father-in-law about the remarriage. The magistrate did not believe him and ordered him to wait for a formal trial. The two fathers and the village head had been summoned to the court. In the hearing, the widow stated that she wanted to remarry and that her parents-in-law agreed; the father-in-law failed to prove that he had not been told this. Then it turned out that, by accusing the widow's family of privately intending to remarry the widow, the father-in-law was actually seeking to secure a debt owed to him by the widow's father. He was using the lawsuit as a bait to recover this. Since the magistrate ruled that the debt be paid to the father-in-law, he felt 'he had nothing to say but close the case willingly (*qingyuan xisu*)'. (Baodi, 162: 147–53)

Case 23

Jiang accused Zhang of preparing to marry his nephew's widow without his agreement. But both Zhang and the widow's family said that Jiang first agreed then withdrew because the gift-money was not enough for him. After the interrogation in court, Zhang agreed to give the uncle more money, then the case was closed. (Baodi, 163: 160–7)

According to law, if the widow's deceased husband's family arranged the second marriage, the betrothal present from the second husband's family was to be received by the widow's parents-in-law. If the widow's own family wanted to remarry her, they should first return the marriage gift received from the deceased husband to the widow's parents-in-law (Case 21), then arrange a second marriage for her, the betrothal present from the second marriage going to the widow's family. The second betrothal gift thus went either to the deceased husband's family or to the widow's family.

From the above cases, we can see that disputes over a widow's remarriage generally concerned the dissatisfaction of the deceased husband's family with the money they obtained from the widow's remarriage. This also clearly shows that, in practice, the right of the husband's family to arrange the widow's remarriage prevailed over the right of the widow's family. If the husband's family was not satisfied with the money it was going to receive or had received, it resorted to the court. The results of the above cases show that the family often received more money. In this sense, disputes over the remarriage of a widow were similar to those over a debt. The privilege of arranging the woman's marriage included the privilege of receiving the marriage gift. It seems that the magistrate, when dealing with such cases, clearly took the deceased husband's family into consideration first.

8.4 Summary

In dealing with marriage cases, the magistrate more often than not applied the law. In fact, the application of the law can be even stricter than in land and debt cases. In other words, the magistrate's court and, even more so, a higher court were less likely to consider human feelings in making a decision. This did not contradict official thinking. Family values were undoubtedly among the most strongly advocated, and, because these values were carefully enshrined in the provisions of the Code, a strict application of the Code was a logical result. Only this conclusion can explain such decisions as that in Case 6 where the judges showed anything but human feeling.

9

Other Relevant Matters Concerning the Resolution of Land, Debt, and Marriage Disputes

A couple of striking characteristics connected with the resolution of land, debt, and marriage cases have already been touched on in the preceding chapters, and some examples have been given. Such matters as physical injury or self-help in taking property and exaggerated or false accusations seem constantly to have come before the magistrate. When civil cases involved these auxiliary matters, it is true that the magistrate often imposed punishment, although he rarely did so on the basis of the primary dispute itself. We have also seen that the magistrate rarely applied custom, ethical notions such as human feelings, or sources other than law. However, the function of custom and human feelings in making judicial decisions still requires a brief discussion. Only once these issues have been grasped can one really understand the magistrate's practice in solving land, debt, and marriage cases. I deal with these issues in three sections: punishment; the function of custom in decisions; and the relation between *qing*, *li*, and law in terms of making decisions.

One point that must be born in mind is that each of these issues — punishment, physical delicts, false accusation, or custom, *qing*, and *li* — is a large topic in itself that deserves much more study and space. What I shall examine in this chapter is only the part that relates to resolving land, debt, and marriage cases. For this reason, the conclusions arrived at in this chapter should not be regarded as necessarily applicable in a different context, although I do make some general points.

9.1 Punishment

Punishment, as one of the coercive methods designed by the law and backed by the state to maintain order in a society, is found in all legal systems. For some scholars, the concepts of law and forcibility are logically and factually inseparable; for example, Del Vecchio concludes: 'Where coercibility is lacking Law, too, is lacking.'[1] Of course, a number of jurisprudential writers do not agree with this view. However, few scholars would object to this application of Del Vecchio's dictum to traditional Chinese law. Indeed, punishment played such an important role in traditional Chinese legal culture that the law was often seen as equivalent to 'penalties' (*xing*). I discussed the features that have often led scholars to describe the Qing Code as a 'penal code' in Chapter 1. The Code took a great deal of trouble to match the physical punishment to the gravity of the offence. 'Situations that called for punishment were scrutinized in the greatest detail by those responsible for recommending law.'[2]

Past assumptions have held that punishment was often used by the magistrate in dealing with civil disputes. However, it is clear from the preceding chapters that in all cases where the magistrate imposed some sort of penalty this was based not on the dispute over land, debt, or marriage itself, but rather on a false accusation or an act of violence.[3] In this section, I first examine these two common reasons for imposing punishment in order to see whether the punishments imposed could be justified in terms of the law.

9.1.1 Cases involving minor injuries

Only when the minor injury (*weishang*) involved was a supplementary aspect of land, debt, and marriage cases were those cases left within the magistrate's sole adjudication. Otherwise, the injury might be serious enough itself to be the main charge and constitute the main problem for the magistrate to solve, with the probability of further review by higher authority. In 69 out of 127 cases in the land section (Table 6.1) and 79 out of 126 cases in the debt section (Table 7.1), some sort of violent behaviour, mainly physical injury, was alleged. The proportion in marriage cases is not clear, but seems to have been much lower. Even so, the proportion is extraordinary. I have pointed out that an allegation of wounding was a successful device for bringing a petition to gain access to the county court, especially when the petition itself had a flaw — for example, lacked strong evidence for a claim, as already seen in Case 10 in Chapter 3.

[1] Del Vecchio 1953: 304. John Austin (1955) also believed that every valid law must have a sanction.

[2] MacCormack 1996b: 200.

[3] Zheng Qin and Zhang Jinfan incorrectly believed that the magistrate routinely combined punishment and mediation in handling civil cases (Zheng Qin 1988: 208–9; Zhang Jinfan 1998: 21).

The most relevant provision in the Code is Article 302: *Douou* (Affrays and Blows):

> Everyone who engages in an affray or inflicts blows (*who fights with another*) and, using hands or feet, strikes another but does not cause injury, will receive 20 strokes of the light bamboo. (*As soon as there is a blow* [the offence] *is committed.*) If he causes injury, or if, by using some other object, he inflicts a blow on another and does not cause injury, he will receive 10 strokes of the light bamboo. (*If he inflicts a blow with some other object*) and does cause injury, then he will receive 40 strokes of the light bamboo. (*If the skin which is struck*) turns blue or red (*and*) there is a swelling, this is an 'injury.' Anything other than hands or feet (*which is held*) is 'another object'.
>
> If, because of an affray, there is mutual striking and injury, then investigate the seriousness of the injuries and affix the penalty. The one who strikes subsequently and has reason to strike will have his penalty reduced from the set penalty two degrees.[4]

Obviously, to produce an injury ('*shang*') as described above, whether or not it was intentional, was easy. 'Injury' was construed so broadly that even the skin becoming red was included, and the Code required cases involving injuries to be dealt with immediately. This can be seen from the fact that cases alleging injuries (for example, Case 9 in Chapter 3) were under the jurisdiction of the *xingfang* (the Office of Punishments) instead of the *hufang* (the Office of Revenue), which in Baodi had particular jurisdiction over land cases, or the *yanfang* (the Salt Office), which had jurisdiction in debt cases, or the *lifang* (the Office of Rites), which had jurisdiction in marriage cases. These petitions were marked with the words '*xingxin*' (new case for the Office of Punishments). If a person alleged a *shang*, he or she was examined immediately by the runners on duty, who took a very brief statement of the allegation.

We have seen a few statements from the court reports concerning examination for injuries in Chapter 3. 'The injuries were examined and Huang Lishi [née Li] had two scratches in the middle of her forehead and three scratches on the left side of her face. They all just broke the skin. No other wound was found' (Baodi, 96: 101).[5] 'Shan and Chuan both had their braids untied. No other injury was found' (Baodi, 97: 136).[6] 'Zhou Fulai had an injury of two scratches on the left of his forehead. No other injury was found' (Baodi, 99: 53).[7] 'Zhu Kun's left hand had a scratch. There was no other

4 Jones 1994: 285–7.

5 See also Case 10 in Chapter 6.

6 See also Case 16 in Chapter 6.

7 See Case 7 below.

injury. Zhu Wanfu had a scratch with a piece of tile in the corner of his left eye. The injury has formed a scab, so it is improper to uncover it and see further. Zhu Fusheng had a scratch on his forehead and no other injury. Zhu Wanjin had a scratch on the left of his forehead and no other injury' (Baodi, 104: 104).[8] These kinds of minor injury were quite typical in the Baodi records, and could hardly be called real injuries. Some of the injuries alleged in the petition were self-inflicted, but most of them had been caused by other people.

The concern of Article 302 in broadening the definition of 'injury' perhaps can be regarded as resulting from the emphasis laid by the Code on 'the value of human life'.[9] A memorial by officials who were ordered to revise the Code in the Yongzheng period (1723–35) stressed: 'the emperors have the virtue of cherishing the welfare of living things. And in the first place they cherish human life' (*Tongkao*: 10). Injury often causes loss of life. So, on the one hand, the Code defined 'injury' in its widest scope and imposed a range of punishments to draw people's attention to the value of life; on the other hand, it provided a policy of keeping the loss of life to a minimum.

The policy was put into effect by Article 303: *Baogu qixian* (Time limit for *baogu*).

> (*Bao means to care for or protect, Gu means crime, Care for the* [victim of] *crime* [*Baogu*] *means that if the injured person* [whose injury was caused by] *blows has not yet died, the official having jurisdiction will set a time limit within which to care for him. Caring for another's injuries really protects* [the offender] *himself from* [the consequences of] *his own offence.*)
>
> In every case of caring for the [victim of the] crime, (*first investigate the seriousness of the injury, whether there was the use of hands or feet, whether another object was used, or whether there was a metal knife. In each case clearly establish a time-limit for responsibility*), and order the guilty person (*who is responsible to care for the* [victim of the] *crime*) to have medical treatment given. . . .
>
> If it is an injury which is a fracture or something more serious [Art. 302], and if, within the period of caring for [the victim of] the crime, it is treated medically and is cured, then each offence will be reduced two degrees. (*If someone strikes with justification, then reduce the penalty for striking two degrees. If there is cure within the time-limits provided for caring for* [the victim of] *the crime, then* [the penalty] *is reduced another two degrees. This is said to be the accumulation of reductions in the penalty for a crime.*). . . .

[8] See Huang 1996: 85, 86.
[9] MacCormack 1996b: 122–37.

> Whenever someone strikes and injures another by use of the hands, feet, or other object (*and the injury is not severe*) the limit is 20 days (*for cure*).[10]

The Article was obviously designed to give the injured person the best possible chance of recovery by placing both victim and offender under the control of the court. At the same time, it permitted mitigation of or exemption from punishment for the offender. There is no doubt that recovery from an injury was an important fact that the magistrate had to take into account when deciding whether or which punishment should be imposed. It was certainly an important guideline for the magistrate's resolution of civil cases when minor injuries were involved. Thus, when the magistrate mentions that 'the minor wound has now healed' in his decision, just as when he mentions other reasons, he was giving the reason, stated in the Code, for his decision in the matter of the injury. He did not 'merely wave the matter off'.[11]

Where an injury was involved and the time limit for recovery was quite lengthy, at least twenty days, many cases were heard after this period had elapsed. The magistrate might deal with the matter of injury first, ordering the parties to go home and wait to be heard again after the injuries had healed (Baodi, 188: 163–84 and 194: 101–14). However, many minor injuries, such as a couple of scratches on the forehead, as we have seen above, certainly did not need twenty days to heal. Nevertheless, the magistrate might still have let the parties wait and conducted his hearing twenty days later. In this case, the law governing recovery from injuries could be used as an excuse for postponing a formal hearing. Concerned about such a situation, Sub-statute 303-4 required that the magistrate should try such cases without necessarily waiting until the wound had healed. However, this principle was not applied to the five courts of the capital (see Chapter 2). Another provision allowed the five courts of the capital to start the time limit for a hearing from the time the wound healed (Sub-statute 405-4). Xue Yunsheng noticed the difference and pointed out that there was a contradiction between these provisions (*Cunyi*: 899, 1222).

The matter of the injury would not have influenced the decision in the dispute itself. We have already seen this from Case 10 in Chapter 3, in which the two creditors were punished for their violence but the debtor was ordered to pay them 400 *wen* each. In another case, the plaintiff accused the defendant of owing him money and hurting him with an object. After the hearing, when the magistrate had ascertained that there was no strong evidence of the debt, although the defendant had done wrong and was

[10] Jones 1994: 287–8.
[11] Huang 1996: 90.

punished for his behaviour, the plaintiff's debt claim was rejected (Baodi, 188: 187–208).[12]

9.1.2 False accusation

Bodde and Morris have estimated that there were a total of 206 false accusation (*wugao*) cases in the *Xingan huilan* (Conspectus of Cases from the Board of Punishments), accounting for a quarter of the whole. They stated: 'The false accusation group, because of its high position on the list and its seemingly peculiarly Chinese characteristics', deserved further study.[13] Some discussion of such serious false accusation cases can be found in studies by Zhou Guangyuan and Macauley, who have both made significant contributions.[14] My focus, as I made clear at the beginning of this chapter, can only be on the aspects relevant to land, debt, and marriage cases, as in the previous subsection on minor injuries.

The statistic given by Bodde and Morris is astonishing. But Wang Huizu's mentioning of the Chinese saying 'there is no petition that can be so called if it does not tell a lie (*wuhuang bucheng zhuang*)' is even more shocking.[15] This proverb, although an exaggeration, reveals the high proportion of petitions that contained one or another untrue element. Thus, Macauley holds that false accusation was very often used by litigants to secure access to the magistrate's court.[16] False accusation was indeed a problem in Qing litigation. In twenty-four cases collected by Lan Dingyuan, nearly one-third involved a serious false accusation framed with the help of the 'litigation masters'.[17]

False accusation was codified in the Qing in a complicated way. At least six Articles (336, 337, 339, 340, 343, and 408) and thirty-four sub-statutes (including all twenty-seven sub-statutes attached to Article 336) were relevant to false accusation. In general, false accusation was liable to severe punishment.

Article 336: *Wugao* (False Accusations), reads:

> In the case of anyone who falsely accuses another of an offence punishable with strokes of the light bamboo, sentence him to the penalty of the offence of which he falsely accused [the other], increased two degrees.

[12] There are other cases like this in which the magistrate's decision might or might not favour one or the other side. I therefore think that one should be very careful about stating that the magistrate ruled in favour of one side.
[13] Bodde and Morris 1973: 164.
[14] Zhou Guangyuan 1995; Macauley 1999.
[15] See *Mulingshu*, *juan* 17.
[16] Macauley 1999: 140–2.
[17] Lan Dingyuan 1729/1989: 22–6, 70–4, 82–3.

> . . . . .
>
> If the one who is falsely accused falsely alleges that which is not true in order to calumniate the guilty person [the original false accuser], then inflict on him the penalty for [the offence of which] he accused the other. The other — the original false accuser — is only punished for his own penalty.
>
> If someone accuses [another] of two or more [offences], and the more serious is true and the defendant makes a false confession of having committed the less serious one, or there are several [offences] (*which are not the same, but the*) penalties (*for them*) and the accusation as to one [offence] is correct, then the accuser avoids penalties for all.
>
> If someone accuse another of two or more [offences] and the least serious is true, but the [defendant] falsely confesses to a more serious matter, or if someone accuse [another] of one offence and falsely states a less serious matter to be a more serious matter, (*then apart from the one falsely accused being given what his offence requires, everything else is surplusage*). In all these cases, sentence [the false accuser] (*on the basis of*) exile (*offences which are not true*). If there has already been a decision that has been executed, (*then regardless of whether it is* [an offence involving penalties of] *light bamboo, heavy bamboo, penal servitude, or exile*) in all cases he will be awarded the penalty for the excess offences. If there has not yet been decision and execution, (*then if* [the offence] *that was the subject of the false accusation entails*) strokes of the light or heavy bamboo, he may redeem. If it is penal servitude or exile, [the punishment] will be limited to 100 strokes of the heavy bamboo. For the rest of the penalty he may redeem.
>
> If the law provides a limit to the punishment, then although there is a false accusation of more, do not punish.
>
> If someone accuses two or more persons, but as to one the accusation is untrue, then although the offence is minor, still sentence on the basis of false accusation. (Jones 1994: 317–20)

The Code did not clearly define what was meant by false accusation, which was the key in this issue. At first glance it gives the impression that, whenever a petition contained untrue information, it amounted to a false accusation. However, by analysing the meaning of the provision, we can see that false accusation, as an offence, consisted of two parts. First, the plaintiff had to know that his accusation was not true, that is, as Shen Zhiqi made clear, the plaintiff 'fabricates events that do not exist'. Second, the aim of making the false accusation had to be to bring about the punishment of the accused, as was explained also by Shen Zhiqi, 'in order to accuse somebody of a crime' (*Jizhu*: 810). In the absence of either factor, false accusation had not occurred. This point is extremely important in clarifying whether or not a case should be regarded as a false accusation, and particularly in understanding whether a false accusation was involved in civil disputes.

Baodi cases rarely meet the two conditions necessary for an accusation to be false. At a rough estimate, the results of the cases show that about thirty out of over three hundred civil cases involved a clear indication of 'false accusation'. The number of cases involving false or incomplete allegations that ended up having little to do with false accusation was certainly much higher. I gave an example in Chapter 3 (Case 9) in which the woman who wanted to redeem her land told only half the story by saying that the defendant had refused to return the land. This allegation was used to justify access to the magistrate's court. She omitted to say that she intended to redeem the land with a contract creating a debt instead of with the full payment. Otherwise, she would not have had a case. Situations such as this do give an explanation of the proverb quoted by Wang Huizu. However, they were not sufficient to constitute the offence of false accusation. The magistrate might not even have mentioned the term 'false accusation' in his interrogation and decision in a situation such as this. This is not enough to clarify the confusion.

The number of civil cases involving false accusation in the Baodi records does remind us of the report by the Board of Punishments to the throne. It blamed officials for acting too leniently towards people who brought false accusations. The memorial stated:

> Of the cases reported to us, hardly one in ten has been thoroughly investigated in advance so as to determine the truth or falsity of the charges. For the most part matters are smoothed over just to bring the case to an end. Serious items are commonly played down while trivial ones are played up. Inconclusive statements appear, such as that 'behind the (false) accusation lies some reasons' or 'there is merely suspicion.' When there is no excuse, then the official writes that the parties on appearing in court immediately confessed, in order to bend the law by being too lenient.[18]

Did magistrates act too leniently, as was said in the memorial? If we refer only to the relatively small number of cases giving a clear indication of an accusation treated as false, the answer is yes. A striking example of the 'leniency' noted by the Board is furnished by next case:

Case 1

Liu accused Wang and others (eleven persons who were building a government road) of severely beating his father when they walked through their land and his father went to ask them to explain. His father was hurt too seriously to

[18] Bodde and Morris 1973: 466; the underlined text indicates the part I retranslated for a better understanding

> rise from his bed. The magistrate took up the matter in a very impressive way. He ordered that the relevant people should at once be summoned in the village instead of in the court for his personal examination and decision. The plaintiff was to go home and provide medical care for his father. (Baodi, 96: 117–34)

In this case, the investigation was started with extraordinary speed. The summons *piao* was prepared on the same day the accusation was brought. The following day, the magistrate went to the village and questioned thirteen people. However, the result dramatically changed the situation. The allegedly seriously injured father was found to be only slightly wounded: a scratch on the forehead and on each arm, according to the examination. The son, the plaintiff, explained this big difference by saying that he had not checked his father's wound on the day he brought the petition. He had heard his father was hit and hurried to the court to bring the complaint. The defendants denied they had hit Wang's father. Several days later, the magistrate heard the case again, and the father confessed that his wounds had not resulted from being hit. Although there was obviously a big difference between the original accusation and the result, the magistrate did not treat the petition as a false accusation. One might think that the magistrate acted too leniently. However, the following sub-statute sheds some light on the explanation for both the magistrate's decision and the parties' recklessness in submitting the petition.

> When a person is accused of homicide, if the circumstances of the accusation are false then sentence the offence in accordance with the Article of the Code on falsely accusing a person of homicide where the matter has not yet been decided. The plaintiff is not allowed personally to withdraw the accusation and to stop it. Sometimes there may occur a case in which one has drawn a mistaken inference from hearing a person's words and hastily brings a wrongful accusation [of homicide]. In such a case, should the true facts have been fully disclosed prior to the coroner's inquiry, and should the accuser personally wish to acknowledge the offence of spreading rumours and to stop the action, it being clear that he had not taken bribes to fabricate a charge, he is to be sentenced in accordance with the article on doing what ought not to be done where the matter is serious, and the matter concluded. If one person has encouraged another to bring the false accusation, the instigator is to be sentenced for the offence in accordance with the Code. Should an official under whose jurisdiction the case fell, influenced by favouritism or bribery, condone the offence, he is to be impeached in writing and reprimanded or sentenced in accordance with the regulations. (Sub-statute 336-9)

The confusion is now almost cleared up. This provision actually provided a loophole for some people who made false accusations. It is true that this provision focused on 'false accusations of homicide', but, if people who made these serious accusations were allowed to walk away without being prosecuted under this provision, those who made less serious false accusations should also be exempt. Some petitioners might simply have changed the original accusation by saying that they had been under a misunderstanding (*wuyiwei*), or were suspicious about something (*yixin*), or whatever. For example, the plaintiff in Case 1 above said that he did not check his father's wound, but rushed to the magistrate's court to resort to the law. Furthermore, even though his original petition was not true, it became clear that he no longer wished to secure the punishment of the defendant.

In marriage cases, the husband often alleged that his wife was illegally sold, then later changed his story, saying that he wrongly submitted the petition in a hurry (*qingji wanggao*) because he did not see his wife when he came home. Thus some cases involving untrue elements were not false accusations in terms of the offence of false accusation. If false accusation is understood strictly in the sense of the definition given by the Code, cases of the commission of the offence were not as numerous as has generally been thought. However, not all cases of untrue accusation created an excuse for the plaintiff, as seen in the next two cases:

Case 2

Song's wife accused Yan of preventing them from putting a manure heap on their [Song's] land. Yan then hit her. Although the land belonged to Song, it had been farmed by Yan under a *dian* contract. Yan did not agree that the manure heap should be put on the land. The magistrate punished Song and ordered him to keep his wife under strict control. (Baodi, 96: 73–7)

Case 3

Wang accused his aunt of owing him a debt. He went to demand payment and was injured by the aunt. The aunt brought a counter-plaint charging the nephew with inventing the debt. She had gone to him to enquire into the matter and was injured by the nephew with a brick. The magistrate had their injuries examined and found that the aunt's wound was self-inflicted deliberately. But she owed no money to the nephew. The magistrate punished both the nephew and the aunt's son, who came as his mother's agent (*baogao*), for their false accusation and false rebuttal. (Baodi, 1836/Daoguang 16, 188: 37–41; closed in one day)[19]

The original charge in Case 2, that the defendant prevented the plaintiff from putting a manure heap on the land, was not true because the defendant actually had the right to manage the land at that time, although Song and

[19] See Chapter 2 on the use of agents.

his wife were the owners. The punishment imposed on the husband as substitute for his wife, who had submitted the untrue petition, suggested there was no excuse for her to bring such an unreasonable lawsuit.

In Case 3, the issues of whether or not one party owed a debt to another, or whether or not he had been injured by another, were not the sort of matter that could be misunderstood. If the accusations were not true, then the petitioner must have known this. So the magistrate punished both parties for making false accusations about each other. Since the woman was allowed exemption from punishment, her son was punished instead according to the law (Sub-statute 339-1).

In some cases, one party made a false accusation, but for some reason the magistrate allowed mitigation of or exemption from punishment.

Case 4

At the end of the court statements, the magistrate wrote the following decision: 'I have investigated and conducted the interrogations to ascertain the truth. Zhang Jinnian acted shamelessly out of poverty. He went to Zhao Zongmei's land and pretended to pick the wheat that was left from the harvest but intended to take more from the land. He was detected and warned by Zhao Zongmei's younger son. But he accused the younger son of hitting and accusing him, and also harassed Zhao Zongmei in his home, insisting that he had put some sheaves of wheat on Zhao Zongmei's land. Through Zhao Er's mediation, Zhao Zongmei agreed to give him (Zhang) twenty sheaves of wheat and it seems he should then have let the matter drop. However, he still comes to the court and falsely accuses [the younger son]. Now I have obtained the truth and [Zhang] should have been severely punished. In consideration that Zhao Zongmei implored over and over again my sympathy for him, he was leniently punished with a slapping as warning. Release all the persons involved. Case decided as such (*ciji*).' [Ends with a tick] (Baodi, 101: 1–6)

Case 5

Xu falsely accused Zhang of cultivating his land and injuring him. The fact was that he had borrowed money from Zhang and pledged his land as security. He could not pay the debt, so the land was handed over to Zhang in front of the middleman. Xu later wanted to have the land back and brought the false accusation. Before the formal hearing was conducted, Xu gathered the harvest of 2 *mu* from the land in question planted by Zhang. Thus, he was put in custody at once when Zhang reported him to the court. At the hearing he confessed that he had wounded himself. The magistrate ruled that Xu should pay the debt within three days and return the corn to Zhang. He was to be kept in custody until his brother-in-law submitted the money to the court. This occurred more than one month later and another Zhang from the city gave a guarantee to have him freed and sent home. (Baodi, 100: 97–111)

Case 6

Someone brought a petition accusing his younger brother. He said that he had borrowed some money from his brother and pledged 1 *mu* of land as security. When he returned the money and wanted the land back, his brother refused and said the land had already been sold to him. The younger brother even let his wife and his daughter-in-law hit his elder brother's wife. The magistrate summoned eight persons involved in the case: the accused (the younger brother), his wife, his son and his daughter-in-law, the witnesses (go-betweens Zhang and Han), and the plaintiffs (the elder bother and his injured wife). It emerged from the investigation that the land had been rented to the younger brother permanently for 100 *diao* and there was a written contract.[20] The elder brother's wife had not been hit. The elder brother confirmed that the contract was in his handwriting and agreed that the land was still farmed by his younger brother. His wife's wound had been received when she fell down herself. The magistrate did not punish the elder brother, but only ordered him to make a statement that he had made a false accusation (*wugao ganjie*). (Baodi, 96: 36–44)

In Case 4, Zhang was leniently punished because the other party pleaded to the magistrate for leniency. In Case 5, Xu was not punished, either because he had confessed or because the accusation had been made in order to obtain the return of his land, or both. Confession could be a legal reason for mitigating the severity of an offence (Article 25), and Xu's intention of obtaining the return of his land could have shown that he did not intend to cause the other party to be punished, this being one of the necessary conditions for the offence of false accusation. In Case 6, no punishment was imposed on the elder brother, perhaps for the same reasons.

These cases show that, once the petition had been revealed to be 'false', some factors were often used by the magistrate, and sometimes by the parties too, to seek a lighter punishment or even exemption from punishment. Excuses that were often used included 'bringing this accusation in a hurry' or 'misunderstanding' or 'suspicion'. Since the law allowed that false accusations could truly arise from misunderstanding or where circumstances gave rise to suspicion, such excuses as misunderstanding were accepted, although it was not always clear which was such a case and which was not. In this sense, we may say it was in fact the Code that provided a number of excuses for both the parties and the magistrate to forgive and not impose a severe punishment even for a genuine 'false accusation'. The frequency with which

[20] Rental of land permanently is a type of tenancy called renting without limitation (*yongdian*). This tenancy can be obtained by paying a sum of money (see Chapter 5 on cases concerning tenancy).

the strategy of false accusation was used reveals the power of this practice in opening the door of the magistrate's court, but not the deeper reason for the efficiency of the method. If people used this strategy to secure judicial acceptance of their cases and eventually received punishment for false accusation, the course of action seems to lack sense. So the fact that many petitioners who made a false accusation received no punishment might be explained by the Code itself.

Perhaps because of the complexity of the legal points, Macauley does not offer a general discussion of the provisions on false accusation, and Huang omits some of the relevant provisions on false accusation, for example Article 337, which made false accusation among family members a less serious offence. When relatives were involved in making false accusations, the matter was even more confusing.

> **Case 7**
> Zhou Fulai falsely charged his younger cousin Zhou Fushun with trying to occupy his land and injuring him with a pair of scissors. The land in question had been bought by the cousin's father, though it originally belonged to Fulai's father. In the magistrate's hall, the accused cousin begged the magistrate not to punish his cousin. The magistrate thus ruled: 'Zhou Fulai inflicted a wound on himself in an attempt to blame his cousin. Since Zhou Fushun (the cousin) asked that Fulai be forgiven, I should have allowed such request. However, he should not have involved so many people in this false accusation to bring them into trouble. He is to be punished with thirty blows (the applicable number) with the heavy stick.' (Baodi, 99: 51–61)

Huang analysed this case to illustrate the matter of false accusation, but his analysis seems misleading. According to Huang, Fulai falsely charged his cousin with trying to occupy 10 *mu* of land, an offence that carried a penalty of seventy blows with the heavy stick (Article 93). Huang argued that the punishment that was actually carried out on Fulai, thirty blows with the heavy stick, was 'one grade more severe than for the offence he accused Fushun of'. Thus Huang concluded that the magistrate had not imposed 'the full severity called for by the letter of the code' (namely 'two grades more severe than the law provided in the case of relatively light crimes punishable by lashes with the light bamboo, and three grades for more serious crimes').[21] However, Huang ignored the fact that the Code had a special provision on false accusation among family members. Article 327 contained a number of complicated provisions. The two relevant to this case were: (1) taking

[21] Huang 1996: 84–5.

property or inflicting physical injury constituted exceptions to the general prohibition on accusations between relatives, and (2) should a senior family member bring a false accusation on these matters against a junior family member, the normal punishment for false accusation was to be reduced by three degrees if the person accused was a relative of the second degree, by two degrees if he was a relative of the third degree, and by one degree if he was a relative of the fourth or fifth degree.[22] So, Fulai, as a superior relative of the third degree of the accused, was allowed to have the penalty for the offence reduced by two degrees. In this case, both Fulai's accusations — trying to occupy land and injuring him with a pair of scissors — were untrue. If the accusations had been true, the offender should have received a penalty of seventy blows with the heavy stick for the offence of trying to occupy land (Article 93), as Huang assumed. For the offence of causing injury, he should have received a penalty of seventy blows with the heavy stick and penal servitude of one and a half years (Article 317), a much more severe punishment. Where there were two offences, Article 26 provided, under the head of Names and General Rules (*Mingli*), that the punishment should be for the more serious offence. Thus, Fulai's reciprocal punishment should have been for the more serious offence of which he accused his cousin — injuring him with a pair of scissors — i.e. a penalty of seventy blows with the heavy stick and penal servitude of one and a half years (Article 317). This penalty should have been reduced by two degrees, which would have made the eventual punishment one hundred blows with the heavy stick.

Thus Huang is wrong on the following points. First, the penalty for hitting an older relative within the third degree was much more severe than that for taking his property. To hit an older relative of the third degree (*dagong*) entailed a penalty of seventy blows with the heavy stick and penal servitude of one and a half years (Article 317). According to Article 26, where two offences came to light the punishment should be based on the more severe offence. Second, the punishment for false accusation of family members was different from that for the ordinary offender. According to Article 337, if the accusation was false, the accuser (who was the older relative) within the third degree should be liable to a penalty of two degrees less than the law provided for the ordinary case. Thus Fulai should have been punished with one hundred blows with the heavy stick. Third, the punishment actually imposed on him, that is, eighty blows with the heavy stick (or the thirty actually carried out), was two degrees less than he should have received. Although this was less than he should have been punished, it was

[22] Jones 1994: 323.

not for the reason given by Huang. The reason, as the magistrate pointed out, was that his cousin had begged the magistrate to be merciful.

The magistrate's practice demonstrated that, in matters of false accusation, one has to differentiate clearly between false accusation as an offence and an untrue petition. The essence of the untrue petition was that the petitioner had omitted something that was usually not in his or her favour. There were also cases in which the truth could not have been known before the investigation had finished. In boundary disputes, for example, the plaintiff was quite likely to accuse the defendant of taking a piece of his land, but the facts could be established only after the runner had measured both parties' land according to their property documents. Apart from this type of case, which essentially was not a matter of false accusation, the law itself was to be blamed if those who made false accusations, whether serious or not, escaped the prescribed punishments.

9.1.3 Other reasons for punishment

Apart from the infliction of an injury or the bringing of a false accusation, there were many other reasons for the imposition of punishment. We have seen a case in Chapter 8 in which an engaged man was punished for taking back the girl who broke the marriage promise. Other improper behaviour, especially the use of violence, constituted the most common reason for causing someone to suffer a penalty.[23] For instance, one individual was punished with sixty blows with the heavy stick for shouting in the hall of the court (Baodi, 187: 159–64). In another case the magistrate wrote:

> **Case 8**
> I have investigated and questioned the parties and obtained the truth. Li Wenan wished to buy some meat on credit from a junior member of the same clan, Li Lun. Owing to his poverty, Wenan behaved like a scoundrel. He took a knife and threatened Lun, which was improper behaviour (*shushu buhe*). Wenan should be severely punished with thirty blows with the heavy stick as a warning for the future. Lun, who had not been polite to Wenan when the latter (for some reason) had been hurt, had behaved improperly too (*yiyou buhe*). He should be lightly punished with ten blows with the light stick. Now Li Wenan should make a bond of confirmation that he will never cause trouble again. The knife is to be kept as evidence. All the persons involved are free to go home. The decision is thus recorded [tick]. (Baodi, 186: 6–18)

[23] In one case, a person was punished for deliberately damaging the other party's cooking pot even though the incident happened one year before the case was brought to the magistrate (Baodi, 187: 135).

This decision reveals that the magistrate was applying Article 386 (Doing What Ought Not to Be Done) to both parties. He punished the senior relative with thirty blows with the heavy stick (the actually administered number) under the provision for the heavier offence (which was eighty blows with the heavy stick). He punished the junior relative with ten blows (also the actually executed number) with the light stick, which was one degree less than that under the provision for more minor cases (which was forty blows with the light stick).[24] This Article was regarded as a catch-all provision. Some scholars believe that it was often applied in dealing with civil disputes, for it is thought to have been very useful in filling the gap in the Code with respect to civil matters.[25] This was not the case in Baodi.[26]

Under Articles 302 and 303, most of the land and debt cases involving fighting and injury attracted a punishment of twenty, thirty, or forty blows with the light stick; for example, fighting without causing injury (*buchengshang*) was punished with twenty blows; fighting with injury, thirty blows; injury caused by an object, forty blows. All these punishments were to be reduced on recovery from the injury. According to the relevant law (Articles 98 and 269), many civil cases involving intentional damage to another's goods perhaps also attracted fewer than fifty blows with the light stick, because of the low value of what was damaged.

[24] I have not found a case in which the punishment actually executed was fifteen blows with the light stick, corresponding to the forty blows provided for by the Code. This suggests that for some reason a punishment of fifteen blows was not used.

[25] Liang Zhiping 1996: 139.

[26] It is true that Article 386 was often used to punish people who were neither a principal nor an accessory in serious crime cases, especially those involving loss of life. In one such case, Chen was punished with thirty blows with the heavy stick under this provision for reclaiming a house that had been sold outright. The act of redeeming land or a house that had been sold outright was prohibited by the law (Sub-statute 95-7). Chen's redemption had 'originated the hostile collision' (*Xingke tiben*, Qianlong reign: No. 5). Obviously, Chen's action was wrong in terms of the law. When this behaviour caused a loss of life, his action was not surprisingly held to fall within the scope of Article 386 on 'doing what ought not to be done'. What I am interested in is the point that Article 386 did not, and could not, supply guidelines for essentially civil matters, i.e. to whom the land should be allocated or the money returned. That was why, in land, debt, or marriage cases in Baodi, the magistrate rarely imposed a penalty on somebody under Article 386. When analysing Qing civil procedure, serious cases such as homicide that also involved civil matters should be used as supplementary rather than primary evidence of the issue of civil law, because the civil matters in such cases were auxiliary to the main issues. Although Article 386 could not supply us with any extra provision for civil matters, it reminds us again of the important criterion concerning the allocation of punishment, i.e. the penalty should be decided according to the level of fault.

Although the exact practice of Baodi magistrates was not always clear in matching the punishments mentioned above, it is obvious that the punishments in civil cases were light. For example, the magistrate imposed a punishment in about twenty debt cases, including eight cases in which both parties were punished. Since the decision or the bond of confirmation might mention only the phrase 'light punishment' and not make it specific, the exact punishment imposed is not always clear. The punishment most often imposed seems to have been slapping the face (*zhangze*).

This was slightly different from what was provided for in the Code, because slapping the face was not a penalty designated by the Code. It was mentioned as one of the physical punishments for torture that officials were allowed to use (Sub-statute 396-6).[27] It was supposed to be less severe than the light stick.[28] In Baodi cases, many injuries were minor and the wounds could easily be cured within twenty days. The penalty of thirty blows with the light stick for this offence, if there was one, should be at least two degrees less. Thus, the wrongdoer should receive ten blows with the light stick. The penalty of ten blows prescribed by the Code was actually counted as four blows. Furthermore, the Qing executed the punishment only in multiples of five and ten. For example, twenty blows counted as eight but only five were imposed. This might be the reason slapping the face was often used. If the penalty of five blows was substituted for four blows, slapping the face would be more lenient and might be substituted for the four blows. For example, in a case from the Baodi records (Baodi, 187: 37–41), the wrongdoer was punished with slapping of the face for hitting a person's right eye and producing swelling. In some cases the punishment could be more severe.

Whether the offender was punished with the light stick or with slapping of the face, or even where no punishment was imposed, the magistrate in most cases gave reasons, such as that the wound had healed, or the offender was old, or blind, or a woman. These factors were all mentioned as reasons for exempting the offender from punishment or for mitigating it. We have seen from Article 303 that punishment was to be reduced on recovery from an injury. The other reasons given by the magistrate. such as being old, blind, or poor, were also permitted by law. As the magistrate made clear in his decision to exempt somebody from punishment: the law allows this person not to be punished (*lide mianjiu*).

[27] An earlier sub-statute of Article 396 (Intentionally Incarcerating Law-abiding Persons and Interrogating Them) prohibited officials who were not chief officials from using torture, including slapping the face (*Tongkao*: 1041).

[28] *Mulingshu*, *juan* 18: *Zuoli yaoyan* [The most important advice on being an official].

MacCormack has analysed in detail the functions of punishment in traditional Chinese law, identifying these as deterrence, retribution, and reform.[29] The light punishments (beatings and the like) imposed in the cases discussed in this book exhibit all three functions, with an emphasis on reform. The legislators announced in the Code that the penalties of *chi* (beating with the light stick) and *zhang* (beating with the heavy stick) were established for 'making one feel ashamed' (Article 1). Perhaps because of this, light punishment was connected with education so closely that the phrase 'beating with a whip' (*pubian zhiyi*)[30] was often used in reference to the education of the people. With respect to beating people, the magistrate was to 'be careful when imposing a penalty' (*shenxing*), that is, to consider carefully whether a beating should be imposed or not.

Consequently, in dealing with minor matters we encounter another feature concerning punishment. The magistrate often practised leniency in mitigating or exempting from punishment when the circumstances allowed such mercy. This is seen in such phrases as 'for lighter punishment' (*congqing*) or 'imposing no punishment for leniency' (*congkuan mianjiu*). As I have already pointed out, this does not mean that the magistrate was bending the law in acting leniently. The reasons given in Baodi county — which included: the offender was a woman, was aged, or was disabled, or had confessed, or had been forgiven by the 'victim' who begged the magistrate for mercy, or was poor — either were clearly made a legal reason for reducing a penalty or for exemption or were mentioned somewhere in the Code. The practice of leniency is also reflected in the fact that slapping the face (*zhangze*), which was regarded as less severe than blows with the light stick, was used as a punishment. Huang Liuhong, when discussing *shenxing*, listed seventeen conditions under which punishment should not be imposed.[31] He also said that the smallest stick should be used in minor matters such as delay in the payment of land tax and minor disputes.[32]

'Be careful when imposing a penalty' (*shenxing*) does not mean not beating. *Shenxing* originated in two facts. First, there was the Confucian dictum that punishment should be imposed after people have been educated. In

[29] MacCormack 1996b: chapter 10.

[30] Huang Liuhong 1850/1972: 126.

[31] Ibid.: 126.

[32] He said: 'There are three kinds of sticks. The heaviest one . . . is for deterring local bullies and evil clerks and runners which was not often to be used. The middle one is used for regular cases (*changxing*). The lightest one is used for matters of paying land tax and minor disputes' (Huang Liuhong 1850/1972: 131).

other words, officials have an unshakeable responsibility to educate people. The official should feel responsible if his subjects did something wrong. That was why reasons such as someone was 'ignorant' (*yumei*) could be the ground for reducing the punishment. Second, as the Code made clear, such punishment could make people feel ashamed, and, once the punishment had been imposed, it could not be undone. As Yuan Shouding said, 'the common people should not be carelessly punished with blows, since once they have been beaten, the disgrace will last for their whole life'.[33] So, if there were circumstances that allowed the magistrate to impose a lighter penalty or no penalty at all, he should so act.

Education implied that right and wrong had to be clearly distinguished. If the level of fault was high, the person should be punished both as a warning to others (as the magistrate stated in the above decision) and as something deserved. In this sense, blows with the light and heavy sticks unavoidably served functions of deterrence and retribution.[34]

9.2 The function of custom in judicial decisions

When the term 'custom' is mentioned in studies of traditional Chinese law, it is usually treated as a source of law for the decisions in disputes. Surprisingly, the scholars who particularly focus on 'custom' rarely hold that this was applied by Qing courts in the same way as law, although their arguments vary dramatically, especially as regards whether customary law existed in the Qing.[35] Quite surprisingly, both Shiga Shūzō and Liang Zhiping deny that Qing custom was applied as a source of law in solving civil disputes. Contrary assumptions in the past resulted only from an illusion, inspired mainly by the conclusion that Qing law did not have detailed provisions on civil matters. They did not derive from analysis of either custom or civil disputes themselves. In contrast, the studies of Shiga and Liang are based to a certain extent on such sources. However, although the two scholars both conclude that custom was not treated as law by the magistrate in solving cases, they actually hold very different opinions. Here I discuss Shiga's study

[33] See *Mulingshu, juan* 18: *Shenxing* [Be careful when imposing a penalty].

[34] However, I did find a couple of cases in which the punishment imposed on the offender exceeded the limits provided by the law. For example, a defendant was punished with 500 blows for injuring the plaintiff's head. This punishment was even said, according to the decision, to be the result of leniency. Because of this mention of being lenient, I suspect 500 might be a mistake (Baodi, 193: 207–21).

[35] Shiga Shūzō 1998b, 1992a; Liang Zhiping 1996.

in a little more detail, because it has had more influence on scholars and is directly relevant to this study.

The definition of 'customary law' or 'custom' is a matter of debate. Shiga even doubts that the Qing possessed a term corresponding to 'custom'. According to Shiga, custom, as unwritten law, can be applied in court when there is no relevant codified law. Customs, generally speaking, are norms that are of general obligation in society. They have the character of being obviously traceable: books might be used to record custom; proverbs express norms of general obligation and right found in old sayings; in court there is a formal procedure for proving custom.[36] On the basis of this general understanding of custom, Shiga comments that such a term 'can not be identified in traditional Chinese vocabulary',[37] because 'custom' is not 'discernible as something bestowed with positivity: as something in which "more objective statement and the provision of criteria for decision" is inherent'.[38] Furthermore, 'there was no compilation for purposes of reference in a law court'.[39] 'No case is found in which the existence of some custom became a point at issue in court. There was no formal procedure resorted to in proof of custom'.[40]

For the purpose of this section, I take local practice as roughly having the meaning of the term 'custom'. Since the focus of this section is the relationship between custom and the magistrate's decisions, especially with respect to the question of whether custom was applied, the function of custom in people's lives and in legislation will be omitted, although it might be occasionally mentioned. Thus, I follow Shiga's approach for examining these local practices, which were often introduced with the phrases *fengsu*, *suli*, *tuli*, or *tufeng* in the magistrate's decisions or proclamations.

I consider first Shiga's argument. His article cites each instance where specific phrases such as *suli*, *tuli*, or *chenggui* were used. He examines the context in which these phrases occurred and concludes 'that they are always used in the meaning of a habit or a practice, not of an unwritten law. They are not something to be abided by but something to be taken into consideration in decisions.'[41] For example, the local practice expressed in the phrase '*zhishi dangwu*' (if the property is worth ten, then the conditional sale

[36] Shiga Shūzō 1998b: 55–61.
[37] Shiga Shūzō 1992a: 414.
[38] Ibid.: 422.
[39] Ibid.: 417.
[40] Ibid.: 423.
[41] Ibid.: 423–4.

price is five) supplied only a commonly accepted calculation to the *dian* maker and *dian* holder for their reference (see more on this later),[42] or referred to an established agreement on a specific matter.[43] Such *suli* or *tuli* were not norms that allocated rights and duties to people, that is, they were not customs in terms of the definition given by Shiga (see above). The role played by *suli* or *tuli* in the Qing court was to help to determine a specific aspect of fact, to decide the particular amount of money due, and so on. In short, *suli* or *tuli* had nothing to do with determining which party was in the right or the wrong in a dispute.

By denying that custom served as a source of law in court, Shiga further points out that, 'with regard to the litigation procedure under the magistrate, . . . the paramount criterion of judgement was not custom as a sort of positive law but "common sense of equity" (*qingli*) that had no positivity in any sense'.[44] I discuss the matter of *qingli* later in this chapter. Now I analyse two cases that Shiga uses in order to consider and reconsider his analysis of the use of custom by the court.

> **Case 9**
> Woman Gao conditionally sold her 3 *mu* of land to her brother-in-law Gao and his sons. She wanted Gao to buy the land outright for an extra price of 150,000 *wen* (50,000 per *mu*). Gao refused such a high price. Woman Gao brought an accusation that Gao had refused to pay extra money to buy her land and had stopped her selling it to another. The magistrate ruled: relations between relatives are more important than financial benefit (*gurou weizhong, qiancai weiqing*). Even if woman Gao did not conditionally sell the 3 *mu* of land to you, could you ignore her when she asked for help? If it is difficult for her to live by herself, could you just leave her alone? Now I have a fair decision. Since she has conditionally sold the land to you, she should, of course, ask the extra price from you. The price she named, i.e., 50,000 for each *mu*, is not acceptable. However, it is established practice (*suyou dingli*) that the amount paid in the conditional sale of land is half the land's real price (*zhishi dangwu*). So apart from the price of 45,000 that Gao Jianshi (woman Gao) had already (had from you and) spent, Gao Shuxing (the brother-in-law) should pay her another 45,000. This decision is fair, so both agree.[45]

Three points are made by Shiga in analysing this case. First, the proverb '*zhishi dangwu*' meant that the price paid in the conditional sale of land was half the land's real price. This was a general point of reference as a price for

[42] Shiga Shūzō 1998b: 56, 57.
[43] Ibid.: 63.
[44] Shiga Shūzō 1992a: 415.
[45] Shiga Shūzō 1998b: 56.

people making such transactions. The magistrate used this proverb to ask the woman to reduce the high price she had demanded. At the same time he persuaded the defendant to give up his opposition and still to buy the land on the ground that he had an obligation to help his relative. Second, although the proverb was employed by the magistrate, it meant neither that there existed a rule that the *dian* holder had an obligation to buy the land and pay the same price as in a conditional sale contract when he was asked by the *dian* maker, nor that the magistrate applied such a rule. Here what Shiga means is that this 'custom' was not a custom in the sense of a norm of general obligation in society. Third, this customary phrase served only as a reference to the price normally expected in the conditional sale of land. It did not express a rule imposing rights and duties.

Case 10

Ren had '*dang*'[46] (conditionally sold) the land to Zhong at the price of 18 *diao*, upon terms that most of the land taxes would be paid by the '*dang*' buyer. This land was later sold to Fan by Zhong. The land tax he used to pay was also transferred to Fan. Many years later, when Ren's family wanted to redeem the land, the Zhong family insisted that the land had been sold, instead of conditionally sold, to them. When the case was brought to the court, the documentary evidence had been lost in a fire. To decide the original relationship between the two parties, the court (the prefecture here) pointed out that because the obligation to pay the land taxes initially rested on Ren, the original relationship between the two should be one of *dang* (conditional sale) and not one of *mai* (sale); second, since Zhong paid only part of the land taxes, the original relationship between the two was also shown to be one of conditional sale. The prefecture concluded: 'In this case, Zhong alleged that the "*dang*" was *mai* (sale) and caused many years of dispute. He has now died and should not be prosecuted. Fan Shoude did not check the previous sale contract (*laoqi*) when he bought the land, which was a mistake. However, by investigating the local practice (*cibang fengsu*) I find that there is no such practice (*fengsu*) of checking the original contract when land and houses are bought. This has been the case for a long time. That was why Zhong's cheating worked. There is no evidence to show that Fan knew the real owner of the land when he bought the land.'[47]

With reference to this case, Shiga explains that the original sale contract of the land was used as proof that the seller obtained the land legally and was

[46] The Chinese translation of this case used '*dian*' rather than '*dang*' in most places. But since the quoted decision in this case uses the term '*dang*' and, furthermore, the *dang* holder had paid an extra price to the *dang* maker apart from the conditional sale price, following Yang Guozhen (1988: 41, 42) I have changed *dian* to *dang*.

[47] Shiga Shūzō 1998b: 59–60.

entitled to sell it. In most places the original contract was given to the new buyer, together with the new contract for the sale of the land. But in some places the original contract was not given to the new buyer. Although it was not clear how the official examined the '*cibang fengsu*' (custom in this area), it was clear that he accepted the existence of a practice by which parties did not check the original sale contract of the land at the time of purchase, and he relied on this as an excuse to exempt Fan (the second buyer) from punishment. This *fengsu* had nothing to do with deciding which side, the plaintiff or the defendant, should or should not have the right to the land.[48]

From the above two examples we can see that Shiga strictly limits his observations on custom to decisions in which specific phrases such as '*zhishi dangwu*' (the price paid in the conditional sale of land is half the land's real price) and *cibang fengsu* (custom in this area) were employed. For instance, the reason that Case 10 is analysed by Shiga is the mention of the phrase '*fengsu*' (practice). And he focuses only on this '*fengsu*', i.e. the practice that 'there is no such practice of checking the original contract when land and houses are bought'. By focusing only on this phrase, he makes no mention of the other custom (*dang*) and the important part it played in the case. There is no doubt that *dang* was an established practice distinguished from *dian* by the addition of an extra price paid to the land owner. It was this characteristic of *dang* that contributed one of the important grounds for the prefecture to decide the essential facts, i.e. the real relationship between the two parties, and finally brought about the position that the two parties 'had nothing to say'.

The narrow scope of Shiga's observations influenced some aspects of his conclusion, for example that Qing customs were not norms of general obligation. On this aspect, Liang Zhiping gives a much more detailed account of Qing custom. Liang points out that Qing customs were capable of allocating rights and duties. Because my focus here is on the function custom played in the magistrate's court, rather than the custom itself, what I am interested in is how custom functioned in Cases 9 and 10 and which rule the magistrate applied to decide the cases. My further analysis of these two cases will make it easier to understand Shiga's analysis.

It is true that, in Case 9, the proverb '*zhishi dangwu*' was not applied as a guideline by the magistrate to rule that the defendant had bought the land. However, nor was his decision based on human feelings (*gurou weizhong*), as Shiga states. The magistrate did mention this factor, but it was no more than to provide extra support for his decision. The real rule he applied was derived

[48] Ibid.: 60, 61.

from the law; as he said, 'Since she (née Gao) has conditionally sold the land to you, she should, of course, ask the extra price from you.' It is worth recalling the statutory rule here. Sub-statute 95-3 made it very clear that, if the *dian* maker could not reclaim the land, he/she could ask for an extra price and make a sale contract with the *dian* holder. The proverb '*zhishi dangwu*' helped in determining the specific selling price of the land. In this case, Shiga fails to notice that it was the law that played the fundamental role in solving the dispute.

As I have already noted above, the custom of *dang*, which is ignored by Shiga, played an important role in helping the official to determine a relevant fact, i.e. the real relationship of the two parties concerning the land. On reconstructing the facts, what the official intended to do was to apply the relevant law. If the parties were a *dian* (*dang*) maker and a *dian* (*dang*) holder, then the land could be redeemed; if they were a seller and a buyer, then the land should not be redeemed (Article 95, Sub-statutes 95-3 and 95-7). As for the *fengsu* (practice) used in the case, it was relied upon to determine whether or not Fan had known the real status of the land when he bought it. If he had known that the land was owned by somebody else, then he had committed the offence of plotting to buy a third person's land (*zhiqing moumai*) and, according to law,[49] should receive a certain punishment. Here, *fengsu* was used as evidence to establish the essential fact that Fan did not know the true status of the land in order for him to escape punishment.

As we have seen clearly, custom was important for determining the essential facts of a case when there was no firm evidence, in order that the official might apply the relevant law, or for a decision concerning some specific aspect, such as the selling price in Case 9 above or the salary agreed between the employer and his employees in Case 10 in Chapter 3. These functions of custom were in fact observed by Shiga. However, because he fails to connect these functions with the law, the relationship between custom and law is distorted.

Custom was not basically a source that the magistrate applied in making decisions. The Code itself had made clear that officials should, of course, apply the law. The logic was that officials were prohibited from applying custom when deciding on a case. This was also the logic of a sub-statute that

[49] The offence of *zhiqing moumai* can often be seen from decisions concerning land matters. Both Article 95 and Sub-statutes 93-4 and 93-5 specified that someone who knew that the land belonged to somebody else when buying or conditionally buying had committed the same offence.

gave officials permission to apply custom in special cases. This sub-statute, attached to Article 422 on Deciding the Punishment Improperly, stated: 'all disputes between *miao* people should be decided in accordance with *miao* custom instead of the official law in order not to cause any trouble' (Sub-statute 422-1). The first part of the sub-statute specified that offences for which the punishment of military exile, exile, or penal servitude should be imposed must be judged according to law. Thus, the cited part clearly refers to discretion within the sole adjudication of the magistrate, as was the case with civil disputes. The Code authorized the magistrate to make a decision that did not follow the law, but it is clear that such permission needed to be specifically given to officials.

It was the duty of officials to follow the law, and they had no obligation to apply custom. This feature has been seen clearly in previous chapters. That Qing civil justice was generally efficient, fair, and predictable was not the result of accident, but was achieved with firm determination by certain means, including the application of the principles and specific provisions of Qing law for making decisions in civil cases.[50]

[50] There were many guilds in the Qing that established rules, derived from the practices of the trade, for regulating that trade within a specific geographical area. The Ba county materials provide many examples of such rules and many cases that clearly show that the magistrate applied guild rules for deciding disputes. For example, the workshops in Chongqing that fluffed cotton were divided into two groups, those working particularly with new cotton and those working with old cotton. This was regulated by the guild rules and approved by the local authority. A case brought to the magistrate by members of group A accused some people from group B of fluffing cotton that only group A was entitled to fluff. The magistrate accepted the case and found out that the accused had once been employed by group B but this employment had ended. They had no fixed base and used a mobile shop working at whatever the customers requested. The magistrate ruled that the workshops belonging to group A and B should stick to their original work (*gezhao jiugui*), whereas those that did not belong to them but moved around and worked in the street might fluff both new and old cotton as requested by customers (*suiren suoqing*) (Ba county records, 1750/Jiaqing 15, *juan* 321). What should be noted is the ground of the case. The plaintiff accused the defendant of '*langui*' (not respecting the guild rules). When the magistrate used the guild rules to guide his judicial hearings, the rules acquired further official approval after being first agreed by the local authority. However, because these rules were confirmed by the local authority and enforced in limited areas, they could be easily changed by authorized officials. A lawsuit provided the opportunity to establish new guild rules.

9.3 *Qing*, *li*, and judicial decisions

Before I turn to the role played by *qing* and *li* in judicial decisions, I first need to discuss the issue of the citing of the law in the magistrate's decisions. Throughout the book I have tried to demonstrate that the magistrate's resolution of relatively simple cases was very clear in terms of right and wrong. The process for handling land, debt, and marriage cases was orderly, logical, and efficient under the guidance of law. However, how are we to explain the fact that many decisions did not cite the law in the same way as officials handling serious cases were required by law to do (Article 415: All Must in Every Instance Quote the Statute or Sub-Statute)? Allee has also pointed out that in only four out of seventy-seven cases in the Dan-xin records was the Code cited.[51] To clarify the point, I need to review the relevant Article.

> Every (*official*) who is deciding a <u>crime</u> must cite the [articles of the] law or the substatutes. Any violation (*failure to cite*) will be punished with 30 strokes of the light bamboo. If ([in the] *law there are*) many [rules] gathered together in one article, (*and the official*) merely refers to the [ones dealing with the] *actual*) offence that was committed, this is permitted. . . . If someone cites one on his own authority (*and analogizes from it*) so that there is an incorrect decrease or increase in the punishment, sentence on the basis of intentional or mistaken [decrease or increase in the sentence Art. 409].[52]

The word 'crime' in the Article implies that the strict citing of a particular Article or sub-statute was required when deciding a crime. However, the term 'crime' was not used for the general situation of disputes, but rather indicated specific 'crimes' that the Code had named. So, for decisions in land, debt, or marriage matters, when there was no need to name a 'crime' in respect of either party, the magistrate should not be regarded as not following Article 415. This Article did not require that laws be cited in such cases in the same way as in deciding 'crime' cases.

Thus, in decisions on what we could call minor matters we see that the magistrate might or might not cite the Code. He might cite the whole relevant provision in his decision, though this was very rare, and on most occasions he did so only in his report to his superior and the other magistrate. Anyway, there were many ways for the magistrate to cite the Code. More often he cited the Code in the following ways:

[51] Allee 1994b.

[52] Jones 1994: 396–7, the underlined word (*zui* in the original) is translated as 'case' in Jones.

1. The name of an Article or sub-statute; for example: *fuzhai lü* or *fuqian sizhai lü* (law concerning being owed a private debt; Article 149 — see Chapter 5); *duodian li* (law on eviction — see Chapter 6); *maixiu maixiu* (buying and selling a divorce — see Chapter 8).
2. Phrases used in the Code; for example: 'the interest charged by a private loan should not exceed the capital no matter how many years have passed' (*jieqian sizhai, nianyue suiduo buguo yibenyili* — Chapter 7); '*zhunqi chumai*' (allow her to sell the land); '*shuiqi*' (pay tax for the sale contract); '*xishu guanye*' (allow the land owner to administer the land); and *dinghun* (marriage agreement).
3. The use of phrases such as 'against the law' (*youwei lijin*) or 'the law allows' (*lide mianjiu*).

The land, debt, and marriage cases discussed in this book are representative of the Qing in terms of their types, although they might not always be simple. The magistrate made an obvious effort based on the evidence to link the established facts with the law in order to bring justice to the parties, i.e. to effect a specific measure or remedy. Although the strict citation of the letter of the law was not required, it is clear that the decisions were made on the basis of the law and that the resolution of those cases closed without a formal hearing was also controlled by the magistrate in the same fashion.

'The law' should be understood, first, as the letter of the law (*lüwen*) and, second, as the spirit of the law or exactly here as *lüyi* or *li*. When the case clearly fell within the scope of a particular provision, the magistrate had no choice but to apply the (letter of) the law. Should the circumstances of the case be complicated and different rights in the case require protection, it was not enough simply to apply a particular provision. In other words, when there was a gap between the law in the strict sense and the case, the magistrate was entitled to use his discretion to decide. Since the magistrate had the sole responsibility for the decision in non-reviewable cases, his discretion need not even be reviewed by a higher authority. In this sense, his discretion was so significant that from our point of view the magistrate might be regarded as creating new law. However, in the eyes of both the magistrates and the government, what the magistrate did was no more than to apply the law in its real, if not literal, sense.

By establishing the essential facts to which to apply (the real meaning of) the law, the magistrate enjoyed significant discretion. To direct the magistrate's discretion in the right direction, to see that he did not abuse his power, several mechanisms were introduced. First, the magistrate's decision had to be willingly accepted by both parties; in other words, the parties' bonds of confirmation meant that they both thought the decision was just. Shiga pointed out this limitation on the magistrate's discretion.[53] The parties could either refuse to submit such bonds or make a further petition to the same magistrate. The case would then continue in some way. Second, there was no limitation on how many appeals the parties could make to higher officials: they could take their case through the prefecture (*fu*), circuit (*dao*), provincial judge (*anchashi*) or provincial treasurer (*buzhengshi*), governor (*xunfu*), right up to the governor-general (*zongdu*). Third, the magistrate was required to write a monthly report (*xunhuanbu*) to higher officials, and the officials supervising the circuit occasionally made inspections.[54] These factors were very important in ensuring that the magistrate applied the law in ordinary cases. In this sense, the magistrate's discretion in dealing with most civil cases was tightly controlled.

Several cases discussed in the preceding chapters involved the exercise of the magistrate's discretion (see Cases 4, 5, and 11 in Chapter 6; Case 5 in Chapter 8). The decisions sometimes do not appear to have been completely in accord with a particular law. In such circumstances, the magistrate might introduce phrases containing the terms *qing* and *li*, as, for example, in a number of the cases discussed in this book. Because decisions utilizing the terms *qing* and *li* often look as though they were not in accordance with a particular law, some scholars have concluded that the magistrate decided civil cases by *qing* and *li*. I have made the meaning of *qing* and *li* clear in my discussion of the cases. But what I have not done is to analyse why it is wrong to see *qing li* as something contradictory to the law or the application of the law.

There is one issue that first needs to be clarified. *Qing* and *li* can have several meanings, and they might assume a particular meaning and play different roles in different contexts. For example, the meaning and function of *qing* and *li* in legislation are different from those in judicial decisions. In the case of the Qing law, we might say that *qing* and *li* were the twin origins for making the law. Because of the focus of this section, I shall not consider *qing* and *li* at the level of legislation.[55] I shall focus only on the specific meaning of *qing* and *li* in the context in which these terms were introduced by the

[53] Shiga Shūzō 1998a: 41.

[54] The rule on sending monthly reports to higher officials might not have been respected all the time in all provinces, but there is no evidence that it was not respected generally. Some officials left many relevant comments on the monthly reports of the magistrates (for example Fan Zengxiang and Ding Richang). Baodi records also contribute some evidence. From the surviving records, we have comments such as: 'this case should be included in the group of "closed cases" in *x* month's report' (Baodi, 104: 134).

[55] For more on *qing li*, see Shiga Shūzō 1998a; Liang Zhiping 1996; Yu Ronggen 1999; Philip Huang 1996; and Zhou Guangyuan 1995.

magistrate in the performance of his judicial task.[56] I shall probe the relation between the application of the law and the introduction of *qing* and *li*. Scholars who regard *qing* and *li* as having nothing to do with the application of the law in deciding civil cases have failed to pay enough attention to the content of the law concerning civil matters. At different stages of civil litigation, *qing* and *li* were used differently:

1. The officials might make comments on petitioners who were bringing lawsuits. For example, Fan Zengxiang said: 'if you have *qing* and have *li* you may come to my court as you wish, those who have not *qing* and have not *li* are better not to come to disturb me' (*youqing youli jinguan qianlai, wuqing wuli shaolai qunao*).[57] He meant that the facts stated in the petition had to be true and that the petitioner's claim should be supported by law, *qing* referring to the 'true facts' and *li* to the 'law'. Another quotation from Fan shows clearly that *li* referred to the law. He said: 'I, the magistrate, am a man of integrity and justice. You can hardly escape from being caught by the arm of the law. If you have *li*, you should come as you wish (*youli zelai*), if not, you had better stop the lawsuit yourself.'[58]
2. When the magistrate was studying the accusation, he sometimes commented '*shufei qingli*' (does not follow *qing li*) or '*yu qingli buhe*' (contrary to *qing li*) to indicate his suspicions of the story told in the petition. *Qing* and *li* here were often combined into one phrase, which on most occasions meant 'the logical or reasonable way that things happens'. This phrase can be found in the Baodi records (Baodi, 190: 61; 187: 71).
3. Once the facts had been ascertained, and the magistrate made the decision for the parties, he might use the phrase '*zhun/hengqing zhuoli*' (consider *li* on the ground of *qing*) or '*zhunqing yongfa*' (apply *fa* on the ground of *qing*) in explaining his reasoning. By this he meant that the facts, the whole facts, had been considered in the light of (the real meaning of) the law.
4. Finally, when magistrates commented on the decisions they had made, they might use the phrase '*qingli*' (or '*qing fa*') '*liangjin*' (both are exhausted) or '*liangping*' (both have their weight). This meant that the decision took into account all the circumstances and all relevant laws.

[56] For the general meaning and the meaning that scholars usually accept of *qing* and *li*, see Chapter 3.
[57] Fan Zengxiang 1912, *juan* 1: 9.
[58] Ibid.

It is the usages of *qing* and *li* in (3) and (4) that reveal the nature of the magistrate's behaviour in resolving civil cases.

For example, in Cases 4, 5, and 11 in Chapter 6, *qing* referred to the facts, the whole facts or a specific fact. In Case 4, the complicating fact was the graves; in Case 5, it referred both to the public benefit and to the individual's obligation to his community; and in Case 11, it pointed to several factors: the land belonged to the whole family and it was sold illegally; the land was and would be used for the purpose of the family's ancestral worship. Another example is cited by Shiga.

> **Case 11**
> A pledged his land of 40 *dan* with B,[59] in order to borrow 40 *liang* of silver at interest of 8 *liang* for the whole year (2 per cent per month). B accused A of only paying him three years' interest and still owing the debt. The magistrate thought A should pay the debt but that the value of the pledged land was much higher than the debt A owed to B. So after '*zhenqing zhuoli*' (consider both *qing* and *li*), the magistrate decided that A should give 22 *dan* of land to B and keep the remaining 18 *dan*. Thus the magistrate felt '*qingli liangping*' (justice was achieved according to both *qing* and *li*).[60]

In this case, *qing* referred to the fact that, if the total land of 40 *dan* was given as repayment of the debt, the debt owed was over-returned, which was not what the law supported or protected. What the law demanded was payment only of what the debtor owed. So clearly *qing* referred to the unjust situation that would result if the debtor gave his 40 *dan* of land to the creditor. *Li* referred to the real meaning of the law (*lüyi*). The principle concerning the repayment of a debt is that the debtor should repay only what he owes.

The above example and Case 5 in Chapter 6 make it very clear that *li* referred to the law or the real meaning of the law and the principle the words reprsented. It is this aspect that scholars have failed to notice. They have stressed that *li* was the source of law, but they never realized that in such particular cases *li* could mean law or the real meaning of law itself. Yan Fu (1854–1921) noticed this aspect of *li*. In the preface to his translation of Montesquieu's *L'Esprit des lois*, he wrote: 'in the thinking of the Chinese, the right and wrong of matters is called *li*, the prohibitions of our country

[59] Land of 40 *dan* refers to the size of the land, i.e. this land was allocated 40 *dan* (1 *dan* =10 *dou*) of land tax. Since different qualities of land were allocated different amounts of land tax, it is hard to know the exact size of the land.
[60] Shiga Shūzō 1998a: 29.

are called *fa*. But Western countries call both of them *fa* (law)'.[61] Thus, *li* or having *li* (*youli*) could mean that one's behaviour was in accordance with law.

Further examples can be seen in Wang Huizu's discussion in three of his works. He mentions *qing* and *li* several times, as follows: 'How will it not do if the law is respected while *qing* is considered as well?. . . The law is limited, while situations are not. It is only when the law is applied in accordance with *qing* that the harmony of nature can be achieved';[62] 'Excellent application of [the law] lies in good knowledge of *renqing*';[63] 'Without introducing *qing* and *li* when hearing a case, though the two parties are forced to obey [the decision], it is in the end an evil [unjust] judgment. When a magistrate does not know how to handle a case, repeated hearings are the consequence . . . this is caused by the fact that he is not familiar with the statutes and sub-statutes'.[64] These may not be all the comments made by Wang Huizu, but it is clear that *qing* and *li* were taken into account to achieve a perfect application of the law. In other words, only after all the circumstances of a case such as the cause (*qianyin* — for example Case 4 in Chapter 6), effect (*houguo* — for example, Case 12 in Chapter 6 and the above example from Shiga), and any special situation (for example, Case 5 in Chapter 6) had been taken into account did the decision accord with what the law intended to support in terms of both the letter of the law or the principle and real meaning of the law. Justice then could be achieved. This is what the phrase '*qing fa/li liangjin*' expressed.

It is clear that the bulk of civil cases made no mention of *qing* and *li*. The Baodi and Ba county records contain no case in which *qing* and *li* appeared as such. Shen's cases contain some examples. Out of 135 cases selected by magistrate Shen, he introduced *qing* and *li* in varying patterns in about sixteen places. This proportion is low, even in terms of the cases he chose to include in his book. Compared with the total number of cases he resolved, the proportion is even smaller. Law was what he basically applied, and most of his cases did not mention *qing* and *li*. Because the law had an unchallengeable position, *qing* and *li* did not constitute a different source that the magistrate might equally or even preferentially follow. When *qingli* was applied in the handling of a case, *qing* was introduced as referring mainly to some particular situation of fact and *li* as referring either to the law or to the

[61] Quoted in Yu Ronggen 1992: 3.
[62] Wang Huizu 1794/1892: 370.
[63] Wang Huizu 1786a/1892: 164.
[64] Wang Huizu 1800/1892: 420.

real meaning of the law. Whether or not they were introduced often, the decision depended on the specific situation of the case. Even where the terms do not appear as such, as shown in the Baodi records, the principle implied by these phrases (i.e. to apply the law through understanding the real meaning of the law in considering all the circumstances and the specific facts) still dominated the magistrate's work, as the phrase *zhunqing zhuoli* ('taking specific circumstances into account to apply the law') on a couple of Baodi magistrates' personal stamps clearly revealed.[65]

If the introduction of *qing* and *li* can be regarded as exemplifying the significant discretion the magistrate enjoyed, this was perhaps the logical consequence of the aim of the Qing's legislature and especially the judicial function, namely the achievement of justice (*zhi* or *pingyun*). No matter how detailed the codified law, it was impossible to cover every situation in the Code. As the legislator Shen Zhiqi often said: the law is stable, whereas reality is not (*Jizhu*: 116). To admit the limitations of the law in covering all circumstances and to aim at justice as the result of hearing cases must have resulted in giving the magistrate discretion. It would be more accurate to say that the magistrate found a balance between the entirety of the facts and the law in determining a just solution, rather than to say that the magistrate struck a compromise between the claims of the two parties. There is a difference between a just solution and one that accorded with a specific law. Many critics have said that the law in the Qing did not enjoy the high respect it deserved. Such a comment does not take into account that the aim of the judicial approach was to secure a just solution, which meant neither sticking to the letter of the law nor a mere compromise.

[65] In the Baodi records, the magistrate's personal stamp containing this phrase can be clearly recognized.

10

Conclusion: Delivering Justice and the Absence of Litigation

I have given a picture, both in general and in detail, of the litigation proceedings and practice at the magistrate's court during the Qing dynasty — discussing how the magistrate was supposed to deal with disputes concerning land, debt, and marriage and how he actually performed this function. Given the existence of the concept of non-crime, I covered minor matters concerning land, debt, and marriage in the sense that remedies were provided without imposing punishment. Thus, in both procedural and substantive terms, laws on civil matters were available, so litigants were able to seek help from a state authority and the magistrate's court was able to resolve disputes with the guidance of the law. The magistrate's performance in making decisions was, at least from the available evidence, free from bias. He usually conducted a thorough investigation, established the facts on the basis of the evidence, and applied the law in favour of the party with the more meritorious claim. In other words, the law constituted the key and almost the sole source for most decisions.

However, the magistrate's purpose was to deliver justice, and justice carries more than just applying the letter of the law. If there was a gap between the facts and the law such that strict application of the law would bring injustice to one party, he might introduce what was often called *zhunqing zhuoli* ('taking specific situations into account before applying the law'). In such cases, the decision was still the result of the real meaning of the law (*lüyi*). In the examples in which *zhunqing zhuoli* was used, *qing* represented the facts and *li* represented the law, sometimes in its broad sense. In this sense, *zhunqing zhuoli* was more a principle governing the application of the law than a means for the magistrate to judge as he wished. He was to introduce *zhunqing zhuoli* only if the strict application of a particular rule would obviously bring injustice. The concept of 'justice' carried a wealth of meanings. It meant a higher closure rate and a lower rate of appeals. It was advocated not only as a criterion for evaluating the magistrate's performance and ability to resolve disputes, but also as a belief by which the magistrate would judge himself. The magistrate was rewarded for achieving good results in both these aspects.[1]

If it was true that the Qing normally accepted and decided civil disputes at the institutional level, how could this be compatible with support for an anti-litigation culture in traditional China to which historians have commonly subscribed? It is usually believed that the root of this so-called anti-litigation culture lay in Confucius' preference for education and his ideal of bringing about a state of affairs in which there were no lawsuits. He stated: 'I can try a lawsuit as well as other men, but surely the great thing is to bring about that there be no lawsuit' (*Analects* 12.13).[2] To explain this apparent contradiction, I shall start with Confucius' ideal of an absence of litigation (*wusong*), then analyse the meaning of numerous verbalized 'anti-litigation' phenomena in the hope of clarifying that the magistrate's performance in delivering justice did not actually go against Confucius' ideal of no litigation, nor was it necessarily incompatible with the so-called anti-litigation culture.

10.1 An absence of litigation

Confucius' famous remark quoted above is usually regarded as firm evidence that he aimed to achieve the absence of litigation (*wusong*) and did not welcome lawsuits at all. Qu Tongzu has observed that Confucius 'considered this state of no litigation as the ultimate end'.[3] However, Confucius' 'ultimate end' represented a rather complex achievement of a society where an absence of litigation was only one aspect.

In the *Li ji* we read:

> When the Grand course was pursued, a public and common spirit ruled all under the sky; they chose men of talents, virtue, and ability; their words were sincere, and what they cultivated was harmony. Thus men did not love their parents only, nor treat as children only their sons. A competent provision was secured for the aged till their death, employment for the able-bodied, and the means of growing up to the young. They showed kindness and compassion to widows, orphans, childless men, and those who were disabled by disease, so that they were all sufficiently maintained. Males had their proper work, and females had their homes. (They accumulated) wishing to keep them for their own gratification. (They laboured) with their strength, disliking that it should not be exerted, but not exerting it (only) with a view to their own advantage. In this way (selfish) schemings were repressed and found no development. Robbers, filchers, and rebellious traitors did not show themselves,

1 Ding Richang 1909: *juan* 34.
2 MacCormack 1996a: 112.
3 Qu Tongzu 1965: 249.

> and hence the outer doors remained open, and were not shut. This was (the period of) what we call the Grand Union.[4]

This passage describes Confucius' perception of the ideal world, that is, a world in which everyone behaves properly with no need for enforcement. In this world, disputes would not arise, thus there is no litigation. The absence of litigation depends upon and is the result of the development of every aspect of the whole society. Although Confucius considered that the period in which he lived was a world in disorder (*shushi*), he believed that the Grand Union could finally be achieved. It was in the light of this belief that he established his theory of virtues (*ren*) and rites (*li*), emphasizing that the people and government should behave according to morality and the rites, because an ideal world could be achieved only in such a way. Another passage from the *Analects* stated clearly: 'if you govern the people by laws and keep them in order by penalties, they will avoid the penalties yet lose their sense of shame. But if you govern them by your moral excellence, and keep them in order by your dutiful conduct, they will retain their sense of shame, and also live up to this standard' (*Analects* 2.3).[5] It is obvious that Confucius did not think that the law and penalties were as effective a means of government as moral education in terms of inducing people to keep their self-respect.[6] The reason for this, as Qu Tongzu has pointed out, was: 'Confucianism believed that no matter whether human nature was good or bad, it was possible to bring about improvement by moral and educational influence. To improve the heart through education enabled a man to become good and to become conscious of shame, without, however, suffering from evil intentions.'[7]

[4] *Li Chi* (*Ji*), vol. 1: 364–5. For more discussion on the influence of Confucianism, see Qu Tongzu (1965), MacCormack (1996b), and Vandermeersch (1985) etc.

[5] Cited in MacCormack 1996b: 192–3.

[6] According to some scholars (for example, Yu Ronggen), 'the enrichment of the people' has an importance equivalent to, if not greater than, education (Yu Ronggen 1992: 254). Yu quoted a paragraph from the *Analects*: 'When Confucius on his travels was on one occasion entering Wei in company with Ran You who was driving the carriage for him, he remarked, "What a large population is here!" "With such a large population," asked Ran You, "what should be done?" "Enrich them," answered Confucius. "And after that?" asked the disciple. "Educate them," replied Confucius' (*Analects* 13.9 cited in Gu Hongming 1996: 444). In another place in the *Analects*, Duke Ai once enquired of Yu, one of Confucius' disciples: '"The year now is one of scarcity: we cannot make the revenue meet the public expenditure. What should be done?" The disciple answered, "why not tithe [take one-tenth from] the people?" "Why," replied the prince, "with two-thirds, even we cannot make ends meet: how should we be able to do so with one-tenth?" To which the disciple answered, "When the people have plenty, the prince will not want. But if the people want, the prince will not have plenty"' (*Analects* 12.9 cited in Gu Hongming 1996: 435).

[7] Qu Tongzu 1965: 247–8; 1981: 286–7.

Yet Confucius did not mean that the law and penalties should not be employed at all. This can be seen from his theories in relation to the law, for example when he mentioned 'penalties properly produced (*xingfa zhong*)' (*Analects* 13.3), 'being sad and showing pity' when examining a legal case (*aijin*) (*Analects* 19.19), and that 'putting men to death, without having taught them (the Right); that is called savagery' (*Analects* 20. 2).[8] As a matter of fact, Confucius had been a judge himself. His achievements as a judge, though not known in detail, were highly valued by Xun Zi (fourth and third centuries BC), Dong Zhongshu (second century BC) and Si Maqian (145 or 135 BC–?).[9] Given this aspect of Confucius' attitude toward the law, his famous remark about no lawsuits, when we re-read it, suggests that if disputes happened he would hear them. But the fundamental point of his hearing was that, instead of just resolving the dispute according to law, he would go further and educate the parties as well in order to achieve his cherished ideal world of no litigation. To treat Confucius as subscribing to the idea of 'no litigation' in the sense that education should replace litigation is to oversimplify his thinking.

Nonetheless, this misunderstanding is by no means confined to modern scholars. It can be traced back to as early as the Han dynasty (206 BC–AD 220), when Confucianization of law occurred. There were many model officials (*xunli*) during the Han and later who were very good at educating people.[10] An extreme example comes from the Jin dynasty (AD 265–420). When Jia Hun showed Deng Yu a legal case and asked him to give a judgment, Deng Yu quoted Confucius' statement 'bring about that there be no lawsuits' and refused to read the case. Jia considered his behaviour so worthy that he gave him his daughter in marriage (*Jin shu*, 90, 7b).[11]

The officials of the Qing dynasty still respected Confucius' idea of no litigation and kept education as one important element of their administration. We may take the magistrate Lan Dingyuan as an example. When two brothers came to him with a dispute over 7 *mu* of land, he took much time and used many artifices to induce the brothers in the end to regret undertaking their litigation. The interesting thing was that the magistrate did not leave out the disputed land when they were both willing to give the land to a temple. He ruled that the land was to serve as their father's worship land forever and each should take turns in farming the land for two years.[12] By

8 Confucius 1997: 265.
9 Yu Ronggen 1992: 195.
10 See Qu Tongzu 1965: 253–4.
11 Cited in Qu Tongzu 1965: 249, n128.
12 Lan Dingyuan 1729/1989: 123–34.

so deciding, the magistrate cleverly applied the law (the equal division of family property among sons — Article 88). It is clear that Qing officials did not act in accordance with the precepts of the model officials (*xunli*) of the Han dynasty. Whereas the Han officials often followed Confucius' ideal of no litigation in the sense of refusing to hear a case, their Qing counterparts understood the ideal much more clearly. They played the roles of both educator and judge. They might combine these roles, but they did not replace the judicial role with the educative one.

10.2 Anti-litigation

Qing official literature, such as promulgations and handbooks, in relation to litigation very often criticized people for irresponsibly bringing lawsuits to the court. Huang Liuhong gives an example of a promulgation — 'Prohibiting Bad Litigation' — that very often was treated as evidence of the so-called anti-litigation culture. Both Philip Huang and Macauley make reference to this promulgation to illuminate officials' attitude. For many scholars, the Qing practice discouraged litigation in a number of ways. Macauley noted that recourse to litigation makers was 'strenuously resisted by imperial authorities, who campaigned to eradicate what they labelled the "litigiousness" of the Chinese people by statutory and rhetorical appeal to traditional structures of harmony'.[13]

When interpreting the meaning of criticism of litigation as referring too widely to litigation as a whole, it is easy to draw a conclusion of this kind. In analysing some typical statements, we should bear in mind that the comments relating to litigation (whether criticism or persuasion) bore specific meanings and were usually made in relation to a particular state of affairs. I shall use the emperor Kangxi's Sacred Edict and Huang Liuhong's article on litigation, including the proclamation noted above, to illustrate the point.

Kangxi's Sacred Edict (1670) was ordered to be read out to the people regularly. Three out of its sixteen maxims concerned litigation. They were: 'Behave with generosity to your kindred in order to demonstrate harmony and affection. Cultivate peace and concord in your neighbourhoods in order to prevent quarrels and litigation. . . . Put a stop to false accusations in order to protect the innocent and good.'[14] Another maxim (the first principle) exhorted family members, and especially brothers, to have harmonious relations, which could be regarded as also avoiding litigation. Kangxi's dictum

[13] Macauley 1994: 85.
[14] MacCormack 1996a: 113.

might be generally representative of the tone of officials in speaking of litigation. It seems that these were their basic approaches. One approach focused on family or social relationships, especially close ones such as those among brothers, other relatives, neighbours, friends, and so on. The other approach focused on litigation or, more precisely, the 'false accusation'.

In focusing on people's relationships, what was emphasized was that people should restrain themselves, so that there would be no cause for disputes. This approach encouraged harmony in society. Officials were playing their parental role in educating their children-subjects in the hope there would be fewer disputes. These words said little about the dispute itself. A lawsuit was inevitably a disaster in terms of the parties' relationship. Even if trivial conflicts occurred, the parties should take their relationship seriously and have another think before taking an action to the court in order to avoid ruining the relationship.

Thus, when officials suggested that people should bear with disputes for a time, they were referring to 'complaints over insignificant squabbles' which involved no substantial matters (see below). So, for Huang Liuhong, '[t]he key to putting an end to litigation consists first in calming one's emotions [*pingqing*], . . . The other party is not necessarily entirely at fault, and I am not necessarily entirely in the right. Besides, [if] there is no deep enmity or accumulated animosity, what purpose does it serve to assert oneself and win? If one calms one's emotions with such thoughts, then the anger will pass, and there can be no reason for litigation.'[15]

The other approach targeted the 'false accusation', which sometimes was the most harshly criticized, as clearly shown in Kangxi's dictum above. The attitude of officials to 'prohibiting' litigation was clearly a response to false accusations. Here, false accusation should be understood as referring to baseless petitions brought merely in order to harm someone else. On many occasions such criticism can be found in reference to *diaosong* (literally 'crafty litigation'). This term, just like that of false accusation, also had a specific meaning. In the terminology of the Qing Six Boards, '*diaosong*' referred to specific practices followed by litigants, such as petitioning more than one court at the same time.[16] The point is that phrases such as 'false accusation' or 'crafty accusation' were usually connected with suits that were false (*wuqing zhici*), or lacked evidence, or were brought improperly. They clearly did not cover all litigation of every kind. Because of this, such phrases were understandably often used in relation to the notorious pettifoggers.[17]

[15] Huang Liuhong, *juan* 11, cited in Philip Huang 1996: 200.
[16] *Qingdai liubu chengyu cidian* 1990: 315.
[17] For the details of pettifoggers, see Macauley 1999 and Fuma 1998.

Let us look at the proclamation mentioned by Huang Liuhong — 'Proclamation to Prohibit Crafty Litigation and to Investigate and Arrest Litigation Masters' — for a further explanation.[18] Huang Liuhong thought that this proclamation from a former magistrate contained points relevant to the litigation evils at that time. In the proclamation, three reasons were given for the proliferation of lawsuits. First, 'they file complaints over insignificant squabbles'. 'Second, there are people who are greedy and mendacious and intend to defraud others. They concoct suits out of trivialities and exaggerate other people's minor lapses. After filing a petition, they send accomplices to seek an out-of-court settlement with the other party. If their schemes do not come to fruition, they keep on filing complaints. Third, there are the litigation instigators whose hearts resemble those of tigers and wolves and whose actions can be compared with those of goblins and demons. They have no permanent occupation. Their only profession is assisting others in drawing up legal papers.'[19] The litigation that is illustrated here was clearly not normal litigation, but rather 'bad' litigation according to any criterion. Huang, using his counterpart's example, was merely giving three examples of litigation that was 'bad'. He was not indicating that all litigation was bad, or saying that all litigation was caused by one of these three reasons. Thus, the target of the 'prohibition' was simply bad litigation.

Officials much more often spoke of litigation as a normal occurrence. One can find many discussions in their handbooks on '*cisong*' (lawsuit) or '*xunchang cisong*' (normal litigation). When discussing such litigation in general, the officials stressed that the magistrate should examine the essential cause and facts of the case in order to make a good decision. These comments have undoubtedly been overlooked because readers have presumed that Confucian orthodoxy prohibited all litigation.

It is worth mentioning that disputes were widely believed to result from a moral failure of, at least, one party. Thus, officials also advocated education to persuade people to practise tolerance. Forbearance was one of the two keys mentioned by Huang Liuhong: 'The key to putting an end to litigation consists first in calming one's emotions [*pingqing*], and next in forbearance [*ren*]. . . . As for forbearance, if the other person is being unreasonable, bystanders will have a just opinion about the matter, [so] what harm can there be to me? . . . With such thoughts, the impulse [to litigate] will disappear. There can be no reason for litigation.'[20]

[18] Huang Liuhong 1850/1972: 125–6.
[19] Ibid.
[20] Huang Liuhong, *juan* 11, cited in Philip Huang 1996: 200.

10.3 Ending litigation

The ideal of Confucians was to put an end to litigation. The role of education was greatly valued in the Qing, as we have seen in the example above of Lan Dingyuan, who, apart from resolving the case, troubled himself to educate the two brothers. Nevertheless, Qing officials held that the most effective way of ending disputes and decreasing litigation was to hold fair and efficient hearings. I shall continue to use Huang Liuhong's discussion as an example.

In his prominent handbook on the work of the magistrate (*Fuhui quanshu*), Huang Liuhong included a special article on 'Advice on Avoiding Litigation', under the general title of *Xingming* (Judicial tasks). He began with the observation that, 'although the magistrate is good at hearing lawsuits, he is weak at letting people bring no lawsuits at all'.[21] His language clearly shows that he did not mean to use education as a substitute for the hearing of lawsuits. Then he advised two 'keys' for ending a lawsuit, as quoted above. But he continued with the observation that what 'the magistrate can do is express his exhortations in his actions by conducting trials in the most scrupulous way. When two parties confront each other the magistrate will uphold the party in the right and repress the party in the wrong. Thus no one will dare to file unsubstantiated claims.'[22] At the end of this discussion, he cited the proclamation from a former magistrate discussed above.

> This proclamation addresses the subject of the suppression of unscrupulous pettifoggers as a means of protecting the people's welfare. Since litigation is both detrimental to the pursuit of a livelihood and is a waste of money, only the ignorant will be involved in it without careful consideration. As soon as a complaint is filed with the court, it becomes an instrument for extortion in the hands of greedy and crafty petty officials. Even if the magistrate is a person of integrity who decides cases with absolute fairness, the parties involved will have to go through tedious routines that cannot be avoided, such as answering summons, waiting for trials, travelling back and forth from villages to cities, and finding lodgings for the duration of trials.[23]

After the description of more of the troubles that litigants might encounter comes the paragraph I discussed above about why there were so many lawsuits. The proclamation ended thus:

[21] Huang Liuhong 1850/1972: *juan* 11: 13.
[22] Huang Liuhong 1984: 259.
[23] Ibid.

> I, the magistrate, have taken upon myself the responsibility of eliminating the sufferings of the multitude and suppressing the evildoing of these cunning rogues. I wish all people, civilian as well as military, to know that except in capital cases involving homicide, fugitive slaves, and robbery, for which complaints must be filed immediately, all other cases — those involving family matters, marriage, landed property, and financial contracts — should be settled between the parties themselves, who should not file complaints without due consideration. As to disputes resulting from occasional altercating or minor squabbles, they should be settled without coming to the court.[24]

The points and the logic that Huang Liuhong intended to communicate can be listed as follows:

1. No matter how capable a magistrate was in hearing cases, hearings alone could not stop disputes.
2. Therefore education was necessary.
3. To educate people to stop disputes involved persuading them to bear with their differences for a time and to calm down.
4. However, the best way was still to try cases justly.
5. Finally, Huang quoted a proclamation from a former magistrate prohibiting three kinds of bad lawsuit.

Huang's argument was not fully logical in order, but his meaning is clear. Not only did he prohibit 'bad' litigation, but he also treated the issue in the context of the exercise of his judicial duty. He emphasized particularly that trials of disputes must be fair. His comments even suggest that he took the judicial hearing to be more important than education.

The same approach can also be seen in many other sources. Emperor Jiaqing's decree of 1807 stated clearly:

> To clear the mass of litigation really depends upon whether the local officials exert themselves to hear trials in a just and clear manner. All matters concerning household, marriage, or land among neighbours should be solved with a clear result as to right and wrong, so that every one who is in the right has his right. (*Huidian shili*, vol. 9: 927)

Many comments and statements by officials at all levels on ending litigation pointed out that the key was to hear disputes justly and efficiently, although education still played an important role. The Basics of the Magisterial Service, approved by emperor Yongzheng, stated under the heading 'Hearing and Deciding [Cases]':

> The task of officials who hear litigation is to carry out the law to educate the good and punish the bad. By hearing litigation, officials should decide the

[24] Ibid.: 261.

> right and wrong (*ming shifei*), distinguish the crooked from the straight (*pou quzhi*), root out bullies (*chu haoqiang*), and protect good citizens. Thus the good will be influenced to concentrate (to be good), the evil will reform, as by changing the skin of the face and washing the heart, finally no-litigation is achieved through litigation being heard. The law is respected, and moral education accomplished.[25]

This paragraph clearly makes the following points: the magistrate must hear litigation justly in accordance with the law; by this means is achieved the purpose of education finally to bring about an absence of litigation; deciding cases according to the law is itself to educate people. We may compare this recommendation with Wang Huizu's belief that the most efficient way to educate people was to conduct formal hearings in the main hall (*datang*) in public session (rather than in a smaller room), during which an audience of hundreds watched, so that his judgment would teach them about right and wrong.[26]

Philip Huang branded the Qing official representation as anti-litigation and the magistrate's practice, in contrast, as regularly playing the role of a judge. So he offered a way of understanding 'those seemingly contradictory aspects of Qing legal culture . . . only in the light of a system that encompassed paradoxical representation and practice'.[27] After all the above discussion, it seems that these aspects of Qing legal culture are not really contradictory. In this sense, the significance of Philip Huang's observation about the magistrate's performance, though generally correct in terms of his role and decisions, is limited. It contains a fundamental misunderstanding of the Qing; that is, that there was a clear inconsistency between the Qing's 'official representation' and its 'practice'. What I have shown in my research is that this supposed inconsistency is often the result of reliance upon too narrow a range of assumptions. In other words, by interpreting the Qing data incorrectly, we are led to misunderstand the Qing system of civil justice as a whole.

In comparison with some Han officials, the Qing adopted a more pragmatic view of Confucius' dream of an absence of litigation. Qing officials relied more heavily on the magistrate's performance in delivering justice. If the absence of litigation represented an ideal approach to the issue and anti-litigation an educational approach, then dealing with lawsuits fairly and efficiently represented the judicial approach. To some extent, therefore, the Qing caught the real meaning of Confucius. A combination of this more

[25] *Qinban zhouxian shiyi*: 20–1.
[26] Wang Huizu 1794/1892: 274.
[27] Philip Huang 1996: 3.

realistic ideology with the Confucian belief in human nature eventually inspired the best magistrates of the Qing to achieve excellent results. Wang Huizu's decisions were never challenged by any party through appeal; Liu Heng received no petition for several months. These achievements actually fulfilled Confucius' ideology of no litigation in one sense. Their outstanding practice illustrates what the Qing system of justice for resolving civil disputes can achieve. Although there certainly were some less qualified magistrates and sometimes in war and natural disaster injustice might occur often enough to argue for the opposite of the above conclusion, in terms of the ordinary magistrate's practice as seen in the above discussion, the general conclusion stands.

If we now return to the story told by Giles in Chapter 1, we can see that it clearly misrepresents the magistrate's judicial role. The two conflicting parties had not, or at least had not yet, entered upon the formal litigation procedure. The official just happened to encounter the quarrel. He then actively interfered in his capacity as a chief official playing a general role rather than as a judge. He showed no intention of bringing the parties into the litigation-solving procedure, as the Ba country magistrate had done in similar circumstances (see Case 1 in Chapter 7). This story vividly illuminates what I have called the multiple roles of a Qing official, especially the aspect of being a 'parental official' to his subjects. In this role he was in a better position to exercise Solomonic wisdom, in this case his preference for upholding honesty. Distinctively, in playing a judicial role he ought to, and usually did, follow the established and restrictive legal provisions in commenting, hearing, and ruling upon submitted cases, though he might still be able to manage some Solomonic practice like magistrate Shao (see section 2.1.1). When stories such as this [28] were used to explain the essence of Qing civil justice, they seriously distorted the truth because they arbitrarily separated the official's performance from its context. Indeed, in understanding, learning, and studying Qing legal culture, it should be a prerequisite to keep in mind the context. That is what this book has tried to do, building a constructive understanding of the magistrate's role in solving civil disputes.

[28] The 'custom' mentioned in this story about the 'thanks' money the finder should receive was long established. Article 151 of the Code (Finding Lost Objects) provides that, 'if [the lost objects] are private property, . . . give half to the finder as a reward and return half to the owner'. This provision can be traced back at least to the Tang code (*Tongkao*, 521). By claiming to have lost two Tls. 50 notes, the putative owner was trying to avoid paying any reward money to the finder.

Appendices

1: Categories of the Imperial Shuntian Prefecture Archive

Category	Total *juan*
The system of officials and official rules	23
Charitable affairs and police tasks	28
Fundamental administration matters	2
Law and lawsuits	192
Suppressing revolutionary movements	6
Military matters	21
Finance and money	29
Manufacture and transportation	3
Agriculture and business	10
Contracts and intercourse	2
Missionary matters and cases concerning missionaries	1
Rites	3
Education and health	3
Other matters	10

2: Details of the Category of Law and Lawsuits (*Juan* 54–245)

Juan number	Category
54	Documents and rules from the Board of Punishments on litigation, prior cases, and legal and judicial statistics (from Daoguang 2 [1822] to Xuantong 2 [1910])
55	Autumn trials and general matters of civil and criminal cases (Baodi county) (from Jiaqing 19 [1814] to Guangxu 34 [1908])
56–62	Matters concerning prison (from Qianlong 1 [1736] to Xuantong 3 [1911])
63–64	Prisoners of Baodi county
65–77	Matters concerning the implementation of the penalty of exile and life servitude and the transfer prisoners (from Qianlong 1 [1736] to Xuantong 3[1911])
78–86	Prisoners at large
87–94	Matters concerning the appointment of the *xiangbao*, *shoushi*, *shushou*, and so on (from Jiaqing 1 [1796] to Xuantong 3 [1911])
95–108.1	**Disputes over land and tenancy matters**
109–112	Disputes over houses and house functions
113–120	Gambling cases
121–152	Theft cases
153–160	Blackmail cases by persons with an official rank, clerks, and the *xiangbao*
161–173	**Cases concerning marriage and illegal sexual relations**
174–179	Cases concerning kidnap and the illegal selling of people and **women**
180–184	Cases concerning adoption, inheritance, and other family matters
185–195	**Debt disputes**
196	Prohibited religious groups
197–245	Cases concerning persons attacking and fighting each other

3: Weights and Measures

Area and distance

1 *qing*	=	100 *mu*
1 *mu*	=	approximately 1/6 of an acre or 675 square metres
1 *gong*	=	5 feet or 1.5 metres
1 *fen*	=	1/100 of a foot or approximately 3 millimetres
1 *li*	=	1/3 of a mile or approximately 500 metres

Volume

1 *shi*	=	approximately 1 bushel or 35 litres
1 *shi*	=	10 *dou*
1 *dou*	=	10 *sheng*

Money

1 *liang*	=	1 ounce of silver
1 *liang*	=	10 *qian*
1 *qian*	=	10 *fen*
1 *diao*	=	1,000 *wen*
1 *wen*	=	1 copper coin
1 *liang*	=	1,200 copper cash (according to Baodi, 187: 39)
1 *liang*	=	over 1,500 copper cash (according to Baxian: 255 and Baxian1: 249)

4: The magistrate's *yamen* of Baodi county (From *Baodi xianzhi*)

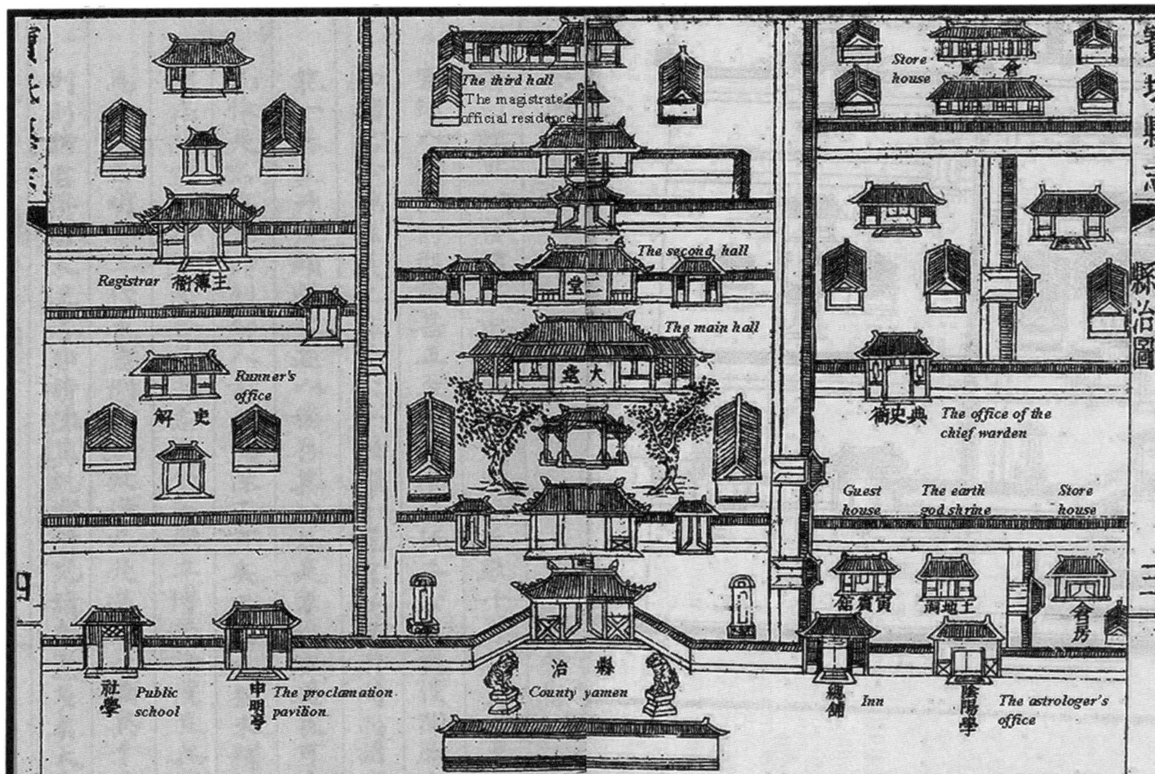

Glossary

aijin	哀矜
anchashi	按察使
anwu xunqing	案无徇情
Anyi	安义
Ba	巴
bao	保
Bao Shichen	包世臣
Baodi	宝坻
baogao	抱告
baogao	宝坻
baogu	保辜
baogu qixian	保辜期限
baojia	保甲
baozhuang	保状
baqi	八旗
beigao / beizao	被告 / 被造
beigao xi x xian ren ziqu x xian konggao keye	被告系某县人自去某县控告可也
beijia qushu	备价取赎
benguan guansi	本管官司
biandi	边地
bianhao	编号
biaozhu	标朱
bici jianmian fuli	彼此见面服礼
bicihehao	彼此和好
bing	禀
boyi	拨役
buchengshang	不成伤
bude	不得
bufu	部复
buhe zequ	不合则去
buwangfa	不枉法
buyi	不义
buying	不应
buyingwei	不应为
buyou	不友
buyuan jizhi	不愿即止
buzhengshi	布政使
buzhun	不准
cha	叉
chai shih (chai shi)	差事
chaipiao / xinpiao	差票 / 信票
chakan	查勘
chaming queshi bingjiu	察明确实禀究
changcun jingwei	常存敬畏
Changping	昌平
changxing	常刑
chanye	产业
chaxun	查讯
chengan	成案
chenggui	成规
chenghun	成婚
cheng zhuang	呈状
chi	笞
chi	饬
chipiao	饬票
chong	冲
chongfu dianmai	重复典卖
chu haoqiang	除豪强
chuanpiao	传票
chushe nianxian	出舍年限
cibang fengsu	此邦风俗
cibi jishi benxian tangduan	此批既是本县堂断
ciji	此记
cinei	词内
cipan	此判
cisong	词讼
ciyao	赐药
congkuan mianjiu	从宽免究
congqing	从轻
cuizhuang	催状
cunfu	村副
cunzheng	村正

Dacheng 大城
dagong 大功
Dai 戴
daishu 代书
daixun 带讯
dali duisuan 大利堆算
dan 石
danbao 担保
dang 当
Dan-xin 淡新
dao 盗
dao gengzhong guanmintian 盗耕种官民田
daogeng 盗耕
daomai 盗卖
daomai tianzhai 盗卖田宅
daoyuan 道员
datang 大堂
di 地
dian 佃
dian 典
diandang 典当
dianmai tianzhai 典卖田宅
dianshi 典史
dianzhong tudi qirong si dian 佃种土地岂容私典
diao 吊
diaosong 刁讼
dinghun 订婚
dingli 定例
diya 抵押
Dongsi *pailou* 东四牌楼
dou 斗
douou 斗殴
duanling guanye 断令管业
duanpiao 短票
dujue 杜绝
duodian li 夺佃例

erdoutian 二斗田
ezha 讹诈

fa 法
falü cisong 法律词讼
fan 繁
Fan 范
Fan Zengxiang 樊增祥
fang 房
fang qianzhai 放钱债
fanggaori 放告日
fei anfen liangmin 非安分良民
feiqi jiuzhang 废弃旧帐
fen 分
fendan 分单
feng shangyu 奉上谕
fengsu 风俗
fu 妇
fu 府
fuhu 富户
Fujian 福建
fuli 附例
fumu zhiming meishuo zhiyan 父母之命媒妁之言
fuqian sizhai lü 负欠私债律
furen 妇人
fuzhai lü 负债律
fuzhuang 副状

ganjie 甘结
ganming fanyi 干名犯义
ganzheng 甘证
gaoshi 告示
gengming guoge 更名过割
gengming tian 更名田
gezhao jiugui 各照旧规
gezhi yici junyuan chuanxun 各执一词均愿传讯
gong 供
gong 公
gong 弓
gong yi shunhe 供已顺和
gongfang 工房
guandaishu chuoji 官代书(某)戳记
guantian 官田
guanye 管业
gugongren 雇工人
guofang 过房
guojia 国家
Guozijian 国子监

gurou weizhong, qiancai weiqing 骨肉为重钱财为轻
han 汉
hanbing 喊禀
hanbingshi 喊禀事
Hankow 汉口
haosong 好讼
hedao 河道
hegong 合供
hezhi yili chizhi yien weizhi yiyi 合之以礼持之以恩维之以义
hongqi 红契
hou jixun 候集讯
hou zhixun 候质讯
houguo 后果
houxun 候讯
Huang Liuhong 黄六鸿
huanyi 换易
huanzhu 换主
hufang 户房
huhun tiantu 户婚田土
huhun tiantu deng xishi 户婚田土等细事
huhun tiantu dengxiang 户婚田土等项
huhun tiantu qianzhai xishi 户婚田土钱债细事
hui 悔
hulü 户律
hunshu 婚书
hunyin 婚姻
hunyin jianqing 婚姻奸情
huopiao 火票

jia 甲
jia shiji 加十级
jiacai tiantu 家财田土
jian 监
Jiangxi 江西
jiansheng 监生
jianzhan 奸占
jiaozhuang 交状
jiaren 家人
jie 结
jieqian sizhai, nianyue suiduo buguo yibenyili 借欠私债年月虽多不过一本一利
jieyue 揭约
jikai 计开
jilu shici 纪录十次
jinshi 进士
jitian 籍田
jiuan 旧案
jiyou siyue 即有私约
ju ganjie 具甘结
juan 卷
juemai 绝卖
junji 军籍
juren 举人

kenhun 措婚
kongci 控词
koutou 叩头
kuaitou 快头

Lan Dingyuan 蓝鼎元
langui 烂规
lanyu 拦舆
laoqi 老契
leshi 勒石
li 利
li 理
li 礼
li 例
li 里
Li Wei 李卫
liang 两
liangjia 两家
liangjin 两尽
liangping 两平
Libu 吏部
lichu 理处
lidan 礼单
lidang zhao benli changhuan 理当照本利偿还
lide mianjiu 例得免究
lifang 礼房

lingzhuang / shouzhuang	领状 / 收状
Liu Heng	刘衡
liubu	六部
long	垄
lougui	陋规
lü	律
luofa shujing	落发数茎
lüwen	律文
lüyi	律意
mai	卖
maixiu maixiu	买休卖休
man	满
manzu	满族
maoren	冒认
mei	媒
meishuo weiyun	媒妁未允
mianxun	免讯
miao	苗
mindi	民地
Ming	明
ming shifei	明是非
mingli	名例
minjian cisong xishi	民间词讼细事
minren	民人
mintian	民田
mobi	墨笔
mu	亩
muting	幕厅
muyou	幕友
nan	难
niandan	粘单
nijia zhuren	你家主人
Ningyuan	宁远
nongmang	农忙
nongmang zhisong	农忙止讼
nüjia zhuhunren	女家主婚人
pai	排
panci	判词
pi	批
pi	疲
pianti	骈体
piao	票
piaogao	票稿
piduan	批断
pincai	聘财
Pinggu	平谷
pingqing	平情
pingyun	平允
pinhu	贫户
pou quzhi	剖曲直
pouduan quzhi	剖断曲直
Poyang	鄱阳
pubian zhiyi	扑鞭之意
putian zhixia mofei wangtu	普天之下莫非王土
qi	旗
qi	契
qian	钱
qianggeng	强耕
qiangzhan	强占
qianyin	前因
qianzhai	钱债
qiaoqu	巧取
qichu	七出
qidi	旗地
qigao shoucheng	期告收呈
qihui	弃毁
qihui qiwu jiaqiang deng	弃毁器物稼穑等
Qijiang	綦江
qimie ziyou	起灭自由
qinan	钦案
qing	情
qing	顷
qing fa/li liangjin	情法 / 理两尽
qingji wanggao	情急妄告
qingli	情理
qingli liangping	情理两平
qingrang	情让
qingyou dan	情由单
qingyuan xisu	情愿息诉
qinzhan	侵占
qiongding	穷丁
qionghu	穷户

qiongyuan jingwei	穷源经纬
qiren	旗人
qiyang	乞养
qizhi	契纸
quanli	权利
quzhi	曲直
raohu	饶户
ren	仁
ren	忍
renming	人命
renqing	人情
renqing wuli	人情物理
ri	日
rubu qianzu, li buzhun chedi	如不欠租例不准撤地
rubu qianzu, li buzhun duodian	如不欠租例不准夺佃
san buqu	三不去
shan	善
Shandong	山东
shang	伤
shanghu	上户
Shangjie li	尚节里
shangyu	上谕
shanshi guaguo	擅食瓜果
shanshi tianyuan guaguo	擅食田园瓜果
Shanxi	陕西
shao youli	稍有力
shaolai qunao	少来取闹
shen	身
Shen Yanqing	沈衍庆
Shen Zhiqi	沈之奇
shendan	审单
sheng	生
shengjian	生监
shengli	省例
shengren	圣人
shengyuan / xiucai	生员 / 秀才
shenyu	审语
shenxing	慎刑
shi bu ganji	事不干己
shi shi	是实
shichan	市产
shie	十恶
shifei	是非
shigu quanwu	尸骨全无
shiju	实据
shoushi	首事
shouyang gulao	收养孤老
shouzhuang	收状
shuangfu	孀妇
shufei qingli	孰非情理
shuiqi	税契
shushi	叔世
shushou	书手
shushu buhe	孰属不合
shuya quejiao	鼠牙雀角
sidian	私佃
siyue	私约
sizhai	私债
sizi gouhe	私自苟合
song	讼
songshi	讼师
su	诉
suiren suoqing	随人所请
suitang shoucheng	随堂收呈
suli	俗例
susong	诉讼
suyou dingli	素有定例
Taihe	泰和
Taiping	太平
Taiwan	台湾
Tanshui-Hsinchu (*Danshui Xinzhu*)	淡水新竹
Tao Xisheng	陶希圣
taowang	逃亡
ti	题
tian	田
Tian Wenjing	田文镜
tianchan	田产
tianchan xishi, tingsong, buzhun	田产细事，停讼，不准。
tianhe	天合
tianli	天理
tianzhai	田宅

tiaochu	调处
tong meishuo	同媒妁
tongli	通例
tongxing	通行
tongyangxi	童养媳
touci	投词
tsu (zu)	族
tuhao	土豪
tuigu bu shouli	推故不受理
tuli/feng	土例/风
Wang Fengsheng	王凤生
Wang Huizu	汪辉祖
wangmao	妄冒
Wangpu (or Wangbu)	王卜
wanjinzhang	万金帐
wei	为
wei chengming cunan shi	为呈明存案事
wei chengming fuqi liyi qingyou enzhun cunan shi	为呈明夫妻离异情由恩准存案事
weijin quli	违禁取利
weishang	微伤
wen	文
wu bujing	无不敬
wu buzhun wu lanzhun	无不准无滥准
Wu Lüfu	吴履福
Wu Tan	吴坛
wu zuiming	无罪名
wucheng chayuan	五城察院
wude hanhun	勿得含混
wufang zaju	五方杂居
wugao	诬告
wugao ganjie	诬告甘结
wugu	无故
wugu xiuqi	无故休弃
wuguan zuiming	无关罪名
wuhuang bucheng zhuang	无谎不成状
wuhui shumu jiaqiang	误毁树木稼樯
wuli	无力
wuping zhixun	无凭质讯
wuqing	无情
wuqing wuli	无情无理
wuqing zhici	无情之词
wusheng	武生
wusong	无讼
wuxin	无心
wuyiwei	误以为
xi	细
xiahu	下户
xian	县
xiancheng	县丞
xiangbao	乡保
xianyou bushi, buzhun	显有不实不准
xiao	销
xiaqing suishun shengcai chuzi tianen	下情虽顺圣裁出自天恩
xin	信
xinan	新案
xing	行
Xingbaoli	兴保里
xingfa zhong	刑罚中
xingfang	刑房
Xingguo	兴国
xingming	刑名
xingxin	刑新
xinpiao	信票
xishi	细事
xishu guanye	悉数管业
xisong	息讼
xiu	休
Xu Wenbi	徐文弼
Xue Yunsheng	薛允升
xuetian	学田
xunchang cisong	寻常词讼
xunfu	巡抚
xunhuanbu	循环簿
xunjian	巡捡
xunli	巡历
xunqi liangzao zhi shifei	讯其两造之是非
xuqian shiqi	虚钱实契
yahang	牙行

yamen	衙门
yan	言
yanfang	盐房
yanglao	养老
yansong	厌讼
yaoque	要缺
yezhu	业主
yi	义
yi	蚁
yibao hunshu	已报婚书
yiben yili	一本一利
yidu jianie zhibi	以杜假捏之蔽
yihu	义户
yijing xiaoyou	以儆效尤
yijue	义绝
yin	印
yindian	引佃
yingqu	迎娶
yinyan	印谳
yipian danxin	一片丹心
yirang	义让
yitian	义田
yiwei zhouxian zhi nanche	以为州县之南车
yiwen	移文
yixin	疑心
yixue	义学
yiyou buhe	亦有不合
yizheng renlun	以正人伦
yongbu huishu	永不回赎
yongdian	永佃
Yongqing	永清
yougan lijin	有干例禁
youli	有力
youli	有理
youli youqing	有理有情
youli zelai	有理则来
youqing youli jinguan qianlai, wuqing wuli shaolai qunao	有情有理尽管前来无情无理少来取闹
youwei lijin	有违例禁
youxin	有心
yu	狱
yu qingli buhe	与情理不合
yuan	元
Yuan Mu	袁牧
yuangao / yuanzao	原告 / 原造
yuangao ziju kangwei najiu	原告自拘抗违拿究
yuannian	远年
yuanyi	原役
yue	月
yue	约
yuedi	约地
yuesu	越诉
yulin ce	鱼鳞册
yumei	愚昧
yuqin	余亲
yushi	御使
yuzhi	谕旨
zaian	在案
zaikong	再控
zang	赃
zaotang	早堂
zaotou	皂头
zeidao	贼盗
zeli	则例
zhai / sizhai	债 / 私债
zhaishi	摘释
zhang	杖
zhangben	帐本
zhangze	掌责
zhao benzhuang guchejia gulan	照本庄雇车价雇揽
Zhaojiapai	赵家排
Zhejiang	浙江
Zheng Banqiao	郑板桥
zhengtang	正堂
zhengzhuang	正状
zhenqing zhuoli	斟情酌理
zhi	直
zhi	职
zhi	智
zhifu	知府
zhijiao	指交
zhiqing moumai	知情谋买
zhiqing shuomei	知情说媒
zhishi dangwu	值十当五
zhixian	知县

zhiye qingdan	执业清单
zhizhou	知州
zhong	忠
zhonghu	中户
zhou	州
zhoupan	州判
zhoutong	州同
zhu	主
zhu	逐
zhuang	状
zhuangbang	状榜
zhuangding	壮丁
zhuangtou	庄头
zhubo	主簿
zhuhunren	主婚人
zhunjie	准结
zhunqi chumai	准其出卖
zhunqing dingduan	准情定断
zhunqing yongfa	准情用法
zhunqing / hengqing zhuoli	准情 / 衡情酌理
zhunzhe	准折
zhuoqing dingduan	酌情定断
zihao	字号
zili anjian	自理案件
zongdu	总督
zou	奏
zouzhun	奏准
zui	罪
zuiming	罪名
zunjie	遵结

Bibliography

Primary sources

Bao Shichen. 1872/1968. *Anwu sizhong* [Four Types of Work of Bao Shichen]. Reprint, Taibei: Wenhai.

Baodi county records, sections (*juan*) 95–195 of *Shuntianfu quanzong* [Imperial Shuntian Prefecture Archive]. Stored in The First Historical Archive of China, Beijing. They are cited by *juan* number and document number — for example, Baodi, 95: 3–6.

Baodi xianzhi [Gazetteer of Baodi County]. Printed in Kangxi. Incomplete, stored in Beijing Library.

Baxian dangan [Ba County Records].Stored in The Sichuan Provincial Archive, Chengdu. They are cited by *juan* number and the document number if available.

Confucius. 1997. *The Analects*. Translated by Arthur Waley. Beijing: Waiyujiaoxue yu yanjiu chubanshe.

Da Qing huidian [Collected Statutes of the Great Qing Administrative Law]. Shanghai: Shanghai shuju, 1899.

Da Qing huidian shili (in the Guangxu reign) [Supplement to the Collected Statutes of the Great Qing Administrative Law]. Beijing, 1991.

Da Qing lü jizhu [Great Qing Code with Collected Commentaries] [ca. 1715], by Shen Zhiqi. Beijing: Falü chubanshe, 1998.

Da Qing lüli [The Great Qing Code], 1740.

Da Qing lüli huiji bianlan [Qing Code with Sub-statutes and Commentaries], 15 vols. Taipei: Chengwen Publishing Co., n.d.

Da Qing lüli huitong xincuan [Comprehensive New Edition of the Qing Code]. 1873 [date of preface]. Yao Run, Hu Zhang.

Da Qing lüli zengxiu tongcuan jicheng [Revised Comprehensive Compilation of the Great Qing]. Shanghai: Wenyuan shanfang, 1900.

Daqing lüli zonglei [Complete Statistics of the Great Qing Code]. 1889. Jiangsu: Jiangsu shuju.

Ding Richang, *Fuwu gongdu* [Documents of a Governor of Zhejiang Province]. Nanyang guan shuju, 1909.

Fan Zengxiang. 1912 [date of Preface]. *Fanshan pandu xubian* [Further Collection of Fanshan Comments], vols 1–3. Lisan shuduan.

Fujian shengli [Regulations of Fujian Province]. In *Guanzhenshu jicheng* [Collections of Official Handbooks]. Hefei: Huangshan shushe, 1997.

Guangxu Shuntian fuzhi [Gazetteer of Imperial Shuntian Prefecture edited in the Guangxu reign]. 1987. Reprint, Beijing: Beijing guji chubanshe.

Gudai pancixuan [Selected Decisions of Traditional China]. 1981. Edited by Gao Chao. Beijing: Qunzhong chubanshe.

Hoang, Pierre. 1898. *Le Mariage Chinois*. Shanghai: Mission Catholique.

Huang Liuhong. 1850/1972. *Fuhui quanshu* [A Complete Book Concerning Happiness and Benevolence]. Japanese annotation alongside the Chinese text by Xiao Tian Xing Jian. Reprint, Japan: Jigu Shuyuan.

——. 1984. *A Complete Book Concerning Happiness and Benevolence: A Manual for Local Magistrates in Seventeenth-Century China*. Translated and edited by Djang Chu. Tucson: University of Arizona Press.

Hubu zeli [Regulations of the Board of Revenue]. In *Zhonghua lüling jicheng* [Complete Book of Statutes and Regulations of China], vol. 5. Changchun: Jilinrenmin chubanshe, 1991.

Jones, William C. 1994. *The Great Qing Code*. Oxford: Clarendon Press.

Lan Dingyuan. 1729/1989. *Luzhou gongan* [The Cases of Mr Luzhou]. Guizhou: Qunzhong chubanshe.

Li Chi [Book of Rites]. 1967. Translated by J. Legge, edited by C. Chai and W. Chai. New Hyde Park, NY: University Book.

Li Liwong (also Li Yu). 1663 [date of Preface]. *Xinzeng zizhi xinshu quanji* [New Extra Complete Book for Assisting Governing]. Tianlutang.

Minshi xiguan diaocha baogao lu [Report Concerning the Investigation of Civil and Commercial Customs]. 2000. Beijing: Zhongguo zhengfa daxue chubanshe.

Muling xuzhi [Necessary Knowledge of Magistrates]. 1889/1970. Edited by Gang Yi. Reprint, Taibei: Wenhai.

Mulingshu [Compendium on the Magisterial Service]. ca. 1838/1865. Edited by Xu Dong, Chengdu.

Qiangu zhinan [Guidance on Tax Matters]. Originally published in the Qianlong reign. In *Ming Qing gongdu miben wuzhong* [Five Secret Collections of Official Documents in the Ming and Qing]. Reprint, edited by Guo Chengwei and Tian Tao, Beijing: Zhongguo zhengfa daxue chubanshe, 1999.

Qinban zhouxian shiyi [The Basics of the Magisterial Service Approved by the Throne]. Originally published in the Yongzheng reign. Drafted by Tian Wenjing and Li Wei. In *Guanzhenshu jicheng* [Collections of Official Handbooks]. Hefei: Huangshan shushe, 1997.

Qingbai leichao [Categorized Recordings of the Qing]. 1915 [date of Preface]. Vols 8 and 9. *Yusong* [Crimes and Litigation], recorded by Xue Ke. Beijing: Shangwu Yinshuguan.

Qingdai Baxian dangan huibian-qianlong juan [Selected Ba County Archives of the Qing Dynasty — Qianlong Reign]. Beijing: Dang'an chubanshe, 1991 (cited as Baxian in the text).

Qingdai mingchen pandu [Collected Decisions of Some Famous Officials of the Qing]. 1924. Shanghai: Guangyi shuju.

Qingdai Qian-Jia-Dao Baxian dangan xuanbian [A Collection from the Ba County Archives in the Qianlong, Jiaqing and Daoguang Eras], vol. 1. Chengdu: Sichuan University Publishing House, 1989 (cited as Baxian1 in the text).

Qingdai Qian-Jia-Dao Baxian dangan xuanbian [A Collection from the Ba County Archives in the Qianlong, Jiaqing and Daoguang Eras], vol. 2. Chengdu: Sichuan University Publishing House, 1996 (cited as Baxian2 in the text).

Qingshi ziliao [Materials on Qing History]. Beijing: Zhonghua shuju chubanshe.

Shen Yanqing, *Huaiqing zhengji* [Administrative Achievement of *Huaiqing*]. In *Jindai Zhongguo shiliao congkan* [Serial Collection of Materials on Modern Ancient Chinese History]. Taiwan: Wenhai chubanshe, 1862.

Shuntian fuzhi [Gazetteer of Shuntian fu]. 1884/1987. Edited by Zhou Jiamei and Miao Quansun. Reprint, Beijing: Beijing guji chubanshe.

Wan Weihan. *Muxue juyao* [Important Skills of a Private Secretary].1892. In *Rumu xuzhi wuzhong* [Five Volumes of Essential Knowledge for Those Entering Private Secretary Work]. Reprint. Taibei: Wenhai.

Wang Huizu. 1786a [date of Preface]/1892. *Zuozhi yaoyan* [Admonitions on Assisting [a Magistrate] with Governance]. In *Rumu xuzhi wuzhong* [Five Volumes of Essential Knowledge for Those Entering Private Secretary Work]. Reprint, Taibei: Wenhai.

——. 1786b [date of Preface]/1892. *Xu zuozhi yaoyan* [Sequel to "Admonitions on Assisting [a Magistrate] with Governance"]. In *Rumu xuzhi wuzhong* [Five Volumes of Essential Knowledge for Those Entering Private Secretary Work]. Reprint, Taibei: Wenhai.

——. 1793 [date of Preface]/1892. *Xuezhi yishuo* [Subjective Views on Learning Governance]. In *Rumu xuzhi wuzhong* [Five Volumes of Essential Knowledge for Those Entering Private Secretary Work]. Reprint, Taibei: Wenhai.

——. 1794 [date of Preface]/1892. *Xuezhi xushuo* [Further Views on Learning Governance]. In *Rumu xuzhi wuzhong* [Five Volumes of Essential Knowledge for Those Entering Private Secretary Work]. Reprint, Taibei: Wenhai.

——. 1800 [date of Preface]/1892. *Xuezhi shuozhui* [Tiresome Views on Learning Governance]. In *Rumu xuzhi wuzhong* [Five Volumes of Essential Knowledge for Those Entering Private Secretary Work]. Reprint, Taibei: Wenhai.

Wang Youhuai. 1987. *Ban'an yaolüe* [Important Strategies in Handling Cases]. Edition with commentary by the Chinese Teaching Section of Huadong College of Political Science and Law. Beijing: Qunzhong chubanshe.

Wu Tan. c.1778. *Da Qing lüli tongkao jiaozhu* [Thorough Examination of the Great Qing *lü* and *li* with annotations]. Edited by Ma Jianshi and Yang Yutang. Beijing: Zhongguo zhengfa daxue chubanshe, 1992.

Xingan huilan [Conspectus of Cases from the Board of Punishments], 1886. Reprint, Taipei: Chengwen, 1968.

Xingfazhi [Legal Monographs]. 1984. Beijing: Qunzhong chubanshe.

Xingke tiben [Memorials to the Board of Punishments]. Stored in The First Historical Archive of China, Beijing.

Xue Yunsheng. c.1905/1970. *Duli cunyi* [Doubts Arising from the Sub-statutes]. Taipei: Chinese Materials and Research Aids Center.

Yuan Huang. 1605. *Liaofan zazhu* [Liaofan's Collected Works]. Yushi keben [printed by Yu], Ming Wanli 33rd year (1605). Stored in Beijing Library.

Yuedong shengli [Regulations of Guangdong Province]. In *Guanzhenshu jicheng* [Collections of Official Handbooks]. Hefei: Huangshan shushe, 1997.

Zhan Yuanxiang. 1983. '*Weizhai riji* [Diary of Weizhai]'. *Qingshi ziliao* 4. Beijing: Zhonghua shuju chubanshe.

Zhishang jinglun [Managing Documents]. Originally published in the Qianlong reign. In *Ming Qing gongdu miben wuzhong* [Five Secret Collections of Official

Documents in the Ming and Qing]. Reprint, edited by Guo Chengwei and Tian Tao. Beijing: Zhongguo zhengfa daxue chubanshe, n.d. 1999.

Zhizhe chenggui [Regulations of Zhejiang Province]. In *Guanzhenshu jicheng* [Collections of Official Handbooks]. Hefei: Huangshan shushe, 1997.

Zhonghua lüling jicheng [Complete Book of Statutes and Regulations of China]. 1991. Vol. 5, edited by Zhang Youyu and Gao Chao. Changchun: Jilinrenmin chubanshe.

Secondary sources

Allee, Mark, A. 1994a. *Law and Society in Late Imperial China: Northern Taiwan in the Nineteenth Century*. Stanford, Calif.: Stanford University Press.

——. 1994b. 'Code, Culture, and Custom: Foundations of Civil Case Verdicts in a Nineteenth-Century County Court'. In *Civil Law in Qing and Republican China*, edited by Kathryn Bernhardt and Philip C. C. Huang, 122–41. Stanford, Calif.: Stanford University Press.

Antony, Robert J. 2002. 'Subcounty Officials, the State, and Local Communities in Guangdong Province, 1644–1860'. In *Dragons, Tigers, and Dogs*, edited by Robert J. Antony and Jane Kate Leonard, 27–59. New York: Cornell University Press.

Austin, John. 1955. *The Province of Jurisprudence Determined*. London: Weidenfeld & Nicolson.

Bernhardt, Kathryn. 1996. 'A Ming–Qing Transition in Chinese Women's History? The Perspective from Law'. In *Remapping China*, edited by Gail Hershatter, Emily Honig, Jonathan N. Lipman, and Randall Stross, 42–58. Stanford, Calif.: Stanford University Press.

Bernhardt, Kathryn and Huang, Philip C. C. 1994. 'Civil Law in Qing and Republican China'. In *Civil Law in Qing and Republican China*, edited by Kathryn Bernhardt and Philip C. C. Huang, 1–12. Stanford, Calif.: Stanford University Press.

Bian Li. 2000. 'Mingdai Huizhou de minshi jiufen yu minshi susong' [Civil Disputes and Litigation of Huizhou Prefecture during the Ming]. *Lishi yanjiu* [Study of History] 1: 94–105.

Bodde, Derk. 1980. 'Age, Youth, and Infirmity in the Law of Ch'ing'. In *Essays on China's Legal Tradition,* edited by Jerome Alan Cohen, R. Randle Edwards, and Fu-mei Chang Chen, 137–69. Princeton, N.J.: Princeton University Press.

Bodde, Derk and Clarence Morris. 1973. *Law in Imperial China: Exemplified by 190 Ch'ing Dynasty Cases*. Philadelphia: University of Pennsylvania Press.

Brenan, Byron. 1897–8. 'The Office of District Magistrate in China'. *Journal of the North China Branch* 32: 36–65.

Brockman, Rosser H. 1980. 'Commercial Contract Law in Late Nineteenth-Century Taiwan'. In *Essays on China's Legal Tradition*, edited by Jerome Alan Cohen, R. Randle Edwards, and Fu-mei Chang Chen, 77–136. Princeton, N.J.: Princeton University Press.

Bryan, Robert T. 1927. *An Outline of Chinese Civil Law*. Shanghai: The Commercial Press.

Buoye, Thomas M. 2000. *Manslaughter, Market, and Moral Economy – Violent Disputes over Property Rights in Eighteenth-century China*. Cambridge: Cambridge University Press.

Buxbaum, David. 1971. 'Some Aspects of Civil Procedure and Practice at the Trial Level in Tanshui and Hsinch from 1789 to 1895'. *Journal of Asian Studies* 30(2): 255–79.

Chen Fu-mei Chang. 1980. 'The Influence of Shen Chih-ch'i's *Chi-chu* Commentary upon Ch'ing Judicial Decisions'. In *Essays on China's Legal Tradition*, edited by Jerome Alan Cohen, R. Randle Edwards, and Fu-mei Chang Chen, 170–221. Princeton, N.J.: Princeton University Press.

Chen Peng. 1990. *Zhongguo hunyin shigao* [A History of Marriage in China]. Beijing: Zhonghua shuju.

Cohen, Jerome A. 1966. 'Chinese Mediation on the Eve of Modernization'. *California Law Review* 54: 1201–26.

Conner, Alison Wayne. 1979. 'The Law of Evidence during the Qing'. PhD dissertation, Cornell University.

Dai Yi (ed.). 1991. *Jianming Qingshi* [Brief History of the Qing]. Beijing: Renmin chubanshe.

Del Vecchio, Giorgio. 1953. *Philosophy of Law*. Translated by Thomas Owen Martin from the 8th edition (1952). Washington DC: Catholic University of America Press.

Du Jiaji. 1997. *Qingchao jianshi* [Brief History of the Qing]. Fuzhou: Fujian chubanshe.

Feng Youlan. 1937. *A History of Chinese Philosophy*. Translated by D. Bodde. Peiping: Henri Vetch and London: Allen & Unwin.

Fuma Susumu. 1998. *Ming Qing shidai de songshe yu susong zhidu* [The Litigation Masters and Litigation System of the Ming and Qing]. Translated by Fan Yu and Wang Yaxin. In *Ming Qing shiqi de minshi shenpan yu minjian qiyue* [Civil Trials and People's Contracts during Ming and Qing], edited by Wang Yaxin and Liang Zhiping, 389–430. Beijing: Falü chubanshe.

Gao Huanyue. 2000. *Qingdai xingming muyou yanjiu* [A Study of the Qing's Private Secretaries]. Beijing: Zhongguo zhengfa daxue chubanshe.

Giles, Herbert. 1876. *Chinese Sketch*. E-version, Seattle, Wash.: The World Wide School™, 2001.

Gu Hongming. 1996. *Gu Hongming wenji* [Collected Works of Gu Hongming]. Edited by Huang Xingtao. Haikou: Hainan Chubanshi.

Guo Jian. 1993. *Gudai faguan mianmian guan* [Judges in Imperial China]. Shanghai: Shanghai guji chubanshe.

Hiroaki Terada. 1998. *Quanli yu yuanni* [Rights and Victims]. Translated by Fan Yu. In *Ming Qing shiqi de minshi shenpan yu minjian qiyue* [Civil Trials and People's Contracts during the Ming and Qing], edited by Wang Yaxin and Liang Zhiping, 191–265. Beijing: Falü chubanshe.

Huang, Philip. 1996. *Civil Justice in China: Representation and Practice in the Qing*. Stanford, Calif.: Stanford University Press.

——. 2001. *Code, Custom, and Legal Practice in China*. Stanford, Calif.: Stanford University Press.

Jamieson, G. 1921/1970. *Chinese Family and Commercial Law*. Reprint, Hong Kong: Vetch and Lee.

Jing Junjian. 1994. 'Legislation Related to the Civil Economy in the Qing Dynasty'. In *Civil Law in Qing and Republican China*, edited by Kathryn Bernhardt and Philip C. C. Huang, 42–84. Stanford, Calif.: Stanford University Press.

Johnson, Wallace. 1979. *The T'ang Code*, vol. 1, *General Principles*. Princeton, N.J.: Princeton University Press.

Jones, William C. 1974. 'Studying the Ch'ing (Qing) Code. The Ta (Da) Ch'ing Lü Li'. *American Journal of Comparative Law* 22: 330–64.

Liang Linxia. 2005. 'Rejection or Acceptance: Finding Reasons for the Late Qing Magistrate's Comments on Land and Debt Petitions'. *Bulletin of SOAS* 68(2): 276–94.

Liang Zhiping. 1996. *Qingdai xiguanfa: shehui yu guojia* [Customary Law in the Qing: Society and the State]. Beijing: Zhongguo zhengfa daxue chubanshe.

Liu Ziyang. 1994. *Qingdai difang guanzhi kao* [Study of the Official System of Local Government in the Qing Dynasty]. Beijing: Zijincheng chubanshe.

McAleavy, Henry. 1955. 'Certain Aspects of Chinese Customary Law in the Light of Japanese Scholarship'. *Bulletin of the School of Oriental and African Studies* 17(3): 535–47.

——. 1958. '*Dien* (*dian*) in China and Vietnam'. *Journal of Asian Studies* 17: 413–15.

Macauley, Melissa. 1999. *Social Power and Legal Culture*. Stanford, Calif.: Stanford University Press.

——. 1994. 'Civil and Uncivil Disputes in Southeast Coastal China, 1723–1820'. In *Civil Law in Qing and Republican China*, edited by Kathryn Bernhardt and Philip C. C. Huang, 85–121. Stanford, Calif.: Stanford University Press.

MacCormack, Geoffrey. 1990. *Traditional Chinese Penal Law*. Edinburgh: Edinburgh University Press.

——. 1996a. 'Assistance in Conflict Resolution'. *Transactions of the Jean Bodin Society* 63: 109–53.

——. 1996b. *The Spirit of Traditional Chinese Law*. Athens, Ga. and London: University of Georgia Press.

Na Silu. 1981. *Qingdai zhouxian yamen shenpan zhidu* [Trial System in the Qing Magistrate's Court]. Taibei: Wenshizhe chubanshe.

Palmer, Michael J. E. 1987. 'The Surface-Subsoil Form of Divided Ownership in Late Imperial China: Some Examples from the New Territories of Hong Kong'. *Modern Asian Studies* 21(1): 1–119.

Pierre-Etienne, Will. '*Ming Qing shiqi de guanzhenshu yu Zhongguo xingzheng wenhua* [Official Handbooks and Administration Culture during the Ming and Qing]'. In *Qingshi yanjiu* [Study of Qing History], 1999(1): 3–20.

Qingdai liubu chengyu cidian [Administrative Idioms of the Qing Six Boards]. 1990. Edited by Li Pengnian, Liu Ziyang and Chen Jiangyi. Tianjin: Tianjin renmin chubanshe.

Qingdai mingan [Selected Cases of the Qing]. 1997. In *Zhonggao lidai mingan* [Selected Cases of Imperial China], edited by Xin Ziniu. Shanghai: Fudan daxue chubanshe.

Qingdai wenshu [The Formula of the Qing Documents]. 1996. Edited by Zhang Wode, Yang Ruohe, and Pei Yansheng. Beijing: People's University Publishing House.

Qu Tongzu. 1965. *Law and Society in Traditional China*. Westport, Conn.: Hyperion Press [ca. 1961].

——. 1969. *Local Government in China under the Chin'ing*. Stanford, Calif.: Stanford University Press.

——. 1980. 'The Qing Law: An Analysis of Continuity and Change'. In *Social Sciences in China*, No. 3: 103–14.

——. 1981. *Zhongguo falü yu zhongguo shehui* [Law and Society in Traditional China]. Beijing: Zhonghua shuju.

Reed, Bradly. 1995. 'Money and Justice: Clerks, Runners, and the Magistrate's Court in Late Imperial Sichuan'. *Modern China* 21(3): 345–82.

——. 2000. *Talons and Teeth: County Clerks and Runners in the Qing Dynasty*. Stanford, Calif.: Stanford University Press.

Shiga Shūzō. 1992a. 'Custom as Source of Law in Traditional China'. *Custom* (Transactions of the Jean Bodin Society for Comparative Institutional History, De Boeck University, Belgium) 53: 413–25.

——. 1992b. *Qingdai zhouxian yamen susong de ruogan yanjiu xinde – yi Dan-xin dan-gan wei shiliao* [Several Observations on Studying Litigation at County Level – Illustrated from the Dan-xin Archives]. In *Riben xuezhe yanjiu zhongguoshi lun-zhu xuanyi* [Selected Translations of Japanese Scholars' Works on Chinese History], vol. 8, edited by Liu Junwen, 522–46. Beijing: Zhonghua shuju.

——. 1998a. *Qingdai susong zhidu zhi minshi fayuan de gaikuoxing kaocha – qing li fa* [Summary Examination of Sources of the Civil Law in Qing Litigation – qing li and fa]. Translated by Fan Yu. In *Ming Qing shiqi de minshi shenpan yu min-jian qiyue* [Civil Trials and People's Contracts during the Ming and Qing], edited by Wang Yaxin and Liang Zhiping, 19–54. Beijing: Falü chubanshe.

——. 1998b. *Qingdai susong zhidu zhi minshi fayuan de kaocha – zuowei fayuan de xiguan* [Examination of Sources of the Civil Law in Qing Litigation – Custom]. Translated by Wang Yaxin. In *Ming Qing shiqi de minshi shenpan yu minjian qiyue* [Civil Trials and People's Contracts during the Ming and Qing], edited by Wang Yaxin and Liang Zhiping, 54–96. Beijing: Falü chubanshe.

——. 2003. *Zhongguo jiazufa yuanli* [Principles of Chinese Family Law]. Translated by Zhang Jianguo, Li Li. Beijing: Falü chubanshe.

Su Yigong. 1999. *Ming Qing lüdian yu tiaoli* [Codes, Statutes, and Sub-statutes in the Ming and Qing]. Beijing: Zhongguo zhengfa daxue chubanshe.

Summer, Matthew H. 2000. *Sex, Law, and Society in Later Imperial China*. Stanford, Calif.: Stanford University Press.

Tao Xisheng. 1972. *Qingdai zhouxian yamen xingshi shenpan zhidu ji chengxu* [Criminal Trial Procedures and Systems at the County Level in the Qing Dynasty]. Taibei: Shihuo chubanshe.

Tian Tao. 2004. *Huangyan susong dangan ji diaocha baogao* [Litigation Documents and Field Work of Huangyan]. Edited together with Xu Chuanxi and Wang Hongzhi. Beijing: Falü chubanshe.

Tong Guangzheng. 1998. 'Mingdai minshi pandu yanjiu' [Study on Civil Decisions of the Ming Dynasty]. PhD dissertation, China University of Political Science and Law, Beijing.

Van der Sprenkel, S. 1966. *Legal Institutions in Manchu China*. London: Athlone Press.

Vandermeersch, Leon. 1985. 'An Enquiry into the Chinese Conception of the Law'. In *The Scope of State Power in China*, edited by Stuart R. Shram, 3–25. Hong Kong: Chinese University Press.

Wang Kan and Lü Li. 1998. '*Ming Qing li bianxi*' [Discussions of Sub-Legislation of the Ming and Qing]. *Faxue yanjiu* [Legal Study] 2: 144–53.

Wang Shirong. 1997a. *Zhongguo gudai panci yanjiu* [Study of Traditional Chinese Legal Decisions]. Beijing: Zhongguo zhengfa daxue chubanshe.

——. 1997b. *Zhongguo gudai panli yanjiu* [Study of Traditional Chinese Legal Cases]. Beijing: Zhongguo zhengfa daxue chubanshe.

Wang Yuesheng. 2003. *Qingdai zhongqi hunyin chongtu toucxi* [Complete Analysis of Marriage in the Middle of the Qing]. Beijing: Shehui kexue wenxian chubanshe.

Watt, John R. 1972. *The District Magistrate in Late Imperial China*. New York: Columbia University Press.

Williams, Glanville. 2002. *Learning the Law*. London: Sweet & Maxwell.

Wu Jiyuan. 1997. *Qingdai difang zhengfu de sifazhineng yanjiu* [Study of Judicial Tasks of Local Government in the Qing Dynasty]. Beijing: Zhongguo shehuikexue chubanshe.

Yang Guozhen. 1988. *Ming Qing tudi qiyue wenshu yanjiu* [Study of Land Contracts of the Ming and Qing Dynasties]. Beijing: Renmin chubanshe.

Ye Xiaoxin (ed.). 1993. *Zhongguo minfashi* [History of Civil Law in China]. Shanghai: Shanghai renmin chubanshe.

Yu Ronggen. 1992. *Rujia fasixiang tonglun* [Thorough Study of Confucian Legal Thought]. Guangxi: Guangxi renmin chubanshe.

——. 1999. *Daotong yu fatong* [Confucian Orthodoxy and Legally Constituted Authority]. Beijing: Falü chubanshe.

Zelin, Madeleine. 1986. 'The Rights of Tenants in Mid-Qing Sichuan: A Study of Land-Related Lawsuits in the Baxian Archives'. *Journal of Asian Studies* 45(3): 499–526.

——. 1994. 'Merchant Dispute Mediation in Twentieth-Century Zigong, Sichuan'. In *Civil Law in Qing and Republican China*, edited by Kathryn Bernhardt and Philip C. C. Huang, 249–86. Stanford, Calif.: Stanford University Press, 1994.

——. 2004. *Contract and Property in Early Modern China*. Edited with Jonathan K. Ocko and Robert Gardella. Stanford, Calif.: Stanford University Press.

Zen Sun, E-tu. 1961. *Ch'ing Administrative Terms*. Cambridge, Mass.: Harvard University Press.

Zhang, Jianguo. 1999. *Diguo shidai de zhongguofa* [Chinese Law during the Imperial Dynasties]. Beijing: Falü chubanshe.

Zhang Jinfan. 1998. *Qingdai minfa zonglun* [Complete Discussion of the Qing Civil Law]. Beijing: Zhonghuo zhengfa daxue chubanshe.

Zhang Yan. 1998. *Qingdai jingji jianshi* [Brief Economic History of the Qing]. Zhengzhou: Zhengzhou guji chubanshe.

Zheng Banqiao nianpu [Records of Zheng Banqiao's Life]. 1991. Qingdao: Shandong meishu chubanshe.

Zheng Qin. 1988. *Qingdai sifa shenpan zhidu yanjiu* [Study of the Trial Proceedings of the Qing Dynasty]. Changsha: Hunan jiaoyu chubanshe.

Zhongguo chuantong falü wenhua cidian [Dictionary of Traditional Chinese Legal Culture]. 1999. Edited by Wu Shuchen. Beijing: Beijing University Chubanshe.

Zhou Guangyuan. 1995. 'Beneath the Law: Chinese Local Legal Culture during the Qing Dynasty'. PhD dissertation, University of California, Los Angeles.

Zweigert, Konrad and Kötz, Hein. 1998. *An Introduction to Comparative Law*. Translated by Tony Weir. 3rd edn. Oxford: Clarendon Press.

Index